DIASPORA SPACE-TIME

DIASPORA SPACE-TIME

Transformations of a Chinese
Emigrant Community

Anne-Christine Trémon

CORNELL UNIVERSITY PRESS   ITHACA AND LONDON

First published 2022 by Cornell University Press

Library of Congress Cataloging-in-Publication Data

Names: Trémon, Anne-Christine, 1976– author.
Title: Diaspora space-time : transformations of a Chinese emigrant community / Anne-Christine Trémon.
Description: Ithaca, NY : Cornell University Press, 2022. | Includes bibliographical references and index.
Identifiers: LCCN 2022007261 (print) | LCCN 2022007262 (ebook) | ISBN 9781501761959 (hardcover) | ISBN 9781501767951 (paperback) | ISBN 9781501765551 (pdf) | ISBN 9781501765568 (epub)
Subjects: LCSH: Chinese diaspora. | China—Emigration and immigration— Social aspects. | China—Emigration and immigration—Economic aspects. | China—Emigration and immigration—History—20th century. | China—Emigration and immigration—History—21st century.
Classification: LCC DS732 .T617 2022 (print) | LCC DS732 (ebook) | DDC 909/.04951—dc23/eng/20220622
LC record available at https://lccn.loc.gov/2022007261
LC ebook record available at https://lccn.loc.gov/2022007262

Contents

Acknowledgments

I am deeply indebted to the people of Pine Mansion and Tahiti for their hospitality and their enthusiasm about my research and hope that this book will live up to the trust they have placed in me. My gratitude also goes to my funders: travel expenses were covered by a grant from the European Network of Institutes of Advanced Studies (EURIAS, Marie Curie Action FP7 COFUND, project No GA# 246561), and subsidies from the Maison des sciences de l'homme Paris Nord, the Foundation for the University of Lausanne, and the University of Lausanne's Bureau for Equality. Luo Jiting, Zhang Rou, and Liu Tingting, now former students of the Chinese University of Hong Kong and Sun Yat-sen University in Guangzhou, helped me during my first stays in Shenzhen and have become friends.

I wish to thank the hosts and audiences of Anthropology and Asian Studies seminars at the Université de Neuchâtel, the Netherlands Institute of Advanced Study, Leiden University, Frije Universiteit Amsterdam, Utrecht University, Max Planck Institute for Social Anthropology in Halle, Chinese University of Hong Kong, University of Hong Kong, University College London, and University of Cambridge. Brigitte Baptandier, Tan Chee-Beng, Ellen Hertz, Frank Pieke, Michael Puett, Pal Nyíri, and Bernard Wong offered encouragement and useful advice when my research was still in its initial stages. Adam Chau, Rebecca Empson, Chris Hann, Chen Ju-Chen, Helene Neveu Kringelbach, Gordon Mathews, Patrick Neveling, Jennifer Robinson, Helen Siu, and Megan Vaughan provided welcoming settings in seminars where I presented my findings and received constructive feedback. I also enjoyed inspiring and stimulating conversations in a diversity of settings with Charlotte Bruckermann, Georges Favraud, Lena Kauffmann, Frédéric Keck, Madlen Kobi, Giacomo Loperfido, and Aïssatou Mbodj-Pouye. During my stay at the Max Planck Institute in the spring of 2016, I spent much time with Meixuan Chen discussing the similarities and differences between the still-rural emigration village in the Meixian region of Guangdong Province that she has studied and Pine Mansion, confirming how much the change in the diasporic relationship owes to the context of economic prosperity and urbanization in Shenzhen.

I am grateful to my colleague in Lausanne, Mark Goodale, for his advice and support, and to numerous colleagues in France who have provided friendly help and criticism: members of the China workshop at the University of Paris-Nanterre,

Brigitte Baptandier, Gladys Chicharro-Saito, Adeline Herrou, Peiyi Ko, and Katiana Le Mentec, and Claire Vidal, and the members of my habilitation jury—Niko Besnier, Alessandro Monsutti, Michel Naepels, Anne de Sales, Pierre Singaravelou, and Isabelle Thireau.

I also wish to express my gratitude to the anonymous readers for their attentive and thoughtful appraisal of my work. Their detailed suggestions and constructive comments provided valuable guidance on improving and finalizing the manuscript. My heartfelt appreciation goes to Cornell University Press's acquisition editor, Jim Lance, and to the members of the press for engaging closely with my book manuscript. My thanks also go to Sally Sutton, freelance editor and proofreader, for her careful editing.

Parts of chapter 4 are derived from the article "Heterotopic Sites, Homochronous Urbanization: Saving Space in a Former Village of Shenzhen, China (1979–2015)," published in *Quaderni Storici* 2 (2015): 439–68. Parts of chapter 5 are derived from "Local Capitalism and Neoliberalization in a Shenzhen Former Lineage-Village," published in *Focaal: Journal of Global and Historical Anthropology* 71 (2015): 71–85. Parts of chapter 6 are derived from the article "Sociodicies of (Im)mobility: Moral Evaluations of Stasis, Departure and Return in an Emigrant Village (Shenzhen, China)," published in *Mobilities* 13, no. 1 (2017): 157–70, copyright Taylor & Francis, available online at https://www.tandfonline.com/doi/abs/10.1080/17450101.2017.1320134.

Finally, I thank Emmanuel for his care and support, which led him to travel from Paris to Hong Kong with our children, then aged one and five, to join me in Shenzhen during my first summer in the field.

I dedicate this book to the memory of my father.

Note on Anonymization, Romanization, and Translation

Pine Mansion is a pseudonym, whose meaning is close to that of the name of the village at the center of this research. Its real name has been shortened in the course of the village being absorbed by a new administrative entity, and it is therefore already partially anonymous. I have also anonymized the urban subdistrict in which Pine Mansion is located and the nearby golf course.

I chose to anonymize the former village's name but not the Chen surname, which is extremely common in China. All the first names mentioned in this book are pseudonyms that respect their French, Tahitian, or Chinese origin. In Tahiti (French Polynesia), the patronym Chen is transcribed as Ching in French, following the Hakka pronunciation. Many Tahiti Chinese frenchified their patronyms when they received French nationality: for instance, Ching has become "Chingues" or "Chanson."

I use the People's Republic of China's pinyin romanization system, with the exception of words in Hakka.

Throughout the book, I use several original Chinese terms rather than translating them: *Huaqiao, hukou,* Qiaolian, and Qiaoban. *Huaqiao* refers to Chinese sojourners or Chinese overseas/overseas Chinese (see introduction). *Hukou,* a legal document, identifies persons as permanent residents of a given area and indicates their rural or urban status, as part of the People's Republic of China's system of household registration. Qiaolian is the short name for *Zhonghua quanguo guiguo huaqiao lianhehui,* the All-China Federation of Returned Overseas Chinese Association. Qiaoban is the short name for *Guowuyuan qiaowu bangongshi,* the State Council's Overseas Chinese Affairs Office.

All translations of quotes from articles, books, and unpublished texts are my own unless otherwise stated.

DIASPORA SPACE-TIME

PART TWO PROCEDURE

SHENZHEN AND THE DIASPORIC RELATIONSHIP

In early August 2011, I alight from the Mass Transit Railway (MTR) at Lo Wu, one of the main checkpoints along the border between Hong Kong and the "continent," *Dalu* or mainland China, and join the flow of pedestrians heading toward Shenzhen.[1] The formalities are brief; the route is marked with arrows and travelers are forbidden to linger or take photos. The enclosed walkway offers views over the river Shamchun, which marks the territorial border, and of the barbed-wire fences and miradors on the Hong Kong hillside. On the other side, Lucien is waiting to pick me up with the hired minivan and driver he uses every time he travels to Shenzhen from Tahiti, French Polynesia's main island, for business. I had met Lucien's cousin Alain during my research in Tahiti in 2000. We had remained in contact since then, and he had asked Lucien to take me to their grandfathers' village of origin, Pine Mansion.[2]

Lucien travels to China three or four times a year on a multi-entry business visa importing construction materials through his company, which bears a Tahitian name. His mother was half-Chinese, half-Tahitian, and he speaks Tahitian fluently. He rarely visits Pine Mansion, which his grandfather left in the 1880s for the South Pacific. As we speed by the skyscrapers and international hotels of Shenzhen's city center, Lucien recalls how the first time he came in 1979 there was only one railway crossing paddy fields and no roads. We continue to head north for about half an hour and leave the highway just before reaching Shenzhen's northern limit. Just beyond the tollgate, large Hollywood-style Chinese characters display the message "Welcome to Miaoyun." Miaoyun is the subdistrict in which the former village of Pine Mansion lies. Lucien points to a large street sign showing the direction of the Quest Peak golf resort. "The biggest in the world," he says in a tone that conveys admiration and pride.

We are still driving at high speed on two-lane roads lined with large multistory factories protected by high walls and gates with closed-circuit television cameras. I see no sign of the village I have been preparing myself to discover over the preceding months. The cover of the Pine Mansion Chen lineage's genealogical book, which I am carrying in my backpack, shows a small ancestral temple, suggesting a rural village rather than an industrial zone. We turn at a footbridge that crosses the boulevard and the van stops in front of a tall white building with the inscription *Zhenneng wenhua dalou* (Zhenneng Cultural Building, hereafter the Zhenneng Building). Zhenneng was the name of the first Chen who settled in what would become Pine Mansion in the middle of the eighteenth century, having migrated from the northeast of Guangdong Province. He is venerated as the founding ancestor of the Pine Mansion Chen lineage.

The Zhenneng Building's wide doorway gives access to a large high-ceilinged room furnished with mahogany chairs, large fans, a water fountain, and paintings of landscapes that confer freshness and a serene atmosphere. A dozen elderly people are gathered around three tables quietly playing mahjong; the silence is interrupted only by the clattering of the tiles and the murmur of the flat-screen television. This place, which manifests a sense of care for the comfort and wellbeing of its occupants and unmistakable tokens of affluence, is the home for the elderly, *laoren yiyuan*. One tall white-haired man is reading a newspaper; Lucien recognizes him immediately and greets him. A little later, he tells me, "We have been lucky to find this old man." He is one of the only people Lucien knows in Pine Mansion and with good cause: Tailai, who was born in Indonesia at the end of the 1920s, was the village Qiaolian, the cadre in charge of liaising with overseas relatives, from the start of the 1980s until his retirement two decades later.

Tailai invites us to sit and have tea. A small circle of curious people gathers around us, but most in the room continue to play. An old woman hurriedly brings a copy of the genealogical book from a small back room and hands it to me. I accept it and open it to page seventy-three, looking for the name of Alain's daughter, who lent me her copy when I visited her in Paris, where she lives. She is mentioned in the Pine Mansion Chen genealogy (2000, hereafter the genealogy) by her French name, transcribed into Chinese characters. I point to it, explaining that I had received the genealogy from her. This is the source of a misunderstanding that I became aware of only later: they conclude that I am Alain's daughter and thus a relative from overseas. My introduction by Lucien and the fact that we act like many overseas Chinese who visit their village of origin, starting with meeting the village Qiaolian, have already created favorable circumstances for this misunderstanding, to which I return later in this introduction.

Continuing to behave like typical overseas visitors, we invite Tailai to lunch at the restaurant nearby which serves traditional Hakka dishes such as stuffed tofu, salt-baked chicken, and braised dog meat. Over lunch, Tailai talks to Lucien about the house that once belonged to his grandfather, which had been demolished a few months earlier along with all the old village houses as part of the redevelopment (*gaizao*) project. Tailai explains that others have pocketed the compensation money of around a million yuan and tells Lucien that he should claim it back. Lucien does not seem very interested and tells me that once converted into Pacific francs and divided among all his uncles, aunts, brothers, sisters, and cousins, it would amount to only small sums. He has an idea who took the compensation money because he has been contacted several times by grandsons of his grandfather's eldest brother, who were born in Tahiti and then sent back to China. We look them up in the genealogy. After lunch, Lucien leaves for a business meeting in downtown Shenzhen; the next time I see him is two years later in Tahiti.

This book explores the changing relationship between Pine Mansion, a Hakka lineage–village community in Shenzhen, and its emigrants and their descendants in Tahiti and around the world. Incorporating insights from my earlier fieldwork in Tahiti and capitalizing on my multisited positionality, it reflects on how the community members' migratory past shapes their outlook on the diasporic relationship and how they reinterpret their relations with their overseas kin in relation to China's changing position in the world. The end of their dependency on financial support from the diaspora is altering the moral foundation on which this relationship has long been based. It is also leading to a reconceptualization of the act of leaving the country: inhabitants of Shenzhen see relatives in the diaspora as remote and emigration as passé, favoring instead practices of transnational mobility such as living abroad for part of the year and in China for the rest. Although overseas Chinese were received with great pomp and a warm welcome in the decades following China's reopening, this is much less common today, as Lucien's low-profile arrival demonstrates. Shenzhen has gone from being an area of emigration to one of immigration from inner China. Its overseas liaison policy has been reoriented accordingly, and this change also reflects a broader shift in China's overseas policy.

This book shows how the relationship between the emigrant community and its migrants and their descendants has altered in a context of accelerated change. Once in the field, I soon realized that if I wanted to understand the emigrant community's current relationship with the diaspora, I would have to understand the changes that have occurred to the village itself. It no longer officially exists, having been absorbed into not only the urban sprawl around it but also Shenzhen's administration system. Shenzhen, located on the eastern shore of the Pearl River Delta (see figure 0.1) is at once particularly representative and an intensified

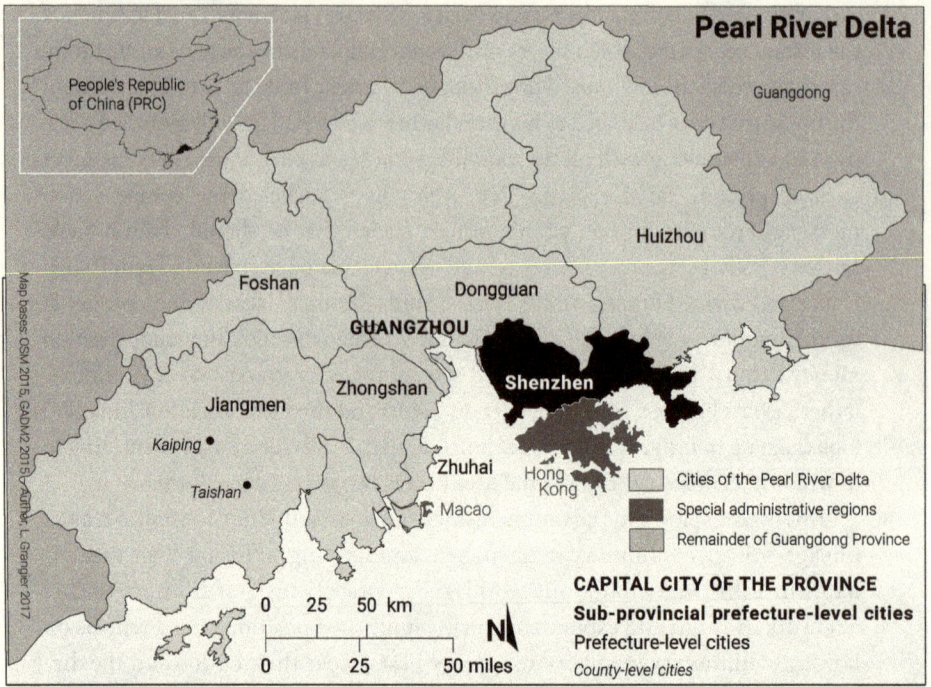

FIGURE 0.1. Shenzhen and the Pearl River delta. Map by Lucien Grangier.

version of Chinese urbanization. In 1978, Shenzhen had 27,366 inhabitants, and the population of the county surrounding it was 300,000–400,000. By the end of 2019, the new city had a population of 13.438 million of which 8.491 million (63%) had resident permits and only 4.947 million (36.8%) had local citizenship (Shenzhen *hukou*) (Shenzhen Statistics Bureau 2020). The population of Pine Mansion has risen from approximately 3,000 at the end of the 1970s to almost 60,000 today, reflecting the city's growth, and only 2.3 percent of these are *hukou* holders. The former village is now part of the new district of Longhua, which was separated from Bao'an District in 2011. The two rural counties of Bao'an, where Pine Mansion was located, and Longgang became urban administrative districts of Shenzhen City in 1993 (see figure 0.2).[3] All of the remaining rural villages in these northern districts, including Pine Mansion, were urbanized (*chengshihua*) in 2004, when they became administratively urban and their inhabitants lost their peasant status to become citizens of Shenzhen.

Shenzhen embodies the launch of China's economic reform and opening (*gaige kaifang*) era. The creation of the Shenzhen Special Economic Zone (SEZ) was both the signal and the instrument of China's opening up to foreign capital and its transition to market socialism (or neosocialism; Pieke 2009) with the clo-

FIGURE 0.2. Shenzhen's districts. Map by Lucien Grangier.

sure of the Mao era. Shenzhen was built from scratch with a very low level of initial state investment (Fenwick 1984; Vogel 1989; Ng 2003); the reform process as a whole has often been described as a businesslike marriage of convenience between the Chinese Communist Party (CCP) and overseas capitalists (Arrighi 2007, 351; see also Lever-Tracy et al. 1996; Cartier 2001). The SEZ brought together foreign capital, mainly from Hong Kong, cheap labor from the mainland, and equally cheap land for factories; this conjunction occurred mainly in Shenzhen's rural villages (Xie 2005; Po 2008; Tian 2008; Liu et al. 2010). Shenzhen's village communities constructed their own infrastructure and other public services using funding from overseas, making it hard to distinguish strictly economic investment from welfare projects funded by overseas kin after China's reopening (Woon 1990; Johnson and Woon 1997; Hoe 2013).

In December 1978, Deng Xiaoping announced the launch of China's economic reform.[4] Four SEZs were opened up in China's southeastern coastal provinces at the start of the reform to experiment with capitalism and develop an export economy, testing the reforms that later spread to the rest of China: the decollectivization of agriculture, the introduction of market principles, the granting of privileges to overseas investors and entrepreneurs, and the encouragement of factory workers in China's inner provinces to migrate to the SEZs (Vogel 1989; Sklair 1991; Ong 2006). The zones' labor-intensive, export-oriented production system (Neveling 2015) turned China into a new workshop of the world. Shenzhen was the first and most ambitious of the SEZs, its global position in the world's production of goods reflected by its container port, Yantian Terminal, which ranks third in the world in terms of volume shifted (World Shipping Council 2019). Although the production of cheaper goods such as clothes and toys has been relocated to other places both within and outside China in the past ten years, Shenzhen still accounts for over 10 percent of China's exports, and it produces an estimated 90 percent of the world's electronic goods (OECD 2017).

The first Chinese SEZs were, significantly, located in the southern coastal provinces from which the large majority of the Chinese diaspora originated (Vogel 1989; O'Donnell 2001). More than twenty million Chinese left China between 1840 and 1940 (McKeown 2010, 98), mostly from Fujian and Guangdong Provinces. After the advent of the Communist regime in 1949, 560,000–1,000,000 people are estimated to have crossed the border to Hong Kong between the mid-1950s and the start of the reforms (Chen 2011). This massive exodus was probably an additional factor in the creation of Shenzhen's large SEZ. The answer to this challenge, in Deng Xiaoping's eyes, lay in economic development on the Chinese side of the border with Hong Kong (Vogel 2011).

From the late 1970s onward, the Chinese authorities invited overseas relatives to visit their villages of origin and contribute to their development with financial donations and investment. To overcome the mistrust created by the confiscations and persecution that they and their families had suffered during the Mao period, the emphasis was on cultural and racial heritage rather than political belief, the goal being to encourage them to reengage with their "ancestral localities" (Thunø 2001, 916; Louie 2004, 50). At the local level, this "politics of native roots" (Siu 1990, 785) was mainly the task of the Qiaolian: overseas liaison officers such as Chen Tailai, whom I met on my first day in Pine Mansion. In the decade following China's reopening, the liaison administration was active in returning property confiscated from overseas Chinese and their families during the agrarian reform, the Great Leap Forward, and the Cultural Revolution, and it was therefore no coincidence that Tailai raised this topic with Lucien.

The Diasporic Relationship

My first day in the field immediately confronted me with the questions that I intended to study: the relationship between an emigrant community in South China and its migrants and their descendants, and changes in the intensity and meaning of these kin-based relations. Lucien's relative lack of interest in Tailai's report on his grandfather's house and obvious delight at coming back to Pine Mansion and showing me its transformation illustrates both a migrant descendant's distance from and his emotional attachment to the village in which his grandfather, who had never returned to China, was born. My earlier research had addressed the formation, persistence, and reconfiguration of a Chinese community in French colonial Tahiti and focused mainly on the inclusion, over several generations, of Chinese migrants and their descendants in French Polynesian society (Trémon 2009, 2010). I had studied the contemporary self-identification of third- and fourth-generation Tahiti Chinese and how they related to their places of origin in China and concluded that their ties with the latter had weakened as a result of several social, legal, and historical factors.

In Pine Mansion, one of their villages of origin, my aim was to examine whether this weakening of ties had been experienced in the same way by its inhabitants, and whether it had occurred with diasporic kin in destinations other than Tahiti. I knew that people had migrated from Pine Mansion and other villages in the area to many parts of the world besides the South Pacific. The main destinations were Southeast Asia and Central America in the 1880s through 1930s, Hong Kong in the late 1950s through late 1970s, and then on from Hong Kong to Europe and North America in the 1960s through 1990s (chapters 1 and 2). I aimed to grasp the perspective of the current inhabitants of the former village and the members of the local Chen lineage community regarding their diaspora.

In the 1990s, the notion of diaspora was extended to what had thus far been referred to as overseas Chinese communities.[5] The boom in diaspora studies in the early 1990s was part of a broader upsurge of interest in migration and other transnational phenomena. This first wave was followed by calls for caution in using the term *diaspora*, which was threatening to become meaningless if too loosely defined (Tölölyan 1996; Brubaker 2005; Dufoix 2011). Researchers also started to reflect critically on the notion of diaspora in the field of Chinese migration studies.[6]

I am less interested in diaspora as an entity than in the diasporic tie that binds, or is supposed to bind, emigrants and their descendants to the place that they or their forebears left behind in China. In this I draw inspiration from Ong and Nonini (1997, 18), who defend the "theoretical respectability" of diaspora, proposing to view it as "a pattern . . . that is continually reconstituted by the literal travel of Chinese persons across and throughout the regions of dispersion, and it is characterized by multiplex and varied connections of family ties, kinship, commerce, sentiments and values about native place in China, shared memberships in transnational organizations, and so on." My work is also guided by the idea that if we are to use the notion of diaspora, we should search for the conditions that allow for an enduring practice of diasporic identity (Gordon and Anderson 1999) without taking for granted that the relationship with the homeland will or must persist.

I started my fieldwork wishing to explore a very precise topic: the history of Pine Mansion's mausoleum. During my fieldwork in French Polynesia, one of my main interlocutors, Alain, who later introduced me to Lucien, showed me photographs of this huge building, which had been completed in 1999. The Tahiti Chens had made large financial donations for its construction but had only a rough idea of the reason behind the decision to build it. I myself only learned later that it had been built over the founding ancestor's tomb to protect it. All Alain knew was that the project was the result of a projected new road that had been a cause for concern. The mystery surrounding this contributed to my designing a new research project in Shenzhen. Taking this enigma as a starting point and collecting oral histories related to it, I was able to trace the processes through which the people of Pine Mansion had succeeded, with the help of their diaspora, in saving some of their most important landmarks and sites from scheduled destruction.

Many studies of the reconnection of diasporic Chinese with their emigrant communities in China were conducted in the 1980s and 1990s, following the launch of China's economic reform and opening.[7] Although some sociological and economic studies have analyzed the impact of overseas and Hong Kong investment and donations on economic development in the Pearl River delta, they pay little attention to local communities' role in this and how they perceive their overseas kin.[8] Much consideration has been given to the initiatives of the overseas Chinese and their effects on the local communities, but only a handful of studies examine these from the point of view of the communities themselves (Thireau and Mak 1996; Ding 2004; Li 2005; Chu 2010; Oxfeld 2010; Chen 2013).[9] This reflects a broader lack of interest in the localities of departure and origin, which were generally not deemed worthy of attention as potential field sites at the time (Chu 2010, 34). This is regrettable in the face of migration-study pioneers' insistence on the importance of the "variables of origin" (Sayad 1977, 60; see also Smith 2006) and the value that a perspective including the locality of origin adds to the understanding of migration.

The reality I discovered did not match what I had read about reconnection in the decade following China's reopening: the literature often depicts overseas Chinese as initiators of and major contributors to cultural and religious revival processes such as the rebuilding of temples and ancestral halls after the Mao era, particularly in South China's coastal provinces (Siu 1990; Dean 1993, 2003; Jing 1996; Kuah 1999; Kuah-Pearce 2011). Not only was the mausoleum project a safeguarding rather than a revitalizing operation, but also the overseas Chinese, at least those in Tahiti, did not take the lead in it and had only a vague idea of its purpose. I found out that the mausoleum had been built to save the founding ancestor's grave from destruction, and that in much the same way, Pine Mansion's primary school had been saved from being shut down with the help of overseas donations. As I traced these histories, I started wondering to what extent people in an emigration community such as Pine Mansion mobilize and even instrumentalize their overseas relatives' emotional attachment to their origins primarily for their own purposes and for causes that cannot legitimately be defended in China. The cases of the mausoleum and the primary school also revealed that the locals resorted to fundraising from their overseas kin only when they faced a critical situation, their reluctance to ask for money reflecting their desire to end their financial dependence on the diaspora.

When China was closed to the rest of the world during part of the Ming and most of the Qing dynasties, any unauthorized departure abroad was considered an act of treason.[10] Following the increase in out-migration starting in the 1880s, the lifting of the imperial ban on emigration in 1893 allowed not only departure but also return (Guerassimoff 2006; Chan 2018). This was accompanied by a requalification and revalorization of Chinese emigrants from "traitors" to "temporary patriotic sojourners" (Salmon 1996; Duara 1997; Wang 1999). The term *huaqiao* was coined at the end of the nineteenth century by the imperial authorities to emphasize Chinese emigrants' loyalty to their country of origin; it literally means Chinese (*hua*) sojourners (*qiao*) and is most often translated as "overseas Chinese" (Wang 1981).[11] The concept of *huaqiao* has worked in tandem with that of the homeland, *zuguo*, suggesting "a mutual constitution of migration and nation" (Chan 2018, 10).

Soon after the establishment of the People's Republic of China (PRC) in 1949, and particularly during the 1966–1976 Cultural Revolution, the official discourse changed and overseas Chinese were labeled capitalist traitors rather than patriots (Fitzgerald 1972). Ties between emigrants and their home communities loosened and even ruptured. Thus, the change that occurred in the late 1970s amounted to a total reversal. The PRC authorities have sought to reestablish the links with those they see as belonging to their diaspora (Wang 1991; Thunø 2001). Although Chinese state discourse distinguishes *huaqiao*—overseas Chinese nationals—from *huayi*—foreign nationals of Chinese descent—both are incorporated via an ethnic and nonterritorial notion of Chineseness in the category *haiwai huaren*—overseas ethnic Chinese (Ong 1999; Nyíri 2002; Xiang 2003; Yeoh and Willis 2004). The people targeted by this discourse may not recognize themselves in such a description. The new politics of the Chinese state caused friction among the overseas Chinese communities originating from the earlier waves of migration prior to 1949. However, it was also conducive to the (re)activation of a sense of belonging to China's diaspora for some members of these communities (Trémon 2009, 2010).

In the 1990s, the emphasis of these politics shifted toward "new emigrants" (*xin yimin*) rather than the old *huaqiao* (Thunø 2001; see chapter 1). Reflecting this change, Pine Mansioners now situate their overseas relatives, and emigration more generally, in the past rather than in the present. Even if they still depart for abroad, they regard themselves as mobile transnationals rather than emigrants, tending to follow the influential model of successful entrepreneurs who regularly commute to the village from abroad. This reflects a broader shift in migration patterns and a diversification of Chinese mobilities (Charney, Yeoh, and Tong 2003; Ho and Kuehn 2009; Nyíri 2010), as well as the latest reorientation of China's overseas policy in the 1990s, away from the old *huaqiao.*

Although I am mainly interested in the perspectives on their diasporic relatives of those who live in Pine Mansion and its surroundings, I also examine the diasporic relationship through overseas travelers' "roots tourism" to the village. These visits and their interactions with the locals allowed me to capture the limits of the lineage-framed relations with the diaspora.

Lineage Ties

Kinship ties, and particularly lineage ties, underpin the diasporic relationship. Pine Mansion's ancestral temple, its primary and secondary schools, and the Zhenneng Building, all named after the founding ancestor, are visible markers of its former status as an almost-single-lineage rural village once chiefly inhabited by members of the same lineage. The vast majority of its native residents (see below) bear the surname Chen and claim common descent from their founding ancestor, Chen Zhenneng. Lineages claim descent from a joint patrilineal ancestor and form corporate entities, regularly coming together for activities such as ancestor worship (Ebrey and Watson 1986, 6). In Guangdong, from which many migrants departed over several centuries, a large number of rural villages were structured into lineages that acted as "emigration agencies" (Watson 1975, 82) and channeled funding from overseas. The lineage tie to the locality of origin was the foundation of the diasporic reconnections that occurred with China's reopening. Lineage ties therefore offer a prism through which the connections, reconnections, and disconnections between the locals and the overseas Chinese can be studied. However, the term *diasporic relationship* refers not so much to the genealogical ties that can be traced from the founding ancestor in Pine Mansion to his descendants worldwide as to the practice of these kinship relations and their social, economic, moral, and symbolic aspects, as well as their strategic uses (Bourdieu 1977).

Although I had started my research in Tahiti with the idea that overseas Chinese in general and Chens originating from Pine Mansion in particular had made important donations for public goods in their locations of origin, in Pine Mansion I faced a discourse that amounted to the fact that overseas contributions were no longer needed. Now a prosperous "village in the city" (*chengzhongcun*), as they are called in China, its native inhabitants are no longer poor peasants who depend on their rich overseas relatives.[12] Still, I also noticed that overseas relatives' commitment to "matters of the public good" (*gongyi shiye*) was not only acknowledged and celebrated but was also presented as being lasting and permanent. This was mainly the case in more official contexts such as the genealogy (2000, 81–82):

> The descendants of [founding ancestor] Zhenneng overseas share a common characteristic: their body is in a foreign nation, but their heart cherishes the native place [*guxiang*].[13] Even those who are born abroad and have mixed blood [*hunxuer*] do not forget that "the source is in Pine Mansion, the roots lie in ancestor Zhenneng." . . . Looking back over a century, our lineage has obtained great success in educational and public good matters, and this is the consequence of the unfailing support of our overseas kin. . . . The *huaqiao* are a forever-shining jewel [*yongyuan shanguang de mingzhu*] in the construction of Pine Mansion.[14]

The contrast between this proclaimed eternity of diasporic support and the less official admission of its decline underscores that this is a moral discourse, held by the members of this globalized lineage, about themselves and their lineage as an institution: the permanence invoked is indicative of a normative expectation, the notion that overseas relatives should always remain committed to their village of origin. The Pine Mansion Chens glorify the global extension of their lineage and the success of their relatives overseas, which contribute to Pine Mansion's local and regional prestige and renown, notably through overseas relatives' visits at times of celebration such as the founding ancestor's birthday. These statements, sometimes voiced by the same interlocutors, that celebrate their contribution to the public good on the one hand and insist on the reduced need for such contributions on the other hand, point to a tension within the Chen lineage between those who have remained local and those who have migrated globally.

Lineages were patriarchal institutions organized around the ancestor cult and forming a patrilineal system of transmission of property, identity, and power. In the early twentieth century, lineages started being seen as cause and evidence of China's economic "backwardness" and vulnerability to Western and Japanese imperialism. The Communist regime outlawed them in 1949. Today, they are still illegal, or at least unrecognized, and the state considers their core religious activities superstitious.

Maurice Freedman's (1958, 1966) foundational work imposed a durably influential lineage paradigm on the anthropology of China.[15] Historians and anthropologists have since pointed out the historically constructed nature of lineage organizations, which have historically been promoted to incorporate local communities into the empire.[16] From the sixteenth to the eighteenth centuries, mainly during the Ming (1368–1644) and early Qing (1644–1911) dynasties, for taxation purposes the Chinese imperial state promoted the formation of local communities into groups that registered their property collectively in the names of their ancestors, thereby creating "lineage trusts." The lineage organization then spread to become the predominant institution in the Pearl River delta. Some criticized Freedman's focus on descent and inheritance in lineage organization (Sangren 1984; R. Watson 1988; Cohen 1990; Chun 1996, 2002). Following, a more recent generation of scholars has drawn attention to other aspects of Chinese kinship.[17]

However, it does not follow from this that studying the lineage should be relinquished altogether. James Watson (1975), who has studied the Man lineage in Hong Kong's New Territories and their migration to the United Kingdom and Canada, reminds us that the lineage is "very much alive" as a form of social organization (2004, 895). Lineages have quietly but largely resurfaced in China.[18] The Chinese authorities' tolerance is linked to the nonregistration of ancestor worship as an official religion and its proximity to the current neo-Confucian revival in China, but it is also due, particularly in southeastern coastal provinces, to local governments' eagerness to attract overseas Chinese capital, which has led them to turn a blind eye to the restoration of social institutions and practices that had been forbidden for almost thirty years.

This book shows that the revived form of the lineage is not identical to that of the past and that there is more involved here than the reestablishment of Confucian modes of social organization (Woon 1990, 147). Prohibited under Maoism, the lineage has resurfaced in broad daylight as a community of worship with its own moral economy, which provides for the public good (*gongyi*) of its members. I follow critiques of functionalist and utilitarian accounts of lineage organization in seeing the lineage primarily as a moral community tied by ritual obligations (Brandstädter 2000; Chun 2002) without excluding the strategic use of lineage ties for economic and political ends. The lineage's moral economy changed and adjusted during the collectivist era and is now readjusting to the new era of urbanization and market socialism. The notion of the public good points to both a Confucian morality long carried by the local lineage and a socialist morality of sacrifice for the common cause and bears an ambiguity that makes it amenable to diverse uses. Moreover, the present ritual economy rests not only on the subsistence ethics (Scott 1977) inherited from the collectivist era but also on "surplus ethics" in the context of renewed local prosperity: income earned from commercial and industrial real estate activities enables the community to cover expenses related to ancestor worship, thereby ensuring the proper functioning of the ritual economy, unlike in the Mao era (chapter 3).

I should clarify from the onset that the lineage as it has resurfaced in Pine Mansion and elsewhere only partly resembles the patriarchal and hierarchical social organization of imperial times. The revived lineage's ancestor-worship rituals, although still exclusively led by senior male leaders, now take the form of inclusive community events in which those who originate from Pine Mansion, men and women, local former peasants and downtown Shenzheners, Hong-Kongers and overseas visitors, participate (chapter 6). In the pre-1949 lineage, patrilineal descent determined residence rights and hence the right to a share in lineage holdings (Potter 1970, 125). Today, there is a separation between descent as a principle determining membership of the lineage on the one hand and residence as a principle determining the right to a share of the collective village economy on the other hand. Not only descendants residing in Hong Kong and abroad but also an increasing number of Chens living in downtown Shenzhen and other localities in the region and visiting the village with any degree of regularity remain members of the lineage as a ritual community.

Although the main focus of this book is the lineage, and the village no longer officially exists as such—it has become an "urban community," the lowest echelon in the urban administrative grid—I still refer to Pine Mansion as a village insofar as it is a reference point of crucial importance, and both those who originate from it and reside locally and those who no longer live there continue to refer to it as such. In the village itself, *hukou* registration as a permanent local resident confers membership of the legal category of "native villagers" (*yuancunmin*) and a share in the collective economy. The majority of this community of natives are Chen men and their wives, and the rest originate from the village but bear minority surnames. Thus, what we have here is at once a corporate group residing locally and a translocal descent group. I refer to this polymorphous entity by the terms *lineage-village community* and *lineage village*.

Building on Maurice Freedman's writings on lineage kinship, I seek to open up new directions in light of Marshall Sahlins's (2013) reflections on the "kinship I" (chapter 8). I use Firth's (1956) insights to propose that lineage ties are a form of "public kinship" and that the lineage should be viewed as a group of potential mobilization: this notion accounts for how the lineage perpetuates itself as an entity by mobilizing its members around projects for the public good in the name of the ancestor.

Processual Anthropology and Diaspora Space-Time

The new prosperity of former emigrant villages in the Pearl River delta has reduced or even ended their financial dependence on overseas relatives. Although I started my fieldwork in 2011 with the idea that overseas Chinese had had an impact on the local changes, I soon came to understand diasporic reconnections had peaked more than two decades ago and were now declining. Moreover, the notion of "impact," much used in development and economic studies of overseas and Hong Kong investment in China, is too unilateral and does not convey the reverse of the coin: how local transformation affects the community's relationship with the diaspora and how the community understands this relationship.

Some macro-anthropological theories treat globalization as a set of flows devoid of order, emphasizing their chaotic aspect (Appadurai 1996). This approach is misguided in two respects: on the one hand, it is hard not to admit the principle that some flows, mainly of capital, have more organizing power than others (Kalb and Tak 2005; Heyman and Campbell 2009); on the other hand, greater attention should be paid to possible ruptures and fragmentation rather than focusing exclusively on the linkages established by flows (Strathern 1996; Tsing 2005). It is therefore necessary to account for the ways in which sites are both connected and disconnected. My multisited positionality (see next section) allowed me to grasp the fractures and discontinuities in the diasporic relationship. Some look for causal explanations of local sociocultural processes in global historical forces (Gupta and Ferguson 1997; Burawoy 1998; Comaroff and Comaroff 1999, 283). Others criticize the ways in which this separation tends to neglect the microprocesses involved (Barth 1966, 1967; Handelman 2005), or the way it locates causal determinations on a scale so large that it is difficult to prove their connection to local sequences of events (Falk Moore 1999).

This book follows a processual approach that is not limited to examining the effects of overseas ties on local transformations, as it pays particular attention to the effects of local changes on the diasporic relationship. I favor an approach that consists of the study of processes (Mitchell 1983), leaving open the possibility that local actors both participate in the shaping of and are shaped by larger-scale transformations. Attention to scale provides an understanding of the "critical junctions" between local and global processes (Kalb and Tak 2005, 2–3), the relational mechanisms between power fields at different levels.

Scale figures centrally in this book in several ways. Shenzhen is an embodiment of what Frank Pieke (2009) refers to as "Chinese globalization": the emergence of China as a dominant center of the world economy and the driving force behind the contemporary transformation of the world system. Following Pieke's (2009, 6) call to identify "how 'China' or parts thereof are differentially constructed in a variety of arenas and circumstances around the globe," my research looks not so much at China as a whole as at the conditions for and consequences and understandings of this emergence on the ground, through the micro-lens of the relations between an emigrant village and its diaspora. China's contemporary globalization has not appeared out of nowhere. The factors and agents behind the

"Shenzhen miracle" are largely to be found below the scale of the city at the level of (pre-)Shenzhen's former emigrant villages. Villages such as Pine Mansion are Shenzhen's building blocks; they are expected to dissolve into the modern city and their native inhabitants, deemed uncivilized and backward, must become modern urban dwellers.

Also at stake, therefore, is the relationship between the centuries-old village at the local scale, and Shenzhen and the Chinese state's modernization plans at the city and national scales. China's state authorities have an ideological discourse that is turned against the kind of territorially rooted local organizations represented by lineage villages such as Pine Mansion (Trémon 2015). However, the resources offered by the scalar properties of their lineage—its global reach and long past—have allowed Pine Mansioners to reestablish their lineage rituals and protect the village's most important ancestral sites in the face of government plans to destroy them. Pine Mansion Chens have used the diaspora as an economic resource and as a pretext, even an alibi, in the development of borderline illegal projects that have skillfully subverted city- and central government policies.

I offer an ethnographic analysis that maintains the analytical value of the local and the global and of core and periphery frameworks but grapples with them as relational rather than absolute terms, paying attention to the scalar and polar dimensions of people's actions.[19] The emigrant village and its overseas relatives is my prime unit of observation for analyzing diaspora space-time—that is, the diasporic relationship's spatiotemporal scales. Diasporas connect scattered people across long distances and over several generations to a real or imagined place of origin.[20] This spatiotemporal extension is not an invariable given; long-distance and long-term links can be loosened to the point of rupture when distant relatives are lost sight of or forgotten.

What I witnessed in Shenzhen was a situation in which this change was under way and translated into scalar struggle. Critical geographers have shifted the focus from scale as size of social entities or preexisting territorial/administrative levels to scale as the result of social actions and political struggles.[21] Scalar action includes scale-jumping (Smith 2008) and rescaling (Brenner 2001). The members of the lineage village community collaborate with projects led by the city, the state, and their diaspora, while also pursuing their own local scalar project. Different timescales are also at play. The importance given to the pre-Maoist past, the Mao era, or the economic reform and opening, the invocation of continuity or rupture, and of tradition or modernity, is also a matter of situational strategies. Spatial and temporal scales interact, as shown for instance in the ways the village territorial organization is still shaped by pre-Mao and Mao-era arrangements but is currently being rescaled as a result of urbanization and increased state involvement, or in the ways the local villagers situate their distant diasporic kin in the past.

Scalar projects concern the scale at which power is exerted (Nonini and Susser 2019, 3) and scalar struggles concern the relevant scale at which social action takes place. I propose an analytical distinction between two dimensions of scale within which social action can be considered: scope and valence. Scale as scope—the extent of actions in time and space—is fairly straightforward. Existing scales are the result of past social action and can be used strategically in struggles for power: far-reaching networks can confer money and prestige; historical legacy can be a source of legitimacy. The desired scale itself can be a goal of such a struggle. This book looks not only at the scope at which actions unfold but also at the values that the actors give to these scales: their valence, a term that connotes both attractiveness—that is, their desirability and potential to generate value—and the importance attached to this potential. Valence is defined as "the degree of attractiveness an individual, activity, or thing possesses as a behavioral goal" (Merriam Webster 2019). The word is derived from the Latin *valentia*, "power, capacity," itself a derivative of *valere*, to be powerful, to prevail. It is a matter of polarity, of being located at the center or the periphery, and it includes a moral dimension.

Although China's ascendance toward the core of the world system makes it a central node in global flows of money and power, it also increases the importance of local and national Chinese scales. Contrasting the diasporic relationship with the Kula circuit's space-time studied by Nancy Munn (2007), I argue that valence is not necessarily a function of scope (chapter 5). In the conclusion, I further develop an argument in favor of a moral economy of scale based on this distinction: scale as the scope of social systems and networks resulting from actions and interactions that lend them a certain extension in space and time, and scale as valence—that is, the attractiveness and desirability of one scale in relation to other scales, resulting from evaluative actions, such as comparing life abroad with life in the village. The micro-unit of the village and its emigrants allow me to observe changing relationships of dependency and the shifting valence of local and global scales. For more than a century, people from Pine Mansion and many other surrounding villages have been migrating from the periphery to the cores and semiperipheries of the world system and making strategic use of the valences of different localities. Today, relations between the homeland and the diaspora are becoming equal, if not reversed, in the context of China's rise to become a core in the world system.

This book examines how the rise of China has affected migration and mobility, arguing that the transformation in the diasporic relationship lies in the emergence of new mobilities and a change in how emigration is conceptualized locally, and, more importantly, in the altered moral economic relationship between the local community and the diaspora. From the point of view of the main focus of this book, the local inhabitants, the revalorization of the local territory's economic potential is morally interpreted as a return to an order of things that is more just than it was in the past, when emigration presented better livelihood opportunities than remaining at home.

The community's relationship with the diaspora is in itself driven by a tension between continuity—the maintenance of kinship ties and the celebration of global brotherhood, epitomized in ritual spatiotemporal fusion, and change, with ties loosened by the passage of time and genealogical distancing, as also by the estrangement generated during the Mao period. From the point of view of emigrants and their descendants, donations from abroad to public projects and the visit from afar to one's village of origin are a moral duty. Moreover, the local community gains prestige from its global extension and the large number of relatives overseas and their contributions to village projects. The ambivalence in its relations with the diaspora is due to tension between recognition of this moral duty and the possibility of capitalizing on it on the one hand and the desire to break away from the relationship of dependence on the other hand. Although the lineage's restored local power draws on its global diasporic networks in some respects, it is complicit with the Chinese state's national scalar project of urbanization, modernization, and economic growth in others. Change is also at stake in the relationship between the local community and its diaspora in matters regarding ritual activities. The revival of the lineage's ritual economy is a local scalar project.

I spent much of my time in the field trying to trace the economic, social, and administrative transformations that have occurred since the start of China's economic reform and opening. At times, I felt that I was losing sight of the diasporic relationship. However, the latter provides the context for a discourse that morally evaluates these transformations. The diaspora is always in the background as a yardstick for comparing livelihoods and as a broader context for the villagers' life choices. It has sometimes been hard to distinguish between the text and the context; for example, although I collected narratives on the improved livelihoods that I thought would provide context for what informants would say about their overseas kin, I came to realize that what they said about these changes was largely filtered through the lens of the diasporic relationship. It was mainly through this prism that I captured these changes, not just as a result of my own analytical choices but also as a result of what I told people in Pine Mansion about my research interests and how they saw me.

Multisited Positionality and Fieldwork

I collected the ethnographic materials on which this book is based over five periods of fieldwork in the former village of Pine Mansion, in August 2011, July 2012,

March and October 2013, and October 2014. Since then, I have returned twice, in March 2017 and April 2018, for a new research project (only limited material from my more recent stays is included here). The book also relies on earlier research in Tahiti between 2000 and 2004. My knowledge of Tahiti Chinese has played an important role in my fieldwork and lent it a multisited positionality even before I traveled back to Tahiti in 2013, in between two stays in Shenzhen (on which more below). In addition to ethnographic observations and interviews, I used written documents, mainly the Chen genealogy, which I read in preparation for my first stay and used as archival material and for fieldwork purposes. I also collected histories of the village written by members of the community and recent historical books about the area. However, I relied mainly on villagers' oral histories.

The genealogical book has two parts: the first is a collection of photographs and texts produced at different times, constituting a rich bundle of historical documentation on the Chen lineage and its overseas connections. The second part contains the genealogical material proper. I used the second part in the field as an instrument for making contacts and as a tool, especially during interviews and casual conversations, for situating people within the lineage and providing background to family histories. Both uses of the genealogy enabled me to analyze the modalities of emigration with regard to kinship ties (chapter 1).

I chose to travel to the field on specific dates in March and October 2013 and October 2014 in order to be present at the two main moments of gathering for rites, which are also opportunities for family reunions when Hong Kongers, downtown Shenzheners, and overseas relatives gather at Pine Mansion. Between the two trips to China in 2013, I traveled to Tahiti in July 2013, not so much with the intention of conducting fieldwork (although it turned out otherwise) as to attend the wedding of a Tahiti Chinese with whom I had become friends at the time of my doctoral research. When the word spread that I was returning to Tahiti, Alain, my key informant and guide, asked me to give a series of talks on the research I had started in Pine Mansion. This detour through French Polynesia added new momentum to the diasporic dimension of my research. Granted the status of an expert in villages of origin, I gathered new material in the form of testimonies from people in the audience about their own travels to find their roots in China. However, the main outcome of this visit was the project it triggered: Alain and a group that formed around him planned to journey to their roots in Shenzhen the following year, when I would be in the field. Thus in October 2014, I found myself together with Tahitian travelers, some of whom I had known for years, in Pine Mansion, where I observed how they experienced their visit to Pine Mansion and other nearby villages.

My decision to conduct my fieldwork as a series of short stays of one to two months over several years rather than in the usual ethnographic way of staying for a long stretch of time was mainly due to my parenting and teaching obligations. There were some logistical reasons as well: my strategy of several short stays allowed me to travel each time on a tourist visa without having to request special authorization. This intermittent presence in the field took on significance that I had not anticipated: it was very similar to the visiting patterns of some diasporic relatives such as the Malaysians whom I met several times on their annual short-but-regular visits to the village. My first visit had immediately likened me to an overseas relative in the villagers' eyes: Lucien's introduction and my copy of the genealogy caused them to mistake me for a *huaqiao* (*fakiao* in Hakka).

My mention of Fuchang, whom I had consulted several times during my earlier research, also played a role. Fuchang was the most illustrious Pine Mansion Chen lineage member in Tahiti.[22] Until he died in 2005, he had been the "connector" (Levitt and Glick Schiller 2004) of Pine Mansion with the Tahiti Chen. Born in the village in 1911, he had worked as a schoolteacher in Pine Mansion before departing in 1937, just before the outbreak of the Sino-Japanese War. In Tahiti, Fuchang had at first worked with his brothers-in-law, later starting his own business. As he was among the last of the Pine Mansioners who migrated to Tahiti, he was nominated as dean of the Tahiti Chens; he became president of one of the major Chinese associations in Tahiti, the Philanthropic Association, and remains the honorary president of the Tahitian Chen (Ching) Family Association. He earned a strong reputation for his culture and calligraphy, and two of his calligraphed parallel verses (*duilian*) decorate the entrance gate to the mausoleum in Pine Mansion.

Perhaps due to my behavior in the village, asking, as *huaqiao* do, to visit the ancestral temple and the mausoleum shortly after my arrival, during the first couple of weeks I was introduced everywhere as an overseas Chinese. I considered it not reasonably possible, considering my features, for me to be seen as of Chinese descent and assumed it was a polite way of situating me and accounting for all the questions I was asking about the village's history, the construction of the mausoleum, and the overseas donations. It was not until I gave the president of the Zhenneng lineage foundation my name card after my first formal interview with him and his surprise at finding nothing resembling the name Chen on it that I realized that this had been a true misunderstanding. Furthermore, when I saw photographs of visiting Canadian Chens with blond hair and blue eyes a few days later, I realized that I could indeed have been taken for a Chen. This amalgamation was all the more plausible because the younger generations abroad understand only a few words of Hakka but do sometimes learn Mandarin at school or university, as I had.[23]

Returning periodically over seven years, I saw the village transforming before my eyes. When I arrived in 2011, only a few tiny old houses were still standing in the center of the village surrounded by an immense field of rubble from the demolition, awaiting their turn. I would walk through the rubble and look at what remained. It was a shortcut between the places where I spent the most time, with the community center for elderly people on one side and the administrative workstation (*gongzuozhan*) and ancestral hall on the other. I had many fortuitous encounters and conducted a series of some thirty or so interviews with community and lineage leaders. These could not be called formal interviews because I seldom found anybody alone: when I arrived, my interviewee would generally be having tea with a fellow villager or visitors from another village, and others would drop in and join the conversation which would then become, for me, an ethnographic observation of discussions between villagers. These others were almost never introduced by their names but only by their function or origin—for instance, "He's a former village head" and "She's come back from Panama." Sometimes they were not introduced at all. Although the lineage leaders had to be contacted beforehand, villagers would refer me to formal community leaders with a good reputation because they kept long working hours and were happy to receive visitors, whether friends or administrative clients, at their office and would ply them with tea and cigarettes at any time during the afternoon.

Even after the misunderstanding was dispelled, my relationships with the Pine Mansion villagers hardly changed. I continued to be regarded, albeit metaphorically, as kin to the Tahiti Chinese. I made contact with Weixin, Fuchang's nephew and the cousin of another prominent (non-Chen) Tahiti Chinese. When I had met him in March 2013, he had come from Guangzhou, where he lives, to spend three weeks in his house and take part in the Chunfen (spring equinox) and Qingming ancestor worship rituals. I met him regularly at these festivals in the following years. Weixin was born the year his uncle Fuchang left Pine Mansion, in 1937. He is extremely grateful to Fuchang for sending him the money to pursue a university degree and become a university professor. Weixin's father had been absent. He had fought on the side of the Kuomintang Party and had left for Taiwan in 1949 and then founded a new family in the United States. Weixin had little contact with him until 1985, when he saw him again in Hong Kong.

Weixin met Fuchang for the first time when he came back to China in 1977, forty years after he had left. Fuchang was a connector. He corresponded with the Pine Mansion villagers and collected donations from fellow Chens in Tahiti, which he sent or brought as cash on several of his trips to the village. His death in particular and the death of the older generation in general, as well as the lack of recent migration to Tahiti have distanced the Tahiti Chens from Pine Mansion. Still, they benefit from an aura of prestige owing to the large donations they made to a variety of projects in the village in the 1980s and 1990s under Fuchang's direction. It is this distance and prestige that I felt and benefited from by my association with them.

My position in the field can be characterized as inscribed in the relationship of the Chens in Pine Mansion with their remote and faraway overseas kin. It had considerable weight, enabling me to collect material by asking questions that would otherwise have been considered intrusive and inappropriate. My apparent proximity to Fuchang made it easy for me to access not only Weixin, who turned out to be extremely talkative and to hold strong views, but also some of the people who had played key roles in the construction of the mausoleum, among them Ganhua, a retired high-ranking cadre who lived in downtown Shenzhen and had led the operation. More generally, mentioning the Tahiti Chens made it easier to ask questions and obtain answers about sensitive subjects such as feng shui (geomancy).

Here, I must briefly digress to underscore that although the focus of my research is transformations over the past decades rather than the anterior past, to trace the village's past I consulted the wide literature on villages of the same type in the region, based on studies of mainland refugees in Hong Kong in the 1950s through 1970s when the mainland was closed to researchers. Of particular comparative (and confirmative) value to my study, as they deal with another lineage village inhabited by Chens in today's Shenzhen, are Richard Madsen's (1984) *Morality and Power in a Chinese Village* and his book with Anita Chan and Jonathan Unger, *Chen Village* (Chan, Madsen, and Unger 2009), although they focus mostly on the collectivist period. *Chen Village*, first published in 1984, was updated in 1990 and 2009, after the authors were able to visit the field (Chan et al. 2009).

I collected very few oral or written allusions to the pre-Mao and Mao periods. Most of my informants knew little about the pre-1949 past and did not like to talk about the Mao period, primarily because of the suffering they had experienced and the divisions in the community that the regime had caused. However, memories of the collectivist period are still active and affect the attitudes and behavior of Chinese citizens (Siu 1989; Yang 1989; Potter and Potter 1990; Yan 1992; Lora-Wainwright 2013). Reference to the past may be negative, acting as a foil and visible in the ways the people of Pine Mansion celebrate the good life they have enjoyed since Deng Xiaoping's reforms. They may also act positively based on a set of moral and political principles that they continue to hold, as in the anachronistic use of Mao-era terms such as *brigades*.

The Chapters

Three moments or phases in my research can be distinguished retrospectively: the first followed my introduction to the village by Lucien, a Tahiti Chinese, and enabled me to capture some aspects of the Pine Mansioners' perspectives on their overseas relatives due to my association with the latter. The second occurred when I traveled to Tahiti and presented my Chinese research there; this displacement gave a truly multisited turn to my research in the sense that it had a heuristic effect, raising new questions and confirming some of my previous conclusions. This restitutive return gave new impetus to my research on the diasporic relationship and triggered the third moment, when I followed a group of Sino-Tahitian travelers' journey to their "roots." This connection of my two fields placed me in an intermediate position ideally suited to observing the diasporic relationship in practice. This book's outline does not strictly follow the chronology of my research.

Chapter 1 is based on the material in the lineage genealogy and recent surveys in the village that estimated the number of kin living abroad and in Hong Kong. Comparison of these two sources reveals the extent to which ties with relatives who are not only geographically remote but also genealogically distant have relaxed. I distinguish between two main migration periods, the first at the end of the nineteenth century (1870s–1890s) and the two decades following the revolution of 1911, and the second following the advent of the Communist regime in 1949. I highlight the difference between these two periods in terms of the mobilization of kinship ties. The number of emigrants leaving Pine Mansion is now much lower than in the past, and a hypermobile class of entrepreneurs has emerged whose members differ from those of the older diaspora and are the focus of the current Chinese authorities' discourse on patriotic migrants.

Not only has migration become less of an option than in the past, but also overseas money is now much less needed. Chapter 2 develops a processual geography and history of the diasporic relationship. I track the changes over time in the amounts donated locally and from overseas to the village school and other public projects from the 1920s to the late 1990s, as well as smaller differences linked to each project's local or global scope. These financial flows reveal changing relations of dependency and the shifting valences of local and global scales. The history of overseas donations also discloses the strategic positioning of migrants and their descendants in the world system. Chapter 2 further shows how the relocation of the lineage foundation from Hong Kong to Pine Mansion in the early 1990s embodied this change in relations and signaled a reterritorialization and relocalization of the lineage and its ritual economy.

The process that unfolded within the lineage ritual economy is similar to that in the village, which is now a real estate rent economy. Chapter 3 traces the transformation of the former agricultural collectives into shareholding companies, showing the persistence of a redistributive system of income drawn from collective land. The moral economy of the lineage has persisted by adjusting pre-1949 moral patterns to the Maoist morality and then to the capitalist era. Despite expectations that the lineage would vanish, continuities in economic and territorial organization account for its contemporary reemergence as a corporate entity, albeit in a different form. The shareholding companies, in which only native villagers are entitled to participate, were established based on subsistence ethics and participate in what I call a moral economy of surplus. Local membership of the former village community has thus gained increased valence in the context of urbanization.

Its global overseas extension offers the lineage economic as well as symbolic resources based on its prestigious past, which the people of Pine Mansion have used to counter some of the changes induced by economic reforms and urbanization. They mobilized to defend two of the village's most important sites: the grave of the founding ancestor and the century-old primary school, both of which were threatened by policies of administrative and spatial rationalization. Chapter 4 analyzes these events in terms of scalar action rather than neoliberal governmentality. The principle of the public good and the figure of the founding ancestor, which stands for the public good, are systematically invoked in calls for local and overseas financial contributions. Diasporic funding has thus been instrumental not only in the revitalization of ancestral worship in villages such as Pine Mansion but also in the cunning circumvention of government-imposed urbanization policies.

How do those who have remained in the village understand migration and the financial relationship with overseas kin? Chapter 5 considers narratives and statements about geomancy (feng shui), the desirability of emigration and the possibility of return, and donations from overseas. They are indicative of how Pine Mansioners question the distribution of value between themselves and those who have left. The improvement in local livelihoods not only reduces the incentive to migrate but also engenders what I call sociodicies of (im)mobility—that is, moralized comparisons of people's trajectories according to whether they have stayed in the village or left. I analyze the implicit moral condemnation of migration by those who have stayed, and the local, more than national, morality revealed by the way some illustrious returnees are considered exemplary figures. How the acts of migrating and returning, or not returning, are morally valued, vary notably according to historical period and social class.

Chapter 6 examines the diasporic relationship through the lens of ritual. I trace how the "revival" of ancestor worship from 1981 was actually its relocalization, since its practice was moved overseas during the period when it was prohibited on the mainland. The way in which the rituals are performed today is the outcome of negotiation between the villagers and Hong Kongers. I analyze how the rituals accomplish the fusion of spatiotemporally distant kin and simultaneously display tensions and differentiation. The symbolic association of the diaspora with the past is very visible in the ways the villagers contrast their overseas relatives' supposed traditionalism with their own ways of performing ancestral worship, which they deem modernized. The fusion and the contrast imply different cultural intimacies: one that the villagers share with their diaspora against the state and another that they share as citizens of the Chinese state against their overseas relatives.

Chapter 7 is based on the visit of a group of Tahitian Chinese to their villages of origin. Although none were first-generation emigrants, they experienced the journey as a return. The travel itself was a continuation of their quest for identity and a response to an absence of knowledge transmission within the family. Because many of the villages of origin have now vanished, searching for their roots is becoming increasingly difficult for diasporic visitors. These two elements account for their approach being largely based on searching for clues and signs, making the journey itself much like a detective game. Deliberately leaving many things to chance, they were searching for (and in several cases achieved) a spiritual reconnection with their ancestors. One of the travelers' paradoxical use of the Tahitian term *mana*, the magical power and energy emanating from the ancestors, reveals the tension at the heart of the diasporic relationship.

The final chapter examines the ambivalence within this relationship, which lies in the tension between the global scale on which kinship with distant overseas relatives is located and the difficulty of maintaining ties when there is no longer a close kin relationship. This global scale is the scale on which the state liaises with the descendants of emigrants who are no longer Chinese nationals, based on a rhetoric of blood ties; it is also the global scale of lineage kinship itself, based on a rhetoric of global brotherhood that confers prestige on the local inhabitants of the former lineage villages. Both are based on a similar rhetoric of global brotherhood and eternal loyalty. Using observational material on emigrants' descendants' visits to the village and their encounter with overseas liaison workers, I examine the ambivalence that characterizes this organization, the Qiaolian, with regard to its attitude to visiting overseas Chinese. I then show how despite the lineage leaders' rhetoric of global brotherhood, interactions between locals and visitors from overseas are limited by the latter's absence of local close kin. Building on Sahlins's (2013) reflections on the "kinship I," I point out a distinction between his terms *mutuality of being* and *mutuality of existence*.

In the conclusion, I discuss what the case of Pine Mansion reveals in terms of the processes and periodization of Chinese globalization, the major feature of the last wave of globalization, which is neither new nor chaotic and occurs within an integrated world system. I review the chapters in light of a moral economy of scale based on the distinction between scale as scope—the extension in time and space of social actions and of the social systems resulting from such actions—and scale as valence—the attractiveness and desirability of scales. The Chen lineage has been globalized by a century of emigration. Although they are still global in reach, the diasporic networks have refocused on the place of origin as a consequence of the creation of Shenzhen and the reopening of China. The generation of value itself is now considered purely local and diasporic relationships are tending to rupture.

A GLOBALIZED LINEAGE

Abroad was better: everyone wanted to go abroad; we Hakkas call it *guofan*. When people came back from abroad there was a lot of rejoicing, they brought cakes, local specialties.

—Mrs. Wang, Pine Mansion inhabitant, October 2014

Overseas relatives still bring their own local specialties when they visit the village, and I had the chance to taste some delicious Surinamese doughnuts during one of my stays in Pine Mansion. Such visits have become sparser, however, and the number of visiting relatives is much smaller today than in the decade following China's reopening, even on occasions for gathering such as the founding ancestor's birthday. Mrs. Wang Cuichun, whose elder son lives in Martinique and whose husband, a Chen, lives in Hong Kong, speaks of people's desire to go abroad in the past tense because it is no longer everyone's obsession as it was up to the late 1970s. Emigration is considered a phenomenon of the past.

In the latest edition of *Genealogy of the Pine Mansion Chen* (henceforth, the genealogy), revised in 2000, the first part, written by two lineage elders, traces the history of the Chen lineage, and the second part presents the genealogical material.[1] Emigration is presented in the first part as an act that followed the same logic of seeking new lands as that of the ancestors' migration to Pine Mansion. "Land is the basis of peasants' livelihood; our lineage . . . has changed residence many times, each time to [seek] land. It was better to leave Pine Mansion to seek other means of subsistence" (Genealogy 2000, 80). Zhenneng, the founding ancestor, is said to have left Changle (today's Wuhua) in northeastern Guangdong, where land had become scarce. Together with his three adult sons and their wives, he traveled all the way to Kowloon, which is now part of Hong Kong, before settling in Pine Mansion in 1751. In the middle of the nineteenth century, some of his descendants settled elsewhere in the area and established separate lineage branches. The text states that the first to go abroad left as indentured laborers and valorizes their audacity: "In the 1870s a few young people who had met with difficulties in life and had courage left for the Nanyang (Southeast Asia), the Pacific, and the Nanyang Islands [to work] as coolies [*kuli*], commonly called 'those who sell themselves as pigs [*mai zhuzaide*].'[2] They were the pioneers (*xianxingzhe*) of the lineage throughout the world, the vanguard who opened up a new life for the Zhenneng lineage" (Genealogy 2000, 80).

Emigration intensified in imitation of these pioneers and as a result of the socioeconomic differences generated by the migrants sending remittances back home. Going abroad (*guofan*) had become everybody's dream by the end of the nineteenth century:

> Around 1900, some people returned to the native village with *huaqiao* status [*huaqiao de shenfen*] to marry and start a family, or to buy land and build a house. They came back from other countries with a large amount of information, bringing things that had previously been inaccessible, and they expanded the worldview of the local farmers. Many people received material assistance from their relatives overseas. "Going abroad" [*guofan*; quotes in original] to earn money became the aspiration of many people in the lineage. This occurred in conjunction with the very strong economic growth of Western countries and the demand for labor. For this reason, from the beginning of the twentieth century onward, more and more people left the native village and "went abroad" [*guofan*] or to Hong Kong to seek a livelihood. (Genealogy 2000, 81–82)

The "*huaqiao* status" mentioned in the text refers to the coining of this category (*huaqiao*) following the revalorization of emigration in the imperial authorities' discourse that accompanied the official lifting of the ban on emigration in 1893. The concepts of *huaqiao* (and *qiaoju*, expatriates) were forged at that time and implied both the right to emigrate and the right to return (Wang 1991). Following the first Sino-Japanese War, which ended in China's defeat and the humiliating Treaty of Shimonoseki in 1895, the discourse on *huaqiao* took on a tone that implied that these emigrants were the Chinese equivalent of European colonizers. They were now seen by the authorities as possible instruments in the struggle against Western and Japanese imperialism, making up for China's economic and technological backwardness and its vulnerability to imperialist onslaughts (Douw, Huang, and Godley 1999, 32). This stance, which was further explored by China's Jinan scholars during the 1920s and 1930s, is echoed in the preface to the genealogy, which discusses emigration as the result of an interaction between the local lack of land and the global demand for labor.[3]

The Chen genealogy traces all the members of the lineage, agnatic descendants of the founding ancestor, without distinction as to where they live. The Chen lineage currently covers ten generations. The genealogy first schematically traces the descendants of generations one to five on four pages and details the descendants of each ancestor of the fifth generation on the next 166 pages. The fifth generation, whose personal names start with the character "Guo," is the organizing principle, as it is halfway between the first-generation ancestor, Zhenneng, and the contemporary generation.[4] The final pages (pages 167–218), however, display lists enumerating them according to their location in Southeast Asia, the Pacific, North and Central America, and Europe. I start by comparing these lists with the Pine Mansion residents' most recent available census of overseas connections. This reveals the extent to which ties with relatives who are not only geographically remote but also genealogically distant have loosened. I then trace the different waves of migration and examine the role of kinship in organizing them. The periods of migration from Pine Mansion village largely reflect those documented in historical studies of Chinese migration (Wang 1991; McKeown 1999, 2000). I distinguish between two main migration periods, the first at the end of the nineteenth century (1870s–1900s and the two decades following the revolution of 1911) and the second following the advent of the Communist regime in 1949. I examine the shift in destinations from one period to another more closely in chapter 2; here, I highlight the difference between the first pioneering period and the second in terms of the mobilization of kinship relations. The chapter ends by showing the change in the desirability of migration since conditions and livelihoods have improved at home and its substitution by a form of transnational mobility that is seen as much less permanent.

Contemporary Links

The first time I went into Pine Mansion's local administrative workstation (*gongzuozhan*) in 2011, I found a sign above a door indicating that this was the office for overseas liaison, the Qiaolian. Inside, I could not find anyone specifically in charge of such matters. The employee I dealt with on this first visit was a young Chen, who took out the *huaqiao* register at my request. I had ventured to ask for it not knowing whether such a file existed. The register he handed to me came from a census of overseas resources in Shenzhen (*Shenzhenshi qiaowu ziyuan*) commissioned by the city of Shenzhen and conducted in 2010.

The census authorities had asked the respondents to provide the following information: the name of an overseas or Hong Kong household head, the nature of their relationship to that person, the number of people in that person's family and her/his nationality, country of residence, and contact number. In the emigration history section of the Shenzhen Museum, overseas Chinese (*haiwai huaqiao*) from the city as a whole are numbered at 120,000, spread across fifty-eight countries which are listed in decreasing order of numerical importance, starting with Malaysia, Indonesia, Jamaica, Tahiti (French Polynesia), Suriname, the United States, the United Kingdom, the Netherlands, and Belgium.[5]

The Pine Mansion community (*shequ*) reported a total of 1,160 people overseas and 1,564 in Hong Kong. I calculated a smaller number of overseas relatives (1,109) after removing all the duplicates (table 1.1.); for instance, the same Tahitian Chen was mentioned by three villagers. This type of redundancy had not been considered by the workstation employees, revealing a lack of zeal that was also evident in the way the respondents had filled in the survey. Only thirty-eight respondents, who had reported forty-four of the 163 overseas household heads, gave their own names and occupations. Since several of these were village cadres, it is likely that they completed the survey for residents under their jurisdiction.[6] In any case, the incompleteness of the answers indicates considerable uncertainty about the requested information. Only nine telephone numbers of overseas household heads are registered, and their relationship to the respondent is only mentioned in cases reported by the same thirty-eight villagers and seems to have been specified mainly when it was a close one (twenty are siblings and fifteen are parents or children). In all the other cases, the nature

TABLE 1.1. Number of Pine Mansion Chens in different overseas locations, Shenzhen census, 2010

United Kingdom	275
Suriname	184
United States	159
Canada	167
Malaysia	76
Tahiti	59
Holland	54
Jamaica	48
French Guiana	46
Belgium	14
Trinidad	11
Singapore	6
Panama	6
Spain	4
Total	**1,109**

Source: Research on overseas resources in Shenzhen (*Shenzhenshi qiaowu ziyuan diaocha wen*), Pine Mansion community workstation, 2010. I was told that the data have not been updated since 2010.

of the respondents' relationship to the overseas head of household is listed as "unclear." Most can probably be characterized as remote lineage kin. Indeed, among the 163 overseas household heads named, only eight are not Chens.

Pine Mansion cadres readily acknowledged that the number of overseas relatives is probably incorrect and highly underestimated: as another Chen workstation employee put it, "Many families have not had contact for almost thirty years, and so they declare five household members when there are probably ten." In fact, having attended the 2003 annual banquet of the Tching (Chen) Family Association, which gathers those claiming to belong to the Chen lineage in Tahiti, I know that well over fifty-nine Chen descendants in Tahiti originate from Pine Mansion.

What these figures therefore signal in most cases is an indication of awareness of the existence of overseas relatives with whom the genealogical ties are mostly unclear and regular contact is seldom maintained. Connections with relatives in Hong Kong are more numerous, and the relationship is closer than that with relatives overseas. Of 215 respondents, 156 gave their names and their relationship to the person they were declaring. The parent-child relationship, which largely prevails, is a two-way street: in forty-four cases, a child declares their father, mother, or both to be living in Hong Kong; in fifty-seven cases, a father or mother declares a son or daughter in Hong Kong.[7] This distribution shows the bidirectional mobility between Pine Mansion and Hong Kong. Children remained in the village, entrusted to their grandparents, when their parents left for Hong Kong. Some continued to live in the village when they reached adulthood, while others in their turn left for Hong Kong. People who left at a young age and had children in Hong Kong returned to retire and spend the rest of their lives in the village while their children stayed in Hong Kong. As shown below, by the end of the 1970s, the village was almost deserted. However, in the first decade after China's reopening, some of those who had left for Hong Kong returned.[8]

In total, the census reports 163 overseas household heads and 278 in Hong Kong in 2010: reckoning the number of households in Pine Mansion at 350, it can be roughly estimated that almost half had relatives overseas, and two-thirds had relatives in Hong Kong.

The numbers given by country at the end of the genealogy are distributed as shown in table 1.2. The genealogical enumeration of overseas relatives proceeds according to a different logic from that of the Shenzhen City census. Unlike the method used by the city authorities, the per-country lists at the end of the genealogy count overseas residents of all generations. They do not include those who migrated but then returned to the village, making it difficult to reach an accurate number of those who left.[9] Moreover, the descendants of those with whom not even indirect contact has been maintained are not included in the records. In the genealogy, lines sometimes end after the fifth, sixth, or seventh generations,

TABLE 1.2. Number of Pine Mansion Chens in different overseas locations

Southeast Asia	338
Tahiti	284
Holland	196
United States	149
Canada	140
Jamaica	135
Suriname	131
Panama	41
United Kingdom	21
French Guiana	16
Belgium	5
Trinidad	3
West Germany	2
Australia	1
Total	**1,462**

Source: Pine Mansion Chen Genealogy, 2000.

indicating loss of contact with these emigrants. For instance, no descendants of twenty-five of the first forty-four men to leave for Southeast Asia are listed. Unlike lines without progeny, which are indicated by a small circle ("o") under the name of the last descendant, these lines come to an end without explanation. In the remaining cases, the names of the wives and children of ninth- or tenth-generation descendants are generally missing. However, this does not necessarily mean that there are no links or that there has been no attempt to reconnect them, although such attempts are the exception. Thus, the Malaysians whom I met twice in the village, at the 2013 and 2014 ritual celebrations of the founding ancestor's birthday, are not named in the genealogy despite the fact that they had been attending the ritual and visiting a close relative of their branch for several years. The figure of 338 Chens in Southeast Asia therefore reflects only a distant historical reality—had all connections been maintained, it would be much higher. This gap indicates the loosened, almost severed ties between this destination and the village.

However, the presence or absence of overseas relatives in the genealogy should not be considered evidence of enduring relationships. Whereas the city census aimed to identify fairly close relatives, the genealogical census listed all generations and relied on the connectors—individuals who are very often leaders of overseas community associations and the main interlocutors of the lineage seniors back in the village—to update the data. These connectors are conveyers of information and resources, and through them other members of the overseas community, especially later-generation descendants, remain indirectly connected to the village of origin. They thus pertain to a transnational social field without being actively involved in transnational practices themselves (Levitt and Glick Schiller 2004, 1009). Descendants (*zisun*) are listed only when connectors have sent data on them. The connectors' mediation allowed the compilers of the genealogy to include those lineage members with whom there are not necessarily close family ties. Thus, the very large difference in numbers between the official and the genealogical censuses regarding Tahiti is explained by the liaison work of the connector Fuchang, who transmitted a lot of material to the compilers. He also translated and transcribed the French, English, and Tahitian first names that have become common in the most recent generations—for example, *Nikelatu* for Nicolas, *Endulou* for Andrew, and *Mouana* for Moana[10]—as well as the lengthy Tahitian names of the emigrants' names into Chinese characters, condensing them, for instance, to *Feliyou* from Tevahine Firuu, *Alihualuo* from Ariifano Tetuaae Teriitehau.

Comparison of the two censuses reveals that whereas the descendants of the few Chens who migrated to Tahiti are well known, those of the many who migrated to Southeast Asia are largely unknown. This difference may be due to the very large donations sent to Pine Mansion by Tahiti Chens, several of whom made huge fortunes (see chapter 2). It cannot be explained by the loosening of ties as a result of assimilation policies, which occurred in both destinations. When Suharto became president of Indonesia in 1967, he closed the country to Chinese immigrants and introduced a policy of assimilation: Chinese schools were closed and the Chinese were encouraged to adopt Indonesian-sounding names (Suryadinata 2004, 14; Hui 2011). The same occurred in Malaysia, although Chinese schools persisted there (Suryadinata 2004, 15). From the mid-1950s, to cultivate good diplomatic relations, the People's Republic of China (PRC) encouraged the Chinese to adopt the nationality of their host country. In Tahiti, Chinese schools were closed following the establishment of diplomatic relations between the PRC and France in 1964, which accelerated the naturalization of the Chinese in Polynesia before French nationality was granted by decree in 1973 (Trémon 2010, 143).[11] Names were frenchified and cultural assimilation was prioritized. The explanation lies in the size of the working class and its political affiliation: many Chinese Malaysians were mine and plantation laborers and were recruited into triads (secret societies) and later as members of the Malaysian Communist Party (Nonini 2015). In contrast, most of Tahiti's plantations had failed by the end of the nineteenth century and most of the Chinese were engaged in business, and although there were class differences between small rural shopkeepers and big urban merchants, upward social mobility was high.

The varying degrees of precision with regard to emigrants' destinations, with Malaysia, Indonesia, and Singapore grouped together as Nanyang (Southeast Asian) in the genealogy in contrast to the very precise count of residents in different European countries in the official census, also indicates a lack of connection with the Southeast Asian Chens. Taken together, these censuses clearly show that due to the distancing that causes kinship relationships to fade over the generations, there are more links with relatives in the countries to which Chens have recently migrated, most often from Hong Kong. These links and ruptures reflect the history of successive migratory waves.

The First Waves

The first migration period from the mid-1860s to the mid-1930s took Pine Mansion villagers to Southeast Asia (Malaysia, Singapore, and Indonesia), the Pacific (Tahiti and Hawai'i), and the Caribbean (Panama, Cuba, Jamaica, British Guiana, Trinidad, and Suriname). They were recruited in the 1860s–1870s as indentured laborers on sugar cane plantations in Hawai'i and the Caribbean, on cotton plantations in Tahiti, and on rubber plantations and in tin mines in Malaysia.[12] According to my estimates, at least 390 men—more than 20 percent of the village's 1,800 male sixth- and seventh-generation Chens—left the village between the 1870s and the late 1920s, with roughly 120 going to Indonesia and Malaysia, two dozen to Tahiti, and the rest to Central America, the Caribbean, and the Indian Ocean. Although this is a low estimate as returnees are not included in the per-country lists, it was still a massive emigration.[13] A large number of men with non-Chen surnames in the village also emigrated as indentured laborers. The proportion of departures were probably higher among them, although it is impossible to provide an estimate without genealogical records for these minority surnames—the donation lists (see chapter 2) are the only source of information.

The pioneer migrants soon left the plantations to set up their own businesses, and some returned home and initiated the migration of their successors who followed them without a contract, taking on debt with their future employer, who was often a lineage relative who sponsored their trip (Woon 1984, 49). Some found employment on the docks or as itinerant vendors. As soon as they could, they engaged in trade (Chen 1939, 60), starting small retail and later wholesale businesses, the most successful becoming traders in exported goods in the early twentieth century (Trémon 2010, 87). Through petty trade, the overseas Chinese hoped to achieve their goal: to provide for their families and increase their socioeconomic status in the home village. Trade was often the only means of accumulating wealth due to colonial administrations restricting their access to employment in agriculture or administration. In the Dutch Indies, the 1870 Land Act prohibited the acquisition of land by the Chinese to protect the indigenous population; in Tahiti, a 1932 decree prohibited land sales to the Chinese for the same reason (Trémon 2010, 129).

Given the small size of Hakka villages, in some cases the establishment of one kinsman overseas was sufficient to trigger the emigration of all of a village's male members (Watson 1975, 82). Watson (1975, 5) coined the term *lineage agency* to describe this triggering mechanism. Once a man had settled overseas, he would advance the sum necessary for the trip to his brothers, cousins, or nephews, who would work for him until they had reimbursed him and then set up independently. It was mainly in this way, through sibling ties, that the men of Pine Mansion emigrated in the early waves. Among the first forty or so emigrants to Southeast Asia were a dozen subgroups of close cousins and brothers. Similarly, among the ten pioneers who left for Tahiti were a father, his son, and his nephew; two cousins; and a set of five brothers, the fifth of whom became so fabulously rich that he was given the nickname Chin Foo (*foo* meaning wealth). These pioneers were of the seventh generation and were the sons of an only son, and therefore an entire lineage segment left Pine Mansion. In short, the pioneers rarely remained alone overseas, although they did not all depart simultaneously: the stories I collected from the Chinese in Tahiti showed that they had arrived successively, each financing the later journey of brothers or cousins.

The lineage also fueled the chain migration of generation after generation. When a father emigrated, his sons born in the village were likely to emigrate themselves to the same or another destination. Studies of Hakka emigrant villages in the 1930s and 1950s all point to the strong predominance of male migrants in the early waves: the men migrated, leaving their wives in the village to serve their mothers-in-law and raise their children. This was a form of guarantee of both the emigrant's return and his biological and social reproduction in the village. The women were in charge of agriculture, which may be an additional explanation for the Hakkas' very high level of emigration. Unlike other emigrant ethnolinguistic groups such as the Cantonese and the Hokkien, the women were responsible for the entire agricultural cycle from tilling to harvesting and for selling their produce at the district market (Pratt 1960, 150; Johnson 1975, 218; Oxfeld 2010, 11). Senior villagers such as Chen Daorong remembered that before 1949, "men did not cultivate the land: it was women who worked in the fields. The men were studying, going abroad, doing trade; many were doing business." A relative feminization of migration began in the early 1920s (Skeldon 1994, 25; Trémon 2010, 59). Women started emigrating as the future wives of well-established emigrants who were rich enough to bring them overseas.

From the 1920s onward, there were also cases of men migrating to join their future fathers-in-law. Chen Fuchang, the most famous Tahiti Chen, departed in 1937 to marry the daughter of a successful merchant who originated from a village farther north. The ship he was on called in at the Philippines on July 7, 1937, when the Marco Polo Bridge incident resulted in the Japanese occupation of China, sharply reducing subsequent emigration (Johnson and Woon 1997, 54).[14] During the Japanese occupation of China and even more so that of Hong Kong (December 1941–August 1945), contact between emigrants and their families was temporarily suspended. Many who had postponed their return to China returned home at the end of World War II, even before the end of the civil war between the Communists and the Nationalists: in 1947 and 1948, 757 returned from Tahiti to Pine Mansion and other villages nearby (Trémon 2010, 137). Many more returned to China from Indonesia and Malaysia in the 1950s due to political turmoil in these newly independent states and discriminatory policy and in response to calls from the Chinese authorities to rebuild the country. In Pine Mansion, I also met people who had returned from places such as Panama and Jamaica as children.

Post-1949 Waves

During the years of China's closure, beginning in 1950, a year after the advent of the PRC and the start of the Korean War, Hong Kong's role as a node through which relations between the diaspora and home villages flowed was strengthened. From 1951 onward, those wishing to cross the border were now required to produce an exit permit from their district's public security authority (Liu 2007, 208). Throughout most of the Mao era, the Chinese authorities saw migrants as traitors (*toudi panguo*). Border guards were ordered to open fire on illegal migrants, and countless numbers were shot and buried on the mountain slopes. Several attempts at crossing the border were often necessary, and some Pine Mansioners told me the number of attempts they had made compared with those of others. The villagers themselves referred to illegal border crossing as *toudu* (*tou* "to steal," *du* "in secret").[15] This "flight to Hong Kong" (*taogang*) is estimated to have ranged between half a million and a million people (Chen 2011). However, four major border-crossing waves, around 1957, 1962, 1972, and 1979, occurred legally. The first three corresponded to district and provincial authorities' relaxation of their control following periods of intense political campaigning and economic reform: the First Leap Forward, an accelerated collectivization campaign; the Great Leap Forward (*Da yue jin*) and its ensuing famine; and the hardest years of the Cultural Revolution. The fourth followed the launch of the economic reform and opening policy.

From the 1960s onward, many returned migrants left Hong Kong, mainly for North and South America and Europe (Fan 1974, 9–10). The wave of migration to the United Kingdom grew dramatically after the 1984 Sino-British declaration planning the Hong Kong handover to China in 1997.[16] When the British government announced that it would not grant preferential UK citizenship to Hong Kongers and started limiting their entry, the migrants turned to Canada and the United States. Remigration to these destinations had already increased following the lifting of barriers to nonwhite immigration in Canada in 1962 and the United States in 1965. Those who remigrated from Hong Kong had generally accumulated some economic capital, with a large proportion migrating under business programs (Skeldon 1994).[17] Whereas pre-1949 destinations such as Tahiti, Indonesia, Malaysia, and Trinidad no longer received migrants, a small but steady flow toward Suriname, which was used from the late 1970s as an entry port for other nearby (French Guiana) and more remote (the Netherlands) destinations, continued until the 1990s.

Chain migration was amplified during this period by state policies discriminating against the dependents of overseas Chinese. Many of those who left in the 1960s and 1970s already had a history of migration, having returned from overseas after 1947 and found themselves categorized as "returnees" from 1957 onward.[18] Although their situation was taken into account in the first years of the new regime, families that were financially dependent on migrant relatives were particularly affected by the grain shortage that followed the introduction of fixed-rate purchases by the state in the second half of the 1950s. These fled in huge numbers (Peterson 2012, 65, 144–45). They left for Hong Kong and from there traveled back to the countries from which they had returned as children, or went to destinations where family members had remained. This continued throughout the 1960s. During the Cultural Revolution, all those with overseas connections (*haiwai guanxi*), especially the cadres, were subjected to criticism, confiscations, and even prison sentences.

From the 1950s, the migratory flows became fully feminized. Under Mao, whoever had the opportunity to leave the village did so. People recalled that the village was virtually empty by the end of the 1970s, the only remaining inhabitants being elderly persons unable to make the trip over the mountains to Hong Kong and some married women who had stayed to care for their young children.[19] When male migrants left first, they arranged for their wives and children (sons and daughters alike) to join them as soon as possible. In Tahiti, several people related their childhood or youth memories of fleeing through the hills to Hong Kong by night, from where, with family in Tahiti or having been born there, they were able to easily obtain a visa to leave.

Even though Chinese citizens with overseas families were allowed to travel abroad after Mao's death in 1976 and with the onset of the reforms, it was still necessary to prove that they had close relatives (*qinshu*) at their destination. In the opinion of the people of Pine Mansion, the "real reforms" (*zhenzheng de gaige*) only began in the 1980s, and it was not until 1985 that conditions for leaving the country were relaxed (Nyíri 2010, 40). One of the last noticeable waves of departure from Pine Mansion took place after this relaxation in 1989–1990, following the Tiananmen Square repression of June 6, 1989. At the time, the situation was chaotic (*luan*), uncertain, Weixin told me. His son had left in 1989 and still lived in Guiana. Weixin introduced me to two lineage cousins to whom he was closely related. They were the same age as his son, whom they had got to know well in Guiana. Both were named Chen Junjie and they too had left China in 1989 and 1990.

The first Junjie had taken French nationality. His motivation was difficult to pin down. Born in 1969, he had left "six months after June 6 [1989]," and although he specified at once that it was unrelated, we can assume that he mentioned the date (*liusi*, 4–6), which is used in Chinese to refer to the Tiananmen Square event, because it had influenced his choice to leave. Financially, he was not so badly off: his father was a prestigious member of the lineage who had established a successful transport company in the 1980s, served on the board of the Zhenneng Foundation, ran one of the village's shareholding companies (see chapter 3), and was a member of the committee for the safeguarding of the ancestral grave (see chapter 4). Junjie was the only one among his age cohort to have completed high school and had found a management job in a US factory based in Pine Mansion where he earned "four times more than the factory workers, 500 Hong Kong dollars a month." He added, thereby admitting that his reasons were not economic, that it was better to be abroad anyway because he could then have "three more children" (he has four).

The second Junjie who had emigrated to French Guiana was born in 1971 and is therefore much younger than Weixin, but like him, he is a ninth-generation emigrant. He noted jokingly that he is Weixin's son's lineage uncle (*tangshu*), although the latter is a little older than him. Junjie had left China in 1991 at the age of twenty after finishing high school. First, he went to Suriname and a little over a year later to Cayenne in French Guiana, where he stayed for thirteen years. He returned permanently to Pine Mansion in 2005. He explained that he had migrated to broaden his horizons and because he did not have much to do in the village. Life was rather difficult there at the time and he wanted to "go and see." On his return, he had invested in real estate in Pine Mansion.

These young men were motivated to depart by the turbulent political context and uncertainty of the time. Like many, they saw the repression of the demonstration in Tiananmen Square as likely to herald a step backward in relation to China's reforms. They were motivated by the prospect of better opportunities because they did not have a university degree and could not therefore seek a prestigious position at home. However, they were not without resources and local employment opportunities existed. They left because leaving the political uncertainty in China behind was attractive and going abroad offered more diverse opportunities than staying in the village. Their departure was facilitated by family precedents and networks.

This last element appears to have been decisive: when asked about the precise circumstances of their departure, they mentioned receiving encouragement from relatives overseas. Weixin stated that his son had chosen French Guiana because he already had a maternal uncle there. This is a relationship of affinity within the lineage, as Weixin's wife is a Chen.[20] More specifically, the uncle in question, Yinghong, is Weixin's wife's cousin, the son of her eldest paternal uncle, and the grandson of her paternal great-uncle, since the great-uncle had adopted his nephew. The lineage relationship between Weixin's son and his mother's uncle is doubled and even tripled, first by the intrabranch adoption and then by the interbranch marriage. Another uncle, Yinghong's brother, lived in Jamaica, from where Weixin's wife had returned as a child in 1947. Yinghong was chosen over his brother to help Weixin's son settle in Guiana because he is the connector of the Chens and a major donor and community leader there.

The second Chen Junjie, who had not changed his nationality, left for Suriname and then French Guiana because he had an older paternal uncle (*bofu*) there to whom he has written asking for help with the necessary paperwork. This uncle, he said, is a "lineage relative, not a close relative" (*tangde, bu shi qinde*). Chen Ganzhong was one of the most successful Chinese in Suriname, a major contributor to lineage works, and a member of the genealogy compilation committee—again, a connector. Junjie was related to this lineage uncle through both parents, who are Pine Mansion Chens, his father belonging to the Guobao branch and his mother to the Wenshan branch. The grandfathers of this uncle and of Junjie's father were brothers. This lineage uncle's only daughter had married a Chen from the Wenshan branch, a third cousin of Junjie's mother, and the couple had given one of their three sons to Ganzhong for adoption so that he could continue his line. Junjie's father and mother therefore share a lineage tie, an affinal tie and an adoption tie with this uncle. The younger brother of the same Junjie had left for Jamaica at the invitation of their maternal aunt (*ayi*), who had emigrated there with her husband in the 1980s. He had departed almost immediately after Junjie, after finishing high school, so they could have traveled to Guiana together, but instead, they left for different destinations. The first Chen Junjie had left for Guiana at the behest of his uncle, a cousin of his mother (not a Chen), who had made a fortune there. These examples show that the uterine relationship plays a role that is as important as the agnatic relationship in the choice of sponsor and destination.

The notion of lineage as a "migration agency" can therefore be nuanced. First of all, close kin or branch relationships (not distant lineage relationships) prevail in the choice of destination. Emigrants join close rather than distant relatives—often their fathers and mothers, or aunts and uncles of the same branch. In cases where a person departs leaving his father and mother in the village, he himself resorts to, or is approached by, an agnatic relative of the same branch or a uterine relative, and sometimes both at once. In cases where agnatic ties are doubled by uterine ties, it is not necessarily the agnatic relationship of "official" kinship (Bourdieu 1977) that prevails in the expression of kinship ties, as the example of Weixin's son shows.

This strategic mobilization of kinship ties signals how the more recent emigration patterns contrast with the pre-1949 waves in terms of kinship relations. Whereas siblings used to migrate to the same destination, after 1949 siblings of the eighth and especially the ninth generations dispersed to a variety of destinations. This is partly the product of a logic of fission, enhanced by the fact that the family estate which, according to the Confucian ideal of four generations under one roof, had to be maintained undivided, no longer existed (Cohen 1976; Li 1982).[21] The villagers were leaving a communist country where there was only one family house to share at best. The individualized choice of destination moreover reflects an individualization of destinies linked to the risk and uncertainty of emigration to Hong Kong and later to other destinations. When done legally with a visa, emigrating from Hong Kong is an individual and domestic matter: the application file is established individually and the wives and children of migrants who make it to Hong Kong follow the same path.

Finally, unlike the early pioneering waves of emigration when an emigrant brother would sponsor his siblings to join him and they would all work in the same business for several years before each was able to set up individually, in the context where emigration takes place to destinations already opened up by predecessors, each individual strategically mobilizes kinship ties in their choice of sponsor and destination and upon arrival works for members of the ascendant generations rather than for the same generation. Each therefore brings different kinship resources into play, calling on different people from the range of available agnatic and uterine relatives. Chapter 5 discusses how this notion of individual choice and destiny supports the ways in which the people of Pine Mansion today formulate moral evaluations based on the comparison of individuals' trajectories. This vision also underlines a change in the conceptualization of international mobility and a reevaluation of the possibilities offered by emigration.

Pioneering at Home: Declining Emigration and New Hypermobility

Incentives to emigrate are much more limited than those of a century ago because Shenzhen now offers opportunities for employment and education, and therefore social advancement, close to the village. People tend to generalize about how "life in China has become better," contrasting the situation in China as a whole with the possibilities offered overseas. They recognize that this improvement owes much to the creation of the Shenzhen Special Economic Zone (SEZ), which they call the "opening" of Shenzhen (*kaihuang*), referring to the pioneering act of clearing land. The SEZ created new construction and transport employment opportunities for the villagers.

The story of Chen Guanxiang and his family is a perfect illustration of this historical change in opportunities (see figure 1.1). Guanxiang's grandfather and his younger brother had emigrated to Sabah in Malaysia. His grandfather had returned to the village for a marriage that had been arranged for him. Guanxiang's father was born in China in 1919, and at about the age of fifteen, he left for Malaysia, where he married a woman from the Chinese community. He died in Malaysia during the height of the British repression of the communist uprising between 1952 and 1954, which had begun in 1948 with the declaration of a state of emergency and lasted officially until 1960 (Nonini 2015, 38–59). Guanxiang's grandmother, his pregnant mother and her eldest child, his elder brother, and his uncles, the three younger sons of his younger great-uncle then left Malaysia, and Guanxiang was born shortly after their return to Pine Mansion. The three uncles all moved to Suriname in the 1960s and their children joined them as adults. Some are still in Suriname, others are in the Netherlands, some have been lost sight of ("unknown" in the diagram), and one, Xianwei, returned to China in the late 1990s (his story is presented in chapter 5). Some relatives remained in Malaysia and Guanxiang had been to see them and to visit his father's grave. Guanxiang's older brother moved to Hong Kong in 1975, and Guanxiang left for Shenzhen shortly afterward. His daughter, who had made the trip with him from downtown Shenzhen to Pine Mansion for the spring equinox festival and to see Guanxiang's aging mother, recalled that her father had gone to Shenzhen

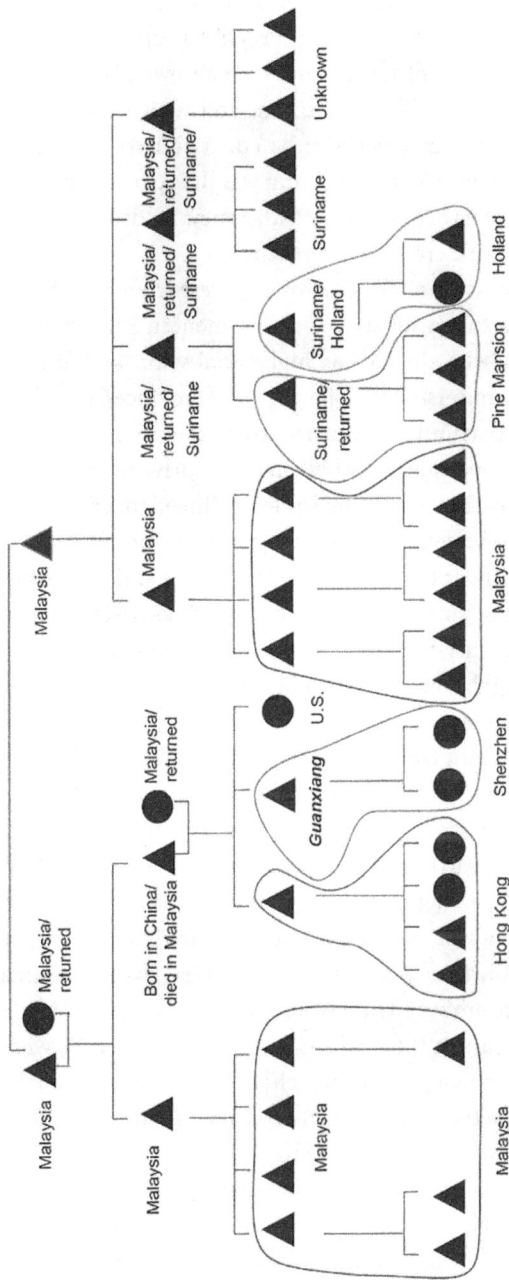

FIGURE 1.1. Guanxiang's family migration history.

as soon as the SEZ had opened, Pine Mansion not being included in the zone initially.[22] "He was one of the very first to 'open' [*kaihuang*] [the SEZ], mending the tanks, repairing the roads, among the very first people who built [Shenzhen]." When he found employment as a driver for a state-owned company, he was able to change his rural *hukou* for an urban one and settled with his wife and two daughters in Luohu, Shenzhen's first urban district, later moving the family to Futian District (see figure 0.2). Guanxiang was thus part of a new generation of pioneers who did not have to move abroad, as new lands were being opened up near the village with the creation of Shenzhen.

In addition to those who, like Guanxiang, were from a modest background and found an opportunity for social advancement in Shenzhen, many people from Pine Mansion who already had high social status and/or had had an urban career in state administration, often in other provinces, found in Shenzhen's urbanization an opportunity to return to live in the city center. They enjoy very comfortable living conditions only half an hour's drive from Pine Mansion, living outside the village but remaining so closely linked to it that they are considered local. This can be seen by comparing two lists of donations: in 1995, 74 donors were listed under the subheading "Shenzhen and Guangzhou" and 167 were listed as living in the village's seven neighborhoods (see chapter 3). In 1998, most of the same seventy-four donors were listed on the list of village donors as residents of the neighborhoods from which they had originated although they no longer lived in them.

Whereas the migrant trajectory stories that I collected show that their selection of destinations has long been guided by a rational calculus of the comparative potential for development (*nenggou fazhan*) in different localities, Shenzhen now appears to be one of the places that is seen as offering the highest potential. When discussing migration, people generally invoke cost-profit calculations to work out whether the sacrifices required to reach the goal of making money are worthwhile. When choosing between possible destinations, they compare promises of profit and the potential for economic development (*fazhan*). My observations confirm those of Andrea Louie (2004, 147), who stress that many people in Guangdong make their choice to migrate a rational decision, an exercise in looking at the options together with an appreciation of the risks. She notes that attitudes toward migration have shifted from blind faith in the American dream to a more nuanced vision of it as a gamble (Louie 2004, 149). Although emigration was unlikely to have been perceived as anything but highly risky in the past (Hsu 2000), it is clear that the change following the region's economic development has generated uncertainty about the relative advantages of migration. The risks of leaving are lowest for those who have inherited a certain amount of economic security and social capital abroad from past remittances and migration, but the chances of gaining a better livelihood are not as high as in the past.

In tandem with these calculations about potential profit, the relative development or backwardness of the possible destinations is also weighed. The case of Suriname is instructive in this respect. According to several people who had gone there in the early 1980s, their decisions had been based on what they saw as its strong potential for development. However, they had ended up resenting the backwardness of the place in comparison to Pine Mansion, where the living standards improved over the following decades to the point where Suriname came to seem much more backward than their former peasant village which is now an urban neighborhood. As living conditions at home become comparable to, if not better than, those in their places abroad, the question of whether leaving home and "eating bitterness" (*chi ku*, working hard to earn money) is worth the trouble becomes all the more acute. There is considerable uncertainty about whether it is easier to make money in Pine Mansion or abroad, and statements made to me on this issue were quite contradictory. Weixin's grandson was now a student at a business school in France. It was he, Weixin (and not his son, he implied), who had sent money for the plane ticket for his grandson to return to China during the holidays; however, in a later conversation, he admitted that were his son to come back to China, he would not be able to earn as much money as he was making from his shop in Guiana.

New mobility strategies in response to this uncertainty are a way of keeping the possibilities open. The increased accessibility of passports and visas for foreign travel (home ownership and villagers' income levels now allow them to obtain tourist visas)[23] has further changed the perception of going abroad. It no longer implies traveling far and staying away for long periods with no guarantee that they will be able to return. As often, it was Weixin who opened my eyes to this phenomenon. "They don't 'emigrate'! They take up citizenship [*dengji*, meaning "to register"] abroad so that they can enter and leave easily," he smilingly answered when I asked how many people he knew had recently emigrated. Even if obtaining foreign citizenship or a long-term residence permit requires remaining abroad for a few years, the residents of Pine Mansion do not define this overseas stay as migration. "Leaving the country" for business or study is viewed as a temporary strategy for cultivating contacts abroad and procuring foreign citizenship, the ultimate goal being to do business in China. In the spring of 2017, Weixin's grandson was an intern with a large French company in Guangzhou, where he lived with his grandparents.

Weixin's lineage cousin Junjie had just spent two years in the village with his eldest daughter and son, aged fourteen and twelve, when I met him in 2013, leaving his wife and youngest twin sons in French Guiana after staying there long enough to obtain French citizenship. Junjie had bought an apartment in a Paris suburb. The reason for this investment became clear the next time I met him. He had set up a small real estate business in the village and relocated his family to the Paris apartment, where he runs a supermarket, and was planning to stay half the year in the village and the other half in France. In 2017, the family left French Guiana and settled in the Paris suburb; Junjie spent six months in the village conducting real estate business and six months in France running his supermarket. When I asked him whether it had been worth emigrating, he replied, "It's hard to tell because you have to work very hard."

Although one must have lived in the country for a sufficient length of time to become eligible for permanent resident status or to take on another nationality, the stay abroad is seen as temporary, with the prospect of returning to China later for long or short periods leaving open the possibility of navigating between countries by securing two types of capital: legal (residence permits) and cultural (diplomas). This mobility is seen as a strategy for cultivating business contacts abroad and gaining foreign citizenship, which provides the mobility necessary to return and do business in China.

Glorious New Migrants, Evasive Mobile Entrepreneurs

Junjie returned to the village intermittently until 2016 and now lives there for six months of each year. He has become a mobile entrepreneur, providing a model for several of his male friends, who consider this the best possible option and aspire to do the same. Some overseas Chens travel more frequently and make much shorter stays in Pine Mansion. The members of this new entrepreneurial class remigrated from Hong Kong to new destinations in the 1980s, and they are a new type of highly mobile sojourner who travel far from China. They came back from overseas in the 1980s and 1990s to invest locally, and many own businesses in Hong Kong and abroad (Suriname, Canada) as well as factories in the village and nearby (figure 1.2). These mobile entrepreneurs are always passing through the village and I only had the opportunity for snippets of conversation with them at festivals, during which they play important parts in rituals (see chapter 5). Their children study in Hong Kong or abroad (Great Britain, the Netherlands, Canada), depending on the family's main place of residence.

The number of these mobile entrepreneurs is difficult to estimate. About ten of them take an active role in the lineage rites, which affords them some visibility, but others are probably less committed and therefore less visible. Theirs are typical instances of the "flexible citizenship strategies" that Aihwa Ong (1999)

FIGURE 1.2. Pine Mansion in 2011, first-generation factories of the 1980s in the foreground. Photo by author, 2011.

highlights in the case of rich Hong Kongers in the 1990s who relocated their families to the United States while running transpacific businesses. They minimize political risk by relocating the family in countries perceived as stable and economic risk by distributing their investments and interests across different localities (Ong 1999, 112). These logics of transnationality aiming to accumulate cultural, economic, social, and legal capital through intense mobility now extend to the newly rich on the other side of the Hong Kong border. In Pine Mansion and many other former emigrant villages in Shenzhen, such strategies are facilitated by the webs of kinship and the history of migration networks that allow the leveraging of former generations' accumulated capital in semiperipheral destinations such as French Guiana or Suriname to move up to core destinations: the former metropoles of these colonial territories (see chapter 2).

The rise of this mobile entrepreneurial class reflects recent changes in China's policy on overseas Chinese. This policy was revised several times under Mao and again since the economic reopening. In September 1979, the privileged status of returned overseas Chinese (*guiqiao*) and families with relatives overseas (called dependents, *qiaojuan*) was restored (Wang 1991, 228; Thunø 2001, 914). When it was first established in the 1950s in hopes of eliciting the financial support of overseas relatives, this status entitled returnees and their dependents not only to some autonomy in their use of relatives' remittances but also the right to spend them on matters officially condemned as "capitalist" and "superstitious" by the Communist regime, such as hiring agricultural laborers and maintaining ancestral tombs. Dependents and returnees were also allowed facilitated access to institutions of higher education.[24] In the context of China's transition to market socialism, the right to use the money in such ways was no longer specific to returnees and dependents, but they continued to be singled out as a particular group, mainly to identify *qiaoxiang* areas, places of origin of overseas Chinese.

Although this policy was first reaffirmed with the 1990 Protection Act,[25] since the mid-1990s the Chinese authorities have reoriented their policy away from "overseas Chinese" (*huaqiao*) toward "new migrants" (*xin yimin*) who left from areas other than Guangdong Province after 1978 to settle in North America, Australia, and Europe (Thunø 2001).[26] Whereas villages or counties were previously categorized as *qiaoxiang* according to the numbers of returnees and emigrants' dependents, they are now defined according to their total number of emigrants. The number of *qiaoxiang* has thus been reduced by considering only villages with large numbers of recent emigrants. In 2001, a new law amended the 1990 Protection Act of returnees' assets: the protection now focuses on their investment in high-tech industries. More generally, the new policy promotes the attraction of capital, technology, and talent—the "three imports" (*san yinjin*). The "new migrants" are mentioned in the official media as the epitome of modernity in implicit contrast to the old *huaqiao*. Natives of the PRC, the new emigrants are presented as more loyal to the country and to Communist power and more educated and modern than overseas Chinese who have lived outside the country for several generations (Nyíri 2002; Zhuang and Zhang 2012; Liao 2015).

The most famous of Pine Mansion's mobile entrepreneurs is Chen Xingchang, a successful businessman. He is halfway between the old *huaqiao* and the new emigrant. Born in 1951, he emigrated before 1978, has little education, and comes from Guangdong Province—that is, the region of origin of the old diaspora. However, he was born in China and displays much loyalty to his homeland. Xingchang left the village for Hong Kong in the early 1960s at the age of fifteen or sixteen and then moved to Canada in the 1970s. He has dual Hong Kong and Canadian nationality. He returned to Pine Mansion in the 1980s, where he established a plant manufacturing electrical material, which he still heads, and later set up the Shenzhen Trading Company.

With their plural nationalities and rights to residence, such hypermobile entrepreneurs are difficult to categorize, further increasing the difficulties and ambiguities of Chinese officials' liaison work with overseas Chinese. In the subdistrict of Miaoyun, Chen Yunxiang, the head of the Qiaolian, or Federation of Returned Overseas Chinese, is also the head of the Qiaoban, or Overseas Chinese Affairs Office.[27] When I asked him if he could give me some statistics on overseas Chinese investment in the subdistrict, he raised his arms to the sky helplessly. He explained that identifying investors is extremely complex: they are often involved in joint ventures using both Chinese and foreign capital, and in the case of foreign companies, it is often hard to tell whether they are using overseas capital (*qiaozi qiye*) or Hong Kong capital (*gangzi qiye*). Moreover, there are people today with multiple citizenship status (*duozhong shenfen*). He gave the example of Chen Xingchang: "He has several identities: he has a residence permit in Canada, an identity card from Hong Kong, and is at home on the continent [China] all at the same time. . . . When he takes out a pen to sign a check and contribute to the public good [*gongyide*], by whom are we fed? By a Hong Konger, right; by a Chinese [*huaren*, Chinese in the ethnic meaning of the term], right; by a member of the [local] chamber of commerce—that's right, too. He plays several roles. Like me: I'm a grandfather, a husband, and a son."

The case of Chen Xingchang illustrates the difficulty, given his emigration to Canada, of disentangling overseas from Hong Kong investments because the former tend to transit through Hong Kong (Bolt 1996, 86; Thunø 2001, 919). Provenances are often mixed in the statistics; it is estimated that "Hong Kong capital combined with that of *huaqiao* has provided more than 90 percent of the starting capital of private companies in the Pearl Delta" (Guldin 1995, 92).[28]

Chen Xingchang above all embodies the major role of Hong Kong in the economic transformation of the villages of the Pearl delta, and particularly Shenzhen. Hong Kongers' investments on the mainland have mainly benefited the eastern part of the Pearl delta along the Guangzhou–Hong Kong corridor, including the cities of Dongguan and Shenzhen. Long a poorer and marginal region, it has been the fastest-growing area economically since the reopening (Woon 1996, 32–33; Johnson 2007). What makes Xingchang famous is the mix of local patriotism and entrepreneurialism that allowed him to persuade Hong Kongers to invest in the area in his capacity as head of the Miaoyun People's Association in Hong Kong. A biographical note estimates that in the early 1990s, more than sixty companies settled in Miaoyun under his influence, investing more than 200 million yuan renminbi (RMB). "Today, total investments amount to 1 billion RMB, a huge contribution to Miaoyun's economic development," according to this note, which enumerates Xingchang's titles and rewards: he is a member of the Shenzhen Chamber of Commerce and the Chinese People's Political Consultative Conference (CPPCC, *zhengxie*), and is vice president of the Bao'an District Chamber of Commerce.[29] He received an invitation from the State Council to attend the military parade in Tiananmen Square on the sixtieth anniversary of the founding of the PRC. He has earned the title of Love and Favor to the Native Village from the State Council's Overseas Chinese Affairs Office (OCAO) and that of Advanced National Patriotic Entrepreneur from the Committee for the Organization of Chinese Patriotic Activities.

Xingchang's status is elusive: he is presented both as a returnee and as an overseas Chinese. His appointment to the CPPCC is a form of party state co-option of entrepreneurs with a right to residence abroad (Edin 2003, 46; Chen and Dickson 2010). The party state has sought to co-opt the business classes by turning them into allies who will not challenge the political regime. As an essential part of its of economic reform and opening policy, the CPPCC's aim has been to integrate personalities such as Chen Xingchang into the state's functioning.[30] The CPPCC's Overseas Chinese and Hong Kong, Macao, and Taiwanese Affairs Committee (*Quanguo zhengxie gang'aotaiqiao weiyuanhui*) is one of the Chinese institutions working in the field of overseas Chinese affairs (*qiaowu gongzuo*) that are all characterized by close interaction between public and private actors (Liu and Van Dongen 2016).[31] Membership of this committee, though mainly honorary, gives the entrepreneurs delegated to the conference the power to influence the party on policy options available to companies and privileges for investors living in Hong Kong or abroad (Chen Minglu 2018).

During my first brief meeting with Chen Xingchang, he showed little interest in my questions, most of which he ignored. The little he said was an illustration of this co-option, but class co-option into the elites rather than political co-option in the sense of allegiance to the regime. He boasted that he had been sitting not far from Hu Jintao's wife at the opening ceremony of the World University Games, which had just been held in Shenzhen in August 2011. He seemed concerned with doing business in China above all and displayed a distant irony about the political regime when he told me that today it is no longer so much a question of "serving the people" (*wei renmin fuwu*, the party's motto) as of making money: "*Wei renminbi fuwu*," serving the money, he joked (*renminbi* is China's currency).

Xingchang has been one of the forty to fifty honorary citizens (*rongyu shimin*) of Shenzhen City that have been appointed every year since 2011. His 2016 listing states that he has contributed more than 10 million RMB to public causes (*gongyi shiye*). He is also a member of the board of the Bao'an District Philanthropic Committee (*cishanhui*). His sustained philanthropic activity is closely linked to his activity as a businessman, as philanthropy is a criterion for being appointed to the Political Consultative Conference and is expected of delegates. However, it must also be understood as meeting a local moral obligation. As chapter 2 shows, Xingchang is one donor among many, part of a long moral economic tradition of donations to the village.

THE SHIFTING LANDSCAPE OF DONATIONS

Migration has become less desirable than short-term mobility, and there is also much less need for overseas money, even for public projects. Until the 1950s, the village served as the center of the diasporic network with regard to its function in the social and cultural reproduction of the members of the main lineage, the Chens, as well as the minority with other surnames. Many emigrants used to send their sons back to the village to study at the local school.[1] This reproduction, however, was heavily dependent on their own financial contributions. The creation of Pine Mansion's first primary school in 1914 was initiated by returned emigrants (see chapter 4). Several fundraising campaigns in the twentieth century financed the building of a secondary school and the rebuilding of the primary school after the reopening of China. Pine Mansion is far from unique in this regard: schools were the major recipients of emigrants' donations in late imperial and republican periods (Chen 1939, 83; Siu 1989, 69–73), and along with other infrastructure such as roads and bridges, they featured prominently in welfare projects funded by overseas kin in the two decades after China's reopening (Hoe 2013).

Even if I had wanted to track the volume of remittances sent to the village in the past, it would have been impossible due to the lack of data. Remittances sent to close kin (wives, parents) generally stopped after one or two generations, once the family ties had loosened.[2] Today, the inhabitants of Pine Mansion no longer receive remittances, and the same seems to be the case throughout the Pearl delta (Hoe 2013, 131). Wang Cuichun used to receive the equivalent of the grain tax (*gongliang*) from her husband in Hong Kong so she could pay it in money instead of in grain. This was a common arrangement at the beginning of the reform era, which, given the number of families with relatives abroad, made up for the People's Republic of China's (PRC's) shortage of foreign currency. The money allowed Cuichun to purchase equipment to ease her hardest tasks. She was the first in her neighborhood to own a gas oven (*meiqizao*), an improvement that development economists cite as freeing up agricultural manpower for other sectors. This meant that she no longer had to cut grass to heat her oven—hard work usually done by men but that fell to women in their absence, as other women from Pine Mansion and surrounding villages told me. The generalization of this piece of domestic equipment was one of the drivers of China's economic take-off, as was the decline in the number of children resulting from family planning and the one-child policy, which did not affect Mrs. Wang's generation, however (Jacka and Sargeson 2001, 54). She was also one of the first to stop farming, allowing villagers who were poorer than she was and had no income from abroad to use her land. Remittances were sent via the bank or through merchant companies to Hong Kong, from where someone either brought the money to the village in cash or it was dispatched by the *xinyongshe* (credit union).[3] Now she withdraws her pension each month, still from the credit union.

Donations, by contrast, continued over several generations because they were made to the lineage and to the village as a whole. There is a considerable amount of material available concerning donations to village projects, with the sums received per country of origin and per donor systematically recorded. These lists are intended to glorify the names of the generous donors (*juankuan rongming*).[4] Some are posted at the entrance of the buildings whose construction they supported, but when a building is replaced, as has happened several times, particularly in the case of the primary school, the donation plaques are destroyed along with the former building, although the genealogy has the records.

Initially, I undertook counting these sums to identify variations in the size and the overseas share of total contributions over time. However, what the data revealed about donations and migratory patterns proved interesting. When we consider the spatial destinations of the Chinese and their social trajectories in the host countries, neat binary frameworks break down. Historians of global migration have come to recognize the extent to which accounts of migration and globalization have long been heavily Eurocentric (McKeown 2010. Until recently, they systematically tended to overlook the fact that, in the course of the nineteenth century, although fifty million people left Europe, mainly for the north, another estimated fifty million left India and China to work in the south on plantations, in mines, and on construction projects. But while offering a necessary corrective to Eurocentric views of world history and making the case for an international racial division of labor, such north-south generalizations tend to give currency to a

Global South–Global North dichotomy that cannot hold when we adopt a processual perspective over a longer-*durée* history.

The Global South–Global North framework is insufficient to account comparatively and cross-historically for the pattern of migration destinations and financial flows sent back to the village and the changes in these over time. A ternary core/periphery/semiperiphery framework is preferable, not only because it avoids simplistic Global South–Global North oppositions, but also because it emphasizes relationality rather than a dichotomous typology. Second, much of the literature on globalization in the 1990s is framed within a teleological perspective that, turning against core-periphery frameworks, emphasizes the disjuncture between deterritorialized flows that were supposed to have replaced former territorially bounded entities (Rouse 1991; Appadurai 1996). The case of Pine Mansion's Chen lineage and its diaspora suggests another type of periodization: several waves of globalization of social and kinship networks between the 1880s and 1980s followed by the reterritorialization and recentering of diasporic networks in the village of origin—that is, by relocalization.

This chapter develops a processual geography and history of this diasporic relationship. Rather than contextualizing my observations within preestablished global typologies such as core and periphery countries or the Global South–Global North, I identify and contextualize core-periphery relations by examining the history of emigration from a south Chinese village to destinations around the world and the changing role of its diaspora in donations to the village's public projects. In other words, although I do take account of available frameworks at the macrolevel of analysis, the micro-unit of the village and its emigrants allow me to observe changing relations of dependency and the shifting valence of local and global scales. I look at not only how the financial flows between the village and its diaspora take shape in terms of shifting center–core periphery relations but also at what the history of overseas donations reveals about the positioning of these migrant networks in the world system. This requires attention to scalar strategies—the actors themselves' strategic use of the values of different localities and how they valorize these—in ways that complicate macro-frameworks and their oversimplification of the global scale.

I compare four main lists of donations to the village schools, in 1929, 1946, 1987, and 1998, totaling the amounts listed individually per donor in different locations.[5] I then consider the donation campaigns for a series of other causes: the house of overseas Chinese (*huaqiao zhijia*), which was built in the mid-1980s to house visiting overseas relatives in the village, the home for the elderly (*laoren yiyuan*) in 1994, the garden around the founding ancestor's grave in 1995, the mausoleum two years later, and the Zhenneng Building, which replaced the home for the elderly in 2004. They reveal that the shares of local and overseas funding varied according to the local or global scope of interest in the cause for which the money was being raised and that local funding gradually outstripped donations from abroad. Today, the lineage and the village no longer rely on overseas funding; the relationship of dependency has ended.

The amounts sent back to the village, which range from very small to very large sums, indicate that the donors were probably representative of the general population in each destination. They did not, however, constitute the entire overseas population originating from the village. The total number of donors is significantly lower than the total number of residents in each overseas destination, and only a small number of donors' names appear in the genealogy's resident lists by country. Where overseas donors are not included in the per-country lists (see chapter 1), this means that they returned to Pine Mansion. Indeed, it seems that the majority of the donors planned to return home. By and large, sending remittances, and especially donations, was a means of securing prestige in the community of origin during their temporary absence and increased status on finally returning to grow old in the village. Of course, not all of the emigrants achieved their goals. In Daniel Kulp's (1925, 53) study of a village in eastern Guangdong in the early 1920s, only one-tenth of the emigrants had returned.

Donations in Times of Crisis and War (1929 and 1946)

In table 2.1 showing donations to the primary school in 1929, the overseas donors' locations reflect the early waves of the migration of indentured laborers to sugar plantations in the Caribbean, the Indian, and Pacific Oceans and to rubber plantations and tin mines in Malaysia. Indentured Chinese laborers were brought to Hawai'i, Cuba, and the British (Guiana, Trinidad, Jamaica), French (Tahiti, La Réunion), and Dutch (Suriname) colonies in the 1850s to 1880s.[6] Workers were also transported to Panama to build the railway and the canal across the isthmus.[7] Most of their destinations were insular or coastal, and in many cases, they were ports. On the lists, the names of the destinations, regardless of whether they refer to a town or the country as a whole, are followed by the mention *bu* (port)—for example, "overseas compatriots (*qiaobao*) residing in port X (*zu X bu*)."

Within the village, the sums donated by residents range from 1 yuan (one donor) to 500 yuan (also one donor). Some of the largest donations are from lineage branches who had established landed trusts in the names of second- and third-generation ancestors. The names of these branches' apical ancestors—Junshi and

TABLE 2.1.   Donations to the primary school in 1929

LOCATION	AMOUNT IN YUAN	NUMBER OF DONORS
Pine Mansion	6,808	196
Colón (Panama)	6,570.66	21
Tahiti	2,475	19
Trinidad	3,875.06	30
Suriname	1,247.35	29
Cuba	210	5
Sarawak (Malaysia)	710	9
Indian Ocean islands	87.1	4
Hawai'i	355	33
Samalang (Aceh, Indonesia)	83.88	None registered
Total amount	**22,422.05**	

Junke (Zhenneng's second and third sons), Wenshan, Wenlin, Wenhe, and Wenhoi (the four sons of Zhenneng's eldest son)—appear on the list with the name of the living donors. Eight official titleholders also feature among the largest donors.[8] There seem to be no titleholders among the overseas Chinese contributors, even though it is well known that at the end of the imperial era, successful overseas Chinese tended to buy a title on their return to China. However, as stated above, several donors may have returned to the village having made large donations in preparation for their return and, having returned, were excluded from the per-country lists. This highlights a divergence that remains today between two types of path leading to two types of status: one, local and based on the acquisition of academic qualifications and a career in administration and education, and the other, overseas and based on the accumulation of economic capital.

The small amounts given by Southeast Asian donors can be accounted for in several ways. First, it is likely that a large proportion of Malaysian and Indonesian sojourners had returned to the village by 1929. This is impossible to confirm because the names of the 1929 donors from Indonesia were lost, as stated in the genealogy, making it impossible to cross-check them against the per-country list. Chen (1939) and Woon (1984) suggest another possible reason: they note a strong contrast in the behavior of Chinese in the United States, where exclusion laws and discriminatory practices spurred the sending of remittances, and Southeast Asia, where the most successful tended to reinvest their savings locally while those who planned to return sent regular but more modest remittances (Chen 1939, 124–25, 142–43; Woon 1984, 49–50, 104). The small Malaysian donations listed are also probably due to the global economic crisis that broke out in 1929 and rapidly affected colonial territories that were heavily dependent on the export of raw materials such as rubber and tin, whose prices collapsed. The Great Depression saw many overseas Chinese return from Southeast Asia to China with no means of subsistence. This may explain the small per-capita donations of migrants from Malaysia, with an average of 80 yuan, compared to 130 yuan from donors in Tahiti, where some wealthy people such as the banker Chin Foo made important investments locally but also sent large contributions to the village.

The overall volume of global monetary remittances and donations to China dropped in the next decade as a result of the economic crisis in the host countries, the decline in migration flows due to Chinese immigration restrictions, and political instability in the regions of origin during this period (Chen 1939, 74–78). With the Japanese invasion, overseas Chinese, mobilized by the Kuomintang government, contributed en masse to resistance against the occupier (Hsu 2000, 151–52), and the 1946 donations must be considered a continuation of this effort as well as in the context of the imminent return of a large number of emigrants to Pine Mansion at the end of the war.

The chaos of the anti-Japanese and civil wars in China, the ensuing economic crisis, and the devaluation of Chinese currency are reflected in the donations supporting the building of a secondary school in 1946 (table 2.2, figure 2.1). The apical ancestors of lineage branches no longer feature among the village donors. In the context of the economic downturn and soaring inflation of the time, their income may have been restricted to covering the operating expenses of the primary school.[9] Donations from Malaysia and Indonesia are altogether absent. This can be explained by their economic devastation during the Japanese occupation, followed by anti-Chinese violence during the 1945–49 Indonesian revolution

TABLE 2.2. Donations to the secondary school in 1946

LOCATION	TOTAL AMOUNT IN DIFFERENT CURRENCIES	TOTAL AMOUNT IN USD	NUMBER OF DONORS
Suriname	£1,286	5,182.58	28
Trinidad	£86	346.58	12
Kingston (Jamaica)	£1,304	323.57	45
Colón (Panama)	US$1,301	1,301	36
Hawai'i	US$175	175	7
Annam (Vietnam)	350,000 yuan	286.41	2
Tahiti	28,450 XPF	573.58	78
Aruba	£60	241.8	8
Hong Kong	HK$86	21.66	5
Pine Mansion	733,000 yuan	599.83	37
Total amount		**9,052.18**	

FIGURE 2.1. Zhenneng secondary school. Photo by author, 2014.

(Hui 2011) and social unrest in Malaysia at a time when the British were attempting to restore their colonial power and profits, leading to the anti-British guerilla war and its repression from 1948, all of which caused many Southeast Asian Chinese to return to China after 1949 (see Guanxiang's family history in chapter 1).

Several destinations had small but significant numbers of non-Chen donors in 1929 and 1946 (see table 2.5). Although the Chens also sent small amounts, non-Chens generally donated the lowest sums, with one exception: a Ye in Kingston, who gave £100 in 1946. This may reflect their previous trajectory as indentured laborers but perhaps also the lesser challenge of making a name for themselves in a Chen-dominated village community. In 1929, there were several non-Chen donors named Liu, He, and Qiu, and in 1946, several named Ye, Wu, Zhang, and Zhong. They were mostly former indentured laborers or their descendants. The gradual economic dominance of the Chen lineage with the increase in their number and the resulting pressure on available land is probably the reason for the high number of minority, non-Chen surnames, among the waves of emigrants leaving to work as indentured laborers.[10] Although the majority of non-Chen donors were in Trinidad, Jamaica, and Panama, a few were in La Réunion and Hawai'i—they were among the main destinations of indentured laborers on the sugar plantations in the nineteenth century (Live 2003; Pan 2000, 353, 357). In 1946, the Indian Ocean Island(s) (most probably La Réunion) recorded in 1929 vanished from the list, and the number of Hawaiian donors was much smaller.[11] One possible explanation might be that former indentured Chinese workers who did not manage to return tended to become assimilated into the local population and to sever their ties with their village of origin, as is very clear in the case of

Tahiti (Trémon 2010). Only a very small number of non-Chen donors are listed in Tahiti and Suriname. Here, the first wave of indentured labor triggered a second and much larger wave of "free migrants": emigration organized by the migrants themselves and framed by lineage ties with the aim of expanding the shops and businesses already set up by the pioneers (Watson 1975; Woon 1984, 49).

Semiperipheral Destinations

The migration pattern that is evident from the donation lists clearly shows a tendency for migration to plantation colonies on the peripheries of the world system rather than to the core—that is, Europe and the United States. This is probably due to the relatively marginalized and dominated position of these migrants as members of the Hakka ethnolinguistic minority. Unlike the Cantonese, the Hakkas did not migrate to the United States and Canada until the 1970s, tending to go instead to where strong minorities of Hakka people from their own region east of the Pearl River delta had first settled and prospered. The Hakkas are generally in the minority in Chinese communities around the world, only constituting the majority in a few destination countries.

Hakkas originating from the Dongguan-Huiyang-Bao'an triangle are overwhelmingly concentrated in Tahiti, Jamaica, Suriname, and Sabah and Sarawak in Malaysia, where they are numerically dominant to the point that Hakka is the lingua franca adopted by Cantonese and other minorities.[12] Although their large numbers and linguistic homogeneity do not themselves explain the large remittances sent back by overseas Pine Mansioners from these destinations, they do explain the number and size of the fortunes amassed. In addition, the rivalry between neighboring lineage villages, transposed overseas, takes the form of competition among the migrants to demonstrate the greatest success and loyalty through conspicuous giving. However, the rivalry between Hakkas was tempered by the fact that the different emigrant villages were interconnected, both in China and overseas, by matrimonial alliance relationships that often underpinned commercial partnerships (Trémon 2010).

Changes in their geographical distribution from 1929 to 1946 suggest remigration, as confirmed by their family histories: in the late 1920s, many moved on from Malaysia to Tahiti, and others left for Suriname after returning temporarily to Pine Mansion; similarly, many of those who returned from Indonesia and Malaysia in the late 1940s and 1950s moved to Suriname in the next decades.

What is particularly striking in the records is the strong presence in 1946 of Chinese immigrants within the imperial territories of the victorious capitalist powers of World War II, including the United States (the Panama Canal), the

United Kingdom (Trinidad, Jamaica, and Hong Kong), the Netherlands (Suriname and Aruba), and France (Annam and Tahiti).[13] Their harbors provided military rear bases for operations in the Atlantic and the Pacific, generating local economic booms that ensured many Chinese traders' fortunes. This can explain the preeminence of migrant donors in Suriname, Tahiti, and Panama. This change in the donation landscape reflects the situation of the Chinese emigrants and their descendants at their places of destination rather than changing migration flows, as emigration stopped with the Japanese invasion of China in 1937 and the war limited remigration flows.

Characterizing the above destinations as peripheries and migration to them as "mobilities within the Global South" presents an oversimplified picture. Although the countries to which the Hakkas migrated are usually classified as peripheries on the national scale, looking at the places where they settled on the local and regional scales, the picture becomes more complex. The economic functions performed by these places and the Chinese immigrants' role in mediating the economic, political, and social activities that linked core and peripheral areas are typically semiperipheral (Wallerstein 1974, 1976; Chase-Dunn and Hall 1997).[14] As soon as they amassed the means to do so, the Chinese immigrants started small retail and wholesale businesses and restaurants (Chen 1939, 60). Those who did well became exporters of goods such as copra and vanilla from Tahiti and played an important role in the monetarization of the local economy and its articulation with the world economy (Trémon 2010, 87). The second wave of Chinese, who migrated at the turn of the nineteenth and twentieth centuries, generally acted as minority middlemen between the natives and the colonial elite (Bonacich 1973; Chun 1989) and in a way characteristic of semiperipheries, served as a political buffer (Wallerstein 1976, 229–33). They were upwardly mobile in many of their destinations: in Trinidad and Suriname (Lowenthal 1972, 204) and in Tahiti the economically successful first-generation Chinese migrants moved up the racialized colonial social ladder toward the levels of the white and creole elites, the wealthiest sending their children to school in the colonial metropoles or the United States, and this was amplified in the next generation, who came of age after World War II.

After China's Economic Reopening

Although remittances from overseas slowed down during the Mao years, they continued to be channeled through Hong Kong during periods when the right to cross the border was relatively relaxed (Vogel 1989, 46). However, fundraising for public projects ceased until the reopening of China in the late 1970s.

By 1987, as table 2.3 shows, the number of individual donors in the village (264) had superseded those from Hong Kong and overseas (214). Overseas donations had declined everywhere: there were none at all from Hawai'i, Trinidad, Annam, or Jamaica, and in Tahiti, Panama, and Suriname, the number of donors had declined sharply. Tahitian donations almost halved, although funding from here, supplied by 20 percent of all donors, constituted one-third of the total amount received from overseas and Hong Kong. In Panama, where the number of donors had dropped by 80 percent, provided under 3 percent of total contributions from just over 3 percent of all donors. In contrast to Tahiti and Panama, whose economies were relatively stable and prosperous at the time, the low Surinamese contributions were due to the end of Holland's economic aid following the country's independence in 1975, its economic crisis since the military coup in 1980, the fall in world bauxite prices, and high inflation reducing the value of the Surinamese guinea to almost nothing. This is further reflected in the emergence of donations from French Guiana, where some Chinese immigrants who had recently arrived in Suriname headed, crossing the Maroni River that forms the boundary between the two territories. Furthermore, with Suriname's independence and again after 1980, large numbers of Chinese remigrated to the Netherlands.

Another significant trend is the emergence of donor couples (*fufu*), particularly in Canada, where the leaders of two overseas Chinese associations made large do-

TABLE 2.3. Donations to the primary school in 1987

LOCATION/SOURCE	TOTAL IN HKD	NUMBER OF DONORS
Bao'an District government	114,670	
Miaoyun township government	45,870	
Pine Mansion Village committee	17,200	
Pine Mansion individuals	43,775	264
Tahiti	121,711	46
Canada	80,295	55
Panama	10,020	7
United Kingdom	13,840	2
French Guiana	10,500	2
Belgium	12,867	1
Suriname	5,734.50	13
United States	1,300	2
Hong Kong	106,821	87
Canada, Hong Kong, or Pine Mansion (impossible to locate)	11,123	10
Total amount	**595,726.50**	

nations together with their wives in 1987.[15] The practice of making conjugal donations had spread to Pine Mansion and elsewhere in the diaspora, particularly the
Netherlands, by 1998. The wives are not Chens: men who settled in Canada had
generally left for Hong Kong at a very young age and married women with other
surnames. Conjugal donations probably reflect both the fact that the couple had
established a business together and the gender equality encouraged in China and
the host country. This equalization was also both the cause and the result of the
change in family emigration patterns: unlike before World War II, the migrants
had not left their wives behind in the village to live on their remittances. In Tahiti,
there are no donating couples, but the proportion of women donors is relatively
high: in 1987, there were eight women among the thirty-seven donors, compared
to the same number in 1946 among seventy-eight donors. Some of these are the
same women, demonstrating their lasting commitment to Pine Mansion and their
great longevity. Three of these were the daughters of the immensely rich Chin Foo,
Chen descendants who gave donations in their own names.

Hong Kong emerges as a major source of funds, reflecting the large wave of
people who fled during the Mao era (see chapter 1). I was unable to determine the
location of 2 percent of these donors, who appear in different country resident
lists in 1987 and 1998 and are clearly the entrepreneurs who regularly commute
to the village from abroad introduced in the previous chapter. The trend of remi-
grating from Hong Kong to North America and Europe can be considered a strategic use of Hong Kong's semiperipheral position as a British colony. Migration to
the United Kingdom rose sharply after the treaty of retrocession to Hong Kong
was signed, but as the 1997 deadline approached, the United Kingdom limited
the entry of Chinese from Hong Kong and migration flows reoriented to Canada.
Canada had already emerged as a major source of donations by 1987, and this
trend is confirmed in 1998. This reflects not only the considerable flow of emigration to that destination from Hong Kong but also remigration to Canada from
the Caribbean and Central America (Lai 2007, 192), the names of some major
Jamaican and Trinidad donors in 1987 resurfacing on the Canada list in 1998. At
around the same time, many Chinese residents in Suriname moved to the Netherlands, some subsequently moving on to other European destinations. Such
strategies were facilitated by kinship webs and the history of migration networks
that allowed the leveraging of former generations' accumulated capital in semiperipheral destinations such as French Guiana or Suriname in order to move to core
destinations—the former colonial metropoles (e.g., Holland in the case of Suriname) or the actual metropoles (e.g., France in the case of French Guiana).

In short, the changes in the donation landscape reveal the distancing from the
village of origin over time and generations and the peripheralization of earlier
destinations in the donation landscape reveal the distancing from the village of

origin over time and generations and the peripheralization of earlier destinations. They also reflect strategies for migration and remigration to the cores of the world system and more generally the upward social mobility of migrants and descendants who remained connected to the village. Although this history of migration could be described as a reorientation of flows from the Global South to the Global North, this would ignore the ways in which earlier migrants were differentially assimilated into their host societies, with some able to move up the social ladder by exploiting semiperipheral positions in the world system on a subnational scale and thereby creating new opportunities for later waves. What must also be considered is the shifting relations of dependence between the village of origin and migrants' destinations.

Local and Global Causes

In 1929, overseas contributions to the school made up 70 percent of its total funding, with the rest provided by local donors. In 1946, overseas contributions represented over 93 percent of the amount collected for the secondary school and local contributions less than 7 percent. In 1987, 38 percent of the cost of building and equipment for the primary school were covered locally, 28 percent by the local governments in the district and township (*zhen*) and 10 percent by the village itself. The remaining two-thirds were covered by overseas (42 percent) and Hong Kong (18 percent) donations; 2 percent were not locatable. Local funding took precedence during the last round of fundraising for the reconstruction of the primary school in 1998. Pressure from the district government, which threatened to close the school unless the villagers provided a new building to the required standard (see chapter 4), stimulated their effort to raise the considerable sum of over 3 million RMB yuan that was needed. The local-overseas ratio is the reverse of that of 1987, with the local share 58.4 percent and the amount from Hong Kong and overseas only 41.6 percent.

In 1998 (see table 2.4), fundraisers sought to attract overseas contributions by recalling the school's importance in the history of the Chen lineage and appealing to the loyalty of emigrants who had been pupils there. In spite of this, the rise in the amount raised locally by this campaign reflects the fact that the modernization of the school was mainly of interest to local Chens and non-Chens alike.[16] The possibility of one's children attending the school appealed not only to Chens but also to native villagers with other family names and to the new settlers who ran successful shops and factories that gave them the right to send their children to this public school (see chapter 4). By 2010, 90 percent of the school's pupils were neither Chens nor inhabitants of Pine Mansion, reflecting the migrant ma-

TABLE 2.4. Donations to the primary school in 1998

DONORS	AMOUNT IN YUAN RMB
Pine Mansion village	
Pine Mansion Village committee	578,000
Collectives and individuals[1]	
Fulou	23,600
Taixing	27,400
Shangwei	33,500
Henan	30,963
Zhongxin	51,069
Dabu	60,609
Xiangxi	100,588
Chen lineage sub-branch in another location (Baopuchi)	7,300
Teachers	14,500
Pine Mansion Security	1,000
Subtotal	**928,529**
Hong Kong and overseas	
Major donors (from Hong Kong and overseas)[2]	840,000
Hong Kong	229,300
Guiana	12,569
United States	8,347
Suriname	19,639
Tahiti	29,168
United Kingdom	34,831
Canada	59,257
Netherlands	69,390
Subtotal	**1,302,501**
Other donors	
Shenzhen companies	767,000
Zhenneng secondary school alumni association	15,000
Other non-Chen donors in Pine Mansion	78,000
Factory managers	33,000
Neighboring village	2,000
Other	3,800
Subtotal	**131,800**
Total	**3,129,830**

[1]Each shareholding company gave 10,000. The rest of the amount was donated by individuals residing or originating from each of the neighborhoods (see chapter 3).

[2]Their donations are listed apart.

jority in the population of the new urban community. Whereas emigrants largely sent their children back to the village to be raised by their grandparents and educated at the local school until 1949, in 2013 there were so few children of recent first-generation migrants at the school that the headmaster counted them on one hand. In the past, Chen pupils had been in the majority. However, the primary school and especially the secondary school had enrolled non-Chen students from the village and the area around it from early on, and the proportion of non-Chen donors to the school was particularly high in 1946 (see their numbers in table 2.5).

Similarly, in 1994 the donations for the home for the elderly (*laoren yiyuan*) were largely local and non-Chen.[17] In this respect, the home for the elderly is at the opposite end to the house of overseas Chinese, for which HK$70,745 were raised in 1981, mainly from overseas. Canada's share in this (30 percent) was the largest, and Trinidad's (20 percent) was also substantial, largely due to the contribution of a single rich benefactor, who later moved to Canada; Panama donated 12 percent and Tahiti, 2.27 percent. The Tahitian Chens, the descendants of migrants, were less interested in this project than in the school in 1987 and 1998, while recent migrants in Canada were more eager to invest in Pine Mansion: the house of overseas Chinese was initially intended to welcome and host visitors from abroad in order to attract their investments and donations. Furthermore, in 1995 and 1999, two rounds of fundraising for strictly lineage-related projects linked to the founding ancestor's grave site attracted a high proportion of overseas funding—namely, over two-thirds of the total amount donated for the garden around the founding ancestor's grave in 1995 and as much as 86 percent for the mausoleum over the same grave in 1998 (see chapter 4).

This confirms that the proportion of local to overseas funding varied according the local or global scope of interest in each cause for which money was required. There is also a clear correlation between strongly local interest in the cause for which the money was raised and the higher proportion of donations from local non-Chens. Although the reform era has seen an overall increase in local contributions and a decrease in overseas contributions, variations can be observed in the respective shares of overseas and Hong Kong donors and in the proportion of non-Chen donors, depending on whether the cause is of more immediate local or more broadly global interest. Activities related to the lineage, in the sense of a group whose members worship their common ancestor, have a much more global reach than projects that transcend the boundaries of the lineage such as school-building projects. This, is partly an illusion, which looking at the longer time span dispels. Since 1929, there has been a slight increase in the number of local donors and a slight decrease in the number of overseas donors. The proportion of non-Chens among local donors has increased over time, while

TABLE 2.5. Summary of contributions to village projects and contributors per cause

YEAR: CAUSE TOTAL AMOUNT COLLECTED/TOTAL NUMBER OF DONORS (NUMBER OF NON-CHEN DONORS)	TOTAL OF LOCAL CONTRIBUTIONS AND PERCENTAGE OF TOTAL COLLECTED	NUMBER OF LOCAL DONORS (NUMBER OF NON-CHEN[a]), PERCENTAGE OF ALL DONORS	TOTAL OF OVERSEAS CONTRIBUTIONS AND PERCENTAGE OF TOTAL COLLECTED	NUMBER OF OVERSEAS DONORS (NUMBER OF NON-CHEN), PERCENTAGE OF ALL DONORS	TOTAL OF HONG KONG CONTRIBUTIONS AND PERCENTAGE OF TOTAL COLLECTED	NUMBER OF HONG KONG DONORS (NUMBER OF NON-CHEN), PERCENTAGE OF ALL DONORS
1929: Primary school 22,422.05 yuan 346 (12)	6,808 30%	196 (0) 57%	15,614.05 70%	150 (12) 43%	0	0
1946: Secondary school US$9,052.18 268 (41)	599.83 6%	37 (1) 14%	8,430.69 93.2%	216 (36) 84%	21,660 2%	5 (4) 2%
1981: House of Overseas Chinese HK$70,745 212 (14)	0	0	49,845 70.4%	153 (10) 72%	20,900 30.6%	59 (4) 28%
1987: Primary school HK$608,540 479 (36)	70,745 37%	264 (25) 55%	256,267 42%	128 (4) 27%	106,821 18%	87 (7) 18%
1995: Grave garden 503,451 RMB 529 (20)	69,998 14%	272 (18) 51%	186,002 37%	142 (1) 27%	247,451 49%	115 (1) 22%
1998: Primary school 3,129,830 RMB 451 (27)	1,827,329 58%	233 (21) 52%	970,700 31%	131 (5) 29%	331,801 11%	87 (1) 19%

[a]Not including non-Chen wives of donors who contributed to their husband's lineage.

that of those overseas reached a peak in 1946 before declining. It is however clear that the lineage tie is a mobilization channel, a powerful rallying force overseas, whereas local causes such as the school may mobilize people beyond the limits of the descent group (see chapter 4 for other examples of mobilizations beyond the limits of descent). Depending on whether the cause is more or less local or global (this may vary over time as in the case of schools) the scope of the lineage as a "group of potential mobilization" (Firth 1956) adapts to the cause at stake.

These successive shifts in the proportion of local versus overseas funding further reveal changes over a century in the village's dependence on its overseas migrants, which peaked just after World War II and the Chinese civil war, and a clear downward trend in the decades following the reopening of China.

The Repatriated Foundation and Its Ambiguous Status

Today, the village no longer depends on overseas contributions. In 2016, the very last round of donations for the renovation of the lineage temple (see chapter 4), which one would expect to be a global rather than a local cause, did not even include overseas emigrants, the contributors being mainly local and from Hong Kong. The relocation of the Zhenneng Foundation, the Chen lineage foundation named after the founding ancestor, from Hong Kong to Pine Mansion in the 1990s was the clearest signal of this change in the relationship between the village and its diaspora. The foundation's headquarters were moved from the Zhenneng Building to the newly renovated ancestral temple (*citang*) in 2016. Established in Yuenlong in Hong Kong's New Territories in the early 1960s after many villagers fled there during the years of the Great Leap Forward, the foundation collected contributions from Hong Kongers and the diaspora and organized ancestral worship in Hong Kong during China's prohibition period.

In the 1980s, lineage activities resumed in the village and the Hong Kong–based foundation was responsible for collecting contributions toward the restoration of the temple and other such public facilities, including the rebuilding of the Zhenneng primary school in 1987. At this time, at the village level, a cadre was in charge of relations with overseas Chinese. This Qiaolian function, abolished in China during the Maoist era, was reinstated with the launch of the reforms. Qiaolian in Chinese usage refers to both the association and the person who chairs it. Pine Mansion's Qiaolian from 1980 to 1990 was Chen Tailai, the first villager I met when I arrived with Lucien (see introduction). He had been imprisoned during the Cultural Revolution and rehabilitated in the late 1970s. During the 1980s and 1990s, he handled correspondence with overseas Chens and collected money for village projects. He was unanimously recognized in the village as the key connector with the diaspora, as the genealogy (2000, 88) relates: "Tailai and those who were part of the Qiaolian, forming a brotherhood dedicated to Zhenneng's cause, established a temporary organization for the purpose of celebrating the two annual festivals, repairing the ancestral temple and tomb, and doing work for the public good with the support of contributions from overseas."

In the mid-1990s, the Zhenneng Foundation was "retransplanted" (*yizhi guolaide*), as the lineage elder Chen Ganhua put it, to the village of Pine Mansion, and Tailai retired. In the eyes of the villagers, the foundation has taken over the function of the Qiaolian. "At the time, it was the Qiaolian who was in charge of these public goods [*gongyi shiye*]. Today, it is the foundation," another lineage elder, Chen Jinyou, told me.[18] Members of the council explained this transition in terms of a generational change on account of Tailai's old age (he died in 2014, aged eighty-five).

The foundation's vice president, Chen Deqi, gave me the following explanation in 2011:

> Today the Qiaolian function no longer exists. . . . The Qiaolian was an organization belonging to the People's Republic of China, each locality with its own overseas relations office, while this foundation was a Hong Kong organization. Now the previous generation is no longer there and in Hong Kong no one organizes [the rites], so we continued it in Pine Mansion, run by people aged fifty, sixty, seventy. Before, it was the Qiaolian, but now these things are the responsibility of the foundation and the foundation's board. We kept using this name. To do public works [*gongyi shiye*] in Pine Mansion, we carried on using the name "Zhenneng Foundation," and now we no longer use Qiaolian or any other [name].

Interestingly, Deqi explains the organizational transformation primarily with reference to generational change, although it is also related to administrative restructuring resulting from legal urbanization. In 2004, the village (*cun*) was redefined as an urban community (*shequ*) under the jurisdiction of the town (*zhen*) of Miaoyun, which became a subdistrict (*jiedao*) of Shenzhen City. As a result, the function of Qiaolian was transferred from its former village level to this higher subdistrict administrative level, coordinated at the city level. The overseas liaison previously carried out by a village cadre with the title Qiaolian no longer exists as such in the new urban community (*shequ*). When I returned to the workstation in 2013, office 802, next to the office of the party secretary, a sign of its previous importance, had been vacated, although the Qiaolian nameplate remained. An employee informed me that the office had moved down to the third floor. In office 301, I met Chen Guanqiu, a local Pine Mansioner employed at the workstation and in charge of social affairs, who advised me to contact the Qiaolian of Miaoyun subdistrict (*Miaoyun guiguo huaqiao lianhehui*). The organization dedicated to liaising with overseas Chinese had been moved up one administrative level from its former village level.

This omission is all the more revealing because Deqi, the Zhenneng Foundation's vice president, chaired the Miaoyun Qiaolian from 2003 to 2005, as I later learned. The Qiaolian organization still exists but beyond the reach of Pine Mansion, and this is why Pine Mansioners conceive the establishment of the Zhenneng Foundation in Pine Mansion as its continuation at the level of the former village. Just after my return in 2014, I thanked Chen Guanqiu for having put me in touch with the Qiaolian during my stay the year before. I was referring to the Miaoyun office, but Guanqiu thought that I was referring to Tailai, the former village Qiaolian and told me that he had died a few months earlier. He offered to put me in touch with Chen Deqi, an indication that the foundation is perceived in the village as a continuation of the Qiaolian.

This unofficial transfer of Qiaolian functions to the Zhenneng Foundation is a way of compensating for the loss of the village's administrative autonomy due to its urbanization (China's rural villages are, at least in theory, autonomous). The Pine Mansion Chens have thus retained control of their overseas relations and lineage affairs. The Zhenneng Foundation today is in close association with the village shareholding companies, the lineage's institutional form. The villagers of Pine Mansion portray it as an organization dedicated to working for the public good within the village (*cunlimian gongyishang de dongxi*), which mainly involves taking care of the mausoleum, the ancestor's temple, the home for the elderly, the main square in front of the temple, and all the activities related to these. The foundation's governing board (*lishihui*) organizes and finances the two annual worship festivals, at the temple and the mausoleum. The board is composed of some fifteen male members who are referred to as village elders (*xiangcun fulao*) and is made up of Hong Kong and overseas residents, returnees (*guiqiao*), local private entrepreneurs (*getihu*), retired civil servants and teachers, and some younger cadres in the urban community of Pine Mansion. The board members are all Chens, but non-Chen workstation managers and influential entrepreneurs are periodically invited to attend the meetings.

The Hong Konger Chen Xingchang, introduced in chapter 1, chairs the Zhenneng Foundation. Through his multiple identities that were mentioned by the Qiaolian, he embodies a perfect synthesis of the village community and their relatives in Hong Kong and overseas. As Chen Shengyu, the head of the workstation in 2011, described him, "He works for the public good and in the industry, which is why we recommended him to the foundation's board." Chen Xingchang was portrayed by villagers as an influential person with many connections (*guanxi*) in government circles. This view and his strong commitment to the lineage's ritual economy suggest that Xingchang not only converts local prestige into regional and national prestige but also operates a local village-level conversion of the regional and national titles and prestige that he has accumulated. His donations range from old photographs of the village displayed in the home for the elderly, bearing the inscription "Given by Xingchang," to large sums of money for rituals and fundraising: he gave HK$2,000 for the school in 1987 (US$245) and 100,000 yuan in 1998 (US$12,100).[19] The foundation contributes to welfare projects and to the improvement and maintenance of Pine Mansion's infrastructure and, in this way, plays a significant role in creating a local environment favorable for economic endeavor. As president of the foundation, Xingchang officiates at the lineage rites and has a decisive role in how they are conducted and the action necessary to maintain the efficacy of the founding ancestor's positive influence on his descendants' economic success (see chapter 5).

Mette Thunø (2001, 928) suggests that "the reconstruction of social structures such as the lineage institution defying the central leadership of the CCP [Chinese Communist Party] has probably caused the redefinition of the *qiaoxiang* concept." The reorientation of China's overseas policy on new migrants in the 1990s (see chapter 1) carried a fairly clear message discouraging coupling investments in *qiaoxiang* areas, places of origin of overseas Chinese, with pre-1949 religious practices. A personality such as Xingchang chairing Pine Mansion's lineage foundation ensures its legitimacy. The Zhenneng Foundation's legal status is uncertain; the subdistrict Qiaolian, Chen Yunxiang, who is not from Pine Mansion, presented it to me as an organization that is "not entirely legally justifiable [*mingzheng yanshunde*]. . . . It is not registered with the state administration [because] it was created spontaneously." Although not officially related to the Qiaolian, it is informally connected to it, as the president and vice president of the foundation sit on the board of the Qiaolian. Chen Yunxiang's opinion discloses the sympathetic complicity that the foundation enjoys despite its illegal nature. "Although is not legally registered, it has been involved in this work for many years and has made real contributions [*gongxian*]. Therefore, we still want to classify it as a mass organization [*shetuan*], a civil organization, even if, legally speaking, it is not. From the government's standpoint, you have to register [as an organization], yet not [being registered] does not mean it is illegal."

This status as an approved organization even though it has not received official approval is due, Yunxiang suggested, to two factors: its longevity and its contributions. Its longevity refers to its Hong Kong origins and is used here to indicate everything the foundation stands for in terms of attracting capital from overseas and above all from Hong Kong, which the Shenzhen authorities still pursue. The foundation has a strong presence within the Miaoyun People's Association in Hong Kong, created in 1985 to encourage investment from Hong Kong residents originating from the Miaoyun area and that Xingchang also chairs. It is therefore a larger entity than the Zhenneng Foundation, which was only intended to bring together people from the Chen lineage of Pine Mansion. Until the early 1990s, both were run by another Pine Mansion native living in Hong Kong, Chen Guanxin, who was more senior than Xingchang and was one of the main donors in the 1987 and 1998 school fundraising campaigns. Chen Xingchang took over from Guanxin as head of the foundation and the Miaoyun People's Association in 1991. It can be assumed that the influence of the unity and numbers of the Pine Mansion Chens acted as a springboard for the leadership of the Miaoyun People's Association in Hong Kong. Several Pine Mansion Chens were appointed to the latter as councillors and vice presidents and are among the association's founding members.

Such territorial associations (*tongxianghui*) have long been the main mechanisms by which migrants have maintained a link to their villages of origin (Sinn 1997). They emerged in Hong Kong as early as the nineteenth century, functioning as guilds and connecting nodes between Chinese living overseas or in Hong Kong and their place of origin, mainly within Guangdong Province (Sinn 1997, 377). They performed the essential function of returning the deceased to their native village, and in the first decades of the twentieth century, they organized the repatriation of overseas Chinese from Southeast Asia (Nanyang) during the Great Depression. From the late 1970s, the Hong Kong associations sent delegations to participate in festivals and lineage rites at the invitation of local Qiaolians (Sinn 1997, 391). They organized group bus tours to older members' home villages, established and cultivated contact with officials to facilitate business in China, and continued to serve as fundraising channels for philanthropic causes, including building schools (Sinn 1997, 392; Kuah-Pearce and Wong 2001, 210).

These associations operate as joint stock companies whose members hold a share equivalent to the amount of their contribution. In 2013, the Miaoyun association had thirty-four members, all but three were men. The president and vice president disbursed 40,000 yuan and the other members 30,000 yuan for their shares. They received symbolic awards and congratulatory letters from the State Council's Overseas Chinese Affairs Office, which are replicated in the activity reports and posted on websites. The website of the Federation of Shenzhen Associations in Hong Kong, of which the Association of the People of Miaoyun is a member, along with thirty-eight other associations representing former villages and towns now subsumed by Shenzhen, shows that it not only actively encourages and defends Hong Kong's economic interests in Shenzhen but also plays a political role supporting Hong Kong's integration into the PRC and promoting pro-China parties during electioneering in Hong Kong. The thirtieth anniversary of the Association of the People of Miaoyun in Hong Kong was celebrated on June 26, 2015, a few days before the eighteenth anniversary of Hong Kong's handover to China on July 1. The Federation of Shenzhen Associations' slogan, which Chen Xingchang included in his speech that day, highlights the triple allegiance promoted by the association: "Love the homeland, love Hong Kong, love the village of origin" (aiguo, aigang, aixiang).

All this is covered by the "longevity" motive invoked by the Qiaolian Chen Yunxiang to explain the authorities' leniency toward the foundation. Other reasons he cited behind this tolerance are the foundation's "contributions" (gongxian) and its action "for the public good of civil society" (wei minjian zuo gongyi de shiqing). Chen Yunxiang here resorted to typically Chinese Communist rhetoric: "If the foundation does good work for this village's popular masses, then it certainly helps the government to some extent; it helps to bring harmony to the urban community. So we support it. We cannot therefore repress it [ya]. . . . If it were another type of organization, if it had a political purpose, it would certainly have to be abolished. But it has no political purpose! It does good deeds [shanshi]! . . . If there is no political content, we won't make a fuss about it. This includes [the former villages of] Yanghe, Pine Mansion—both have the same essential qualities: they are central communities [zhongdian shequ]. The others do not [have a foundation]."

This last sentence reveals the complicity between the neighboring village of Yanghe, from which the Qiaolian Yunxiang himself originates, and Pine Mansion, the two villages being related through their founding ancestors, who were both Chens from Wuhua. The villages are both rich in overseas connections and have similar lineage foundations. Coming from a lineage village similar to Pine Mansion, Yunxiang is careful not to mention the ritual activities that are liable to be labeled superstitious and that are one of the main purposes of the Zhenneng Foundation. He restricts himself to pointing out the absence of political aims—a very vague characterization that could be said to mean that an organization is innocent of these unless accused of harboring them. This is what happened to the Wenzhou migrants in Beijing's Loving Heart Society, which was dismantled when it was seen as a locus of power likely to reveal the corruption of local officials, rather than simply a provider of public services (Zhang 2001, 112). The ambiguity around the nature of the foundation is skillfully maintained, and since its leaders know that they have the tacit support of the government authorities, they do not seek to hide their status as an unregistered organization. Its strictly private nature protects the foundation from government incursions into its internal business, which is thus protected from any possible inquisitive scrutiny, while at the same time, its commitment to the public good protects it from the repression that its illegal status could attract. The lineage can thus take on an institutional form and openly act as an organization.

Today, the Zhenneng Foundation derives most of its income from local sources rather than from the diaspora. It no longer issues an annual call for contributions for worship funding. In the minds of its members, this transition coincided with the establishment of the foundation in Pine Mansion. One member said, "You can still make contributions to the foundation, but we no longer need them for the large or small activities we organize." It has a stable income that allows it to accept the occasional contribution as an extra. Its income is the direct result of investments made by the diaspora in the village during the 1980s and 1990s. One source of income is rental from the house of overseas Chinese. Because it soon became obvious that overseas visitors preferred to stay in hotels rather than in what they considered the uncomfortable conditions that this house offers, an additional building housing a small factory has been built next to it and is rented to a migrant from Hubei, with the house of overseas Chinese serving as a dormitory for factory workers from the same province. The second source of income, the Zhenneng Building, was built in 1994, financed by a Chen in Belgium and his wife and rebuilt in 2004. The additional floors of the new, taller building contain rooms that are rented to migrant workers and the headquarters of the foundation, now rented out as office space since the headquarters were moved to the renovated ancestral temple complex in 2015. The third source of income is the rental of commercial premises in a large building that houses the largest supermarket in Pine Mansion on the other side of the Guanpinglu, the main thoroughfare that runs alongside the foundation building (see map 3 in chapter 3). In 2011, the foundation's annual income was estimated at 500,000–600,000 yuan (US$70,000–$90,000).

In the village today, the foundation receives most of its income from renting these buildings, which were originally financed by overseas donations. The overseas contributions raised in the two first decades of the economic reform and opening era have thus created conditions for local financial autonomy in the ritual and overall economy. In this context, it is therefore not surprising that several Chen leaders pointed out that money from overseas was no longer necessary—"From the moment we had the foundation, it was no longer necessary for *huaqiao* to send money back [*bu xuyao huaqiao jiqian huilaile*]"—and that they no longer needed a Qiaolian, which is another way of stating the same thing.

The history of China and its diaspora is useful for rethinking binary oppositions such as the Global South and Global North. Chapter 1 pointed out how grassroots understandings break down dualist categorization in the context of considerable uncertainty about migration strategies. The migration patterns delineated in this chapter show the need for a more multiscalar understanding of phenomena that are usually referred to in macro-frameworks from a one-dimensional perspective. Heyman and Campbell (2009, 145) write that "there is much justice in critiquing the use of core (or center) and periphery as aprocessual spatial labels that are laid over more complex realities. But this objection holds less water if we view 'core' and 'periphery' as pointing to a strategic relationship that gives rise, through enormously complex processes, to contingent outcomes distributed unequally across space and social groups." Core-periphery relations remain a useful analytical tool when used processually and on the ground to account for spatial mobility strategies and social actors' use of varying opportunities within the world system according to the value they attribute to different localities.

The repatriation of the foundation to Pine Mansion is part of the village's re-territorialization and refocalization. Although the lineage was deterritorialized by massive migration in the early twentieth century and worship activities were delocalized to Hong Kong during the Maoist era (see chapter 6), the return of the foundation has provided an institutional grounding for the lineage in the village, which has recovered its position as a center for decision making on lineage-related activities. Although the foundation in Hong Kong was disconnected from any territorial source of income, its funding is now essentially drawn from real estate in the village, further highlighting this shift. These processes are less contradictory than a single dialectical process: the diaspora's financial contributions have enabled the creation of this local source of income. The process that unfolded within the lineage ritual economy is similar to what occurred as a whole in the village's economy, which is now a real estate rent economy. The vice president of the Zhenneng Foundation drew a link between several elements to explain the end of the fundraising campaigns: "In recent years, there have been no activities and therefore no contributions. The collective economy has grown [*jiti jingji zhuangdale*], and that is why we no longer solicit contributions: they are voluntary." This collective economy is described in the next chapter.

COLLECTIVE FUNDS AND THE MORAL ECONOMY OF SURPLUS

When they make speeches at meetings and ceremonies, local leaders address the crowd as "*Gewei fulao xiangqin*" (villagers/local people). Yet, Pine Mansion is no longer a village: it was legally urbanized in 2004 through a process officially called the urbanization of peasant villages (*nongcun chengshihua* or simply *chengshihua*) through which the villagers lost their peasant *hukou* and became urban citizens (*jumin*) of Shenzhen. This made Shenzhen the "first Chinese city without villages", with no peasants on its official population register. Pine Mansion has also seen a demographic explosion as a result of the inflow of migrant workers from inland China. All of the Pine Mansioners aged fifty and over whom I met had started their lives as peasants or had been peasants for most of their lives and had experienced the radical break from the Mao era. They stressed the tremendous changes introduced by China's reform and opening, using hyperbolic expressions such as "heaven and earth turned upside down" (*tianfan difu*) and emphasizing how much better life in China has become.

Urbanization and industrialization have allowed those living in the village to retire from their agricultural livelihoods a decade before they legally became urban citizens. They have largely benefited from the economic boom generated by the creation of the Special Economic Zone (SEZ) and even took an active part in it by creating the infrastructure for the zone.[1] As this chapter will show, nowadays many do not have to work for a living, and the young have study and employment opportunities nearby.

This chapter outlines the history of Pine Mansion's transition to communism and land collectivization, and then to capitalism and the conversion of their land to industrial and residential use. There has been a striking continuity from the pre-1949 period until today in the territorial structuring of the village in spite of its urbanization. The territory is a fundamental identity marker. All who originate from Pine Mansion strongly identify with their *cun*, which means both the community of native inhabitants and their residential neighborhood, which they also call *cun*, or *wei*. People introduce themselves saying they are "from Zhongxin *cun*" or "from Xiangxi *wei*." They also make statements such as "There are very few Huang; they are in Fulou [*cun*]." When two Chen donors listed in the donation tables have the same name, their neighborhoods are indicated in brackets to differentiate them.

This chapter traces how the transformation following the creation of the Shenzhen SEZ paradoxically brought about an economic and moral valorization of territorial belonging to the villages that were dissolved as part of this transformation. Local membership of the former village community has increased in importance and value in the context of the urbanization, especially since only native villagers are entitled to a share in the collective economy. Village collectives, whether government enterprises or shareholding companies such as in the Shenzhen villages, have been the main agents of China's rural industrialization in the reform era (Oi 1989; Zhe 1997; Pei 2002). In Shenzhen, the village companies draw income from the management of industrial and commercial real estate and distribute annual dividends as well as welfare benefits to their shareholders. Chan, Madsen, and Unger (2009, 346) note that most villages in the area function as mini welfare states; most of these villages are also lineages, social organizations that act as welfare providers (Chan 2012).

Despite the urbanization and transition to market socialism, the territorial continuity also inheres in the way the shareholding companies, as heirs of the Mao-era collectives, are coterminous with the lineage organization. Together, they form a moral economic community. This chapter shows how despite membership of the shareholding companies being no longer strictly based on descent but rather mainly on native origin and residence, the organization of these companies largely continues the lineage's organizational logic. David Faure (2006, 40–41) emphasizes the relevance of Maurice Freedman's view of lineages as enterprises. In Pine Mansion, the lineage is referred to not only as a descent group (*zu* or *zongzu*) but also as an enterprise and a cause (*ye* or *shiye*). The term *ye* is used to describe the foundational act of ancestor Chen Zhenneng, who cleared the land and laid the foundations of his descendants' prosperity. The lineage in itself is a corporate entity that aims to continue Zhenneng's enterprise or cause. "He is actively contributing to Zhenneng's cause" is a standard laudatory formula for a benefactor. This entrepreneurial ethic blends with moral principles that emphasize equity and collective solidarity among members of the same lineage and village. The chapter ends by showing how the shareholding companies were established based on subsistence ethics and participate in what I call a moral economy of surplus.

From Lineage Segments to Collectives

Historically, the creation of the lineage as a corporate group was the result of the extension of state power to local communities, mainly in the Ming and early Qing dynasties in the sixteenth and seventeenth centuries (Faure 1989, 2007). In the twentieth century, the lineage started to be seen as a feudal social entity that was responsible for China's economic backwardness and the root cause of social inequality. After the Communist Party took power, it sought to wipe out the lineage system through land reform (Parish and Whyte 1978, 97; Madsen 1984, 2). Speculating from a distance, some predicted that the seizure of their property would lead to the demise of the lineages (Freedman 1966, 176; Potter 1970, 130). However, once able to access the field after China's reopening, several authors found that many inhabitants of lineage villages had maintained their communal identity, reinforced by kinship ties (Chan et al. 2009; Madsen 1984; Woon 1984; Siu 1989; Potter and Potter 1990). Lineages remained "anchored in villages" (Parish and White 1978, 28).

Prior to 1949, the majority of the population was poor, and a large amount of land was collectively owned as lineage land and branch land. The Chen Pine Mansion lineage collectively held a portion of land, called lineage land (*zudi*), in the name of first-generation ancestor Zhenneng. "Before the liberation [*jiefang*, in 1949], Zhenneng's land was rented; whoever wanted to cultivate it had to rent it," an elderly lady recalled. Furthermore, the lineage was divided into several branches, some of which collectively held land in the name of the next generations' apical ancestors, the *gongtou* (*gong*, ancestor, *tou*, head). The segmentation into branches was generally asymmetric: some held more land and had more members, and members with higher status, than others. At the beginning of the twentieth century, at least nine branches, or segments, were prosperous enough to have established a private school (*sishu*) in Pine Mansion, which they managed themselves and financed with income from "school lands" (*xuetian*), plots held in the name of *gongtou*, ancestors of the third, fourth, or fifth generations.

In this type of lineage, which was particularly widespread in southern China, an individual member of a prosperous segment would belong to several corporate groups and was therefore entitled to a share of the income from several ancestral domains corresponding to different generational levels of segmentation

(Freedman 1958, 131; Freedman 1966; Potter 1970, 125). Tenants cultivating common land held by the lineage or a lineage segment were chosen preferentially from the poorer branches of the descent group (Potter 1970, 128). Members of the wealthier branches received a share of the income from the jointly owned estate after the expenses for ancestor worship rituals had been deducted. The richest could support their families without having to work and devoted their time to studying for imperial examinations or engaging in trade, further increasing the wealth, power, and prestige of their segment and lineage. Although most of the benefits went to their own close relatives, this elite used its power to ensure that the humbler members of the lineage received minimal benefits (Madsen 1984, 59). Therefore, large lineages were marked by both strong inequality and interclassist solidarity (Freedman 1958, 127; Watson 1985; Faure and Siu 1995, 6; Unger 2002, 37).

The members of lineage segments tended to live together in distinct residential clusters called *weiwu*, which the people of Pine Mansion simply call *wei*. They formed compact housing complexes surrounded by a wall (*wei* means "to surround"), distinguishing one complex from one another by the alignment of the houses. These houses were torn down in 2010 and 2011 as part of Pine Mansion's urban redevelopment project, to which I return at the end of this chapter. The Zhongxin and Xiangxi *wei* are in the central and oldest part of the village at the foot of Beifu Hill, where the founding ancestor had built his house and his temple was later constructed (see figure 3.1). Following the geomancy (feng shui) of this site, the houses of Zhongxin, which were closest to the temple, turned their backs to the hill and looked toward the south while those of Xiangxi faced (*xiang*) west (*xi*). In the nineteenth century, the population expanded to form the new *wei* of Shangwei and Henan on each side of the small river that flows through Pine Mansion. Farther west was Dabu *wei*, and in the southeast, Fulou and Taixing seem to have been inhabited largely by non-Chens.

With the creation of the People's Republic of China, revolutionary programs were implemented in rural areas through a succession of reforms and mass campaigns. The Land Reform (*tudi gaige*) launched in October 1950 in Guangdong and implemented by teams sent to the villages from 1951 onward aimed to reform the social order by redistributing the land equally among all villagers. The land of large landowners and that held in common by the lineages was confiscated.

The neighborhoods (*wei*) formed the basis for the creation of production teams after 1949. They were first identified and categorized as natural villages (*ziran cun*)—hence the reason they are also called *cun*—which were in turn gathered into administrative villages (*xingzheng cun*). In Pine Mansion, the Chens were grouped together with those with other surnames in this new administrative entity, while farther south, Baopuchi, a neighborhood populated by a segment of the Chen

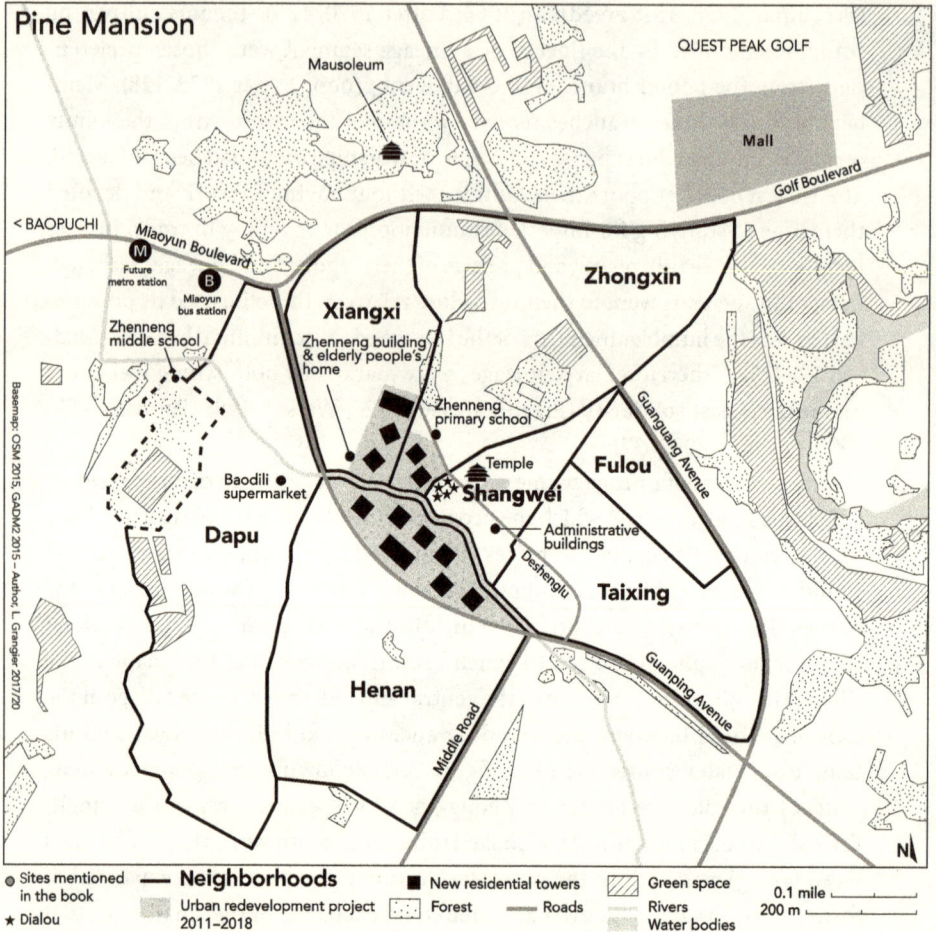

FIGURE 3.1.   Pine Mansion. Map by Lucien Grangier.

lineage, was included in another administrative village.[2] This agrarian reform policy forged a new village identity by adding new dimensions of social interaction (Ruf 1998, 71–72). New territorial bases for political ceremonies, meetings, and mobilization replaced the old ones (Feuchtwang 1998, 60). In Guangdong Province, this policy was intended to bring together rival ethnic groups and lineages such as the Chen Hakka majority and the Huang Cantonese minority in Pine Mansion, dismantling lineage solidarity.

Full collectivization began in the summer of 1955 (Parish and Whyte 1978, 32). Cooperatives, previously voluntary, were now mandatory and became the owners of collective land. In Pine Mansion, seven small production teams were supervised by three larger production teams (*shengchandui*) which were themselves subordinate to the production brigade (*shengchan dadui*) at the administrative village level. From 1958 onward, Pine Mansion's production brigades were controlled by the Miaoyun commune (*gongshe*). Each commune included several production brigades and an average of one hundred production teams, involving about fifteen thousand people (Oi 1989, 5). The Great Leap Forward introduced self-sufficiency and the collectivization of resources at the commune and province levels, and Guangdong Province, which had previously grown many specialized cash crops and imported some of its grain, was now to be self-sufficient in grain. The poorly controlled reorganization and use of the labor force for nonagricultural tasks quickly led to a major economic and demographic disaster. The management of labor and income was decentralized in 1961, and the communes were reorganized into small teams (*xiaozu*), each of about thirty households (about 150 people) which were now the basic units of collective ownership and management.

Equality was achieved by abolishing the lineage estates without breaking up the segmentary lineage structure itself. The collectivization gave groups of inhabitants united by close kinship and neighborhood ties ownership of the land they farmed and enshrined the genealogical subdivisions of the lineage in the territory of Pine Mansion where, as elsewhere, the production teams corresponded to the lineage segments. Several authors have pointed out that this is what made the collective agricultural system acceptable to the peasants (Parish and Whyte 1978, 301; Siu 1989, 157). The way the elders still use the term *gongtou* indicates that the principle of lineage branching has been kept alive to some extent until today.

That the collectivization of land contributed to ensuring a degree of continuity in terms of lineage-based social organization and its moral economy is further demonstrated by the existence of collective funds. Payments in grain to the households of each team corresponded to about 60 percent of team's total income, just over 20 percent of the remainder being absorbed by production costs and the rest by levies of two types. First, the grain tax (*gongliang*), paid to the state in kind, accounted for 3–8 percent of a team's income (Parish and Whyte 1978, 50). Second, deductions made by the brigade and the team went into several funds: the capital fund, intended for future expenditure on equipment; the cash fund, for future expenditure on fertilizer and other production-related necessities; the grain reserve, *yuliang*, made up of the crop remaining after distribution to the families of the team and reinstated during the Cultural Revolution to provide a safety net in the event of famine or war; and the public charity fund (*gongyi jin*) that provided relief for members in need and covered the team's education, health, and public ceremony expenses (Parish and Whyte 1978, 50).

Chen Guizhen, born in the early 1940s, was probably referring to this last fund, which made it possible for her to pursue her education, when she explained,

"For example, my family was poor, but we could study for free; this lineage [*zongzu*] granted you 100 *jin* [110 pounds] of rice to support you in your studies." She is descended from Zhenneng's third grandson, an apical ancestor to whom she refers as a *gong* or *gongtou*. "In the past, many of us were poor, but if someone wanted to study, his *gong* would help him a little. The *gong* helped a little, and the person's own family [*ziji de jia*] would also be looking for a solution. Back then, there was no foundation."[3] There is therefore continuity between the pre-1949 reserve system consisting of the grain harvest from land in the name of an apical ancestor (*gongtou*) and the public charity fund for public welfare and education formed from a portion of the production team's harvest on its collectively owned land. Although collective revenues were no longer used to finance sacrificial rites under Mao, they continued to support traditional philanthropic duties. There was thus a generalization of the principles of collective ownership and redistribution that had previously coexisted with the exploitation of tenants by landowners of the same lineage.

From Collectives to Shareholding Companies

According to elderly Pine Mansioners, living conditions were extremely difficult in the wake of Deng Xiaoping's reforms. Massive emigration greatly reduced the labor force, hampering teamwork as each team was left with only a few members, mainly women whose husbands had left for Hong Kong. The families survived thanks to plots of land (*ziliudi*) allocated to them by the brigade on which they grew vegetables, sweet potatoes, and sugar cane. Still, they could barely meet their needs. They earned only 3 or 4 *mao* (0.3 or 0.4 yuan RMB) a day. One of the first major changes was introduced by the Household Responsibility System in 1981, which made each household responsible for the cultivation of its own plot of land (*zerentian*), a process that the villagers called *fentian daohu*, the division of land between households.[4]

The decollectivization led to a 30 percent increase in agricultural income during the first half of the 1980s and a drop in collective income to near zero.[5] The communes had been definitively dismantled in 1978 and the village-level collectives were now empty shells. However, they soon made a comeback in Pine Mansion, as elsewhere in Guangdong, under new guises (Po 2008, 1610; Chan et al. 2009, 323). From the mid-1980s onward, a new form of collective economic entity, separate from the corresponding administrative entities, emerged.[6] Economic development companies (*jingji fazhan gongsi*) were established at the level of the former brigades, and at the lower level of the natural villages, the cultivation groups were replaced by cooperatives (*jingji hezuoshe*). Each head of household held a share in its cooperative and received dividends (*fenhong*) on condition that they had previously held farmland as a member of an agricultural collective, had been born in or married into the village, and had complied with the single-child policy.

At this time, the new collectives, now allowed to engage in nonagricultural activities, began to use their agricultural land for factory buildings. The villagers called on their kin in Hong Kong and overseas for funding and pooled their money to build factories, which they rented to Hong Kong and Taiwanese corporations. Overseas contributions and investments thus made it possible to maintain a collective sector against the general trend of decollectivization and privatization (Woon 1990, 150; Johnson and Woon 1997, 55). The leaders of Pine Mansion dated the beginning of the economically profitable collectives back to this period. After the brief break in the early 1980s, there was a return to a form of collective economy (*jiti jingji*), as I explain below.

China's urban land is owned by the state, and rural land are owned by rural village collectives.[7] The latter have been the major agents in the large-scale transformation from agricultural to industrial land (Po 2008, 1612). The resulting low cost of land has facilitated industrialization; it is estimated that since the late 1970s, more than half of the factories in the Pearl River delta have been built on rural collective land (Po 2008, 1609), mainly by Hong Kong and Taiwanese investors. In this context, shareholding cooperatives emerged as a solution to the problem of distributing the industrial rental income among the villages' peasant inhabitants. This kind of land-based rural shareholding, initiated in Guangdong, later spread to many localities in China in various forms (Po 2008, 1604).

In the early 1990s, while some villagers had embarked on commercial enterprises such as construction and transport companies, many Pine Mansioners were still growing sugar cane and sweet potatoes. This changed after 1992, when large tracts of agricultural land were converted to residential land in eighty-square-meter plots, which the collectives distributed among the villagers by lot (*chouqian*). By 1994, most villagers had built four- or five-story houses on these plots, having leveled part of the land, and had moved from the old compounds to these new modern buildings, often occupying one floor while renting the others to migrant workers. At about the same time, the village cooperative (former brigade) was forced to sell a significant portion of its land in the northeast of the village to a state-owned company that resold it two years later to a private foreign company, which turned it into what has become one of the world's largest golf courses. Another part was sold to Shenliang, a state-owned agroindustrial company.

One village leader stated that by 1994, agricultural land was no longer being cultivated in Pine Mansion and that the environment had been completely destroyed. The landscape has been radically transformed by the construction of factories and residential buildings and an expressway, and the village has merged into the urban agglomeration. In the past, a villager told me, the landscape had been one of green hills and clear rivers (*qingshan lüshui*), an expression denoting a pleasant rural landscape. However, the descriptions are not all nostalgic, and some evoked negative aspects of the scenery: "It was a 100 percent peasant village; there were stinking pig houses, and the toilets were chaotic [*luanqi bazao*]," according to Chen Weixin, who lived in Guangzhou but visited his wife and mother in the village regularly. Worse, the hills were not green at all but denuded (*guangtutu de*), as all the trees had been cut down for firewood. And whereas the flat ground around the village was used for rice paddies, the more rugged terrain was seen as *huangdi*, wasteland.

Despite this radical change to the landscape, the territorial structure has remained largely the same. Newly constructed residential areas around the core of the old village have been named after each of the old neighborhoods preceded by *xin* (new)—for instance, xin Xiangxi. Only the main roads in Pine Mansion bear distinctive names, the streets bearing the names of the neighborhoods. In short, there has been a centrifugal expansion of the ancient neighborhoods (*wei*). Thus, while the land reform had territorialized the lineage subdivisions by granting them collective ownership of the land, urbanization, despite partial individualization of ownership, perpetuated this territorial organization by giving newly built residential districts the names of the collectives that used to own the land and still owned large plots in common.

The shareholding companies that evolved from the Mao-era cultivation groups are now the major economic agents in the urbanized villages. Following Pine Mansion's urbanization, in 2004 the cooperative development companies were reformed as seven small cooperative shareholding companies (*gufen hezuo gongsi*) at the neighborhood level and one large one at the former village level. The companies manage the collective's real estate assets—the factories and shops rented to foreign companies and local entrepreneurs—and distribute the dividends to their shareholders. "We receive factory rent every month and we do the maintenance" is how the manager of the larger company, Chen Yunyan, summarized their activity. The large company holds use rights to part of the industrial zone (see figure 3.1) and rents out several major industrial buildings. Between 2004 and 2011, its annual rental income increased from 4 to 15 million RMB, according to Chen Yunyan. The seven small companies have far smaller earnings, which vary according to the number and condition of the factories and other sources of real estate income on their territory (*dipan*). In Pine Mansion, the factories mainly specialize in machinery, tools, plastic, and electronic components. The smaller factories are rented to locals or migrants from Guangdong or other provinces, while others on the outskirts of the former village are much larger and are leased to Taiwanese or US multinationals.

In theory, the legal urbanization and transformation of the village into an urban community entailed the state, in the form of the municipal government, taking over land previously owned by the collectives. In Pine Mansion, it took over only a very small part of the collective land, mainly comprising uncultivated forest and hills, paying 46 RMB per square meter in compensation; in Shenzhen, only unused land (*shaowei*)—that is, land not cultivated or used for real estate—with a surface area of more than two hundred square meters was requisitioned. The village collectives retained their right to the collective use (*jiti shiyongquan*) of everything else. This is a right of use and not a right of ownership, as urban land in China belongs to the state, hence the ambiguity around the term *expropriation* (*zhengshou*). The senior company manager Chen Yunyan used it while clarifying that it is not legally expropriation but "a societal reform of the whole city of Shenzhen through the urbanization of villages."

Elsewhere in China, entire village communities have been deprived of their lands. In many cases, the local government buys the land at a low price and sells the use rights to real estate development companies at a higher price. Land requisition followed by its sale has become local governments' main source of income (Cartier 2001; Zhu 2004; Ma and Wu 2005; Zhang 2010). It has also been one of the main causes of conflict and revolt in rural China over the past decades (Perry and Selden 2000; Guo 2001; Zhao 2009; Bruun 2013; He and Xue 2014). In Shenzhen, and more generally in the Pearl River delta region, rural village communities undergoing legal urbanization have generally retained the land use rights to their former collective land (Fu 2003; Tan 2005; Po 2008; Zha 2008), mainly due to lack of government resources. The new Shenzhen municipal government was small, financially weak, and unable to pay compensation. It refrained from taking over all the collective land to ensure villages' self-development and self-provision of public goods (Po 2008, 2841).[8]

In Pine Mansion, as in other lineage villages in the Pearl delta (Zou 2014), the underlying lineage structure confers unity on the former village community. The leadership is dominated by the Chen lineage, with the elected heads (*dongshizhang*) of the seven small shareholding companies in 2015 all Chens, as shown in table 3.1.

The village's large shareholding company is located in one of the two eight-story buildings that rise side by side in the heart of the old village near the ancestor's temple and next to the pond that lends it good feng shui, the other housing the community workstation (*gongzuo zhan*) that supervises the new urban community (*shequ*) that has replaced the village. Workstation employees are directly appointed at the higher subdistrict level (*jiedao*).[9] While the village was

TABLE 3.1. Leaders of shareholding companies in 2015

THE THREE MAIN PARTS OF PINE MANSION	RESIDENTS' COMMITTEES	SMALL SHAREHOLDING COMPANIES	LEADER (PSEUDONYMS)
Center-East	Pine Mansion	Zhongxin	Chen Zhimin
		Xiangxi	Chen Guoxin
West	Nandafu	Henan	Chen Xiaohai
		Dabu	Chen Chunxian
Southwest	Fuxingwei	Shangwei	Chen Jianming
		Taixing	Chen Chunhui
		Fulou	Chen Guoyuan

administratively autonomous before 2004 because it was run solely by the village committee. Although urbanization has generated greater subordination to the municipal power hierarchy, it has also created a duality of power. Company leaders still form a powerful alternative body of power within the urban community, and they and other lineage village members hold leadership positions at the workstation. The three neighborhood resident committees (*juweihui*) are headed by the elected directors (*dongshizhang*) of a shareholding company from which they receive funding. Over a period of seven years, I have seen the main leadership positions of party vice secretary, community workstation head and vice head, and head of a large shareholding company rotating regularly among the same small group of people.

From One Classification to Another: Urbanization and the New Natives

Apart from the few who have been able to pursue studies and an urban career outside the village, which in some cases made them eligible for an urban *hukou* prior to 2004, the people of Pine Mansion have long held rural *hukou*. Under Mao, they were classified into different peasant categories by the five-category social class system introduced in the countryside with the land reform (Vogel 1969; Shue 1980; Ruf 1998). Intended to rebalance socioeconomic status through debt cancellation and property equalization, this became a rigid caste system (Wu 2014, 39). Households were categorized as landowners (*dizhu*), rich peasants (*funong*), medium-rich peasants (*zhongnong*)—subdivided into "medium high" and "medium low"—and poor peasants (*pinnong*) based on their pre-1949 standing. In practice, it was the opposition between the first two and the second three categories that mattered most. The brigades discriminated against the landowners and rich peasants, particularly in terms of the amount of work to be done and their access to education, and favored medium-rich and poor peasants.

In Pine Mansion, the biggest categories were those of poor farmers and medium-low peasants. Some families with overseas relatives were classified as rich peasants, and I was told that there were also "quite a few medium-high peasants." Wang Cui-chun, whose family was in categorized as poor peasants, had a large poster of Mao at home and went to see the "real portrait," as she put it, at Tiananmen Square during a trip to Beijing: "Mao was very good to us poor farmers: he denounced the landowners [*pidou*]." She talked for a while about the unequal workload be-tween members of the work teams that the system had created, and with a slightly embarrassed laugh, she pointed to one of the elderly men sitting at a nearby table in the restaurant where we were having morning tea: "He was a rich farmer."

Most Pine Mansioners do not like to talk about these issues, and when asked, they generally make evasive comments. When they do talk about it, it is in gen-eral terms, as a matter of history over which they had no control, and a now-defunct parenthesis. "This happened when Mao took power," explained Chen Zhimin, one of the village leaders, who had been categorized as medium high. "People were classified by the government. . . . It is a problem of past history [*guoqu de lishi wenti*]. It disappeared naturally, naturally, in the 1980s: it wasn't canceled." By repeating "naturally" (*zi ran er ran*), he stressed the arbitrariness of the class system. Indeed, the system fell into disuse during the 1980s rather than being officially repealed (Unger 2002, 46–48; Thireau and Hua 2010, 190). This change was accompanied by rehabilitation of the victims of the Cultural Revolution and the anti-rights movement.

Those who suffered most during the Cultural Revolution were the "intellectuals"—all those with a secondary education—and in the countryside, "bad class" villagers—landowners, rich peasants, and particularly people with overseas ties—who constituted nearly 60 percent of the cadres in Guangdong Province (Vogel 1989, 37). In Pine Mansion and elsewhere, the latter were the tar-get of attacks and public criticism, and several had been imprisoned.[10] Many fled to Hong Kong (see chapter 1), to return in the 1980s when they could be rehabili-tated (*pingfan*) and resume possession of their confiscated property. Wang Cui-hun stated that her stepfather had returned from Southeast Asia in the early 1950s and then moved to Hong Kong in the mid-1970s, but "it was only when Deng Xiaoping ratified [*pizhun le*] that he was able to come back." The verb she used, *pizhun*, which also means "approved," probably refers to Deng Xiaoping's 1978 declaration signaling the change in policy, which now saw foreign ties as beneficial (OCAO 2000).

At least two of the leaders who created the impetus for the resumption of lin-eage activities and ties with the diaspora from the early 1980s onward were categorized as landowners or rich peasants and had been imprisoned in the 1970s. One of these was Maoxin, one of the authors of the 2000 genealogy and the former school headmaster, but he had died before I began my research and I have very little information about him. Tailai, the other, whom I had met on my first day in Pine Mansion, was born in Indonesia in the late 1920s. His parents returned to the village following the anti-Chinese pogroms at the end of the 1940s and were classified as rich peasants. He was imprisoned for five years during the Cultural Revolution. At the end of the 1970s, he was rehabilitated, became a production team leader and then the village Qiaolian in charge of relations with migrants overseas. He retired as a cadre (*ganbu*) in the early 2000s.

This return to power in the early 1980s of middle-aged people born in the 1930s and early 1940s who had been politically persecuted and socially discriminated against under Mao is not unique to Pine Mansion. In localities with diasporic ties and resources, the rebuilding of former temples and lineage halls using money from overseas favored a return to traditional power structures (Jing 1996, 176) or empowered alternative organizations such as Associations of Elderly Persons led by village elders as mediators between the village and overseas Chinese (Chen 2013, 84–93, 99). It is not surprising that people such as Tailai, who had both a high level of education and close family ties overseas, once again became village leaders in the context of the 1980s, when being able to contact or reconnect with overseas Chinese was of strategic importance. Communication took place mainly through letters written by local connectors to their interlocutors abroad. Tailai, who used to read the newspapers daily at the home for the elderly (*laoren yiyuan*), passed on both national and local news to Chens living overseas.

Tailai, who died in 2014 at an advanced age, had become a bitter man who would launch into somewhat incoherent diatribes in which he railed against his fate, the Maoist leaders, especially the Band of Four, and the most recent changes in Pine Manson. Apart from the Cultural Revolution, which is the only episode to have been officially condemned, land reform, the Great Leap Forward, the political persecution of local elites, and the suppression of religious practices are not officially open to criticism in China and are still considered by the government to have laid the foundations of socialist society. This official repression relegates the memories of punishments endured and of the deceased victims of persecution to private reminiscence. These can be discerned between the lines of public rites (Watson 1994). Tailai's lamentations in my presence recalled the funerals (Watson 1994, 73) and healing rites (Mueggler 2001, 50) that act as public outlets for the suffering experienced under Mao.

Perhaps more particularly in Shenzhen, whose creation embodies China's opening and reform, the triumphalist discourse on national success may act even more as an agent of oblivion and the repression of memories of the past, making open criticism of the state exceptional. The people of Pine Mansion consider their classification into social classes past and forgotten due both to the psychic repression of this painful history and the divisions it created and to the later historical strata overlying it, the amnesiac effect of the rehabilitation and restoration to leading positions of the main bearers of such memories, and more recently, the passing away of this generation.

The fact that nobody is classified as a peasant any longer also plays a role in this omission. With legal urbanization in 2004, the residential status of the villagers was officially changed to urban (nonpeasant, *feinong*). The "natural" disappearance, rather than the official abolishment, of the social categories that separated the villagers was formalized by this new categorization which the villagers call Shenzhen classification (*Shenzhen de huafen*). The very phrase that was previously used to mark divisions within the village community ("how the family was classified" [*jia shi shenme huafen*]) is now used to mark the categorization of all of its members as citizens of Shenzhen. However, whereas the old categorization was a source of inequality and political persecution, the new classification not only offers those who worked the land as farmers a form of compensation but also equalizes all former villagers. The collective social promotion to urban citizen status further contributes to the contemporary reinterpretation of past suffering as compensated, if not rewarded, in a certain way by present prosperity (see chapter 5).

Table 3.2 shows the categorization of Pine Mansion's population in the 2010 official census.

The table shows that the rural-urban dichotomy hardly matters any longer and has been replaced by the separation of natives from outsiders: the category of "native villagers," *yuancunmin*, literally villagers of origin or inhabitants of the village of origin, is counted separately and makes up only 2.4 percent (1,441)

TABLE 3.2. Categorization of Pine Mansion's population in 2010

CATEGORY (*FENLEI*)	RESIDENT POPULATION NUMBERS
Pine Mansion committee	15,547
Nandafu committee	18,110
Fuxingwei committee	13,001
Factory dormitories	11,881
Native villagers	1,441
Total	**59,980**

Source: 2010 official census.

of the total population. Administrative urbanization has given birth to this new legal category for people of Pine Mansion who had a peasant *hukou* at the time of urbanization in 2004. This helps to explain why native Pine Mansioners continue to refer to themselves as simply "villagers": one easily slips from "original villager," *yuancunmin*, to "villager," *cunmin*, and most former villagers use the latter term, although this may also be due to the vagueness of the word *cunmin*.

All those whose *hukou* was registered elsewhere are excluded from this official category. This includes not only migrants from other parts of Guangdong and other provinces but also those who, having been born in the village, left it and obtained an urban *hukou* in Shenzhen or residence in Hong Kong before returning to settle in Pine Mansion. Chens who have returned from Hong Kong and overseas seldom hold local *hukou*: I learned of only two cases who had been able to restore their local *hukou*.[11] Those who left to follow an urban career in major cities in Guangdong Province and elsewhere in China and changed their *hukou* before 2004 generally have their urban *hukou* registered elsewhere. However, among the younger generations, not all those who left have changed their *hukou*. Some one hundred to two hundred Chens among the much larger, but impossible to estimate, population originating from Pine Mansion who now live in central Shenzhen have retained their Pine Mansion *hukou* registration. Some of these left the village in the 1980s and 1990s, usually to work in downtown Shenzhen, and remain in the category of native villagers and shareholders although they do not live in Pine Mansion. Others left the village after its legal urbanization to live in downtown Shenzhen and are reluctant to transfer their *hukou* to other parts of the city, as they would lose the benefits associated with shareholdership.

Even so, it remains that the officially registered *yuancunmin* are fewer in number than the population considered truly native to Pine Mansion. Chen Zhimin, the village leader with whom I met most often due to his availability and outspokenness, told me that "our current number is a little vague [*muhu*]. . . . It's been a bit of a sensitive issue in recent years." The sensitivity is related to the rights arising from holding local *hukou*—for instance, the possibility of enrolling their children at the primary and middle schools. The mobile entrepreneur Chen Junjie, who lived in the village for two years with two of his children while his wife and younger children were in Guiana, was only able to register them at the school thanks to the goodwill of the headmaster, a local Chen. Previous detention also determines the right to a share in the collectives and thus to dividends and pensions. However, all Pine Mansioners in the extended sense—that is, including nonofficial natives but excluding migrants from other provinces—have become rentiers.

A Village in the City: Booming Population and Rental Boon

Pine Mansion belongs in the category of places called villages in the city, *chengzhongcun* (Lan 2004; Li 2004; Yeh 2005; Lin 2006; Wang, Wang, and Wu 2009). In 2005, there were 241 of these in Shenzhen, 91 within the SEZ, and 150 in Longgang and Bao'an Districts (Wang et al. 2009, 959). Villages in the city are considered anomalies, stigmatized as incompatible with the spatial order that the civilizing ideology of urbanization intends to produce as a vehicle for modernization (O'Donnell 2001, 419; Zhang 2001, 19; Siu 2007, 239; Bach 2010, 422). Due to their "spontaneous urbanization" (Shen, Wong, and Feng 2002; Tian 2008) in contrast to the planned urbanization of central Shenzhen, they are characterized by a particular and somewhat chaotic landscape in which increasingly tall factory and residential buildings stand beside older buildings. One should not imagine a looser mesh of urban fabric here than in the planned city: on the contrary, while the latter is aired by large avenues and has much higher buildings, the villages within the city convey an impression of extreme human density.

On the surface, the village has physically disappeared. Once surrounded by fields and hills, the old residential areas are now lost among factories and buildings. The boundaries of the village are traced to the north and east by the boulevard that leads to the golf course (see figure 3.1). The village is crossed from north to south by another two-lane artery, Guanping Avenue. On either side of these roads are dusty, bumpy streets rarely used by cars and best accessed on foot or motorcycle. During the day after school has started, elderly natives walk or cycle, idle youths parade in their sports cars, and migrant grandparents look after toddlers or exercise in the tiny public squares. In the afternoons, especially in summer, a languid atmosphere prevails and the elders and construction workers rest in the shade of the longan and banyan trees. In the evenings, gym and dance sessions gather a more typically urban crowd.

Rural villages on the outskirts of the planned urban area of the city have welcomed migrants, who find affordable housing there as the authorities have made no provision for any accommodation except by requiring factories to provide dormitories for their workers (Song, Zenou, and Ding 2008).[12] Migrants come from northern Guangdong, nearby provinces such as Guangxi, and further afield (Sichuan, Hunan, Henan). Some 95 percent of these hold temporary residence permits and work in factories or run stores, restaurants, or factories. The proportion of immigrants in the population of Pine Mansion is higher than in Shenzhen in general, where it stands at 70 percent (Li 2006). Internal migrants generally constitute more than 80 percent of the total population of the urbanized villages all over China (Tang and Chung 2002; Zhang, Bao, and Tian 2003; Chung 2010; Kipnis 2016).

During my first stay in the summer of 2011, from five o'clock in the afternoon when the sun was going down and the heat was easing, a human tide would suddenly sweep through Pine Mansion. The workers in their factory uniforms would go to eat dinner in the canteens, surf the internet and play pool in the open air, then return along the straight avenues bordered by newly planted palm trees to their dormitories. Couples strolled around comparing the menus of the small Sichuan or Hunan restaurants and the shoes and bags in shops run by the Wenzhounese. Families wandered along Guanping Avenue examining the stalls of other more-recent immigrants on which counterfeit items were arrayed: "Calvin Klain" boxers, "Samsmug" phones, socks, watches, and toys.

From stay to stay, I saw these stalls disappear in favor of clothing and food stores, including bakeries. Internet bars were replaced by karaoke bars, and the number of workers diminished. It seems that there has been a reflux of migrants toward Guangzhou, where rents and food are less expensive. The average wage of workers in Shenzhen was about 2,000–2,500 RMB per month (about US$300), while the cost of living in the city had increased significantly. Another reason for this change was that the old village houses in which the native villagers had lived until the early 1990s and then rented to migrants after building new apartments for themselves, have been demolished in the 2010s under the urban renewal program.

Many of the people I met in the village did not have to work for a living and displayed an idleness that, by the early 2000s, had become a sign of status in similar formerly rural villages in the area (Chan et al. 2009, 293). Siu (2007, 334) calls the native inhabitants "Maoist landlords" (see also Liu 2009). They take care of their grandchildren and collect the rent from their apartments, but many have plenty of time to sit outdoors chatting with fellow native villagers and playing mahjong. Until the beginning of the 1990s, the main means of subsistence was agricultural, supplemented with remittances sent by relatives in Hong Kong or overseas. The land from which they once earned a meager agricultural income now generates a much larger rental income. In addition to this individual revenue, Pine Mansioners had also started to receive annual dividends from the collective income shareholding companies draw from the rental of factories to foreign companies.

Data from a census of overseas and Hong Kong relatives (see chapter 1) provides information on the professional occupations of 193 household heads in Pine Mansion. Table 3.3 shows that two-thirds of the native population in 2010 were either unemployed or retired.[13]

One Saturday morning, I joined Wang Cuichun and her retired women friends from the village in a restaurant on the outskirts of the old town of Miaoyun,

TABLE 3.3. Occupations of native villager household heads in 2010

OCCUPATIONS	PERCENTAGE
Cadres	6
Employees, skilled professions	7
Low or unskilled occupations	18
Entrepreneurs and factory managers	7
Unemployed or retired	62

Source: 2010 population census of overseas and Hong Kong relatives.

whose boundaries are no longer marked, the road leading to it being entirely lined by high buildings. They go there to shop almost every morning, as the market is better stocked than the very small one in Pine Mansion. Before or after buying their vegetables, they often have tea and dumplings together at a large restaurant that is very popular with the locals. At noon, they go home to cook and then come back out to play mahjong or cards in the afternoon. Even though seniors receive a bus pass for free public transport throughout Shenzhen, they rarely go downtown. They used to go from time to time fifteen years ago, when there were few shops in Miaoyun, but now they can find everything they need nearby. Wang Cuichun passes through Shenzhen only once a year on her way to Hong Kong, where her husband lives. Village life is quiet and comfortable; the accommodation is more spacious than in downtown Shenzhen and Hong Kong, and everybody knows one another.

Pine Mansion's native villagers (*yuancunmin*) have benefited considerably over the past thirty years from the real estate income generated by the economic boom, as have those who live downtown in Miaoyun or in the center of Shenzhen and those who have returned from Hong Kong and elsewhere to settle in the village. Members of these two latter categories, although mostly nonlocal *hukou* holders, have, thanks to lineage complicity, received plots on which they have been able to build. One of the villagers I met at the beginning of my first stay was Chen Jinhe, a well-known local figure who had studied in Guangzhou during the Cultural Revolution and became a propagandist painter. He later painted in an artists' village in Shenzhen and ended his career teaching at the Shenzhen Academy of Fine Arts in the late 1990s. Jinhe is famous for painting several propaganda posters celebrating Deng Xiaoping's visit to Shenzhen and particularly his famous Southern Tour (*Nanxun*) in the spring of 1992.[14] He also painted founding ancestor Zhenneng's portrait, which hangs in the ancestral temple, and carved the stone statue which stands at the foot of the hill where Zhenneng is buried (see chapter 4, photo 3). He showed me a TV report aired in 2004, when

Shenzhen was declared China's first city without villages, in which he gives a short interview standing in front of his poster in downtown Shenzhen, followed by interviews with other Shenzheners expressing how much they owe to Deng.

After moving back to the village, Jinhe supplemented his retirement pension with rental income. He is not a *yuancunmin*, as he changed his *hukou* in the 1980s, but he is tied to the village by his marriage to a woman from an older branch of the lineage, he himself being from the younger branch. We climb a small path to his house on the hill above the ancestral temple. On the left is a building belonging his brother who lives in Hong Kong. On the landing, we meet Jinhe's sister-in-law who has come to take care of various matters. It is an eight-story building built with Jinhe's own money. The first six floors have eight rooms each, which are rented to immigrants with a total of forty-eight tenant households. He occupies the top two floors, with his studio on the lower floor full of his paintings and portraits of his parents, grandchildren, and other family, a self-portrait, and photographs of his students.

Chen Guizhen, whom I met on the day she and her sons and daughter were worshipping her husband's ancestor, had been able to study with the help of her *gongtou* but never became a teacher as she intended. Like everyone who graduated from high school in 1961, she and her husband, whom she married the same year, had to go down to the countryside (*xiafang*, literally, being transferred to a lower level) to participate in agricultural work.[15] She did not "get out" until she was forty-seven years old. Her husband then became a teacher while she worked in the school canteen. She came back to settle in the village at the end of the 1980s and asked the village committee for "a house"—a buildable plot of land. She drew lots for a plot and received one on Guanping Avenue on which she built a five-story building with a loan from the *gongtou* for the construction, which was completed in 1995. Now she has paid off her debt. When I went to visit her for the first time, she was living on the third floor and renting the apartments on the other four floors.

The native villagers persist in speaking of Pine Mansion as "their village," both to distinguish it from the city of Shenzhen, even though they are formally Shenzheners, and to refer to the close-knit, face-to-face community to which they belong within the wider urban community with all its new inhabitants. It is also a moral economic community.

The Native Community's Moral Economy

The creation of the shareholding companies emphasized territorial bonds and gave importance to the new social category of the native villager, which defines who is entitled to a share in the collectives. The collectives' dual-level organization is reminiscent to that of the pre-1949 lineage in which an individual was likely to belong to several corporate groups and to have shares in several ancestral domains held in trust by different branches. However, the right to hold a share is no longer determined by patrilineal descent but above all by local residence, and therefore, women can now own shares if they have local *hukou* status.[16]

The main condition for becoming a shareholder was local peasant residential status (*hukou*) before the village's urbanization in 2004. When the shareholding companies were established in April 2004, those who had never left the village paid a much lower price per share than those who had left temporarily, mostly for Hong Kong, and then returned. The villagers call this process of price determination "arranging a share" (*yugu*). The cost of a share for each individual who met the basic conditions was decided according to several criteria, called qualifications (*zige*): age, with older people paying less, land use rights, and the duration of a person's stay in the village. Elderly people paid about 1,000 RMB, adults 2,000–3,000 RMB, children 4,000–5,000 RMB, and those who did not have use rights to the so-called responsibility land, because they had left the village prior to its distribution in 1981 (see above) and only recently returned, paid up to 10,000 RMB.[17] The result is equality between the shareholders, a principle on which the villagers always insist when they refer to the shares: "one share per person" (*meiren yigu*). The system for buying shares worked as an equalization mechanism, with the payment of unequal amounts making the shares equal for all. The head of a small company insisted on this: "Different amounts of money were paid out in order to obtain identical shares" (*xiangtong de gufen*).

Similar processes for the distribution of shares were employed in other villages in the Pearl River delta. Anita Chan et al. (2009, 340) write that in another nearby Chen village, such a logic of equalization and equity testifies to the endurance of the communal values central to the collectivist period. However, the system of equal shares of collective property can also be traced to before 1949, when the lineage organization was predominant and the principle of equality between brothers prevailed. Here, there is a syncretic combination of the lineage's ethics of entitlement to land held in trust in the name of an ancestor and the collectivist ethics of equal rights and duties to the land held by the collective, in a "mobilization of past principles" (Thireau and Hua 2001). These normative principles are still present and were used to evaluate people's entry rights based on their past. In Pine Mansion, it was essentially the duration of time spent working in the fields—and therefore the amount of past work in the collective economy—that was considered when calculating the price of shares. The system was a mechanism for equalization guided by a logic of equity—namely, the principle that those who had remained to work the land when many went abroad, and therefore had participated most in the collective agriculture, paid the lowest entry fee. In other words, an expanded labor theory of value is at play in these moral calculations, which took place at the crucial moment when the villagers lost their peasant livelihoods, responding to this valuation crisis with a revaluation project (Collins 2017).

Shareholders do not legally own their shares. They only have the right to a share (*guquan* or *fenquan*)—that is, a share of the income generated by the collective economy. They are not free to transfer their share, which can only be inherited by their child, provided that the child's residence is registered locally. This is important, as holding a share entitles to welfare rights—companies distribute not only annual dividends but also social benefits (*fuli*), and in particular, retirement pensions. The concern about equal access to these rights on the basis of past work is then all the more understandable.

This is where the main change due to the legal urbanization lies for the villagers. Before urbanization, there were virtually no social benefits. The Maoist era was characterized by the establishment of a strong duality between urban and rural citizens in terms of the standard of living and benefits that Chinese citizens could claim (Solinger 1999; Smart and Smart 2001; Zhang 2001). Urbanization brought about a legal framework that gave new urban dwellers the rights associated with urban residence—namely, access to retirement pensions and social and health insurance. In urbanized Shenzhen villages, the former village collectives, now transformed into shareholding companies, are responsible for paying these benefits. The system was designed by the authorities as a social insurance system: women over fifty and men over sixty receive a pension from the company in which they hold a share. In addition, the companies provide social insurance (*shebao*) and health insurance (*yibao*), either buying these in and providing them directly to their shareholders or reimbursing shareholders who purchase their own insurance.

Chen Xiuhuan a forty-year-old woman born in Pine Mansion, paid a small amount for her share. Coming from a very modest family, she had not studied and had farmed the land until the early 1990s. She married a Chen, also a native villager. They each receive a minimum of 9,000 RMB from the annual dividends of their corporations. Members of households with two shareholders do not need to work. Wang Cuichun, who married in the village in 1972, lives with her grandson in a house in Xiangxi. She holds a share, and her grandson has inherited a share from her father-in-law. Her retirement pension amounts to 2,400 RMB per month (more than her husband's in Hong Kong, as she noted). She also received 20,000 RMB in compensation for the loss of her husband's old house, which she had rented to migrants for 100 RMB per month before it was torn down for the redevelopment of the village. She has no other rental income, having sold the additional building she had built for her son, to pay his—and possibly also her own—gambling debts.

The development of shareholding companies was designed to ensure a smooth transition to a socialist market economy. On the one hand, it encouraged the industrialization of Shenzhen, leaving it to the village collectives to invest in the real estate infrastructure that has enabled the establishment of manufacturing production in the area. Shareholding companies have been an essential instrument in this infrastructural development. On the other hand, they have ensured former rural dwellers' transition to urban status and guaranteed them an income despite the strong competition on the labor market generated by the influx of migrant workers. These companies are hybrids (Gu 1999, 2010) which, although part of the Chinese conversion to capitalism, still operate partly according to the old collectivist system. Prior to 1949, most lineage land was held in trust in the name of the founding ancestor or later ancestors (Faure 2007, 219), and part of its income was used to fund ancestral worship, philanthropic works, and lineage schools. The small and large shareholding companies perpetuate this system by making large donations at the times of the ancestral festivals that contribute to the cost of the worship and the meal together (part of the expense is also covered by the lineage foundation). The large shareholding company gives 1,000 RMB to each elderly villager in a red envelope on New Year's Day and 500 RMB on several other holidays, including the Mid-Autumn and Chongyang Festivals, and 500 RMB to children on Youth Day. In collaboration with the lineage foundation, it also funds scholarships of up to 10,000 RMB per year for young Pine Mansioners who succeed in gaining a university place.

The vice president of the lineage foundation explained that during the Mao era, the foundation and the collectives did not have the means to pay such expenses, but now that they have a surplus, they can afford to be generous. Freedman (1968, 126) defines the lineage-based economy as a "surplus economy." Surplus is used to accumulate land and to finance rituals, which in turn consolidate the lineage as a property holding group. Both Patricia Ebrey (1986, 29) and Allen Chun (2002, 178) reverse this functionalist conception: landed property ensures the lineage's continuity through the perpetuation of ancestral worship, hence the moral prohibition on selling ancestral land. Although this is not a sine qua non condition for the existence of a lineage (Cohen 1990), the ownership of property facilitates the funding of worship and welfare. Surplus is not a goal that worship functionally supports but a facilitator: the lineage has a dual economic and moral nature. Lineages are "both corporate interest groups and at the same time institutions of a 'moral economy'" (Brandstädter 2000, 70).

In Edward Thompson's (1971) and James Scott's (1977) definitions, "moral economy" has two connotations: in the economic sense, it implies the subsistence ethics that guarantee all individuals living in a community the right to enough to eat; in the moral sense, it is the set of principles by which individuals act in a way not purely driven by profit or utilitarian interests (Brandstädter 2000, 40; Fassin 2009). Whereas the principles of equity and equality that underlie the shareholding system relate to the former, the lineage foundation and shareholding companies' distribution of monetary gifts and the funding of ancestral worship pertains to the latter. I call this second dimension "surplus ethics." Rentals generate income that not only allows its distribution to the members of the lineage but also ensures the proper functioning of the ritual economy by covering the most essential expenses, those related to ancestor worship, thanks to the existence of a surplus. This goes against William Booth's (1994) criticism of the concept of the moral economy on the grounds that it is only applicable to situations of scarcity and famine, as it involves only the guarantee of a livelihood—"subsistence ethics." A moral economy is indeed contextual but does not disappear with prosperity and is compatible with a market economy (Hann 2011; Palomera and Vetta 2016).

Income earned from commercial and industrial real estate activities enables the community to abide by surplus ethics in addition to subsistence ethics: its moral economy is not only a moral economy of subsistence but also a *moral economy of surplus*. Paradoxically, the existence of this surplus is rendered fragile by surplus ethics. Since share ownership gives rise to the right to social benefits, they are distributed by the shareholding companies independently of profit. Elected heads of companies are also prompted by voters to be generous to ensure their reelection. Surplus ethics, however, is not the only culprit. The global economic crisis of 2008 and the ensuing closure of factories reduced the shareholding companies' rental income. In addition, these companies are responsible for the maintenance of the industrial buildings under their management and, until recently, that of much of the village infrastructure. For all of these reasons, by the early 2010s, most companies were in deficit, not only in Pine Mansion but also in all of the villages in the Miaoyun constituency and more broadly, the Pearl delta (Xue and Wu 2015).[18]

For example, Zhongxin's financial statement for March 2012 revealed that a small company's revenue had amounted to 180,600 RMB and its expenses to 328,100 RMB. Almost all of the income came from real estate rental from factories, with an additional 10 percent of the total from compensation paid in the context of urban redevelopment. Its expenses were mainly irreducible social expenditure on pensions and social benefits but also included other less-vital expenses that are nonetheless considered socially useful, such as contributions to the two sacrifices to the ancestor and outings in China for which a bus is chartered twice a year, some shareholder groups even going abroad to Singapore and

Malaysia. This kind of group trip, a common practice in such villages, has of course the effect and purpose of "strengthening and celebrating feelings of belonging to the collectives" (Chan et al. 2009, 322).

The people of the generation that experienced the collectivist period continue to think of themselves as members of a village collective, as demonstrated by their use of the old terms. Wang Cuichun, for example, said that she had benefited greatly from the trips "organized with the *shengchandui* [production team] by *lingdao* [leader] Chen Guoxing." This sense of continuity is also generated by the names of the companies, which include those of the old neighborhoods (*wei*) as well as of the three residents' committees, two of which, Nandafu and Fuxingwei, combine the names of the individual *wei* (see table 3.1). The third, consisting of Xiangxi and Zhongxin, was renamed Pine Mansion. Its leader, Chen Zhimin, justified this takeover of the village's former name by the fact that "its population is the largest," since it represents nearly half of the native Pine Mansion inhabitants. He added that "it was necessary to continue [*yanyong*] the name because it has value" (*you dian jiazhi*).

This naming occurred at a time when the neighborhoods that had formed the heart of the old village had been completely destroyed as part of an operation aimed at generating increased real estate value. In early 2011, three shareholding companies, Xiangxi, Zhongxin, and Henan, signed an agreement with the local district government and a private developer to implement a project of "cooperative development for the renovation of the old village" (*jiucun gaizao hezuo kaifa xiangmu*). The project's goal was to build a new block of a dozen high-rise buildings (see chapter 4) as part of the policy started in 2009 by Guangdong Province to promote the redevelopment of old towns, old factories, and old villages ("the three olds"). Aimed at producing a uniformly modernized urban landscape, this policy can also be understood in the context of the consequences of the world economic crisis that broke out in 2008. Boosting the construction sector was intended to reduce the risk of rising unemployment, and the increased area of real estate was to increase the income of the shareholding companies. This adds to the systematic policy of industrial upgrading promoted by the government over the past few years that has helped the shareholding companies to offset their deficits. They are once again in surplus, at least for now.

The collectives, which are the urban reincarnation in China of the Mao-era agricultural production team, have been the main actors in the industrialization and urbanization of the villages in the city and are the main vectors through which the people of Pine Mansion persist in conceiving themselves as a village community. They have increased the importance of the territorial definition of local identity and its value, making "villagers of origin" a now-privileged category and one that can be inherited. It remains to be seen how those of subsequent generations who are born in urban areas will identify themselves.

Shareholding companies act at the interface between capitalist investors in the SEZ, the state, and the local community. Hybrid in nature, they embody the community's moral economy, set up according to principles of subsistence ethics and distributing money in accordance with surplus ethics. They allow for "local capitalism," capitalist practices shaped by "kinship or social networks that provide non-market frameworks within which the locality engages in external market transactions to accumulate collective capital" (Smart and Lin 2007, 285). As chapter 4 shows, while this community morality is partly congruent with the state's modernization and neoliberalization projects, it also differs from them to an extent that can be considered subversive.

4

SAVING THE ANCESTRAL SITES, MOBILIZING FOR THE PUBLIC GOOD

Shenzhen grew at the astonishing pace of over 27 percent a year from 1980 to 2006, generating the expression "Shenzhen speed" (*Shenzhen sudu*). This high-speed growth continued over the next decades and spread to the former villages lying outside the city's central districts. Between 2011 and 2018, I witnessed Pine Mansion undergoing the same kind of erasure that had initially taken place in the core of the city—namely, the wholesale destruction of old houses to make space for new apartment buildings. Although this kind of destruction is occurring all over China, it is particularly spectacular in Shenzhen, where in March 2005, the municipal government declared the "reformation of villages in the city" as its major mission (Du 2008, 202). Far from passively accepting this policy, the people of Pine Mansion have taken an active part in it. In the previous two decades, they had already thoroughly transformed their formal rural village landscape into an urban one, as chapter 3 has shown.

However, they also collectively mobilized in the face of urban policies and spatial planning that threatened some of the landmarks at the heart of their enduring unity as a lineage village community. Although the villages in the northern districts of the city were officially pronounced urban only in 2004, they had been affected by urbanization plans and related administrative rationalization policies in the 1990s after Longgang and Bao'an became urban districts in 1993. The first community mobilization in Pine Mansion, at the end of the 1990s, was to save the founding ancestor's grave from China's funeral reform, which ordered the disinterment of all buried human remains and their storage in public cemeteries outside the villages. Another mobilization followed shortly after this to save the village's primary school, which was under threat of being shut down in accordance with the district government's rationalization of school management. The third and more recent mobilization was to renovate the ancestral temple (*citang*) just after the core of the old village had been destroyed as part of the urban village redevelopment policy.

This chapter's title adopts the typical form and punctuation of the slogans that spurred the Pine Mansioners' mobilization to save these sites and of Chinese slogans more generally. I refer here to mobilizations in both the sociological sense of collective action and the emic sense, inherited from the Maoist technique of governance through political campaigns (Hertz 1998), of all Pine Mansioners locally and abroad being called to action (*fadong*) by the village and lineage leaders. Whereas the first two mobilizations were critical and succeeded only thanks to massive financial support from overseas Chens, the third, for the temple, involved the latter only slightly, if at all, reflecting the end of the village's dependence on outside help (see chapter 2). The mobilizations aimed to preserve particular places—the ancestral tomb, the primary school, and the ancestral temple—and their associated rituals and festivals.

These sites correspond to what Michel Foucault (1998, 178) calls heterotopias and heterochronias: alternative places and temporalities that differ from the spatial rationalization and fast pace of urbanization and their related policies. In his reflection on heterotopias, Foucault somewhat changes the direction of his thought on the "order of the discourse" (*l'ordre du discours*) by making room for attention to the social use of spaces. However, more is at stake than just the social use of space: these sites—the cemetery, the school, and the temple and public square in front of it—are also public goods in the economic sense, as well as things that are part of the public good in a more abstract, moral sense, which the figure of the founding ancestor embodies. The villagers emphasize the principle of one share per person and define public goods as "the things everyone uses" (*dajia yongde dongxi*).[1] The notion of the public good is thus closely linked to the equalizing and redistributive principles central to the community's moral economy (see chapter 3). These two dimensions are therefore inseparable, and this is further shown by the fact that the word *gongyi*, the public good, takes an adjectival form with the addition of the suffix "de" (*gongyide*) to designate the "public goodness" of things.

Retracing the mobilizations to save these public goods requires adopting a perspective from below on economic rationalization and modernization projects and management schemes that are often studied from above. This type of issue has been dealt with primarily in terms of neoliberal governmentality in analyses inspired by Foucault's reflections on the rationalities of government and forms of knowledge that shape the conduct of individuals and populations (Rose

1999; Inda 2005; Ong 2006). More often than not, such top-down accounts lead to an overstatement of the totalizing character of governmentality and a "residualization of the social" (Barnett et al. 2008, 634). In the case of China, scholars making claims for an overriding neoliberal hegemony tend to focus on individuals, elites, and lifestyles rather than on social groups, subalterns, and protest (Nonini 2008, 146). The cases examined here invite a perspective on how local communities mobilize to defend some of their most valuable sites that goes beyond analyses of neoliberal governmentality. These sites have value, in the double sense of social worth and economic value, and therefore constitute public goods.

"Saving space" plays on the double connotation of saving: what is at stake is both saving in the sense of accumulating as much space as possible for the purpose of economic exploitation for urban development, and safeguarding particularly meaningful sites and valuable public goods. This chapter shows how, while their ritual uses signal them as heterotopic and heterochronic, the strategies adopted for their protection are also homotopic and homochronic with urban development at "Shenzhen speed." The mobilizations for the ancestor's grave and the school aimed to counter the effects of neoliberal urbanization but did not challenge the policies themselves. The third mobilization, for the temple, was even less overtly a matter of resistance. These valued sites are the main territorial anchors of the local community and its diaspora, and the process of mobilizing for their protection intensified this territoriality.

Heterotopic/Heterochronic Places

A line of critique regrets superficial use of the concept of heterotopias, which is often confined to labeling certain places and tends to ignore "how places and localized ways of life are relationally constructed by a variety of intersecting socioecological processes occurring at quite different spatiotemporal scales" (Harvey 2000, 538). I take up the challenge of this critique and pay attention to the ways in which the preservation of these sites is at stake in historical and geographical processes of place and space construction, at both the local scale of the community and the larger scale of central and local state-led policies. Foucault's vague definition of heterotopias as "different spaces" has precisely the advantage of leaving room for exploration of how these sites are constructed relationally.

The sites concerned here, which were marked out at the very foundation of Pine Mansion, are ritual spaces. Heterotopic places are most often sacred, set apart from the profane, reserved for the accomplishment of specific life-cycle rituals (Foucault 1998, 179). It can be argued that ritual action is par excellence linked to the shaping of heterotopias, since it operates "by emphasizing the disjunction between the world being created by the ritual space and the world that exists outside of that ritual space" (Puett 2013, 97). At the entrance to the ancestral temple, the lines of a two-line verse are painted on wooden boards that hang on either side of the door proclaiming, "The source rises in Changle, the enterprise starts in Bao'an," (*yuan cong Changle, ye chuang Bao'an*). These lines constitute a slogan in the etymological sense of the word, like the rallying cry of Scottish clans (Makovicky, Trémon, and Zandonai 2018). It encapsulates and celebrates the founding act of ancestor Chen Zhenneng, who migrated from Changle, in the north of Guangdong Province, to Bao'an, which is now a district of Shenzhen.

The parallel verses (*duilian*) had been hand-painted by a famous calligrapher from Guangzhou in 1925 when the ancestral hall was restored and embellished with contributions from Chens who had migrated overseas. Such verses, consisting of two counterbalanced phrases with matching semantic and phonic properties, are often used to frame the main entrance to a residence or official building. *Duilian* are propitiatory and beneficial (Delahaye 2002, 49; Thornton 2002, 31). They also have a special ability to create a close relationship between particular people and specific places. As graphic speech acts, they are intended to underscore the importance of a new situation or a crossing, and they act as a marker for the visitor, flagging that he or she is entering a different space (Delahaye 2002, 43). Here, they act by signaling and singling out the foundational spaces of Pine Mansion's Chen lineage.

The slogan "*Cong zheli kaishi, bu yiyang de jingcai*" appeared everywhere in downtown Shenzhen during the summer of 2011. Along with its English version, "Start here; Make a difference" (the literal translation being "from here start, not the same wonderfulness"), it was posted in two vertical lines in the manner typical of a *duilian* on banners that hung at regular intervals along the sides of the motorway. This slogan was the official motto of the World University Games held in Shenzhen in mid-August, and with it, Shenzhen City was advertising itself, more than the games, as a place of new beginnings.

The resonance of the Shenzhen and lineage slogans seems to suggest a perfect accord between the history of Shenzhen and the Pearl River delta region, as they are currently presented in museums and other official narratives, and the history of the Pine Mansion Chen lineage. It also appears to offer a fine match between the entrepreneurial spirit promoted by the Chinese government and that which guides the lineage as an enterprise. The overall narratives that encapsulate them both are very similar: the city slogan depicts Shenzhen as a pioneering place, a new frontier where people dare to launch new enterprises and are animated by an entrepreneurial spirit, while the lineage hall *duilian* celebrates the pioneer ancestor Zhenneng's start of a new enterprise, its second line reading "*ye chuang Bao'an*," which can be translated as "the enterprise [or the estate] starts here [in Bao'an]."[2]

The Shenzhen and Chen lineage slogans chime with each other not only in their representational content but more importantly in their pragmatics, insofar as they participate in the shaping of a new space. Yet, despite their similarities, the ideologies and logics of practice that they express and enact differ. Whereas one verse of each pair is similar to the other in proclaiming a new start, the other verse opposes them. The village slogan's first line, "the source is in Changle," acknowledges the origins of the lineage. It is a reminder of the Confucian moral imperative "When you drink the water, remember the source" that is central to the religious cult of ancestors. It is on this precise point that the state-promoted enterprise of neoliberalization, which faces the future ("start here"), differs from the aim of the lineage enterprise: to perpetuate the estate created in the past. The city slogan's second line ("not the same wonderfulness") celebrates Shenzhen as a new city turned toward the future.

The local lineage village's slogan stands in a part-whole relationship to the larger-scale city slogan—the city contains the village, and the village is one of the city's building blocks. Yet, this part-whole relationship is meant to be suppressed: villages are supposed to dissolve into the modern city and their native inhabitants, deemed uncivilized and backward, are meant to become modern urban dwellers. The Shenzhen slogan can be seen as condensing all inhabitants of the city into a new undifferentiated ensemble of modern citizens. It is a synthesis of a larger discourse that is turned against the kind of territorially rooted local organizations represented by lineage villages such as Pine Mansion.

Two main sites are fundamental to this territorial anchorage. One is the ancestor's tomb, which contains the ancestor's bodily remains. The other is the ancestor's temple, where his spirit tablet is lodged. The rituals performed at these sites are sacrificial rituals aimed at prolonging, year by year, the afterlife existence of the founding ancestor. They are guided by the goal of transforming the dead into ancestors and preventing them becoming evil and vengeful spirits, *gui* (Ahern 1973, 125; Baptandier 2001, 15). Ancestors who are properly cared for and receive regular ritual attention are expected to be benevolent to their descendants (Hsu 1963, 45; Wolf 1974, 165).[3] The manner in which the rituals at the ancestral temple and the grave are conducted in Pine Mansion has been largely simplified in comparison to the past (see chapter 6) but still follows the main principles and the same sequence (Thompson 1988; J. Watson 1988a): the ritual is led by male lineage elders and involves offerings of food, drink, and sacrificial money, accompanied by an oration calling for the founding ancestor's blessing and beneficial influence on the community of descendants. After the ritual, a communal meal of pork and rice, cooked in the morning, ends the half-day festive gathering of people from the village and their kin, many of whom have returned to the village from elsewhere for the occasion.

Both sites are said to be geomantic power spots due to the conjunction of their topographic features and the presence of the ancestor in his bodily remains and his spirit tablet. According to Chinese geomancy, or feng shui, it is important to bury a dead relative at a propitious site, the form and shape of which channels the vital energy (qi) contained in the bones, which is a source of vitality and fertility for descendants (Feuchtwang 1974; Bruun 2003; Paton 2007). Ancestors can be more beneficial to their descendants when they are buried at sites endowed with good geomancy.

In the Chinese context, where such beliefs are considered superstitious and the expression of a backward peasant mentality, few Pine Mansioners are willing to talk to outsiders about feng shui (see chapter 5). According to the history narrated in the Chen genealogy, before he left northern Guangdong for Bao'an, ancestor Zhenneng was taught geomancy by a feng shui master, which endowed him with a special ability to select propitious places. Whether it is due to their beneficial influence or simply to respect for sites inherited from the founding ancestor, from a more secular viewpoint there is the idea that these places belong or pertain to the founding ancestor and must be preserved. The sites were chosen by the founding ancestor himself and continue, not metaphorically but in a very real way, to belong to him. Today, they are not said to be the property of any individual or shareholding company, or even of the lineage village as a whole; even the village leaders, who otherwise abide by the doxa that urban land belongs to the state, point out that these sites belong to the ancestor. They use the term *shu*, meaning "belong, dependent." *Shu* has the virtue of being vague and not appearing to be a claim to the right of possession or even use, while at the same time, it clearly reflects the fundamental idea of belonging not to the living individuals who make up the village collective but to the ancestor and the ideal that ancestral land should be held in perpetuity (Faure 2007, 219).

The ancestral sites are directly related to another time, which could be called foundational time. The communal gatherings for rituals on these sites amount to both an evocation and an invocation of the origin of the village that is more than simply a commemoration of history, although some of my interlocutors coined it as such. "The source rises in Changle, the enterprise starts in Bao'an" is a foundational statement in that it refers to both the origin and the future. In this regard, these heterotopias are also heterochronias. Foucault (1998, 182) distinguishes between the "quasi eternity" of cemeteries as "heterotopias of time that accumulates indefinitely," akin to libraries and museums, and heterotopias that are "absolutely chronic," linked to time in its most "transitory and precarious aspect" in the form of the festival or events such as fairs. The grave and the temple are heterochronias in that they are eternal and "chronic": they are sites destined to keep the ancestor's bones and soul forever, beyond his life on earth, and where a huge festive celebration is held twice a year. Thus, the *duilian* that frames the entrance of the temple links two sociospatial frames: they not only set the place apart as a place of worship devoted to the apical ancestor, a defining feature of heterotopias, but also frame the space of the (former) village itself, bringing together two temporalities, the ephemeral and the eternal.

The Mausoleum: A Response to the Funeral Reform

In 1995, the Chens' founding ancestor's grave was threatened by the proposed construction of a road leading to the Quest Peak golf course, which had just opened to the north of the village. Pine Mansioners prevented its destruction by forming a human barrier in front of the bulldozer and sending a protest letter to the district government. They protected the site by raising money for erecting a fence around the hill where the grave lies with an entrance gate that names the site as a garden (see chapter 4). This piece of land has remained lineage property, and the other side of the hill behind the grave was made a public park. The road was built, but it goes around the site (see village map, figure 3.1).

Four years later, the Chens built a mausoleum around the tomb of the founding ancestor Zhenneng. They took this decision following the introduction of the funeral reform (*binzang gaige*) in Shenzhen in 1997. Wishing to maintain Shenzhen's image as a pioneering city in the field of reforms, the municipal authorities immediately implemented the national regulations issued that year by the Chinese State Council, anticipating the Guangdong provincial government's decision to generalize cremation (*huozang*) the following year, 1998. A decision was made to achieve 100 percent cremation across Shenzhen within ten years and to prohibit burial (*tuzang*). Moreover, the authorities ordered that all buried remains be exhumed and cremated and the ashes scattered or stored in a publicly accredited cemetery.

This reform was justified in the name of building a "socialist spiritual civilization." Its stated goals were to "eliminate superstitious activities (*mixin huodong*) in funeral customs," a goal the Communist Party had had on its agenda since the generalization of cremation was established as a national objective in 1956 and had achieved, under Mao, mainly in urban areas (Whyte 1988).[4] The reform clashes with the widespread principle that a deceased person must rest in the earth, as expressed in the phrase *rutu wei'an*, literally "enter the earth to [be] at peace." It also goes against the idea that animates burial practices and ancestor worship rituals—namely, that the ancestors can be more beneficial to their descendants when they are buried in sites endowed with good geomancy. The funeral reform seeks to suppress these ancient and powerful burial places by replacing them with abstract modern spaces.[5]

China has a long history of state control of funeral practices (Ebrey 1991, 2003; Goossaert and Fang 2008) and a long tradition of orthodox Confucian criticism of "superstitious" funeral customs (Yang 1957, 276). Confucianism is not opposed to respect for and remembrance of deceased family members, filial piety (*xiao*) lying at the very heart of the Confucian doctrine. Nor does the official state atheism that the Communist Party has endorsed since 1949 oppose all forms of remembering the dead; the funeral reform, implemented to varying degrees since 1956, seeks to replace traditional funeral customs and ancestor worship with commemorative ceremonies. In this, the ideology of the state conflates with a particular strand of Confucian thought that opposes the material, corporeal dimension of ancestor worship (the continued territorial presence of the ancestors through the medium of their bones) and argues that it should be replaced by spiritual commemoration and symbolic gestures.[6] Ancestral temples are better tolerated than graves for this reason.

The ideological mix driving the funeral reform comes close to neoliberalism, as described by the tenets of the governmentality school, in its encouragement of a rational and individually rooted way of remembering ancestors that is more compatible with economic efficiency than with the collective worship of ancestors at their tombs. The main goal of the reform, apart from its anti-superstitious ideological overtone, is of course the freeing up of space. Confucian principles and state-promoted secularism serve as arguments to justify the clearing of graves and requisition of the land occupied by tombs for economic development, even though it is hard to reduce this to merely a form of legitimization. The ideology that carries the funeral reform forward cannot solely be accounted for in terms of neoliberalism (Nonini 2008); it rests on a combination of economic goals and an alliance of orthodox Confucian and atheist state rejection of traditional customs that are seen as backward.

In Pine Mansion, as in all the surrounding villages, the graves lay scattered across the hills around the village.[7] The new policy aimed to concentrate all the dead's remains in one or two public cemeteries per district, requiring the rural villages in each district to renounce what the government saw as a waste of space. A government team came to Pine Mansion in 1998 to proceed with the exhumation. The villagers were threatened with losing their shares in their companies if they did not comply. I estimate that about a thousand graves were dug up and the remains cremated and placed in urns, which were temporarily stored in the ancestral temple and then removed to the mausoleum when its construction was finalized two years later.

The mausoleum (figures 4.1, 4.2) was a clever solution to a double challenge: how to protect at least the remains of the collective founding ancestor, and how and where to store the ashes of ancestors that the villagers could not avoid exhuming and burning. It was built over Zhenneng's tomb, whose remains were thereby kept entire and buried. On either side of the tomb, a set of steps leads to two wings that are connected on the first floor by an arched walk with a balustrade from which one can see the tomb. On the second floor, a cement cloche with small openings for ventilation overhangs the tomb. The wings offer storage space for the ashes of all Zhenneng's descendants and of the deceased relatives of non-Chen native villagers. The remains of Zhenneng's wife had also escaped cremation, the reason for which I did not manage to grasp; I was told rather vaguely that she had been buried at a site that became part of the Quest Peaks golf course in 1995, and it can be supposed that the villagers negotiated with the company that owns the course. Her remains were later removed from the grave when the Quest Peaks managers planned to build villas on the site, and they are now in the mausoleum.

The layout of the building presents a structural homology with the written genealogy. In both, the ancestors of the fifth generation, the common denominator whose two-character name is Guo, serve as the ordering principle. The urns

FIGURE 4.1. View from downhill of the mausoleum, founding ancestor Zhenneng's statue. Photo by author, 2018.

FIGURE 4.2. The mausoleum. Photo by author, 2013.

of the second- to fourth-generation ancestors are kept in a special room next to Zhenneng's grave. At the entrance to the mausoleum, a list indicates the room number of each Guo ancestor, who has been allocated to a determined area based on the number of his descendants. In addition to the obvious practicality, since contemporary descendants have now reached the tenth generation, the choice of the Guo generation is also understandable in terms of another factor: fewer of the fifth generation emigrated than those of the following Hua and Deng generations. The choice of Guos therefore guarantees that all descendants are included in the mausoleum.

The entrance to the building was newly framed by the same *duilian* as that on the ancestral temple: "The source rises in Changle, the enterprise starts in Bao'an." This iteration of the lineage slogan underlines the importance of the site and defiantly recalls the successful erection of the mausoleum itself in contravention of government policy. The mausoleum was designed and constructed in two years under the leadership of a lineage member, Chen Ganhua, a high-level government cadre who had retired from his position as vice president of Shenzhen airport and was living in downtown Shenzhen. In 1997, Ganhua had temporarily returned to Pine Mansion to assist a cousin living in Belgium who, with his wife, wanted to finance the building of a home for the elderly as a contribution to the community (chapter 2). His first reaction was to think of his great-grandfather Guobao, the wealthy and illustrious apical ancestor of the lineage segment to which he belongs.

He deemed depositing his ashes in a public cemetery unimaginable and considered placing them in a towery building (*diaolou*) that had once served as a school (see later in this chapter). This would not be easy, as it could be considered a contravention of the funeral reform, and he first had to make sure that the village leaders would back him up. He went to see them and explained that his plan included nothing illegal: "They told me 'Uncle Hua'—that's what they call me—'this way of doing things, we can make it bigger, we can take it to a larger scale [*daxing de*]. You shouldn't be thinking only of yourself: wouldn't it be possible to do the same for our Lord Zhenneng? This wouldn't violate the law either, would it?'"

When these leaders, his remote lineage cousins, asked him if he thought he could work for the whole village rather than just for himself, Ganhua accepted their proposal and took the lead on three conditions. The first was that the village leaders should have the approval of the majority of Pine Mansioners. A consultation was launched, and the villagers approved unanimously. The second condition was that in the event of a government incursion ("if government people came to ask questions"), the village leaders would "receive them and present a united front" (*cunwei limian quanmian jiedai*). Ganhua's third condition was a call for financial contributions from the overseas Chinese. The mausoleum was built thanks to his connections overseas as well as in the government and the construction industry. The first set of connections allowed the speedy mobilization of the Chen diaspora in Asia Pacific and Northern and Central America and the swift collection of the huge amount necessary to build the mausoleum, with over 1 million RMB gathered in a few months. The second meant that the mausoleum was built rapidly, reducing the possibility that governmental opposition would prevent the initiative.

The mausoleum is officially called the Pine Mansion Historical and Memorial Hall, although I have rarely heard it called by this name: generally, the word *lingyuan*, meaning mausoleum or cemetery, prevails. The same strategy was pursued in the village of Dachuan in northwest China with the Confucius Temple, which is officially "a public site dedicated to cultural education" (Jing 1996, 64–67). Ganhua and the village leaders played with the official definition of "public cemetery" where the funeral urns were to be stored, cleverly dealing with the government authorities by using the gray zones and interstices that decades of authoritarian rule have lent the Chinese people. Since the reform required urns to be placed in public cemeteries, therefore, the community created its own. Allowing non-Chen native villagers to store their dead's funeral urns in the mausoleum prevents it from appearing to be a private family site. Its maintenance and management are ensured and financed by the lineage foundation, which allows all members of the community to place the urns of their deceased in it free of charge. Moreover, with its Heritage Bureau listing as one of Bao'an District's heritage spots (*wenwu dian*), there is public recognition of its importance and need for protection. Pine Mansion is not the only village where an ancestral tomb has been accorded heritage protection, showing that there has been some district government leniency regarding these initiatives.

Such collective mobilization to save the grave site from destruction is at odds with the state-driven policy of neoliberal urbanization. By protecting the founding ancestor's tomb, the villagers have succeeded in exempting this piece of land from future appropriation by the state for economic development. The duplication of the lineage slogan at the entrance of the mausoleum is as provocative as it is performative: it states the continued presence of the Chen lineage and its control over the territory. Clearly, the funeral reform did not meet the goal of getting rid of practices considered superstitious, since worship of the founding ancestor and of each family's close relatives continues at the spring equinox (Chunfen) and fifteen days later at Qingming. Such practices continue in the new public cemeteries, but in Pine Mansion, the rites are performed in front of the relatives' urns at the mausoleum, rather than on their tombs, as was the custom before the reform (see chapter 6).

Territorialization and the Public Good

The safeguarding of Zhenneng's tomb was presented as a categorical imperative, a necessity so obvious that no explanation was required. My interlocutors often referred to the expected result: I was told that if the mausoleum had not been built, the ancestor's remains (*haigu*) would not have been safe (*baobuwen*). In short, the answer was somewhat tautological; they had to be saved because they were threatened.

It was difficult to persuade the villagers to talk about this sensitive issue, and when I asked about it at the municipal office, they at once suspected me and asked, "Aren't these questions political?" A comparison with what happened in a nearby village shows that the people from Pine Mansion did have some room for maneuver. In the other village, the inhabitants accepted the order to store their ancestors' remains in the district's public cemetery, but it was the bones and not the ashes that they transferred, avoiding the required cremation. In another rural village in Meixian County, in the northeast of Guangdong Province, the authorities were so keen to attract funds from the diaspora that they allowed the village's *huaqiao* not to cremate the dead and to bury them in the surrounding hills (Chen 2013). Other villagers, who had to proceed with the cremation, exploited the gap thus opened to obtain the right to bury their ancestors' cinerary urns. In Pine Mansion, the leveling of land and the urban density deprived the villagers of such a possibility. The only remaining hills are Beifu Hill behind the ancestral temple and the hill on which Zhenneng's tomb is located. Not only is there simply less available space in Shenzhen, but also the current prosperity of the city and its former villages reduces the need for investment and donations from overseas Chinese, whose good graces the district authorities no longer need to preserve.

The people of Pine Mansion therefore made a virtue of necessity by placing the cinerary urns above ground but beside the founding ancestor's tomb. Although there may have been some ex post rationalization in their accounts, what people told me about the dangers of the deceased remains' dispersal and the benefits of gathering them all in the mausoleum offered further explanations of their choice. First, emigration reinforces the desire of many emigrants and their descendants to root themselves in the village. In Pine Mansion, the long migratory past makes maintaining the village as an anchorage point for the diaspora crucial, and the growing trend of people from Pine Mansion moving to Shenzhen and other major cities increases this need. It guarantees that they will be able to return to the village and receive postmortem care, while their placement in a large public cemetery outside the village could risk their being forgotten or neglected. In 2011, Chen Yunyan, the manager of the large shareholding company who lived in downtown Shenzhen, explained the decision: "We could not allow that to happen. So we thought of the following: build a building over his grave to protect the ancestor's bones and bring the whole village together without separating the lineage [*jiang quancun bufen xingshi*]." The construction of the mausoleum can in this sense be interpreted as participating in the process of refocusing and relocalizing the lineage in Pine Mansion since China's reopening: it plays a role in anchoring the lineage as a deterritorialized and globalized collective to the village as a place.

Second, the Pine Mansioners voted in favor of a solution that compelled them to burn the bones of their closest ancestors down to ashes but allowed them to keep them within the territorial boundaries of their village. Many of the villagers stressed that at all costs, they wanted to avoid their ancestors' dispersion (*fensan*). This surprised me because I had also heard it with reference to the graves prior to the reform: people insisted that before the construction of the mausoleum, the graves had been scattered (*fensan*) all around the village. People considered the mausoleum an improvement on the past, when they had had to "run all day" from one tomb to the next: "Now everyone comes here. . . . We no longer have to run around," said a woman I met at Chunfen, the day of the spring equinox, when ancestor Zhenneng, his wife, and his sons are worshiped. The construction of the mausoleum and cooking facilities at the foot of the hill made it possible for this ritual to be followed by a shared meal as was already the tradition on the ancestor's fall birthday. In the past, each family had returned home for the meal. The mauso-leum reinforced the focality of the tomb, creating a gathering point for all of the ancestors whose graves had been scattered and also for the living, who now have an additional opportunity to come together. This is a process of territorialization in the sense defined by Feuchtwang (2002, 250): the creation of a physical place characterized more by its focal point than by its borders and a place of collective effervescence where social interactions are concentrated.

The people of Pine Mansion found another advantage in the gathering that the creation of the mausoleum allowed. Their choice was one of maximal con-centration of their dead's remains in a minimum amount of space. Yet, the space where this concentration took place was not just any space: it surrounded the founding ancestor's tomb, lending it its particular geomancy. There seems to have been a geomantic collectivization. The centralization (*jizhong*) of the ashes around Zhenneng's tomb is believed to infuse them with the bones and soil in which the ancestor is buried. Burton Pasternak (1973) reports that among the Hakkas of southern Taiwan, the deceased were in some cases grouped in "com-posite tombs" for the collective maximization of geomantic effects. One woman with whom I talked casually at one of the ritual gatherings spontaneously al-luded to this geomancy. She mentioned the threat posed by the funeral reform: "Placing all the other descendants elsewhere! That was impossible—everyone had to be protected. This place [Zhenneng's tomb] is most likely a precious geoman-tic place [*fengshui baodi*]!" Another woman told me during Chunfen, "After fu-nerals were banned, [the mausoleum] was built here because they thought this feng shui was better, something like that." This gathering and concentration thus embraces the same logic that guides urban development: maximal exploitation of the available space.

The focalization also affects the founding ancestor in the sense that his grave being located at the entrance of the mausoleum makes him a presence who meets every Chen who visits the building. Having all the dead gathered around him guarantees that all their visiting descendants will make a sacrifice to Zhenneng together with their sacrifice to their deceased close relatives, even when they have not come at Chunfen. The preservation of Zhenneng's bones is of prime impor-tance because they are the agnatic substance shared in common by all descen-dants, the common denominator of lineage. Zhenneng unifies all the ancestors by substituting for the materiality of their disappeared remains. His name is also used as a rallying cry, as in the following quotation from an interview with Chen Deqi, the vice president of the Zhenneng Foundation, about the mobilization: "Using the name of Lord Zhenneng [*yong Zhennenggong de ming*] we have united [*tuanjie*] compatriots here and overseas in the cause of Pine Mansion, in its eco-nomic construction, and in the public good [*gongyi shiye*]. We encouraged overseas leaders to mobilize [members of their communities], and all of them, hearing that something had to be done for Pine Mansion, for Zhenneng, answered the call as one man." The use of the expression *tuanjie*, to unite or rally, underlines the political role of lineages as corporations (Sangren 1984, 400). The same is true of the verb *fadong*, to mobilize.

Zhenneng is both the cause of the mobilization and the means by which it was able to be carried out. The evocation of his name encourages mobilization for the sake of the common cause that he embodies. Through his founding gesture—his migration to and settlement in Pine Mansion—he is a "heroic figure" (Sahlins 1985, 47). One of the hallmarks of the "heroic historical mode," according to Sahlins, is leaders' use of the "heroic self" as they tell the story of the entire kingdom in the first person, the "I" standing for the whole polity. The founding ancestor is an operator of unity, a structuring and guiding principle of the public good. Lord Zhenneng embodies the public. *Gong* following a name translates as "lord" but has taken on the modern meaning of public.[8] "The public/private opposition in China is rather the opposition between a whole and the different parts of it" (Thireau and Hua 2001, 89), and just as the village community as an entity is crossed by tension between the whole public and its private (Chen) part, the Chen lineage is itself crossed by a tension between the public kinship of the lineage and the private kinship of the families and segments.

Protecting the remains of the founding ancestor was not a foregone conclusion and did not come about naturally but required collective coordination. The uncertainty in the months following the announcement of the funeral reform revealed that the first impulse was for each to take care of their own ancestors. This duality between the founding ancestor and close ancestors normally expressed through the two forms of ancestral worship was overcome in a time of crisis thanks to the Chens' capacity for unity. The solution that was found, to house the ashes of the close ancestors alongside the protected grave, reveals the founding ancestor's status both as an operator of the collective and as a public principle.

Unity, Desegmentation, and the School Protest

Although in retrospect it is difficult to compare his current importance with that of the past, to think that the founding ancestor has always occupied the place he occupies today would be an anachronism. There are some clues to support the idea of what can be called a desegmentation of the lineage—that is, a unification of its segments around the figure of the founding ancestor.

Accounts of the mobilization for the mausoleum suggest that it entailed some lineage members working for everyone and not only for their own ancestors. Other elements along the same lines are evident in the way segmentation is subject to internal criticism within the lineage. When I discussed the question of branch membership with lineage leaders, they produced a normative discourse condemning the tendency to think of oneself as belonging to a branch rather than to the lineage in its entirety. I received a detailed account on this point during a conversation with Zhimin, a village leader, and his friend Xianwei (see chapter 6). As I often did, I raised the issue on behalf of the Tahiti Chens, some of whom say that they are proud to be descendants of the first branch. I asked their opinion on the matter. Xianwei, who belongs to this branch, answered, "We could say that there are many people [in this branch], and their level of culture is a little higher [than that of people of other lineage branches]." Zhimin replied, "Certainly, there are more people and people who have money and culture. But we don't think this branch is more honorable [*guangrong*]." He went on to say that if I asked such questions, then people would focus on such things, and they should not: "I don't agree with these ways of seeing. Why? Because it is like making divisions among the descendants of Zhenneng. . . . 'I am not from the same branch as them': this tendency [*qinxiang*] is not good because we are a family; we are all descendants of Zhenneng."

Zhimin speaks here not only as a lineage leader but also as a local cadre and party member. Using the term *qingxiang*, tendencies, to morally condemn factionalism is obviously reminiscent of the Chinese Communist Party's use of the term to condemn incorrect ways of thinking associated with the influence of bourgeois capitalist and Western thought. Zhimin's reasoning merges two Chinese moral registers: that carried by the lineage and Maoist sacrifice for the common cause. What is at stake, as evidenced by the fact that Zhimin made this statement to me, a foreigner, is on the one hand concern about presenting a dignified image, using the word "honor" and elsewhere, "face," as Chen Ganhua referred to the "united front" presented to the outside world, and on the other hand, the unity and solidarity of the group in the political sense of the term, and its ability to mobilize unitarily for the public good.

Desegmentation was accelerated by the funeral reform, but it had already begun eighty years earlier when the lineage founded Pine Mansion's primary school. The establishment of the school, like that of the mausoleum, achieved through a collectivization of private segment interests. The school was founded in 1914 after members of the Chen lineage council, propelled by returned emigrants and in the wider context of the overthrow of the Qing dynasty, the proclamation of the Republic of China in 1911, and the imperial court's reform of the education system in the years preceding the revolution, decided to merge the lineage's nine existing private schools (*sishu*) into one. The schools had been run by the lineage branches, funded by income from the "school fields" (*xuetian*), which was used for school expenses and teachers' salaries (see chapter 3). The revolutionary context of the 1910s encouraged the lineages to adapt to the requirements of modernization, which in turn required the modernization of lineage organization itself and thus its desegmentation.[9]

The process of lineage desegmentation can be traced back to this merging of the segments' private schools. Lineage desegmentation is both a response to emigration, as it is a means of channeling funding for a unitary cause by invoking the founding ancestor's name, and a result of emigration, as migrants tended to bring funding as well as new ideas home from overseas. In his study of emigrant communities in northeastern Guangdong and southeastern Fujian in the 1930s, Chen Ta (1939, 197) found that in response to the many ills affecting their regions of origin in the 1930s, emigrants in Southeast Asia who had discovered "more comprehensive public security of life and property" sought to import it to China by financing and organizing police forces, hospitals and schools. Pine Mansion Chens claimed to have been the precursors of public schooling in Bao'an District, thanks to the influence of emigrants (*huaqiao*), described as "pioneers of education" (*xianzhe xianxue*), who brought back Western ideas.[10] Drawing students from not only Pine Mansion but also the entire surrounding area, the Chens were the earliest supporters of "the education of all citizens" (*quanmin*).[11] Overseas Chens sent their children back for a Chinese education, and there were also students with Chen fathers and foreign mothers who had "white skin and blond hair, or black skin and curly hair."[12]

In 1923, after a returned emigrant smashed the ancestral tablet, an unfortunate event that threatened to bring down misfortune (see chapter 6), the school was offered to the ancestor and named after him. The money raised by a call to villagers and overseas kin and income from the school fields was used to build a larger school that was inaugurated in 1929 on the birthday of the founding ancestor, the celebration of its anniversary therefore coinciding with the commemoration of his birth. In 1946, a new round of fundraising, this time entirely from overseas, made it possible to build a middle school, also named after the ancestor. Both schools were taken over by the government after 1949 and renamed, neutrally, Bao'an Number Two Middle School and Pine Mansion Primary School after the district and the village, yet they continued to be managed by the lineage village community. At the start of the reform and opening era, the schools resumed their original names. In 1987, a new call for funding was circulated among the diaspora that enabled the construction of a new, larger primary school building.

Because it bears the name of their founding ancestor and was built by their forefathers, ten years later when they heard of the district government's plans to merge it with one in a nearby village, the people of Pine Mansion found the idea of the primary school closing down unbearable. Saving space by merging schools was a way for the district government to save money through economies of scale and meet municipal and provincial requirements and targets in terms of size and facilities. After the Chinese state introduced reforms in the 1980s to expand and strengthen its educational system and then decentralized administrative and financial responsibilities to local government, many schools were closed under a policy of school consolidation in which local education bureaus tied investment in new facilities to the closing of small schools (Kipnis 2006).

The villagers mobilized to defend their school and sent an open letter of protest (*gongkaixin*) to the district government. They framed their argument in ways that the authorities could hear: transporting students to the other village was impractical; the school had been largely financed by overseas Chinese and therefore closing it did not conform to "national policies regarding overseas affairs work"; and although the village committee itself and village inhabitants had also contributed to the school, they had not been consulted. The government replied that a school bus could remedy the first problem but took the other arguments into consideration. It gave the villagers a year to build a school conforming to the new, higher standards; otherwise, the merger would go ahead.

The village leaders appointed a preparatory committee (*choubei weiyuanhui*) that launched a funding campaign. In just a few months, they had collected over 2 million RMB. The village committee sacrificed the 500,000 RMB that it had saved for a new office building, and over two hundred Chens and non-Chens living in the village or nearby, among them schoolteachers and factory managers, contributed approximately 500,000 RMB (see table 2.4). Hong Kongers and overseas Chens in French Guiana, the United States, Suriname, Tahiti, Canada, the United Kingdom, and Holland donated 1.3 million RMB. It was only after the old building had been destroyed, the new school building had been completed, and the merger had been canceled that the municipal government and two state-owned enterprises based in Shenzhen granted the project almost 1 million RMB and 700,000 RMB, respectively, which were used to equip the new multistory building with multimedia teaching rooms, a library, a large dormitory, basketball, volleyball, and football grounds, and even a Ping-Pong room. The teaching rooms were named after the donors, and hanging in the auditorium is a large portrait of one of the more generous contributors, a Hong Konger (see chapter 2).

In Pine Mansion village, the government had struck a sensitive chord by threatening to close down a school that had nominally belonged to the state since the early 1950s but was still considered the property of the lineage. In this way, the district government was able to compensate for its lack of resources by relying on citizens' private investment. The primary school was already formally a public school, even though the village committee had been paying half of the teachers' salaries. Now the school was entirely government funded, and it moved up from its ranking as a local school in 2000 to that of a municipal school in 2003, reaching the highest level as a provincial school in 2005.[13] In 2017, the school has over nine hundred students, only 10 percent of whom are children of Chen Pine Mansion villagers. Most are from migrant families who fulfill the admission criteria— complying with the single-child policy, working in the area, and holding a residence permit, a housing certificate, and social insurance. The school became entirely free in 2015, like all public schools in Shenzhen, and is now run by the district's Bureau of Education without interference from the Chens, although a Chen was appointed headmaster in 1998. He was appointed to another school and replaced by someone from outside the village in 2017.

The school is still named after ancestor Zhenneng and is still an important part of Pine Mansion's community life. When facing the ancestral temple, one can see the school on Beifu Hill with "Zhenneng Xuexiao" painted on the school's facade in large characters (figure 4.3). On each occasion of the annual ancestor worship ritual on Zhenneng's birthday, which I attended in October 2013 and October 2014, the school sends a delegation of students (Chens and non-Chens) down to the temple, and the village community sends part of the meal of pork and rice up to the school. The arrival of the school delegation signals the start of the ritual of sacrifice to the ancestor, which begins when the school parade, led

FIGURE 4.3. The renovated ancestral temple and the primary school on Beifu Hill. Photo by author, 2018.

by a unicorn dancer, has come down the road, passed by the administrative buildings, circled around the pond facing the temple (see figure 3.1), and come to a standstill in lines in front of the entrance gate on which the portrait of ancestor Zhenneng hangs. Once the ritual is accomplished, the schoolchildren leave the ancestral hall line by line and head back up the hill to the school. The parade frames the ritual, and the entire ceremony underscores the extent to which Pine Mansion community members consider themselves fully part of the new urbanized and educated society of Shenzhen.

Public Space and Value Generation

The school parade circles the contours of the public space where the former peasants living in the village, the returned retirees, their higher-status kin from Shenzhen and other cities, and their kin from Hong Kong and abroad gather annually. This space is now being enhanced in the context of the "redevelopment of the old villages" (*jiucun gaizao*). Pine Mansion's redevelopment started with the center of the former village in the neighborhoods surrounding the ancestral temple. The small, single-floor houses with their tiled roofs were torn down in 2011 and 2012 to make room for a "garden residence" (*huayuanshi zhuzhai*) (figure 4.4). This was decided after a majority of each of the participating small companies' shareholders voted in favor of the project and the municipal government approved the plan.[14] The residential towers that have since been built form three clusters, one for each shareholding company involved. Each cluster rises above a first floor housing a commercial concourse, which will be partly topped with a roof garden; their construction was almost complete in 2018. A footpath along the river runs from the wide Guanping Avenue, which adjoins the new neighborhood to the west, to the east of the residential area and the ancestral temple and administrative buildings.

Facing the western wall of the ancestral temple complex and next to the administrative buildings at the intersection of the new residential area and the street up to the school is a plot of land that is not scheduled for redevelopment. The *diaolou*, the only buildings that have escaped demolition, have been moved and placed together here to clear space for the construction of the high-rise buildings (figure 4.5). *Diaolou* were built at the end of the nineteenth and in the early twentieth century by the village's most prosperous members. These tower buildings, finely decorated with colorful wall paintings, displayed their owners' wealth and served as places of storage and safety at a time when the region was caught in political turmoil, interethnic conflict, and banditry. There were five of them in the old compounds, but only four remain, one having broken up during its transportation.

FIGURE 4.4. Old houses to be demolished as part of the first phase of the redevelopment plan, new houses, and one surviving *diaolou*. Photo by author, 2011.

FIGURE 4.5. Clustered *diaolou* and new high-rise buildings. Photo by author, 2018.

The *diaolou* have been clustered in the corner of a public space made up of the tiny square in front of the temple, the basketball courts on the other side of the pond, and the small space next to the administrative buildings. On days of ancestral worship, the entire space is used for a variety of purposes, with tables for collecting donations and for selling firecrackers, billboards listing the donations collected, and a stage for musical performances and dance. The participants sit on plastic stools around a hundred tables to eat the celebratory meal of pork and rice, which is cooked on several large stoves in a small annex behind the administrative building, where several hundred kilos of meat are spread over braided mats on the floor. People walk back and forth between the ancestral temple and the kitchen, greeting one another and exchanging news.

The latest major collective mobilization in the village was for the renovation of the ancestral temple. In the spring of 2014, the lineage foundation decided to announce the renovation plan publicly on the day of ancestral worship, October 13, which that year was a particularly large and lavish celebration because in addition to ancestor Zhenneng's 321st birthday, it was the primary school's centennial. Facing the administrative building, next to the usual board beside the pond listing the birthday donations stood another large board which displayed an open letter from the foundation's vice president calling for mobilization and donations, with a list of the members of the temple's renovation committee.

The committee's office shared the same space as the village renovation program on the fifth floor of the building housing the larger shareholding company, highlighting how these two projects were seen as part of the same move toward the renewal of the former village's built environment, even if the first entailed total reconstruction and the second only a revamp. The temple had not been renovated since it was rebuilt in 1925 and had deteriorated under the Cultural Revolution. The open letter's call for contributions revealed that its renovation was seen as indissociable from the construction of the modern garden residence because it was above all a matter of matching the aspect of the temple to that of the new buildings. The temple must be on a par with the high-standard "world-class" residential apartments, as they were advertised. In a way, then, the temple was to be made homotopic with the new urban neighborhood.

This is the case regarding not only the prestige and "face" (*mianzi*) of the entire community, as the open letter emphasizes, but also the economic standpoint since a newly decorated temple next door adds value to the future apartments. For the prioritized buyers who had lost their old houses, the presence of the ancestral temple nearby not only embellishes the neighborhood but is also the main reason for having an apartment in that precise place. Many have left the village to live elsewhere but wish to own something in the village as a duty of thanks to their ancestors. Of course, although the real estate company—the main investor and profit maker in such a program—did not make the decision to renovate the temple, it did contribute to its funding. More generally, the village lineage community's work to save and upgrade some of the village sites has very probably gained them bargaining power in negotiating the finances for the redevelopment—the compensation for the old houses and government funding for the repositioning of the *diaolou*. Along with the proximity of the golf course, the nearby provincial primary school and a secondary school are all highlighted as attractions in the company's sales material. In other words, the village's landmarks are used to market the apartments and to generate value in the sense of both commercial value and social worth.

The ancestor's grave and the school have been saved to preserve the community from the tendency in Shenzhen to erase traces of the past and replace "uncivilized" villages with modern urban compounds. Yet, the very strategies for their protection, entailing the construction of larger and taller buildings (the mausoleum, the school) and concentration around geomantic spots (the gathering of urns around the ancestral tomb and the *diaolou* around the public space) were not at odds with the state-driven policy of making way for urban development: on the contrary, they formally espoused the visible properties and logics of urbanization, with vertically dense properties and logics of spatial clearing for the maximal exploitation of space. In the same process, the figure of the founding ancestor, who embodies the public good, has been both a cause in itself and a means of spurring mobilization, his centrality enhanced and the community's territoriality accentuated by focalization on the most important sites.

These strategies were not only homotopic to urban policies but also homochronic. When the mobilizations for the grave site and the school took place, the game amounted to overtaking the authorities, acting even faster than they had planned and presenting them with a fait accompli by erecting monumental buildings that corresponded to the expectations and standards of Shenzhen modernity. The mobilizations for their protection did not involve open opposition to the urban authorities so much as the exploitation of gray areas left open to interpretation, and it was therefore crucial to act fast—at Shenzhen speed. To this extent, it is possible to argue that the very act of preserving heterotopic and heterochronic sites eventually brings homotopia and homochronia into play.

Urbanization and its associated policies of rationalization constitute technologies of subjection (Ong 2006) that aim to shape "backward" peasants into modern, civilized citizens. However, although the people of Pine Mansion cannot escape the effects of power and ideological discourse, urbanization, far from being entirely imposed from above, is inscribed in a logic of development that is also theirs. What the members of the lineage village community celebrate and wish for in their annual ritual gatherings is the continual pursuit of village development. By preserving these sites, the Pine Mansioners continue a line of transmission tied to a specific origin and place in a way that they hope will continue to be beneficial. Their rationale is the maximization of geomantic-territorial value and thus includes both social worth and economic value. The mausoleum, the school, and the temple are sites that generate value in the broadest sense. They are public goods, or parts of the public good, in that they enable the community to care for their dead, educate their children, and gather with visiting relatives. In this way, they ensure the social reproduction of the local community over time and maintain a territorial reference point for the global community of overseas descendants.

REVERSED FENG SHUI AND SOCIODICIES OF (IM)MOBILITY

The overseas Chens were symbolically rewarded for their crucial financial contributions to the safeguarding of the ancestor's grave in the form of donor plaques detailing the amounts they had donated. However, this overseas financial participation was perhaps not considered desirable by everybody within the lineage and may have led to internal debate, as shown in chapter 4 with the fact that Chen Ganhua had imposed it as a precondition for launching the mausoleum project. Dependence on financial support from overseas Chens had already decreased by the end of the 1990s, and it is quite possible that without this force majeure event the Pine Mansion Chens would have dispensed with it altogether. Beyond their reduced dependence (chapter 2), community members' insistence that they no longer solicited money from overseas highlights their subjective apprehension about their financial relationship with their overseas relatives and its social and moral implications.

This chapter considers the ambivalent and nuanced morally laden discourse about migration and financial relations with overseas relatives from the perspective of those who have remained in the village. Although transnational mobility is very much a commonsense part of their everyday lives as members of a community with long-standing overseas connections, they clearly see migration overseas as a phenomenon of the past. Even though there have been times when many migrated and everybody aspired to do so, today this desire has largely disappeared (chapter 1). Recent change in the village has resulted in the revalorization of locality in the sense of both its increased economic value and the resulting heightened value of being a native villager, along with the moral valorization of those who have stayed (chapter 3). In this chapter, I consider understandings of migration and the relationship with overseas kin as they are framed by this changing context. They surface in debates about the geomancy of the founding ancestor's grave site, narratives about the desirability and possibility of emigration and return, and statements about remittances and financial donations from overseas.

Sociodicies, or secular theodicies (theodicy, from the Greek *theos*, god, and *dike*, justice), are explanatory schemes that offer theoretical and ethical responses to and justifications of "meaningless" afflictions, injustices, and social inequalities (Weber 1970; Herzfeld 1992; Bourdieu 1994). In using the term *sociodicies*, my purpose is not to retrace a coherent conception of order that presupposes a relatively stable system of meaning. Rather, I am interested in how narratives of migration and representations of the diasporic relationship constitute attempts to make sense of a complex and changing historical and sociological reality. I build on Luc Boltanski's sociology of critique, which focuses on the ways in which social actors propose justifications for themselves or others in disputed situations, and the ethical principles they invoke when making comparisons between people (Boltanski and Chiapello 2005; Boltanski and Thévenot 2006). I examine how the people of Pine Mansion voice *sociodicies of (im)mobility*: more or less explicit moral justifications of success or lack of success that surface when they compare the trajectories of people who have emigrated or remained in the village. I argue that the region's economic development has not only led to a perceived equalization of Pine Mansioners' socioeconomic position with that of those living overseas and in Hong Kong but has also made the order of things commensurable and thus evaluable in moral terms.

Feng shui discourse explains inequalities; it is itself a sociodicy. The first section provides an analysis of the interpretations of the founding ancestor's tomb's feng shui, which was seen as responsible for the inequalities between those who remained in the village and those who left it, although now this is said to have changed. In the next two sections, I move to a more general analysis of justifications of emigration and nonmigration, return and nonreturn. I look at the types of moral justification that are used to account for both the inequalities generated by emigration in the past in the form of the disparities in fortune between those living in the village during the Mao era and those who managed to leave for Hong Kong and abroad, and those of the present, when migration is no longer one of the main means of social mobility and villagers who have remained in Pine Mansion have seen their livelihoods improve. I consider how evaluations of departure and return as morally assessable individual choices are tempered by a macrostructural theory explaining the difficulty of returning. In the course of my analysis, I highlight how categorical nationalist imperatives to remain Chinese play only one part in these reflections.[1] The last two sections focus on the relationship between the local community and its diaspora through the question of remittances—financial support for family left behind—and donations to the good works of the village and lineage community. Donations are in general far less conflictive than remittances, and their much higher valuation reveals the Pine Mansion villagers' contrasting perceptions of the diaspora according to social class.

Change as a Test in Feng Shui Discourse

Not only has migration become less of an option than it was in the past, but also overseas money is now needed far less than it was in the two decades following China's reopening. The meaning that Pine Mansioners conferred on the change that led to their reduced financial dependence on the diaspora can be grasped through their discourses on the feng shui of the founding ancestor's grave.

Feng shui, or geomancy, is a technique that consists of harmonizing and channeling flows of energy or the "cosmic current," *qi*, by aligning and situating buildings and graves in a particular way. Its practitioners aim to increase their wealth, happiness, longevity, and fertility (Feuchtwang 1974; Bruun 2003). The term *feng shui* also refers to the results of applying this technique. In the present case, it refers to the influence exerted by the ancestor on his descendants' destinies through the combination of his bodily remains and the features of the environment in which he is buried.

Although the reform-era authorities have shown greater tolerance of feng shui and popular religion more generally, it is still officially seen as superstitious. In this context, it is not surprising that my questions about the feng shui of the ancestral tomb were often met with a display of distance and ambiguity.[2] Some strongly adhered to the idea that it is pure nonsense and a backward superstition while others justified its existence as common sense or tradition. Many people rejected it as a belief of peasants hoping for a good harvest, thus associating it with Pine Mansion's past. Several insisted that it was a belief to which Hong Kong and overseas Chinese cling, and Weixin stated that rich Hong Kongers are the most superstitious of all. This heteroglossia (Besnier 1996) is due to the fact that feng shui lends itself to a diversity of interpretations. My aim here is not so much to reach a true interpretation of how the feng shui of the founding ancestor's tomb works or to ascertain whether Pine Mansioners really believe in it; my interest lies in analyzing the discourse in all its complexity insofar as it reveals something about the diasporic relationship.

One prevailing interpretation appeared in several corroborating testimonies—namely, that for a long time, the length of which was undefined in people's accounts, the feng shui of the founding ancestor's grave was said to "reach out to far away, not close by, and to women, not men" (*guan yuan buguan jin, guan nü buguan nan*). It was said to benefit those who left the village most of all and thus acted positively on migrants who left the village to seek a livelihood abroad and women who "married out" of the village. Until inter-Chen marriage was permitted in the late 1950s (see chapter 1), Chen women who married out generally left the village to live elsewhere with their non-Chen husband. From the 1920s onward, village women increasingly married migrants. Moreover, the daughters of some emigrants seemed particularly favored. Those of some of the Tahiti Chens were immensely wealthy and made large donations to the village (chapter 2). In Tahiti, the prevailing oral tradition was that the feng shui of the ancestor's tomb primarily benefited women. In Pine Mansion, the interpretation was wider in that it was said to have benefited emigrants in general and particularly women. I suspect that this interpretation arose not only because of the perceived gap in fortunes but also because the ancestral cult was delocalized to Hong Kong and overseas during the Mao period. It should, then, be logical that those who perform the rites benefit most from the ancestor's blessings.

Generally, the geomantic properties of a burial site have positive effects on different categories of people to greater or lesser degrees, depending on how the grave is situated and oriented (Freedman 1970, 178). The main cause of the particular effect of feng shui in Pine Mansion seems to have been the inversion of the founding ancestor and his wife's burial sites: the ancestor is said to have been buried in a feminine, *yin*, site, whereas his wife was buried in a masculine, *yang*, site. Zhenneng's wife was buried not beside her husband but at a fair distance from him on a mound facing Zhenneng's grave. Zhenneng's burial place is said to have the shape of a winnowing fan (*boji*), a tool used to separate grain from chaff, while his wife was buried in a monticule in the shape of a pile of grain (*gudui*). Whereas both sites exhibited favorable agricultural features, their forms may also be read as uterine and phallic, respectively.

Freedman (1966, 131) was struck by the recurrence of female graves in feng shui matters, with women buried separately from their husbands in places with particular geomantic virtues in contravention of the Confucian order that subordinates the female to the male. Such practices may be a remnant of Taoism, which emphasizes the blurring of categories and hierarchy as the complementary interaction of dualities (Thompson 1988).[3] Raising women to the rank of founding ancestors by not burying them next to their husbands, to the point where the geomancy of their grave is of equal importance to that of the male ancestor, appears to be a distinctively Hakka practice (Lagerwey 1996, 9; Johnson 1988, 142). Likewise, the prominent positioning of Zhenneng's wife's name on the ancestral spirit tablet (*shenzhupai*) at the temple contradicts what is commonly reported in the literature, which mentions only the presence of male ancestors' names on the tablets. If the wife is listed, her name is secondary to that of her husband (Watson 1985, 41).[4] Although Zhenneng's wife is generally only named by her surname, Zeng, she occupies the same amount of space on the tablet as her husband. Now that she has been exhumed (see chapter 4), her remains have been placed in a large jar next to Zhenneng's tomb bearing the inscriptions "Great ancestor" (*tai po zu*) and "Grandmother of the Chen." She is worshipped at Chunfen along with Zhenneng's three sons and their wives and his servant, who traveled with him from Wuhua.[5] Her exhumation and the geomantic collectivization that resulted from gathering all the deceased at the mausoleum are said to be among the reasons why the feng shui of the ancestor's tomb in Pine Mansion has changed.

Feng shui is a way of talking about and explaining differences in fortune between individuals, families, and lineage segments (Naquin and Rawski 1987, 179). In this sense, it is a discourse of causal imputation based on a "principle of equality" (R. Watson 1988, 215) in that it is both a technical tool for achieving equality and a discursive tool for explaining inequalities. In this respect, geomantic discourse can be considered a sociodicy (or geodicy). In this particular case, feng shui explains the differences in economic fortune among the founding ancestor's descendants—who are supposed to be equal—according to whether they lived in the village or overseas. Although not all the emigrants made their fortune, many did, and the failures were largely overshadowed by the publicity given to the most spectacular successes.

The fact that feng shui supposedly benefited those who had left the village was invoked both as part of the imputation of superstitious beliefs to the emigrants (*huaqiao*) and to justify protecting the founding ancestor's tomb (chapter 4). Chen Shengyu, the former village head, explained that the launch of the funeral reform in 1997 made the Hong Kongers and overseas Chinese very anxious about the geomantic consequences of cremating the ancestor's remains. He related this to the long-standing interpretation of the effect of feng shui "because the [ancestor's] remains act far away and toward the outside [*guanyuande, guan waimiande*]."

The imputation of superstitious beliefs to overseas Chinese makes them a convenient alibi for the (illegal) protection and maintenance of the founding ancestor's tomb and for masking beliefs that have been officially condemned as superstitious. While at the time of this mobilization the relatives abroad and in Hong Kong may have been most involved in safeguarding the tomb and its feng shui, local people did allude to the beneficial feng shui of the grave site in conversation without reference to them. Even those who initially declared their skepticism later conceded that feng shui might exist. For instance, Chen Junjie (the one who had returned from Guiana without taking French citizenship; see chapter 1) said at first that he did not believe in it, but added that anyway, when the Hakkas had arrived in the area in the eighteenth century, all the powerful feng shui spots had already been picked by preestablished Cantonese (*bendiren*).[6] On another occasion, he stated that Zhenneng's grave had been "covered" (*gaile*) by the mausoleum in such a way as to preserve the site's geomantic layout. Some, referring to their own houses, for instance, stressed that it is just a matter of common sense, of being more comfortable when well seated. Others pointed to the village's present prosperity as proof that the founding ancestor, a skilled geomancer, had made a judicious choice in picking Pine Mansion as a place to settle.

Some went further, suggesting that the grave's feng shui has changed for the better. For instance, I was told that "before the liberation [*jiefang* in 1949], there was feng shui, and it had not changed much, but since the reopening [*gaige kaifang* in 1979], it has changed a lot." Even Chen Weixin, the retired university professor who had earlier rejected feng shui as superstitious nonsense that mostly Hong Kongers believe in, told me that "buildings are better than hills," referring to the factory that now faces the founding ancestor's grave. Several other people suggested that the feng shui might have, if not "turned" to the advantage of Pine Mansioners, at least become more equal, now benefiting them as well. Andrea Louie (2004, 155) also overheard the expression "the feng shui has turned" (*feng shui lunliu zhuan*) with reference to changes in the perception of emigration among Pearl delta inhabitants and the equalization of the status of Hong Kong visitors and local Chinese.

The profound ambivalence of and contradictions between these statements is due to the fact that the improvement in local people's living conditions may be deductively interpreted in two ways: although it may be seen as proof that feng shui is nonsense, it may also prove that interpreting it as beneficial for those who left the village is no longer valid. Both views are ways of expressing and possibly explaining the changes in the lives of those who inhabit the village. If feng shui is used to explain the difference between the fortunes of those who stayed and those who left, both the suggestion that people no longer believe in it and the statement that it has changed emphasize the disappearance of this difference with the equalization of their living conditions.

Central to Boltanski's theory is the notion of "test" (*épreuve*), which "concerns the selection process governing the differential distribution of persons between positions of unequal value, and the more or less just character of this distribution" (Boltanski and Chiapello 2005, 32). In this case, it can be considered that people conceptualize the development of the region, and more generally of China as a whole, as a "legitimate test"—that is, one that has moral implications (Boltanski and Chiapello 2005, 31).[7] It is seen as such because it makes situations on the mainland and overseas commensurable and thus evaluable in moral terms. It signals not only the advent of a more just order of things in that people can now stay and enjoy a good life at home but also that this order is more just because the trajectories of those who stay and those who emigrate are morally evaluable, as their positions and living conditions are now comparable, in contrast to pre-1949 and the collectivist period when the gap was so large that it rendered comparison absurd.

The inversion or rebalancing of the living conditions of those who went abroad and those who stayed finds its expression in these declarations about the feng shui of the founding ancestor's tomb. There is something more to it, though: suggesting that its influence has changed to benefit the locals is also a way of stressing the resolution of a moral dilemma raised by the manner in which it operated in the past, when leaving the village often led to greater rewards in terms of economic success.

The Moral Reward for Staying

The social and economic change in the village following the reform and opening policy and its inclusion in what is now the Shenzhen Special Economic Zone have reduced the difference between the living conditions of the locals and those abroad to the point that it has become possible for them to compare the benefits of remaining versus leaving and of returning versus staying abroad. These retrospective comparisons reveal the moral dimension of such evaluations. Today, villagers in their fifties and older who have remained in the village tend to stress, in a posteriori rationalization, that their choice to stay at a time when everybody wanted to leave was judicious. Ronald Skeldon (1994), a scholar of Chinese migration, writes that one of the major problems researchers face in trying to explain why people move is post facto rationalization.[8] Here, I consider such rationalization not so much a hindrance as an object worthy of analysis per se.

These narratives tend to present both departure and nondeparture from the village as the result of individuals' decisions and therefore morally assessable. This does not mean that such decisions were not affected by obligations to kin or the availability of the resources needed to migrate. Although these are acknowledged, in retrospective narratives the emphasis is placed on the choice a person made at some point during his or her lifetime. Wang Cuichun described the situation at the end of the 1970s: "The village had been totally emptied of its inhabitants, everybody had fled [*toudu*], but I did not leave. I wanted to look after my children. . . . [In my team,] only I and three other women who worked in the fields were left. Many people asked, 'Are they stupid [*meng*]? Everybody has left for Hong Kong and these women remain there, working.' . . . People thought I was stupid."

Not leaving, and especially not taking the opportunity to cross the Hong Kong border while it was somewhat relaxed at the beginning of the reforms, was seen as stupid in the sense that it represented inability to intelligently seize an opportunity. This shows how the act of emigrating is perceived as the result of a personal decision based on rational calculation.

The contemporary comments of those who had not left systematically rest on a posteriori rationalization that presents the choice to stay as a felicitous decision that later led to an improved livelihood. Cuichun's husband left for Hong Kong in 1979. In the years that followed her husband's departure, she was alone at home with her children to care for and the land to cultivate. She told me that she had not wanted to go and immediately started to explain how "here at home, life has become much better; there are pensions for old people, several thousand RMB a year." She is a shareholder and also receives a pension of 2,400 RMB per month. All three of her children, the daughter and two sons, left for Hong Kong in the 1990s. "If I had left for Hong Kong, I would not have had so much," she remarked.

On the day of the 2013 spring equinox festival, I met Xiuhuan, a woman in her late forties, who had the sunbaked skin of someone who has long worked in the fields. Most of her family live abroad, her paternal cousins in the United States and her maternal cousins in Hong Kong and the United States. She also has other remote kin overseas, although she does not know exactly where. Her paternal aunt and uncle left toward the end of the 1970s when she was in her teens. When I asked her why she had not emigrated herself, she answered, "They did not apply for me to go [meiyou shenqing wo guoqu; referring to the letters of invitation generally issued by relatives abroad and required for a visa application]. Why am I not over there? Here it is very good; over there it is hard [xinku] and very cold!" During the course of my fieldwork in the village I call Pine Mansion, I heard this type of retrospective rejoicing about having stayed behind many times.

Put differently, this improvement in living conditions in Pine Mansion allows people to retrospectively present the act of staying as a decision that was as rational and courageous as the act of leaving. What sustains these narratives is a meritory logic of past virtue rewarded in the present. They see their native villager status, which allows them to reap the fruits of the village's economic development as a reward; when they established the shareholding companies, those who had never left the village paid a much lower price per share than those who had left temporarily and then returned (chapter 3). Although the people of Pine Mansion experienced the difficulties and poverty of the Mao period, they now perceive their present prosperity as their reward for choosing to stay. As landlords, they now reap the fruits of the land that they had such a hard time cultivating and living on until the 1980s.

These narratives further suggest that ultimately staying in the village and its surroundings is preferable to living overseas. One clear illustration can be found in the biographical portrayal of Chen Deqi, the vice president of the lineage foundation, in a book released for the village primary school's centennial. Deqi's biography follows that of his grandfather and father under the heading "Three Generations of a Renowned *Huaqiao* Family." The description of Deqi's grandfather begins with his decision to leave the village and the turbulence that followed the overthrow of the Qing dynasty in 1911. The text insists on the courage and strength of will that he had to muster to leave for Southeast Asia, where he worked first on rubber plantations and then as a dockworker. He later emigrated to Panama, where he opened first a shop then a sugar factory. He sent regular remittances back to his wife, whose hardship raising her children alone is mentioned, and made substantial donations to the school.

Deqi's father left for Hong Kong and from there, applied for a visa to join his father in Panama in 1955 without success. His wife joined him in 1962, leaving her two sons in the village, but later Deqi's older brother left for Hong Kong while Deqi remained in Pine Mansion. The text on Deqi begins, "It is quite interesting that his grandfather and father were *huaqiao* but that he himself has always stayed in China [*zai neidi*]." The reason for this was that his parents "did not want to cut off their 'roots' [quotation marks in the original] in the native place [*jiaxiang*]." The text goes on, "At the time life was extremely difficult." This alludes to the fact that Deqi's studies at the Institute for Foreign Languages in Guangzhou were interrupted by the Cultural Revolution in 1966 and he had to go back to the village to cultivate the land. "But looking back, his parents' conservatism [*baoshou*] was not without reason. . . . In thirty years of reform and opening, Shenzhen's economy developed very quickly: all the families in Pine Mansion have become 'property owners' [*yezhu*; quotation marks in the original] and Deqi's life has become more prosperous and comfortable than his brother's life in Hong Kong." Deqi's biography thus states that he ended up better off than his brother and that the historical changes have proved his parents right. The individualization of emigration, enhanced by competitive relations between brothers (Freedman 1970, 4; Potter 1974, 229), accounts for their frequent dispersion across destinations post-1949 (see chapter 1) and allows for ex post facto comparisons of this kind.

In the past, the decision to migrate was unambiguously motivated by the desire to earn a better living and was validated when a migrant such as Deqi's grandfather succeeded and sent back remittances and donations. Today, however, emigration is less likely to be justified in the same way. There was considerable uncertainty in people's statements about their overseas relatives' economic success (chapter 1). Chen Weixin, whose son left for Guiana and whose grandson studies in France, joked about his lineage cousin Junjie, who had returned from Guiana: "Look at him; . . . now he's back, but he doesn't look that well-off [*hai bu shi zhege yangzi*]." He stressed that the living conditions of people in China, compared to those of the same generation in Hong Kong, "are not that much worse and tend to be improving." Yet, he made it clear in another conversation that his son in Guiana would not be able to make as much money in China.

The challenge to abstain from methodological nationalism (Glick Schiller and Salazar 2012, 9) is even greater when the focus is on cross-border mobility because the tendency to see such mobility through the eyes of the nation-state is more tempting as national and state discourse on migration pervades people's understandings of it. This is visible, for instance, in the fact that people refer to migrants using the official term *huaqiao*, to which I return later in this chapter. One way out of this is the methodological suspension or "bracketing" (Dzenovska 2012, 205) of such categories when analyzing people's practices and discourses to identify the extent to which the nation-state's discourse interferes with their representations of migration.

Dace Dzenovska's (2013, 213) observation about the Latvians is also true of the people of Pine Mansion: "The stories of concrete individuals both departing (and staying) exhibit a great degree of variety and cannot be easily subsumed under stable ethical configurations." However, she contrasts this with the discourse upheld by the Latvian state, which consistently tends to portray emigration as an aberration. In China, the ambivalence about the act of leaving is all the greater because there have been several reversals over time. Throughout Chinese history, leaving the homeland has been alternately discredited as an act of disloyalty to the emperor or the nation and hailed as an act of potential patriotism (Wang 2000). The same sequence of rejection and acceptance can also be found in the twentieth century. After a period of severing ties and the political stigmatization of emigrants and people with overseas connections (Fitzgerald 1972), since the 1970s emigrants have once again been valorized for the resources they might bring to the nation (Nyíri 2002, 2010).

Conservatism, rather than patriotism, is invoked in Deqi's portrait of his parents, possibly because their decision was based on attachment to the native place on the local scale rather than to the nation. Furthermore, Deqi's parents were themselves emigrants, and emigration is never presented as an act of disloyalty to one's country, although non-emigration may be presented as patriotic. Weixin, for instance, reacted quite vehemently when I asked if he had ever considered migrating himself. He answered, "No, because I am Chinese." While staying can thus be hailed as patriotic, departure from China, even under Mao when it was described as *toudu* (crossing the border illegally), is never presented as unpatriotic, and not simply because it is justified by another ethical principle: that of caring for one's family and filial duty to one's parents. There was also a suspension of the official interpretation of migration as immoral at a time when the policies of the state itself were illegitimate. The portrait of Deqi's parents included the caveat that the use of the term *toudu* to describe his mother crossing the border in 1962 is "not totally accurate." She had benefited from one of the periodic policies of relaxation adopted by the local government of Guangdong Province. More generally, the chaos of the Maoist period diminishes the illegitimacy of what was officially illegal migration. Weixin himself later admitted that he had contemplated migrating during the Cultural Revolution because it was "a time of great confusion." His own son had left for Guyana following the Tiananmen Square repression of June 4, 1989 (see chapter 1).

Return and Nonreturn

The fact that state evaluations of mobility and grassroots notions of what is desirable only partly coincide is further demonstrated by Xianwei's trajectory, which was presented to me as morally exemplary. Xianwei legally left Pine Mansion for Suriname, where his parents had settled, in 1979 and returned to the village at the end of the 1990s with his wife and three sons. Xianwei himself and his friend Zhimin, an influential village leader, presented his return as the result of a radical resolution.

First, they both stressed the uncompromising and irreversible character of his decision. He came "straight back to the continent [*dalu*]," Xianwei said. Returning to "the continent"—the People's Republic of China—is implicitly set against living in Hong Kong, which would have facilitated transnational mobility and kept the possibility of returning to Suriname open. On his return, Xianwei opened a small restaurant. He made it clear that he had "given up the idea of making money, that kind of thing" because, he justified by generalizing, "for Chinese people, as long as you have enough to eat you are content." "Being Chinese" is defined here as living a modest and frugal life at home in China, in contrast to striving to accumulate wealth abroad or in Hong Kong. Although loyalty and return accord with the official patriotic discourse on migration, his lack of interest in accumulating wealth is at odds with the Chinese state's glorification of successful entrepreneurial individuals who invest large sums in China upon their return. It can also be seen as an implicit critique of the group of hypermobile entrepreneurs who commute regularly between Pine Mansion, Hong Kong, and elsewhere abroad, embodying this official ideal (see chapter 1).

This narrative does not highlight the "un-Chineseness" of emigration so much as potentially losing one's Chineseness as a consequence of emigration. Xianwei came back at the end of the 1990s mainly for the sake of his family. He explained that his three children were still only seven, eight, and ten years old when they all returned, and he wanted them to go to school in the village. He voiced the expression "pure Chinese" (*chuncui zhongguo ren*) several times and explained that he had feared becoming "assimilated" (*bei tonghua le*). Yet as shown above, far from being seen as ineluctable and self-evident, the choice to return to China is considered a personal decision that implies a moral choice, just as departure is. The reason Xianwei's trajectory was singled out and presented as a model by the village leader—and indeed his is the only case I found of return in middle age—is then precisely the awareness and common recognition that things generally go otherwise. Xianwei's decision is valorized all the more because it went against a phenomenon of estrangement that is perceived as almost inescapable, unavoidable by individual effort, the tendency to become habituated to another way of life and at least partly assimilated into a foreign culture.

This narrative of high morality, strength of will, and righteous decision contains its own reverse: a discourse that exonerates those who have not returned. Parallel to the moral valorization of those who did not leave and the few who returned is a generalized discourse that invokes a repertoire of justifications for the impossibility of returning. The fact that most emigrants do not return is explained by the theory that the longer they stay abroad, the more they become estranged from China to the point of inability to return. This is considered inevitable. According to the same village leader, Zhimin, "When one stays abroad for a long time, naturally [*zi ran er ran*] one no longer understands/knows [*bu liaojie*] the Chinese way of life. Uncle Wei [Xianwei] did not stay away for a long time and so his understanding of China is quite deep." He contrasted this situation with that of the Tahiti emigrants and their descendants: "Tahiti is different. The duration [of their stay] was very long, and in the '50s, '60s, and '70s their view of China [the continent] was bad, and life in China was bad, so they no longer identify with it [*renting*]."

Besides the political context, what is implied here is a progressive dishabituation from living in China that makes returning to live in the village impossible. This way of justifying not returning reveals an underlying sociological theory that is very close to Pierre Bourdieu's (1977) theory of dispositions and habitus. People in Pine Mansion generally emphasize their habituation to (*xiguan*) living in the village, where life is so good, to explain why they would not want to live in downtown Shenzhen or Hong Kong, for instance, and that people who have emigrated do not return because their habituation to foreign life and ensuing preference for it creates a disinclination to return. Pine Mansioners behave like Bourdieusian sociologists when they use the word *xiguan*, which is close to *habitus* in Bourdieu's theory of dispositions; the idea that over time, the unconscious and nonverbal incorporation of the social world generates dispositions and propensities to behave in certain ways and to adopt certain tastes and worldviews.[9]

This theory and the explanatory regime it constitutes rest on the idea of causalities and forces beyond individual agency: people do not return due to reasons over which they have no control. Nonreturn, then, is attributable to this process, which is seen not as suppressing the will to return but as working against that will. As Zhimin, referring to both *huaqiao* and people who had left the village to live in downtown Shenzhen, said several times, "It's not that they don't want to come back; it's that they're more accustomed to being there."

My main focus here has been on moral evaluations of immobility in the narrow sense of not having taken part in international migration and more widely of preferring to remain in the place of origin. This does not mean that those who have stayed are socially or even physically immobile, since not only have many former inhabitants of the village moved to downtown Shenzhen and nearby cities, but those who have stayed have been socially mobile despite physically remaining in the same locality. The village's inhabitants voice two distinct sociodicies to account for the destinies of those who have stayed and those who have left. What prevails for the former is a theory that places the emphasis on agency and a posteriori rationalizes staying as a decision based on personal choice, the soundness of which is demonstrated by their improved lives; feng shui discourse constitutes a less agentive, more collective and impersonal but complementary variant of this sociodicy. This stands in contrast to a second, structural theory that accounts for the difficulty of returning on the part of those who have left, thereby justifying their estrangement from the village. These retrospective accounts thus reverse the narratives that tend to present stasis as the result of deprivation of agency, a set of constraints that bind people to a locality, and departure abroad as the expression of agency and courageous self-liberation from constraints and attachments.

The Usual Suspects: *Huaqiao* as a Separate Class

In a conversation near the home for the elderly, a woman told me that there is now little difference between Pine Mansion villagers and their overseas relatives. She explained that she no longer dresses as the peasant she once was, so emigrants no longer look different from the villagers when they visit. However, even though surface differences may have faded, the memory of past inequalities vividly remains in present narratives about past choices and the discourse that sees overseas relatives as a separate class.

When I asked another of my female interlocutors, Chen Xiuhuan, whether her cousins sent her money despite not having offered to help her migrate to join them, she replied. "No, why? We divided the family assets [*fenle jia*]—why would they send money back? We rely on ourselves [*kao ziji*]." Xiuhuan's laconic answer reveals several aspects of the relationship between those who stayed and those who left. First, those who left had benefited from the financial support of close agnatic and uterine kin who had already emigrated (see chapter 1). Emigrating requires the means to do so or the sponsorship of close relatives. Furthermore, remittances (*huikuan*) are only sent back to close family: father and mother, and brothers and sisters where there has been no division of the family's property (*fenjia*)—that is, when the family still forms an economic unit (Cohen 1976). This is what Chen Xiuhan was referring to when she stated that since the family property had been divided, there was no reason for her cousins to send her money. The most wide-spread type of remittance was that sent by a husband to his wife. For instance, Wang Cuichun received remittances from her husband in Hong Kong, and while her father-in-law was still alive, the household also received biannual remittances from his brother in Panama and his elder sister in Canada.

Second, the emigration of some family members distanced them socially and economically from those who remained to the point of creating a clearly percep-tible division between "them" (the emigrants, *huaqiao*) and "us," doubling the difference between "rich" and "poor." When I asked Chen Guizhen why some families had many relatives abroad and some did not, she replied, "When your family is poor, no one takes any notice of you [*kanzhong ni*]. For example, my hus-band's uncle [*ashu*, father's younger brother], . . . he is a *huaqiao*, he despises you, your family is poor, he doesn't invite you to go—how are you going to get there?"

This illustrates the difference between rich and poor families in terms of their relations with emigrant relatives. Families that were rich prior to 1949 had many overseas relatives, the most successful of whom helped those who had stayed in the village to join them abroad or sponsored their studies. Chen Fuchang, who migrated to Tahiti in the 1930s, did the latter for his nephew Weixin until the late 1950s, and Weixin was thus able to become a university professor. Poor fam-ilies generally lacked such beneficial overseas connections: fewer migrated because they were poor, and they were poor because they had fewer overseas rela-tives and thus less financial help. Among them, those who managed to flee to Hong Kong during Mao's rule left without capital or overseas connections, and those who succeeded financially took many years to do so. Chen Guizhen's state-ment also reveals the distancing in the relationship between mainlanders and overseas relatives as a result of their socioeconomic differences up to the 1990s. This distance, which increased with the lack of communication under Mao's rule, in turn contributed to reduced family solidarity and a relationship dominated by suspicion.

Pine Mansioners often complained of emigrants' stinginess about helping close kin. This is not unique to Pine Mansion: James Watson (1975, 137) and more recently Louie (2004, 150–52) and Ellen Oxfeld (2010, 169) also mention recriminations of and gossip about overseas Chinese and their remittances. The relationship is very complex, as it is underpinned by not only ethical considerations but also the importance of maintaining face; as much as they blamed emigrants for their manifest lack of desire to help family left in the village, the villagers also claimed that they did not want to beg. On the one hand, overseas Chinese were perceived as individualistic and selfish, having lost the sense of their ethical obligation to their loved ones, while on the other hand, the inhabitants of the emigrant villages did not want to be indebted to their overseas relatives. Chen Guizhen described this relationship: "Yes, we have an emigrant [*Huaqiao*] in the family: it's pointless, he has never had anything to do with us [*gen women conglai meiyou guanxi*]. One day he came back, called us to come and sit with him for a while and told us how much poorer than us he was. He was afraid we would ask him for money. . . . Because he was afraid that we'd ask him for money, he said he was very miserable. After he came home [to Pine Mansion], I went to see him only once; then I never went to see him again."

Another woman told a similar story: "My husband has two *huaqiao* little brothers. Ten years ago, he said with his own mouth that each of them had 30 million RMB. Last year, my husband was in hospital. His brother's son went to see him and told him that now his father is poor and can't even feed himself."

Chen Guizhen framed the relationship as one between separate classes: "It is these rich people who are most afraid of us, the poor. . . . The rich have this way of thinking [*sixiang*]." This type of judgment, although widespread, is not systematic. The two cases above are judgments on collateral members of their spouse's family. A person such as Mrs. Wang, whose husband sent her remittances for years, has a more sympathetic view of emigrants' behavior and pointed out the misunderstanding at the heart of the villagers' relationship with them. When I told her "some people say that the emigrants are afraid that when they return they will be asked for money," she replied, "No, who wants [their] money? These emigrants [*Huaqiao*] who have worked hard [*xinxinkuku de*] making money outside [China]. When they come back, they don't want to give it to people here, so their relatives [*qinqi*] may think they're stingy, but there are many people who don't want their money." The monetary relationship is largely based on mutual suspicion, with overseas relatives afraid of being asked for money and villagers afraid of being suspected of wanting to ask for it. When Mrs. Wang points out that many do not want to ask the emigrants for anything, it is clear that they want to save face.[10]

It is also plausible, although the women mentioned above appeared not to have considered this, that their migrant relatives had experienced setbacks that prevented them from being generous to their relatives in the village. The women did not appear to be aware of the possibility that living overseas may not always be synonymous with wealth. But along with the opposition of the "rich" (emigrants) to the "poor" (villagers) that emerges in their discourse, this lack of acknowledgment reveals precisely this dual categorization of overseas Chinese and villagers, which generates a dichotomy within the lineage community.

I have so far followed the villagers in their naming of the overseas Chinese (*huaqiao*) as a group distinct from their own without commenting on this remarkable propensity to adopt an official category forged by the Chinese imperial authorities at the end of the nineteenth century to refer to emigrant members of almost every family in the village. Although such categorization is not surprising in leaders' speeches about the history of the lineage as a whole or speeches with a sociological tone attributing feng shui beliefs to emigrants, it is striking that individuals use the same term for close family members. There is no alternative word for migrants who are also close relatives. *Qiaokun* and *qiaoqin*, overseas relatives, are the generic and formal terms in written form.

Considering the very flexible possibilities for combination in the Chinese language, one might imagine that terms could be coined that qualify both the specific kinship relationship and the fact that this family member has emigrated: for instance, "*qiaoshu*" (a contraction of *huaqiao* and uncle). However, this potential has not been realized—at least not in Pine Mansion, where speakers first use the *huaqiao* category ("we have a *huaqiao* in the family") and then the reference term that indicates the kinship relationship (for instance, *shu*, uncle) or vice versa. The maintenance of this kinship terminology on the one hand and official categorization on the other hand reveals a gap and a potential contradiction between being a relative and the geographical and social distance produced by emigration.

Moral Expectations and Differing Perceptions of Migrants

Although they are individually linked to families in the village, the *huaqiao* are collectively categorized as a separate class. This is heightened by the fact that those who return and are generous are so especially with regard to the lineage works as a whole. The terms *huikuan* (remittances, money sent back by close relatives) and *juankuan* (donations of money for lineage projects) are very similar, sharing the morpheme *kuan*. *Kuan* refers to an element constituting part of a whole and to the logic of the gift—to an amount given or an amount collected— and as an adjective, it describes the act of hospitality, as in *kuandai*, to offer a guest food and entertainment. However, whereas *huikuan*, which is also a verb meaning "to remit," emphasizes the act of sending money back to relatives who have remained in the village with the emphasis on the recipient (*hui* meaning "to converge, to gather, things collected"), *juankuan* underlines the deliberate act of contributing money to village and lineage works (*juan* meaning "to contribute, to make a donation, to relinquish, to subscribe").[11] While *huikuan* is also used in the village to refer to the action of receiving remittances ("I go to the bank to collect the remittance," *wo qu yinhang huikuan*), *juankuan* is used exclusively to refer to the action of contributing to the public good, whether this is done by overseas Chinese or local people. This difference points out that, although remitting money to the family and sending contributions to village lineage institutions evoke a common notion of giving, they are seen and valued as two distinctly different types of action. Sending money back to the family is expected, the fulfilment of an obligation, ideally without the family asking for it; sending money to the collective is highly esteemed as devotion to a cause and all the more valuable as less obligation is involved. This is similar to Oxfeld's (2010, 58) observation in a Hakka village in the Meizhou region: "While no one would describe an overseas relative who did not contribute to a [collective] project as lacking moral conscience (*liangxin*), someone who could afford it and did not help their own family would be [morally condemned]."

The call written by the foundation's vice president on the ancestor's 2014 birthday celebration for contributions to the renovation of the temple (see chapter 4) explicitly underlined the link between the act of giving as a virtuous and meritorious act and the reputation that the donor would gain from it: when the "eminent benefactors of society [*shehui xianda shanren*]" perform "infinite virtuous achievements [*gongde wuliang*]," their "virtuous names [*fangming*] will forever be engraved." The renovation was described as "meritorious action" (*shanshi*). *Shan*, compassion, is one of the foundation stones of Buddhism. Other terms in the same moral lexical field include *rexin*, warmheartedness, and *youxin*, heartfelt.[12] The vice head of the workstation, Chen Lijun, explained that by making a donation on the ancestor's birthday, the workstation was "expressing its regard" (*daibiao yipian xinyi*). When I asked Chen Jinyou, a member of the lineage council, if everyone agreed that Xingchang should be president of the foundation, he replied, "Yes, because money is needed for the public good [*gongyi shiye*]." Another council member added, "One condition is that [the president] must have money; another is that he is devoted [*rexin*]. If he wasn't devoted, the money would be no use."

Whereas the notion of devotion to the public good is also part of the social-ist morality, the specific act of giving is part of a long Buddhist tradition, which continues to influence lineage organizations despite their historical emergence as a Neo-Confucian reaction against Buddhism (Faure 2007). Chinese Bud-dhism's emphasis on the creation and accumulation of merit and the notion that common effort multiplies the value of small offerings (Gernet 1995, 216) are founding principles of philanthropic funding. Donations take on an additional dimension in the context of the remoteness of diasporic members of the village lineage and community and are celebrated as deeds that express strong moral commitment to the village of origin. They resolve the dilemma brought about by the individual quest for wealth at the cost of a distance perceived as betrayal of family and patriotic attachments, since they testify to the continuation of moral commitment despite the departure. They also give the overseas relatives a presence and lasting prestige in the form of the inscription of their names on the village's most important infrastructure in appreciation of the well-being that they have provided for the villagers, and in the final part of the genealogy.

We are dealing here with what Nancy Munn (2007, 11) describes in her study of Gawa society's participation in the inter-island-wide ceremonial exchange sys-tem, or Kula circuit, as an "extension of the intersubjective space-time domain" consisting of "the capacity for developing space-time relations that go beyond the self." Becoming a Guyaw, a partner in the Kula, requires others' recognition of this status (Munn 2007, 51). Both the Kula shells and the fame of the com-munity as a whole are produced via a process of exchanging elements internal to Gawa with people of other islands. The circuit is based on a set of dyadic re-lationships between partners. The memory of transactions—the conversion of an objective gift into subjective recollection—helps to maintain connectivity.

In Pine Mansion, the circuit is not based on the principle of reciprocal dona-tion; it is a Sino- or village-centered circuit in which the migrants constitute a population flow to the periphery, with the money they return establishing a fi-nancial flow to the center. The inscription of their names on the donation plaques placed in the most important symbolic locations in the village and on infrastruc-ture that supports the villagers' material well-being both enhances and ensures the visibility of their existence, as they are seen to be participating in the per-petuation of the lineage village community through its social reproduction. There is therefore a disparity between the limited financial solidarity that links migrants and their relatives who remain in the village and the important con-tributions sent by the most prosperous migrants for projects for the public good at the level of the village lineage complex. This reflects the duality between the shared remote ancestor and individuals' close ancestors, between public and pri-vate kinship (see chapter 8). Thus, the ambivalence in the diasporic relationship partly stems from the fact that the relationship itself is valued differently according to the standpoint adopted, being much more positive at the village and lineage levels than at the level of the family unit.

However, it is important not to overstate the opposition between each party's suspicions about the moral intentions of the other in intrafamily financial relationships on the one hand and the trust in financial relations between the local and overseas communities on the other hand. There are also doubts about the use of funds from overseas. It was rumored in Tahiti that the sums sent by the Tahiti Chens had been recorded on the list of donations to the mausoleum as less than they actually were. When I went to the mausoleum with Alain, one of the visiting Tahiti Chens (chapter 7), we stopped to read this list (figures 5.1 and 5.2). Alain recognized the names of several donors. The amounts they had given were listed as about 20,000 RMB *Daxidi bi* (the Chinese translation of Pacific francs) per person. Alain stated that as far as he remembered, this did not seem consistent with the amounts that had been sent. In the village, I also gathered hearsay about some overseas Chens' complaints about the use of their donations, which they did not see as proportionate to the amounts they had sent.

These statements were not related to specific facts or to donations made for a particular cause, and I hardly dared to explore them further, especially since time had passed since they had been voiced. Although there may have been

FIGURE 5.1.   Alain reading the donations' plaque at the mausoleum. Photo by author, October 2014.

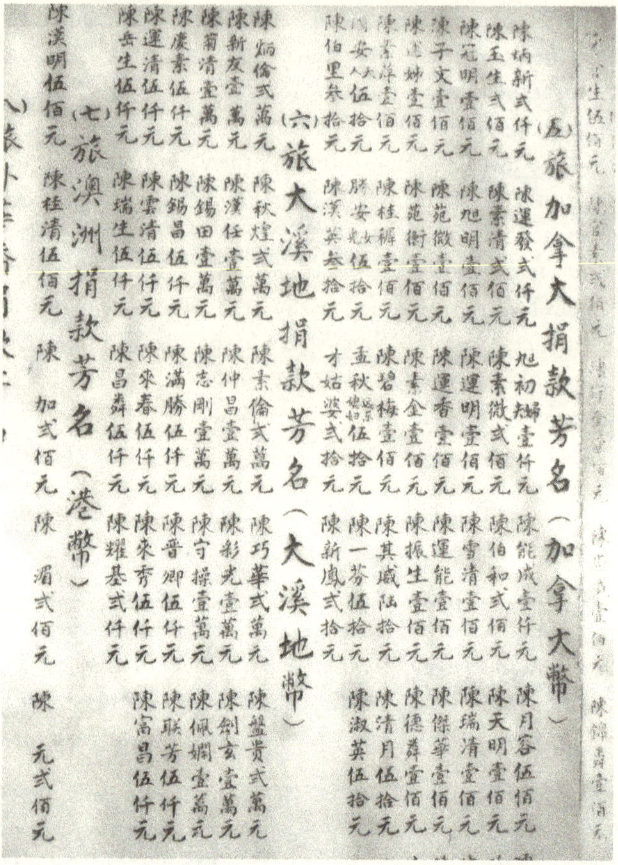
(五)旅加拿大捐款芳名(加拿大幣)
陳炳新式仟元
陳玉生式佰元
陳冠明壹佰元
陳子文壹佰元
陳述娣壹佰元
陳素萍壹佰元
陳安人大伍拾元
陳伯里叁拾元
陳運發式仟元
陳素清式佰元
陳旭明壹佰元
陳苑微壹佰元
陳苑衛壹佰元
陳桂稱壹佰元
勝安伍拾元
陳漢英叁拾元
旭初夫婦壹仟元
陳素微式佰元
陳運明壹佰元
陳運香壹佰元
陳素金壹佰元
陳碧梅壹佰元
孟秋伍拾元
才姑婆式拾元
陳能成壹仟元
陳伯和式佰元
陳雪清壹佰元
陳運能壹佰元
陳振生壹佰元
陳其威陆拾元
陳一芬伍拾元
陳新鳳式拾元
陳月容伍佰元
陳天明壹佰元
陳瑞清壹佰元
陳傑華壹佰元
陳德彝壹佰元
陳清月伍拾元
陳淑英伍拾元
(六)旅大溪地捐款芳名(大溪地幣)
陳焔倫式萬元
陳新友壹萬元
陳菊清壹萬元
陳慶素伍仟元
陳運清伍仟元
陳岳生伍仟元
陳秋煌式萬元
陳漢任壹萬元
陳錫田壹萬元
陳錫昌伍仟元
陳雲清伍仟元
陳瑞生伍仟元
陳素倫式萬元
陳仲昌壹萬元
陳志剛壹萬元
陳滿勝伍仟元
陳來春伍仟元
陳昌彝伍仟元
陳巧華式萬元
陳彩光壹萬元
陳守操壹萬元
陳晉卿伍仟元
陳來秀伍仟元
陳耀基式仟元
陳盤貴式萬元
陳劍玄壹萬元
陳佩嫻壹萬元
陳联芳伍仟元
陳富昌伍仟元
(七)旅澳洲捐款芳名(港幣)
陳漢明伍佰元
陳桂清伍佰元
陳加式佰元
陳湄式佰元
陳元式佰元

FIGURE 5.2. Tahiti Chinese donations. Photo by author, 2014.

embezzlement or misappropriation, it is likely that at the least errors have been made in record keeping and currency conversion, and the discontent expressed by some overseas Chens could explain the villagers' reluctance to launch new appeals for funds, probably for fear of rejection. Hence, the emphasis on the reduced need for overseas money and the strictly free and voluntary nature of such donations. It could also be that if there has been any misuse of funds, it occurred not at the point of arrival but at the level of the intermediaries who channel the money collected to the village. Contributions from the diaspora in the 1980s and 1990s were gathered in each overseas community by a "head" (*tou*) and sent to Hong Kong, and brought from there to Chen Tailai, the village's Qiaolian.

Unlike remittances, therefore, which were sent to a specific person via bank transfer or entrusted to a friend or relative in cash, the donations were channeled via a series of intermediaries who were not necessarily known to the distant donors. The most effective way to ensure that money sent is used properly was, and remains, to take it to the village in person. This was why the Belgian Chens returned to the village to oversee the construction of the building of the home for the elderly; it is also what Chen Xingchang is doing by giving material gifts bearing his name, such as an air conditioner for the home for the elderly, in addition to his big financial donations. Sending contributions from afar is therefore risky, but in many cases, it is the only possibility for second- and third-generation emigrants with no close kin or friends in the village who might oversee the use of their money.

Finally, the duality of sending remittances to close family and contributions to the collective requires qualification in the case of intermediate forms of organization—the lineage branches. Of these, the most illustrious is the Guobao branch, which is particularly rich in people who have achieved superior diplomas and high social position as a result of both inheriting the immense wealth accumulated by Guobao at the end of the nineteenth century and the continued solidarity of its members, who meet once a month and manage their own branch funds. Raising funds from overseas was one of Ganhua's conditions when he agreed to carry out the mausoleum project. As a descendant of Guobao, he had close connections (*guanxi*) with influential people abroad who were all part of the same Guobao branch: his brother in Hong Kong, Fuchang in Tahiti, and others in the United States, Canada, and Belgium. If Ganhua was able to impose the principle of overseas participation, it was therefore not only because he considered it necessary, given the large amount required for the construction of the mausoleum, but also because he was able to act as an intermediary, a broker, which in itself is a source of social prestige, with these key people who themselves acted as connectors.

Thus, the villagers' perception of a dichotomy between the two social categories—overseas Chinese and themselves as former peasant villagers who had been unable to migrate—coexists alongside a class-based difference that is partly inscribed in space. On the one hand, most of the prominent members of the lineage live in the center of Shenzhen and other surrounding cities such as Guangzhou, although some have retired to the village and these are closely related through intrabranch kinship to well-to-do overseas Chinese who wish to participate in philanthropic activities. On the other hand, there are former farmers who have lived in the village all their lives and are despised by those living in the city center for their lack of social and cultural capital, some downtown Shenzhen Chens commenting negatively on the lack of *suzhi*, "human quality," evident in their rough manners and language. The difference is mainly one of education, considering the amount of wealth that some former villagers have achieved as shareholders. Between these two poles, there is a continuum along which are village leaders who have lived in Pine Mansion for most of their lives and people who followed a career outside the village or overseas but have returned to live there.

Most former peasant villagers also have relatives overseas with whom their relationship is generally distant and problematic due to differences in wealth and education, which do not help to make trusting relationships. Relationships weaken in poor families when relatives have left without capital, either because they have not succeeded in making their fortune and no longer return to the village or because they have succeeded, widening the economic gap between themselves and their close relatives in the village and fueling mutual suspicion about one another's financial intentions. Relations also decline when communication is difficult due to villagers' lack of cultural skills in contrast to those who, having graduated and reached average or even high social status, have been able to maintain a continuous written correspondence with emigrants of their generation on an equal footing. In short, social differences lead to different local perceptions and varying degrees of suspicion or confidence that exclude their overseas relatives to a greater or lesser extent.

There is a striking oscillation between the evaluations in the narratives I collected in Pine Mansion. Whereas the acts of leaving, remaining, and returning are seen as the result of individual choice and are morally evaluable and glorified as such, the choice to stay away is generally impossible to evaluate, explained by macro-historical forces that escape social actors' agency. The condemnation of emigration implied by the moral valorization of stasis and the ethical principles of caring for kin and donating to the community are tempered by Pine Mansioners' explanatory theories on migrants' estrangement and distancing from the village of origin due to historical and sociological forces. Paying attention to these situationally variable sociodicies fosters an understanding of the dynamics of change in the collective representations of migration while taking account of the interplay between local appraisals of the desirability of migration and state discourses that have historically fluctuated in their evaluation of the figure of the migrant.

In addition to individual narratives that present the choice to stay in the village as contemporarily rewarded, there is a collective discourse that sets those who have remained and those who have left apart and reflects the change that has occurred. This discourse emerges through comments on the current irrelevance of overseas donations and the feng shui of the ancestral tomb. The almost unanimous discourse on the part of both those who have stayed and those who have returned amounts to the claim that the new local prosperity now allows people to live a good life without leaving the village. Pine Mansion's economic development is thus conceptualized as a test, in Boltanski's sense, and the restoration of the right order of things. This moral accounting for prosperity also underlies the principle according to which money ought to flow back from the diaspora to the village as center.

The diasporic relationship is permeated by moral considerations and underpinned by social relationships of kinship and class that vary its tonality. Yet overall, comparisons of individual destinies are made possible through a mechanism that dichotomizes the overseas relatives, "the *huaqiao*," and the locals into separate categories. This is also the case regarding other noneconomic aspects of the diasporic relationship, as I discuss in the following chapters.

RITUAL RENEWAL AND
SPATIOTEMPORAL FUSION

The ambivalence of lineage and family units' relations with the diaspora is due to tension between the desire to break away from the relationship of dependence and the prestige that the local community derives from its large number of relatives overseas. I was told many times, including by a leader from a nearby village, that although they are fewer in number today than in the 1980s and 1990s, many relatives living in the diaspora come back to China to worship the founding ancestor, Zhenneng. This chapter examines the diasporic relationship through the lens of ritual, which generates a spatiotemporal fusion between persons who are both geographically and temporally disconnected. However, although the collective rituals are an occasion for gathering with overseas relatives, they also highlight what separates them.

Ancestor worship is based on the idea that all deceased relatives must receive ritual care to prevent them returning to haunt and harm the living. The living maintain them in their ancestral status by ensuring that they receive everything they need. Food and drink are therefore provided, and all kinds of paper objects representing homes, clothing, mobile phones, passports, and so forth are transmitted by combustion. Large amounts of ritual paper money are also burned, multiplying its value in the afterlife to enable the dead to lead a comfortable post-mortem life (Gates 1987, 268–69). In return for the well-being thus supplied, the ancestors will provide benefits to their descendants in the form of prosperity, academic success, numerous descendants, longevity, and so on. In line with the surplus ethics charted in chapter 3, money is thus recycled to ancestors, not so much to make it harmless (Parry and Bloch 1989) as to make it

FIGURE 6.1.   Burning ritual paper and lighting firecrackers on the weekend before Qingming. Photo by author, 2013.

productive (Chu 2010, 205) by feeding the ancestors as a source of value creation for the living (figure 6.1).

Until the funeral reform of 1997, the Pine Mansion Chens practiced worship of their closest relatives on their tombs (see chapter 4). This "domestic" worship, which Maurice Freedman (1970, 167–68) differentiated from collective "lineage" worship, is now performed at the mausoleum at Qingming, the third day of the third lunar month, which falls on or around April 5. Although Qingming is a national holiday, some people also gather during the preceding weekend either to pay their respects to their maternal ancestors and then visit their paternal ancestors at Qingming, or because their Hong Kong kin can more conveniently spend the weekend in Pine Mansion. Families usually take their urns out of the mausoleum and line them up on the edge of the low wall at the foot of the building. When the weather is wet, some leave the urns inside the mausoleum and place their offerings on the floor beneath the shelves on which they stand. The villagers perform the same actions at the mausoleum as they did at the graves, except that instead of sweeping the graves, they now dust off the urns, although they still call it "tomb sweeping" (*saomu*), and refer to the rites of sacrificing to the ancestors with the expression "worshipping the mountain" (*baishan* in Mandarin, *kasan* in Hakka).[1]

There seem to be as many ways of doing this as there are individuals, but the overwhelming majority start by worshipping ancestor Zhenneng. Some pray in front of the tomb, others behind the large incense burner tripod (*ding*) facing the tomb. Some say prayers aloud, others keep them to themselves. I overheard an elderly woman asking to win at mahjong. Another elderly woman knelt in front of the tomb. A mother and her daughters who lived in Hong Kong explained that they were only burning incense without asking for a blessing because they were Christian. However, most people asked Zhenneng to bless them (*baoyou*) and addressed him as "Great Lord" (*taigong*).

This chapter focuses on the collective lineage worship rituals, which are performed twice a year: at the temple on the founding ancestor's birthday on the twentieth day of the ninth lunar month, around mid-October, and at his grave at the spring equinox, Chunfen, the fourth solar period in the Chinese calendar, or March 20 in the Gregorian calendar, about two weeks before Qingming.[2] The collective ancestor's birthday ceremony was first invented in the 1920s in response to the danger posed to the ancestral spirit by the destructive action of a returned emigrant. During the Mao era, the cult was relocated mainly to Hong Kong. The delocalization of ancestor worship in this way preserved the ritual and accounts for its swift resumption in Pine Mansion in the early 1980s. However, ancestor worship as it is practiced today has required some amendments to make it officially acceptable.

Although ancestor worship activities are seen as less potentially subversive than cults that worship deities, the Maoist campaign targeted them as much as any other. Some scholars interpret their revival in the reform era, and the general revitalization of popular religion, as a reaffirmation of historical memories (Jing 1996) that bears witness to the resilience of local communities (Yang 1994, 2000, 2004; Feuchtwang 2000). Although this is largely true, the notion of resumption or revival suggests a discontinuity that does not apply to emigrant communities such as Pine Mansion. What happened was rather the return or relocalization of worship. The people of Pine Mansion did not have to recover their memories of actions and words that had not been performed for at least two decades, as the cult's relocation to Hong Kong ensured its continuity and therefore the transmission of ritual knowledge.

And yet, this local renewal is also a re-creation, deeply influenced by the years of Maoist anti-religious campaigns and answering the need to seek legitimacy in the eyes of the state and its local representatives in the post-Mao context of controlled tolerance (Siu 1989; Thireau and Hua 2001; Chau 2011; Flower 2004). The simplified and modernized version of the ritual is the result not of loss but of a deliberate desire for local adjustment, a compromise between Hong Kongers and local people. Local lineage members tend to favor simplicity and claim that their way of performing the rituals is modern, distinguishing themselves in this way from their Hong Kong and overseas relatives whom they situate in a symbolic past.

This raises a paradox: the local villagers see the *huaqiao* as both estranged and at the same time conservative, having kept up the old traditions. The chapter conclusion's explains this paradox by pointing out the coexistence of two cultural intimacies (Herzfeld 2016): between the local villagers and their diaspora on the one hand, and between the locals and the Chinese state on the other.

The Invention and Revitalization of the Lineage Cult

The lineage is a community of worship whose members collectively perform rituals for their common ancestor(s). Such practices have built up over time and have fluctuated in form and frequency. The genealogy reports that tomb sweeping at Chunfen began in 1842 after Zhenneng was buried at Huang Song Wo (Genealogy 2000, 87), where the mausoleum now stands over his tomb.

The celebration held on Zhenneng's birthday is said to have come about after an unfortunate event in the early 1920s. According to the genealogy, the lineage, whose first generations had laid the foundations for future prosperity but themselves experienced difficult times, only performed the Chunfen rite on the tomb and another simple rite at the ancestor's temple, and had not yet held a big celebration. "Regarding the establishment of the ancestor's birthday, here is an interesting anecdote," write the authors. "In 1922, a lineage brother, Linjiao, who had returned from Southeast Asia and had a mental illness, complained that the ancestor had not allowed him to make a fortune, and smashed the ancestral tablet on the floor." This caused a "great commotion across the community. . . . But because he was sick, there was nothing we could do" (Genealogy 2000, 78). This last may imply either that he could not be punished or that his destructive action could not be avoided. The lineage council members then discussed renaming the school after Zhenneng, as proposed by the school headmaster and another influential lineage member and enthusiastically agreed by the members of the assembly. The first celebration was held in 1923 on the twentieth day of the ninth lunar month. The schoolchildren presented a show, overseas relatives sent donations, the villagers sacrificed pigs, chickens, and ducks, and a large banquet was held. This festival thus became "the traditional celebration, the great ceremony of the entire lineage, and all this was due to Linjiao's mental illness and the broken tablet" (Genealogy 2000, 79). Since then, the commemoration of Zhenneng's birthday (*Zhenneng gong dansheng de jinian ri*) has coincided with the school anniversary (*xiaoqing*), with the pupils taking part each year.

The invention of this tradition was therefore the result of the collective will to remedy the potentially negative effects of the returned and probably depressed emigrant's destructive act, which was not only highly disrespectful but also contained the dangerous potential to turn the ancestor into an evil spirit, as the tablet is believed to contain his spirit. A deceased person who does not receive at least the minimum of ritual care is at risk of becoming a *gui*, a wandering soul, a harmful spirit hungry for revenge (Ahern 1973; Harrell 1974; Baptandier 2001). Naming the school after Zhenneng can be considered a sacrificial gift of the school to the ancestor, and seems to have been intended to satisfy him by magnifying his symbolic place in village life, as further shown by the particularly lively celebration during which the sacrificial rite takes place.

Religious practices were banned when the Communist regime came to power in the late 1950s. According to the genealogy (2000, 87), the rituals were stopped following attacks on and persecution of the lineage leaders who conducted them. During the Cultural Revolution from 1966 onward, many ancestral temples were closed or converted to schools, as in Pine Mansion, warehouses, as in another Chen village (Chan, Madsen, and Unger 2009, 87). Many ancestral tablets were also destroyed; in Pine Mansion, the tablet of ancestor Zhenneng, which had been newly manufactured and placed in the ancestral temple after its 1922 misadventure, was salvaged after an event mentioned in the genealogy (2000, 86) with a brief reference to the Cultural Revolution's Red Guards, when "some unfilial descendants oblivious to their own ancestors" damaged the tomb and the temple. Some even went so far as to take the tablet, break it in two and put it on the pile of firewood. Fortunately, the school headmaster, Chen Tianxi, was able to retrieve it and hid it. The stele on the ancestral grave was allegedly thrown into a pigsty.

All this explains why the villagers associate the ban on worship with the Cultural Revolution, which started in 1966 and to which they refer by the expression "destruction of the four olds" (*po sijiu*)—old ideas, old culture, old habits, and old customs: "during *po sijiu* worship was forbidden (*buzhun bai*)." The chronology is frequently muddled. Actually, it appears that ancestral worship was no longer practiced after the mid-1950s, with the anti-right campaign and Great Leap Forward, when increasing numbers of villagers fled to Hong Kong, many settling in the village of Yuenlong in the northwest of the New Territories, which the Hong Kong authorities developed as a new town in the 1970s. In 1961, these emigrants established the Zhenneng Foundation (*Zhenneng jijinhui*) to finance the annual birthday ceremony for which a new tablet was made. Although it is likely that the cult was delocalized to Hong Kong as a result of this massive inflow of Pine Mansioners, the people of Pine Mansion present it as an intended purpose of their flight to Hong Kong. As one villager put it, "At the time of the Cultural Revolution it was required to get rid of these superstitious things [*saochu zhexie mixin dongxi*] so the villagers took them to Yuenlong."

From 1961 to 1980, "everyone worshipped in Hong Kong." There was no worship at the grave, unless clandestinely. The man whose words I have just quoted also told me that they worshipped the ancestors "inwardly" (*bai xinli*), in their minds and hearts. William Parish and Martin Whyte (1978, 267) note the "decline of the role of lineages as a focal point for collective ritual life" in the early 1970s, and in their sample of sixty-odd villages, they found that Hakka villages had a higher propensity for simple or "modernized" life cycle rites—modest wedding celebrations and no domestic ancestral tablets (Parish and Whyte 1978, 271).[3] Although the rites related to the life cycle were maintained, albeit in a simpler and more austere form, they involved only close relatives and not the lineage community; for example, weddings no longer involved a visit to the temple to present the bride and groom to the ancestor. Although I have very limited data on this subject, the life cycle ceremonies do not appear to have been re-embedded in the lineage rites. It is clear that the lineage has not fully recovered its previous function of asserting a patriarchal and hierarchical order, and as I will show, the relative erasure of the hierarchy is one of the major features of the rites as they have returned to the forefront.

However, as Richard Madsen (1984, 60–61) notes, while the Communists eliminated the formal trappings of the lineage structure and the villagers abandoned their religious traditions apparently without regret, the Confucian moral principles supporting the lineage remained deeply rooted (see also Parish and Whyte 1978, 254). Although people retained them in their minds and hearts (*xinli*), the political and financial conditions for performing the rites were not met. The failure to hold the rites, and especially the collective rites, was the result not only of their prohibition as superstitious and the expression of a feudal order but also the removal of the economic basis that allowed the holding of collective property in the name of the ancestor: quite simply, money and, above all, food were lacking. "When food was scarce, how could we feed the ancestors?" a lineage council member asked (see Jing 1996, 82 for a similar testimony). By the late 1950s, collective rituals had completely ceased in Pine Mansion and were held instead in Hong Kong, where there was the infrastructure to finance them (the foundation) and greater freedom.

This leads to a qualification of the idea of the resumption of worship after its interruption. The cult's practices were not interrupted but relocated overseas, Hong Kong as well as elsewhere in the diaspora. I became aware of how the people of Pine Mansion understand this continuity when in one of my first interviews with Ganhua, he showed me the photographs in the historical part of the genealogy that testify to the fact that Zhenneng's birthday was celebrated overseas. The section devoted to activities celebrating the ancestor's birthday begins with photographs of the rites on the tricentenary of Zhenneng's birth in

1994, then those in 1999, and goes back in time to pictures of what was probably the last village celebration under Mao in 1957, and then of the rites held in 1956, 1961, and 1971 in Hong Kong. These are followed by a reproduction of the ritual eulogy drafted in Hong Kong in 1972 (see below), photographs of the Pine Mansion Chen banquet in Tahiti in 1956, of a meeting in Suriname in 1983, and finally of the banquet, firecrackers, and dance performances in Pine Mansion in 1999, the year before the genealogy was published. These materials thus chronicle the narrative of the rite's historical continuity. Considering the massive emigration to Hong Kong in the 1960s, it is likely that this continuation by relocation also occurred in other villages in the region.[4]

In Pine Mansion, the biannual rites performed for the ancestor Zhenneng, the one at the ancestral temple and the other at his tomb, resumed in 1981. Photographs in the genealogy show the Hong Kong president of the foundation, Chen Guanxin (who has since died and been succeeded by Xingchang, another Hong Konger), leading the rite. It is highly likely, as some studies have shown (Woon 1990) and as the villagers themselves suggested, that worship was reestablished in China on the initiative of the Hong Kongers. Parish and Whyte (1978, 295–96) found in the late 1970s that lineage villages with strong overseas connections were the first to reintroduce the rites. As early as 1981, Zhenneng's tomb was recemented, a new tombstone was affixed, and the ancestor's tablet was reinstalled in the ancestral temple. The repairs and restorations were largely financed as part of the construction and reconstruction of diverse village infrastructure by Hong Kong and overseas Chen (chapter 2). Ancestral worship is no longer held in Yuenlong; the people there travel to Pine Mansion to join the villagers.

The Relocalization and Reinvention of Ancestral Worship

As noted in chapter 4, one effect of building the mausoleum has been the additional opportunity for communal gathering at this new site, although Chunfen is considered less important than the Zhenneng's birthday, as shown by the smaller number of participants. The traditional Hakka dish of pork and salted vegetables (*xiancai zhurou*) (Chun 2002, 210) is consumed after the collective ritual. It is served with rice, the staple food in southern China, which, like bones, it is also an ancestral substance (Thompson 1988, 93–94). Pork, the meat that is always consumed at Chinese lineage rituals, is a female substance which, in conjunction with the male rice, generates fertility: pig with rice, blood with bones (Thompson 1998, 93–94). The rice for this meal was once grown on the ancestor's land (*zudi*), and as Rubie Watson (1988, 222) notes, in a way it is the ancestor himself who purchases his own offerings, as the pigs are paid for from the ancestral estate. The rice and pork are still financed by income from the land held in the ancestor's name (see chapter 4).

Several signs indicate that these gatherings and the rituals themselves are at once simpler and more egalitarian than they were before 1949. On the weekends between Chunfen and Qingming, people gather to worship *gongtou* (see chapter 1), the three sons of Zhenneng's eldest son, whom they refer to as Zhenneng's grandsons. These ancestors are subject to particular ritual attention, probably due to their important role in the history of the lineage but perhaps also to the idea of the symbolic preeminence of the oldest branch.[5] The oldest branch is not given special consideration otherwise, and during the collective rite for Zhenneng, there was nothing to indicate that participants belonged to one branch or another; in other words, there was no principle of segmental representation.

In the past, pork was distributed only to male members of the lineage, as evidenced by the people of Pine Mansion and earlier ethnographic accounts. Members aged over sixty were entitled to a double share, and those in official positions were given a quadruple share (Woon 1984, 32–33). The distribution of pork reflected the value hierarchy among the lineage members, and "a right to a share of the ancestor's pig . . . amounts to a public acknowledgement of lineage membership" (R. Watson 1988, 222). Although the meal's consumption by all symbolizes the lineage members' common kinship, it also generates kinship and commonality as it may be offered to nonrelatives such as carriers of minority surnames in the community or a visiting anthropologist. This commensality is more pronounced today than in the past, with equal portions for all members of the lineage, old and young, male and female alike (figure 6.2). Meal vouchers are handed to each household head who makes a monetary contribution, whether small or large. Although the food for the communal meal at Chunfen and the ancestor's birthday is partly covered by individual contributions, it is largely financed by the foundation, which draws its income from ancestral land (chapter 3). In contrast, apart from the wealthy Guobao branch, the lineage branches whose members gather between Chunfen and Qingming do not have a foundation, and the meals they share are entirely paid for by individual contributions.

Although meal shares are no longer distributed based on a segmental and senior hierarchy but in a strictly egalitarian way between families, seniority is still acknowledged in the additional symbolic handouts at New Year and on the ancestor's birthday, when the oldest men and women are given money in red envelopes and a piece of the suckling pig (*ruzhu*) that is offered to the ancestor.[6] As a symbol of longevity, the pig is wrapped in thin red paper and placed in a cardboard box labeled "one meter" (*yi mi*) next to offerings of chicken and chicken giblets, more pork, fruit, and tea on the table facing the tomb.

FIGURE 6.2.   The communal meal at Chunfen. Photo by author, March 2013.

Some degree of social hierarchy is also marked in the order of arrival at the mausoleum, differentiating those who contribute more through their labor from those who contribute money. When I entered through the gate decorated with Fuchang's handwritten parallel verses at around eight in the morning, I saw only three cars in the parking lot at the entrance to the site. There were motorbikes and bicycles belonging to the forty or so elderly men and women already sitting on plastic stools around wooden coffee tables and busily cutting up pork, garlic, mushrooms, and vegetables. Others were hard at work in the open kitchen, where the stew was cooking in huge pots on large wood-burning stoves. These volunteers receive a small amount of money for their efforts: 100 yuan for the cooks and 50 yuan for those who prepare the food. Liao Yuzhen, a native villager seated in the shade of a tree keeping a list of volunteers and contributions, told me that "those who come for the preparations arrive early; the cadres and officials [*ganbu dang-guande*] will arrive a little later." She and her women friends also explained that the latter give the largest contributions to the meal. The primary principle is that those who have money contribute. A woman explained, "There are also young men [for instance someone] who has left the village to work [*chuqu dagong*]; we won't be asking him for money and [we] will contribute a little in his place. But someone who's richer, he'll contribute 5,000 [RMB]. That's the way it works."

Xingchang, the wealthy Hong Konger and president of the Zhenneng Foundation, arrived at 8:45 a.m. He greeted the volunteers and then headed toward

Chen Jinyou, a lineage council member who was directing operations. Chen Jinyou is a calm, shy man, a civil servant who worked for the state rail company before retiring in the village to enjoy a quiet and simple life. Like many elderly native villagers, he rides a bicycle. He was holding a roll of paper on which were noted the formulas for the ritual prayer (*jiwen*). He handed it to Xingchang, who refused to take it. Jinyou insisted, stressing that these were the authentic formulas. Xingchang continued to refuse and pronounced the formulas aloud, as if to show that he knew them by heart. I later understood that the text proposed by Jinyou was the one on which the lineage council had agreed (I return to this in the next section). It was much longer than the version that Xingchang, who appeared to want to get straight to the point, recited.

Chen Xingchang led the collective ritual just before noon. Only a small group of persons go up the steps to the mausoleum to perform the ritual in front of the tomb while the rest remain seated at the foot of the hill. The sixteen participants were Hong Kong and overseas entrepreneurs and senior executives of the shareholding companies and the workstation and were mainly men, with only two elderly women. Chen Junjie and Chen Lijun, both in their forties, distributed bundles of incense sticks. The mobile entrepreneur Chen Junjie was representing his father, a prominent member of the lineage (chapter 2) who was ill and unable to attend. Chen Lijun, a graduate from Shenzhen University, was the recently appointed vice director of the workstation. Chen Junjie asked everyone to quickly arrange themselves in three rows and then Chen Xingchang declaimed the formulas he had announced earlier in the morning. The others repeated each one loudly. I noticed the somewhat awkward attitude of some of the participants, their shy body posture and embarrassed smiles. This repetition of the formulas does not occur on the ancestor's birthday, when the verses are read only once (see next section).

The ritual formulas ended with "Prosperous population, good health, long, prosperous life, high status and great wealth for eternity!" I did not understand the first lines. A few months later, on the ancestor's birthday, Xingchang repeated them and explained, "When we worship the ancestor, there where our Lord Zhenneng is, this is the place with the best feng shui. On the top of the hill [*shantou*], that's where he is buried. [When] we, the descendants, worship him, the feng shui is made manifest [*xian*] by saying it." The prayer begins with an evocation of the mountainous site where the ancestor is buried, and of a powerful spirit at the convergence of the five cardinal points. It invokes the site's geomantic power, which is then channeled in the direction of the ancestors' descendants by the formulas' performativity, which makes the feng shui "manifest," as Xingchang put it.

The official version, which Xingchang did not follow, is quite different and much longer. It consists of twenty-eight verses, each with four characters, and was read aloud by Chen Deqi, the vice president of the foundation, at the birthday rituals that I attended in 2013 and 2014. It is called "Zhenneng *song*," which can be translated as "eulogy to Zhenneng." *Song* are pieces "that praise the outward appearance of flourishing virtuous power, in order to announce its accomplishments and merits to the spirits."[7] These formulas successively spell out Zhenneng's virtue, his descent from the mythical King Shun, his will and ambition, his ability and culture, his migration and choice of an auspicious place to settle, the prosperity that followed and the increase in the number of his descendants, the ceremonial repetition that prohibits forgetting, the importance of remembering his virtue and of cultivating filial piety, the sacrifice he made, his efficacious presence, and his coming to taste the sacrifice. The last verses, in larger characters, evoke the mountains and the water, which were hostile at first until Zhenneng's power domesticated them. They refer to feng shui and are most likely a concession to the Hong Konger Xingchang, whose attention to this issue was clear in the formulas he pronounced in front of the tomb during the Chunfen rite. The closing formula is the standard ending to any eulogistic address (*shangxiang*): "We ask you to partake in this sacrifice" (Yang 1961, 40; Ebrey 1991, 177).

Rituals are totalities formed of speech and action (Tambiah 1985a).[8] On the one hand, the eulogy expresses a cosmological order that includes humans' interaction with the deities. Here, the ancestor is positioned in a genealogy that originated in the mythical times of China's foundation and is praised as the model of virtue and initiator of the lineage. Virtue is attributed to the civilizing hero. On the other hand, the pragmatics of ritual action bring about the order that is being invoked. The ancestor's founding gesture is fused with the geomantic energy that he has domesticated and extends into the present. The magical power of the ancestor, *ling*, is identified here with the hierarchical logic that subdues disorder. Virtue is a Confucian notion of official religion, and *ling* its equivalent in popular religion (Sangren 1987, 217). These ideas about order constitute an ideology, a set of value structures that praise order and legitimate existing institutions and authority. However, *ling* is not only defined by a set of structurally interconnected contrasts and symbolic and logical operations, but it must also be authenticated in local historical tradition (Sangren 1987, 211)—the one that the ritual here recalls.

The rite as it is performed conforms to tradition but with creative adjustments. It is the product of the lineage council's decisions about the best way to do it with regard to their appreciation of which parts of the tradition must be kept and which discarded. Below the written eulogy from which Xingchang read is a note stating, "After discussion, it was considered that the original verses [*yuanci*] should be revised, condensed, and purified." The current eulogy represents just a third as long as the Hong Kong version of 1972.[9] Several verses enumerating a series of locations and cardinal directions, including Yuenlong, where many Pine Mansion exiles settled in the 1960s, have been deleted. The relocation of the cult to Hong Kong, the distance between Hong Kong and the village as the center of the rituals, and the ancestor's presence in the tablet made it necessary to precisely locate and establish a link between the two places. Another notable difference from the 1972 version is the reference to Zhenneng as "descendant of Emperor Shun." This genealogical linkage to the last of China's five legendary emperors, who were model rulers and exemplars of virtue, includes Zhenneng in the Chinese cosmological order and, drawing from the broader genealogical revival in China (Pieke 2003), lends further legitimacy to lineage revival.

The 2014 Birthday Celebration: Spatiotemporal Fusion

I attended Zhenneng's 320th anniversary on October 24, 2013, and his 321st birthday on October 13, 2014.[10] In 2014, the Zhenneng Foundation doubled its efforts as it was also celebrating the centenary of the school established by the lineage. Some of the French Polynesian Chinese whom I knew from previous fieldwork took part in the celebration. Vice president Deqi, who hosted the event with frequent announcements and proclamations through the microphone, mentioned the Tahiti *huaqiao* several times. They were invited to take part in the group meal for which they were assigned two tables in the room next to the temple. While the villagers sat on stools around folding plastic tables under the large inflatable tent stretched over the basketball court facing the temple, the relatives from Hong Kong and overseas were invited to enjoy their meal in the cool of the ancestral temple building. A young girl had written "*Huaqiao*—Overseas Chinese" in Chinese and English on a sheet of paper with an arrow pointing the way to the room in which were seated elderly people who had returned from Canada and Hong Kong, some joined by friends from the village who had been their classmates at the Zhenneng School, and the group of Chinese from Malaysia whom I had met the previous year, who return to the village every year.

The landing at the top of the steps leading up to the workstation entrance, on which a red carpet had been laid for the occasion, was used as a stage. The festivities started there with a *qilin* dance that the Tahitians, like other travelers from overseas, filmed and photographed. The *qilin* is a cow and dragon combined and is one of China's mythological animals alongside the phoenix and the dragon. It is an auspicious bearer of male offspring and a symbol of justice.[11] The dance was followed by the ceremony of donations (*juankuan yishi*) for the banquet that evening celebrating the centenary of the founding of Zhenneng Primary School.

Each small shareholding company donated 20,000 yuan and the big company contributed 100,000 yuan; two Chen brothers who own a large restaurant in the area also donated a large sum, a mobile entrepreneur gave 100,000 yuan, and Deqi himself gave 10,000 yuan. With each donation, Deqi called the donor up onto the stage and invited the audience to applaud, and Xingchang posed for the photographers alongside each one, each holding a corner of the giant cardboard check from the Shenzhen Commercial Bank with the amount in large characters. The cost of the show and the dinner amounted to a million yuan, the balance provided by the Zhenneng Foundation. It followed the same redistributive principle as that of the banquet that follows each anniversary, although this special occasion involved more pomp and spectacle: everyone contributed to the meal according to their means. On this occasion, there were more than a thousand participants at the lunch and the evening dinner rather than the five hundred to six hundred who attend in other years.

This year of splendid celebration saw increased calls for donor generosity. In addition to the usual list of donations of firecrackers and cash for the anniversary, there was the donation ceremony for the banquet and fundraising for the renovation of the temple. The ideological discourse of the call for funding (chapter 4) contains a call to action and constitutes an ideopraxis that states that remembering the ancestor means working for the future by ensuring the prosperity of the descendants and therefore the economic development of the village. This conjunction of past and future was strongly present in the ritual formulas that were declaimed and in the commentary by Deqi, the foundation's vice president, during the ritual.

The presence of so many overseas Chens seemed to have triggered his particularly metapragmatic speech in comparison to his much plainer speech the previous year. He commented on how they were about to carry out the ritual, interlocking this with an announcement of the presence of overseas relatives. At 1:00 p.m., just before the start of the ritual, Deqi invited all the male elders visiting from overseas, including Alain and Michel from Tahiti and the Malaysian and Toronto Chens, to stand at the front with the other senior members of the lineage to burn the incense (figure 6.3). Alain and Michel had connections with the village: Alain's paternal grandfather and Michel's maternal grandfather had originated from Pine Mansion.

He invited them to line up to light the incense, saying that they represented all of Zhenneng's descendants, and then invited them all to present the incense and bow. In addition to these usual performative instructions, he explained that in the past there had been three *koutou*, prostrations, and nine *bai*, upper-body bows. "But now," he added, "we no longer *kou* because now we are a civilized society [*wenming shehui*], we do civilized activities, and we have kept some old

FIGURE 6.3. Schoolchildren, Qilin dancers, and the Tahiti Chinese around Vice President Chen. Photo by author, October 2014.

customs like the *qilin* but we also have new ones." When I asked Deqi later what has changed in the performance of the rite compared to that in the past, he told me that they no longer *koutou*. Already in the Republican era, a major innovation of the national funeral liturgy (*guozang*) that was being promoted had allowed relatives of the deceased to bow without prostrating themselves (Goossaert and Fang 2008, 55).[12] With the advent of the Communist regime, such symbolic subservience was banned altogether. The end of Deqi's introductory speech was indicated by a drum roll followed by the announcement and execution of three salutes (*jugong*) to the ancestor.

The Communist authorities condemned lineage groups not only for the superstitious (*mixin*) elements in their rites but also for the feudal hierarchy they enshrined. This dual dimension is encapsulated in the expression "feudal superstition" (*fengjian mixin*), which in post-Mao political discourse continues to stand for "backwardness," a category that is not fixed but can label any ritual practice that the Party devalues. It "can be paired oppositionally with 'civilization' (*wenming*)," which is closely identified with modernity (Anagnost 1994, 224). This progress toward modernity requires "raising the quality" (*suzhi*) of Chinese citizens by turning them into valued modern urbanites in contrast to "backward" peasants (Anagnost 1994, 224). It also commands a break from the past, which is in tension with the nationalist discourse on a specific Chinese modernity that requires the retention of some elements of the past. The reconstruction of local traditions in the post-Mao era is therefore highly selective, as Deqi highlighted by pointing out that they have kept some old customs and introduced new ones.

Relayed by loudspeakers at each corner of the public square, this speech has a fourfold audience. It addresses the founding ancestor, emphasizing to him the remarkable presence of descendants from afar at the sacrifice. It also addresses the spectators who do not play an active part in the collective rite but are reminded of its importance. To the Hong Kong and overseas participants, it explains what has changed since they or their ancestors migrated. In 2013, Deqi had invited participants to "*koutou*," even if the gesture accomplished was a simple salute. In 2014, he used the word *jugong* (salute). This conspicuous distinction from the customary traditions and beliefs attributed to Hong Kongers and the diaspora denotes the cultural intimacy (Herzfeld 2016) shared by those who experienced Mao's campaign against superstition and its contemporary prolongation. The discourse finally also addresses the state; even though the presence of the overseas visitors lends it additional legitimacy, Deqi explicitly locates the rite within the limits of what the state considers "civilized."

The different modalities of participation in the ritual, with its enactment entrusted to the elders of the lineage and the public standing at a distance, indexes the traditional social hierarchy of the lineage as an agnatic order based on seniority. The discontinuation of prostration and everyone's participation in the meal following the sacrifice, however, testify to a desire to euphemize the old hierarchy and adjust the rite to the context of contemporary Chinese society. Participation in the ritual is seen as each individual's personal choice and a matter of personal responsibility. This notion of responsibility (*zeren*) is a central moral principle, particularly in relations between villagers and ancestors (Ku 2003). This was negatively reflected in the very embarrassing outburst by Shengyu, the former village chief, who, busy in the kitchens, did not hear the call to attend the ritual and, arriving there at the point between two bows, cried out something expressing deep discontent and immediately left. Ganhua did not want to comment on this, telling me that we should not be dwelling on this kind of stuff, but a Hong Kong participant told me that it was Shengyu's responsibility to be there on time and he could only blame himself (*kao ziji*) if he was late.

The talkative Hong Konger took the opportunity to mention that in his opinion, Deqi should not have said "second bow" and "third bow" but "bow again" (*cai jugong*), a point of detail but an indication of the ongoing discussion about the proper way to perform the rite. The modern minimalism adopted highlights the components of the ritual action that are considered essential and irremovable: the senior and male members of the lineage lighting the incense, the gestures of sacrificial offering, and the evocation of the ancestor's beneficent virtue and power. The participants are animated by tension about accomplishing the ritual in a fairly short period of time: the action lasts about ten minutes, and in contrast to the relaxed prolonged festivities of much of the rest of the day, the sacrificial rite itself is an extreme concentration of noise (music and explosions from firecrackers) and linguistic and gestural actions (bodily inclinations, oratory formulas, the presentation of incense and offerings) over a very short period, creating the "sensation of a total fused experience" (Tambiah 1985b, 165).

The collective effervescence, the *renao* (literally, "heat and noise"), then reaches its peak. *Renao* is the general atmosphere at the festivities that individual participants both seek and arouse by their presence; it is also the very particular noise and excitement that immediately precedes the moment of the ritual itself. *Renao* is a goal to be reached at many public events in China (Chau 2006, 147) and offers a minimum motive for people to attend. Weixin, the person with the most negative criticism of superstitious practices of all the people I met in the village, stated that he had come to Chunfen to *chao renao*—that is, to make noise and contribute to the animation. Some migrant workers from Hubei in the audience stated that they were there to enjoy the spectacle of the crowd and all the noise and heat (*kan renao*).

The ritual produces a spatiotemporal fusion through the momentary gathering in one spot, the center of the village, of beings who are usually separate in time and space—the ancestor, the villagers, the relatives living in the city, and the visitors from overseas and Hong Kong. This meeting of people who have been apart for a long time causes a lot of excitement. Present were, among others, four sisters from Suriname who had left Pine Mansion in 1979 in their late teens, first to join their uncle in Hong Kong and then to go on to Suriname, where their father and mother had been since 1965. Their mother spent thirty years in Suriname and returned to the village after their father's death, and the sisters had not seen her for several years. I posed for a group photograph with them in front of the temple (figure 6.4).

The copresence of all creates this momentary gathering at a focal point. In this respect, the rite is the culmination of the perpetual cycle of arrivals and departures that is central to Chinese conceptions of local attachment (Stafford 1999, 2000b). Such comings and goings may be more significant in some relationships than a fixed state of "being together," and constantly repeating this practice produces attachment to a particular locality. The coming of the founding ancestor and expectation of his beneficial action in return for caring for him during the meeting perpetuates his descendants' attachment to his person and the locality he founded. The rare presence of overseas Chinese living in remote locations, permanently separated from the local community, paradoxically underlines the

FIGURE 6.4. Group photograph with Surinamese visitors in the ancestral temple. Photo by author, October 2013.

importance of their relationship with the village and at the same time demonstrates the importance of their own presence to the other participants.

Great Honor and Happy Coincidence: The *Huaqiao* at the Origins of the Lineage

After commenting on old and new ways of performing the ritual, Chen Deqi returned his attention to the *huaqiao*, praising the fact that they had come from far away. "And to ask for what?" he asked into the microphone. "To ask for good health, so when we worship the ancestor [*bai zuzong*] we ask him to bless everyone. We toast you, we invite you to drink. Lord Zhenneng will eat and drink until he gets drunk [*chizui hezui*]."

The back and forth in this discourse between the announcement of the presence of the overseas visitors and that of the ancestor, the commentary on things retained from the past and those that are new, connect the distant and the near, the past, the present, and the future. This discourse is based on an association of ideas that establishes a homology between *huaqiao* and the past or origins of the lineage, Pine Mansion, and the present. The diaspora is placed discursively in a distant past, closer to the origins of the lineage than to the present, but nonetheless, representatives from overseas have traveled to ask for the ancestor's blessing future prosperity and numerous descendants just as the people of Pine Mansion do.

Alain, one of the Tahiti travelers, received a warm welcome when he met Deqi in October 2014, a few days before the ancestor's birthday and the school celebration. One morning, I joined him at the workstation in Chen Guanqiu's office, and after some small talk, Guanqiu phoned Deqi to ask if he could join us. Deqi arrived a quarter of an hour later, greeted us in Mandarin and gave me a bag with the school's one hundredth anniversary logo on it containing the book, the album, and the DVD about the school, released for the occasion. He sat at the end of the table close to Alain, and Guanqiu introduced them to each other. Deqi referred to the famous Tahiti banker Chin foo, then asked how many people there were in the group he was traveling with. Alain told him fourteen, adding that he was the only one from Pine Mansion apart from Michel, his maternal cousin, whose mother was a Pine Mansion Chen. His attention was momentarily diverted by a workstation employee showing him the yellow cloth banner made for the birthday celebration three days away. Deqi asked Alain where he was staying and if he had been born in Tahiti. He inquired about his age and his astrological sign (*shengxiao*): was he an ox, a dog? Alain replied that he was a rooster. They laughed. Alain added that he could not become a *jiagong* (grandfather, ancestor), and Deqi replied, "Ah! You have no son?" Alain answered jokingly that he could perhaps find a new wife and have sons. Deqi asked him how many daughters he had, and Alain said he had five, pointing them out in the genealogy.

The conversation went on in a jesting mode. Alain said with some pride that he was from the oldest branch and Deqi pointed out that he himself was of the third branch—that is, from Zhenneng's third son. At that point, our fellow travelers David, Elsa, and Manoa walked into the office and stood behind the desk. Alain pointed to David, saying, "He is from Chang Hang Gang" (a nearby former village), and Deqi invited him to sit at the table. The two women remained at the back of the room. A discussion ensued about the surnames in David's village: the Chens, the Lins, the Lius. The conversation became more serious when Deqi started talking to Alain in Hakka about his preparations for the birthday.

> DEQI: Big brother [*ah-ko* in Hakka], Zhenneng's birthday, I will tell you
> a little bit about it. I'm younger than you; I am sixty-eight years old.
> ALAIN: I am an older brother. (He repeats this with a laugh.)
> DEQI: This year is your first time in Pine Mansion.
> [Alain replied he had been here once twenty years ago, but Deqi did
> not seem to understand him.]

Deqi: Chen, Chen Zhigang. [Alain's surname followed by his personal name]

Alain: Chen Zhigang.

Deqi: Do you have any relatives in Pine Mansion?

Alain: Of course, of course there must be; I'm checking it out. My ancestor lived here—it's not easy to find [close relatives]. If I find some, it will be even better.

Deqi: There must be some. The Guobaos are quite numerous. Guoxuan [Alain's ancestor] and Guobao are lineage brothers; if you look for descendants of Lord Guobao you should find some Guoxuan [descendants].

[There was a new interruption to discuss the finishing touches to the birthday banner. Deqi took Alain's hand in his own.]

Deqi: Big brother.

Alain: (Looking very pleased) Ah! Big brother!

Deqi: Big brother, our Lord Zhenneng is the grandfather of your grandfather's grandfather's grandfather [*ah-gong de ah-gong de ah-gong de ah-gong de ah-gong*].

Deqi got it exactly right: Alain is a ninth-generation descendant of Zhenneng. Still holding Alain's hand, he told him that although the school was now a state school, the people of Pine Mansion had built it and that they would therefore hold a joint celebration to commemorate the ancestor's birthday and the school's centennial. Alain replied that he had come especially for this anniversary. Deqi went on to explain that the people of Pine Mansion do not go by the solar date but by the lunar calendar (*nongli*). "Remember, the twentieth day of the ninth lunar month, each lunar year." Alain replied that he would like to come every year. Deqi then told him that some people in the community were also celebrating their one hundredth birthday this year and that this coincided (*pengdao*) with the one hundredth anniversary of the school: "This a great honor!" (*hao rongxingle*), continuing, "And you, big brother, you have come this year; we are all very honored, it coincides precisely with [*zhenghao pengdao*] the one hundredth anniversary of the school, so we are very honored. Therefore we can say that this year people are coming from all sides, we are making very comprehensive preparations for a solemn celebration [*longzhong qingzhu*] on the thirteenth."

Deqi spoke at great length about the birthday and how it was to be celebrated, holding Alain's hand all the while. In all of this, the emphasis was on the vertical link between Deqi and Alain's common ancestor in the person of Zhenneng. This vertical link to the lineage's point of origin was also emphasized in Deqi's association between the celebration of the past—or more precisely, the foundations or origins of the school—and Alain's visit. The parallel he drew between the honor to the community of having people the same age as the century-old school among its members and pride in seeing people returning to the village from overseas shows how the latter are symbolically situated in the past, as if they were themselves a hundred years old.

The idea of a chance encounter, the happy coincidences of the centenaries of the people and of the school, and of the centenary of the school and Alain's arrival, which Deqi expressed using the verb *pengdao*, implies the idea of destinies that have been separated and now meet again. Alain's return on this anniversary is perceived as a happy coincidence due to fate rather than chance. The encounter was destined to take place due to the original lineage relationship, and the fact that it had happened was a sign that this relationship had predisposed them to the encounter. My own visits to the village for the birthday were also interpreted as a sign of a predestined relationship, *yuanfen*, intended to bring people together: "Anne must have a *yuanfen* with us; she has been coming [he used a variation of *pengdao*, *pengshang*, which means to "bump into"] precisely on the birthday for three [in fact, two] years in a row."

This is reflected in the title of the sixth chapter of the book published for the school's centenary: *Zhenneng zhimu, huaqiao*, which literally means "Zhenneng's mother, the overseas Chinese," *mu* being the mother, and here, by extension, the family, the origin. This expression is reminiscent of the more widespread and generic expression *qiaobao*, "overseas compatriots," an abbreviation of *huaqiao tongbao*. Bao means "matrix, placenta, born of the same parents" (Hui 2011, 36). The use of this term therefore refers to the idea of uterine kinship, possibly via a female ancestor.

The symbolic classification of overseas Chinese as belonging to the past is materially enhanced throughout the village by the inscription of their names on the commemorative plaques affixed to buildings to which they have donated (chapters 2 and 5). However, the destruction of certain village remains also leads to selective erasure of this memory. Before the old village center was torn down, there was a small stone bridge bearing the inscriptions of those who had built it in the 1920s. I took a picture of it during my first stay in 2011, and when I returned the next year, it had disappeared. Similarly, the building originally constructed on the initiative of a Belgian Chen in 1994 as the home for the elderly, *laoren yiyuan*, was demolished and replaced in 2004 by a taller building in a context in which the state was encouraging the formation of an official association for the elderly (*laoren xiehui*). This parallels the destruction for the same reason of the Old People's Association building in 2005, with no resources to build a new one, in the village that Chen Meixuan studied. However, in that rural village, which is considerably less economically developed than Pine Mansion, overseas connections are still crucially important and the lineage leaders who allowed the building to be destroyed lost their legitimacy (Chen 2013, 107) due to discontent on the part of the overseas Chinese who had financed it. In Pine Mansion, the list of donations for the 1994 building can be found in the genealogy, but the plaque on the wall disappeared during the demolition. To the right of the entrance to the new building, there is now a plaque listing the donors and the sums they contributed for its construction in 2004. Apart from a few Hong Kong contributions, overseas Chens did not finance this new project.

Chen Tailai had never really recovered from the decision to replace the building, even though it was passed by an overwhelming majority at the native villagers' assembly. He made it clear that he had had to fight to ensure that the portraits of the man who had conceived the idea for the previous building, and his wife who had cofinanced it, the two very rich Belgian Chens, continued to be displayed in the main room with an inscription celebrating their generosity and recalling their inaugural action. Tailai died in the late spring of 2014, and with his retirement and then his death, the memory of the overseas contributions for the modernization of the village and the lineage renewal, of which he had been one of the main actors during the decades following China's opening up, vanished, the generation of already elderly leaders who had occupied positions as executives and lineage leaders in the 1980s by virtue of their ties and influence overseas lost. The very fact that Tailai had to insist that this memory was not completely erased is indicative of the people of Pine Mansion's ambivalent attitude to their distant overseas relatives' financial support.

Although both of the collective rites display the same differentiation between high-status individuals—that is, members of the lineage council—most of whom participate in the collective ritual, and everybody else who worships the ancestor individually, they differ in one respect: the rite held at Chunfen is more religious with its sacrifice to the ancestor Zhenneng in front of his grave, while the other rite is more commemorative, closer to the Confucian spirit, and celebrates his birthday more officially. This event draws wider support and a larger number of officials than the ritual at the tomb, which is mainly performed by Hong Kongers and successful mobile entrepreneurs.

The locals contrast the beliefs and practices of overseas Chinese with their own ways of worshiping the ancestors, which they deem more modern. Overseas Chinese are categorized as of the past, and this is strengthened by the structural theory about the almost inevitable estrangement of migrants and their descendants (chapter 5). This does not mean that the people of Pine Mansion consider that they no longer have any overseas relatives—quite the contrary—

but they associate ideas about things of the past with the *huaqiao*. Village and lineage leaders tended to reject feng shui as a belief once held by peasants hoping for good harvests, thus associating it with Pine Mansion's rural past, and saw Chinese living overseas and in Hong Kong as still believing this.

Michael Herzfeld's (2016) concept of cultural intimacy applies very well to this ambivalent attitude. They are torn between recognizing the importance of the rites and their centrality in their lineage village identity, and the unease with which they handle them—and as I have mentioned, the main ritual gestures are left to the Hong Kong entrepreneur who is head of the foundation to perform. This suggests that a scalar strategy of legitimization is at play: the participation of overseas relatives in the ancestral ritual legitimizes lineage practices that the state sees as heterodox in the secular modernity that it advocates, while the categorization of *huaqiao* as belonging to the past suggests a form of complicity (Steinmüller 2013) between the local community and the state. The apparent paradox of seeing the *huaqiao* as estranged and at the same time conservative, having kept up the old traditions, is in fact not so paradoxical. The ritual way of expressing a Chinese identity and maintaining a link to the origins in the diaspora is, officially at least, not considered essential to being Chinese in today's China. It can also be explained by the fact that it is the more recent emigrants and Hong Kong mobile entrepreneurs, on the one hand, and descendants of emigrants searching for their roots, on the other hand, who return to the village and display the greatest interest in the ritual. The next chapter turns to the latter's travels to find their roots.

RETURNING TO ONE'S ROOTS THROUGH JOURNEYS AND QUESTS

Alain had been talking about his desire to travel to China to visit the village his grandfather had left in 1910 since I first met him in 2002.[1] Alain had been one of my main informants when I was carrying out research among the Chinese community in French Polynesia. At that time, I had been led to conclude that its members' ties with their fathers and grandfathers' villages of provenance in South China were weakening. However, I had collected only indirect evidence based on interviews and informal conversations about their relations with their forebears' homeland. This changed when I began to conduct field research in Pine Mansion. When I returned to French Polynesia in 2013, I was seen as an expert in villages of origin, and Alain and the leaders of other Chinese associations asked me to present several public talks about my research, which attracted large crowds and allowed me to obtain in-depth accounts of some people's journeys to China.

Most importantly, my stay in French Polynesia gave Alain the impetus he needed to carry out a plan he had long contemplated: to visit his village of origin, which I had chosen as my main field site (see introduction). As a result, he and a group of other Chinese from French Polynesia made the journey and were in Pine Mansion during my fifth stay there in October 2014. It should be noted from the outset that these travelers and other diasporic visitors whom I met in Pine Mansion organized their own tours independently of the Chinese government, unlike the Chinese American participants in the youth festival sponsored by the Guangdong Province Office of Overseas Chinese Affairs (*qiaoban*) (Louie 2000).

In this chapter, I discuss the practices of diasporic identification (Gordon and Anderson 1999) as they take place in and through travel as an embodied search for knowledge. Diasporic tourist experiences can be analyzed as part of the larger investigation of travel (Clifford 1988, 1997). Whereas Clifford (1997, 2) invites anthropologists to look at fieldwork as "less a matter of localized dwelling and more a series of travel encounters," here I am less interested in "fieldwork as a travel practice" (Clifford 1997, 8) than in what the proximity of the practice of "roots" travel to my fieldwork practice reveals about modes of diasporic identification.[2]

Directly observing the methods and means that the travelers employed in their search made it possible for me to analyze these as a set of meaningful practices rather than taking the common substantializing and reifying discourses about diasporic and transnational identities at face value. It also allowed me to grasp and make sense of how they experienced their quest for identity. Accounts of globalization, defined as an ensemble of cultural flows liberated from their local moorings, tend to adopt a bird's-eye view that looks down on the planet as a multicultural bazaar and to emphasize discursive approaches and textual materials (Kapferer 2000, 188; Friedman 2002, 27–28). Ironically, homelands embrace and prescribe this view of transnational cultural identity flows regarding their diasporas, as China does in its effort to reconnect with its diasporic communities around the world.

We should be wary of narratives that blindly attach diasporic subjects to their "roots," and avoid essentializing identities by assuming that such reconnections are constitutive of a pan-Chinese cultural scape (Louie 2000, 645; 2001). While we run the risk of essentialization when we conflate migrants' visits to their native places with their descendants' visits to their places of origin, labeling them both "(transnational) returns," it is impossible to deny that the descendants of migrants subjectively frame such journeys as returning. French Polynesian Chinese commonly refer to such individual and group journeys as "searching for their roots" or "returning to their roots."[3] None of the participants in the travel were first-generation emigrants and their project is therefore more appropriately described as a search rather than a return. However, the fact that they did refer to the notion of return and used the two phrases interchangeably closely resembles other descriptions of diasporic experiences of traveling to a lost "homeland" (Bruner 1996; Ebron 1999; Leite 2005). Although the subjective experiences of migrants' descendants on their first encounter with their family's village of origin may differ significantly from those of migrants returning to their native place, it is nonetheless true that the travelers whom I followed expressed emotions framed in terms of their reconnection with something that they saw as a lost part of themselves.

Accounting for the travelers' practices on their journey to find their roots requires taking the idea that drives their quest—that they are searching for something that is or should somehow be part of themselves but has been lost, forgotten, or not transmitted—seriously. To account for this search for essence in nonessentializing terms, I draw from Jean-Paul Sartre's (2003 (1969)) existentialist theory with his distinction between being-in-itself (*en-soi*) and being-for-itself (*pour-soi*). The starting point is an ontological split: identity as an analytical principle that proposes that one is what one is never actually realized (Sartre 2003, 123): we may tend toward this identity in itself by defining ourselves according to the givens of our situation such as our language, our environment, our previous choices. This reduction of the self in its function of being-in-itself constitutes our facticity. However, facticity coexists with transcendence, which characterizes the mode of being-for-itself: we are condemned to be separated from our selves.[4] It is precisely this gap between being-for-itself and being-in-itself that gives meaning to human reality (Sartre 2003, 123).

Identity-as-practice in the course of traveling amounts to a quest to fill this gap in the form of sensorial encounters with places and people. Such a search involves particular approaches and procedures that shape the contours of this specific mode of travel. I show how the journey itself is apprehended and realized as a type of detective game and thus entails what Carlo Ginzburg (1989) terms an "evidentiary paradigm," anchored in concrete empirical experience. The French Polynesian travelers were strangers in China, either because it was their first visit or because the changed landscape provoked estrangement, and yet although none were familiar with the places they visited, they adopted an evidentiary method of research which shaped a way of traveling that closely resembled Tim Ingold's (2011) notion of wayfinding.

This chapter argues that the search for one's roots is experienced as a return because it allows experiential recovery of knowledge and refamiliarization: in the course of the journey, what one has been estranged from becomes familiar again. Having flown in from opposite directions, the Tahitian Chinese visitors and I met in Pine Mansion village and stayed in the same hotel for two weeks, during which time the group shared their experiences of discovering Pine Mansion and other villages nearby with me. Although the ethnographic material that forms the basis of this chapter is drawn primarily from this short but intense stay, I would not have reached the same depths of information and understanding had I not known several of the travelers from earlier fieldwork in French Polynesia and had I not already conducted fieldwork in Pine Mansion and the surrounding area. On previous occasions, I had, more or less by happenstance, come across French Polynesian acquaintances who were visiting the area. These meetings also inform my analysis of the material presented here. However, it was traveling alongside the group and sharing their searches and discoveries in a place with which I had already become familiar that allowed me to closely observe how they proceeded in their search, and to reach an understanding of its implications.

In this chapter, I follow the travelers on their quests, starting with their preparations for traveling, the constitution of the group, and their motivations and approaches to the journey. Their approach was based on proceeding from clues and signs in order to trace tracks and paths and fill in gaps, making the journey itself much like a detective game. Armed with a few clues, and in some cases none at all, the travelers sought their way by deliberately leaving much to chance. The connections that some managed to establish during their quest as part of their practice of a diasporic identity are most powerfully encapsulated in Alain's paradoxical use of the Tahitian term *mana* to describe his experience.

Searching for One's Roots

As in many overseas Chinese communities created by the major wave of migration in the nineteenth and early twentieth centuries, a colonial politics of othering coupled with a logic of boundary maintenance accounts for the fact that in French Polynesia today, the ethnic group identified as Chinese is estimated to make up about one-fifth of the total population of three hundred thousand. About five thousand mainly Hakka-speaking immigrants from Guangdong Province arrived in the French Establishments of Oceania, later renamed French Polynesia, in the last two decades of the nineteenth and first three decades of the twentieth century. The majority settled on Tahiti, where they formed an urban community in Papeete, the capital, while others dispersed widely across the Society Islands and the other South Pacific archipelagos that the French had recently annexed.

The first-generation Chinese stayed in close connection with their villages of origin in China, often traveling back and forth, and many returned to China after a few years or sometimes a few decades in Tahiti. As jus soli (citizenship based on birth) did not apply in France's colonies and overseas territories, their children remained Chinese. However, stories of the hardship that met those who returned to China in 1947, some of whom managed to get back to French Polynesia, brought about a change in the way they perceived the homeland state, whose hostility toward and even persecution of overseas Chinese led them to abandon any prospect of returning. President de Gaulle's decision to transfer France's nuclear testing infrastructure to the Polynesian atolls in 1962 and his diplomatic recognition of the People's Republic of China (PRC) in 1964 made the French authorities fearful of having to deal with a large group of dependents under the jurisdiction of a communist regime.[5] A few years before China's reopening in 1979, France began to afford its overseas territories increasing political autonomy, and a 1973 decree extended French nationality law to its overseas territories, granting French citizenship to all French Polynesian–born Chinese.

After China launched its reform and opening policy (*gaige kaifang*) in 1979, a "politics of native roots" (Siu 1994, 32) was deployed within China which cast overseas Chinese visitors as potential investors or donors whose contributions were seen as both acts of patriotism and their filial duty to their ancestors buried in China. The Chinese authorities also made attempts to reconnect with the diaspora. In French Polynesia, several visits by top Chinese officials were followed by the opening of a PRC consulate in 2005 and a Confucius Institute in 2013. All of this provides "fertile grounds for the rediscovery of 'Chinese' identity" (Dirlik 2004, 146). Identification as ethnic Chinese, and even as a member of the Chinese community through participation in its activities, cannot be equated with a diasporic orientation to the Chinese "homeland." Many descendants of Chinese immigrants in French Polynesia have never been to China, or they have been but did not visit their villages of origin. However, in this context, many who identify as members of the Chinese community have been encouraged to not only take part in cultural activities promoted by Chinese associations as part of the revival of Chinese cultural identity in French Polynesia but also engage in a search for their roots.

Alain, born in 1945, was one of the founders of one such association and planned the October 2014 trip. He met his first French wife in Paris, where he had graduated as an engineer, and later remarried a Tahitian woman. For many years, he had dreamed of traveling to his paternal grandfather's village, as he told me when I first met him in Tahiti in the early 2000s. He had devoted an ever-increasing part of his leisure time to genealogical research, and after retiring from a decreasingly successful career as a businessman had opened a small office from which he conducts research into his own family as well as those of others, mostly gratis. This genealogical activity is, for him, a way of actively engaging with the knowledge of his origins and of Chinese culture. Alain's goal was to bring together a group of people interested in searching for their origins and travel with them to China.

Many Polynesians with Chinese backgrounds perceive their relationship to what they call their origins, or their roots, as highly problematic. Retracing their past and identifying the provenance of their forebears in China is a tortuous route strewn with obstacles. The process of gathering knowledge is extremely difficult. The main reason for this is the linguistic barrier: although almost all second- and third-generation descendants of emigrants attended Chinese schools, this was generally only for a maximum of four years prior to going to a French school, and even in the years before the French government closed the Chinese schools in 1964 as part of its turn toward an assimilative policy, they had started teaching more than half of their courses in French. Most of those aged forty and over still speak fairly good Hakka, the dominant language in the Chinese community, but they do not speak Mandarin and cannot read Chinese characters.

The acquisition of French citizenship in the late 1960s and early 1970s included the frenchification of surnames, many of which now differ widely from the original Chinese patronym. Although many French Polynesian Chinese know their original surname, they are unable to read or write it in Chinese. The language obstacle also has further consequences: some are obvious, such as difficulty communicating in China, especially since they are expected to speak the language on the basis of their appearance. There were other problems of which I only became aware when several people in Tahiti who were considering traveling to China asked me to point out Pine Mansion and other villages on Google Maps. In sum, the linguistic obstacle generates difficulties that include not only the impossibility of locating oneself in time—in their genealogy—but also in space at the precise location of their forebears' provenance, rendering the very act of retracing tremendously difficult.

Even those who read Chinese or can at least recognize the characters that make up the village's name will not be able to find it on a map. The difficulty in locating a village of origin is exacerbated by the transformation of the region around it. Like most migrants of the nineteenth- and twentieth-century exoduses, the Chinese who migrated to French Polynesia came from what is now the northern part of Shenzhen. Not only has rapid urbanization absorbed the once-rural villages in its sprawl, but the villages have also lost their original names in their administrative transformation into "communities" (shequ). In order to find a village's whereabouts, one has to use stratagems; for example, I located one group member's village thanks to the fact that a bus station was named after it. Moreover, with these changes there is little chance that Hakka-speaking travelers will find a taxi driver who understands them and knows the places they seek—most of whom are migrants from inner China.

Distance in time accounts for the fact that only a few descendants of migrants still have close kin in China, let alone living in the villages. None of the travelers had close relatives (qinqi) in their villages of origin. Only one person I met in French Polynesia and another in Pine Mansion had a half brother and a half sister, respectively, whom they had not met until they traveled to China. The half siblings were the result of their fathers' past transnational mobility. This degree of relatedness facilitates transnational business ventures (both men had established such partnerships). Apart from these exceptions, remoteness in kinship relations explains why, unlike the more recent emigrants who left in the 1950s and 1960s, and especially those who settled in Hong Kong, the descendants of emigrants do not invest in Shenzhen.

This is the outcome of family dispersion through tumultuous transnational migration and of geopolitical factors that made visits and communication difficult (Trémon 2017). The three Mao decades from 1949 to 1976 increased the distance that grows between kin with the passing of generations. In many cases, grandfathers and fathers who migrated to French Polynesia remained in correspondence with their kin in the village or relations who had fled to Hong Kong, and visited the villages when China reopened at the end of the 1970s. However, they did not always transmit precise knowledge about these villages to later generations, and much of the information the latter did manage to gather about the locality or whom to contact is now outdated. The rise in income and living standards in Shenzhen has allowed many native inhabitants to move to new houses outside of the old village centers (see chapter 3) or even to other neighborhoods beyond their former villages.

Alain, as the main initiator of the collective travel project, spent the first part of 2014 looking for at least ten travel companions, the minimum number for plane tickets at the group rate. In August, he emailed me a list of travelers, and I offered to book them into a hotel where I had stayed several times, praising its ideal location in the center of Pine Mansion and its proximity to the temple, where the ancestral festival was to be held during our stay. I knew that not all of the group would have come from Pine Mansion, but most of the French Polynesian Chinese's villages of origin are within a twelve-kilometer radius of it.

A group of thirteen formed around Alain on an ad hoc basis. They decided to join him because they were tied to him by either kin or friendship, and a few others simply seized the opportunity. André and Michel, his remote maternal cousins, had known him since childhood. Michel was accompanied by his son and daughter-in-law, who live in California. Others had become acquainted with Alain more recently through his activity as a genealogist or through Chinese community networks. David is the current leader of one of the older (Kuomintang) Chinese associations and is very active in French Polynesian and overseas Chinese Catholic networks.[6] Maurice is the owner of a famous restaurant that plays a central role in the community and is accompanied by his wife. Elsa works at the Bureau of Land Affairs and is therefore regularly confronted with genealogical questions for which she often consults Alain or his Tahitian wife. The group was completed by three people enrolled by André who, like him, had started attending Mandarin classes at the Confucius Institute: André's paternal cousin René, who had already traveled in the area and had a good level of Mandarin; Loïc, the oldest in the group at eighty, and Jean, the youngest in his early fifties, both of whom, like André, were beginners at Mandarin. Elsa had recruited two Tahitian women friends, Heinui and Manoa.

The party of thirteen travelers were only loosely connected. Only Alain's grandfather originated from Pine Mansion, while the others' fathers and grandparents had come from other villages in the area. The three women in the group whom Alain had described to me as Tahitian did not know the name of their villages of origin when they set out: both Heinui and Manoa's Chinese grandfathers had returned to China in the 1930s or 1940s, leaving their spouses and female offspring in Tahiti, and Elsa's Chinese father had died when she was a child, without passing on any knowledge about their village.

Bridging a Gap and Preparing for Revelations

The search for information about China and their villages of origin was intended to bridge a gap that the travelers saw as the result of a lack of or an interruption to their families' transmission of knowledge. It is significant that Alain, Michel, David, André, and Elsa had all lost their fathers in their childhood or early youth. Others regretted that their grandfathers and fathers had been too busy earning money to pass on what they knew. For most, their acquisition of Chinese culture had been limited to the few years they had spent at the Chinese school as young children. The members of the group shared the same desire to fill this gap and saw their journey as a means of recovery and rediscovery of what they had forgotten or been deprived of.

They all, especially the three women who did not know the precise name of their grandfathers' villages, conceptualized and even deliberately constructed the journey as an enigma to be deciphered. However, those who knew the name they would seek and even those who had already visited their village also had mysteries to solve: finding their genealogy or filling the gaps in their own genealogical knowledge, finding people who might have known their fathers or grandfathers, tracing kin who had remained in China, often after being sent back as children in the 1930s or returning in the 1940s, and from whom they had had no news. Although each traveler had his or her own personal enigmas to solve, the journey itself, at least in the early days, took the form of a collective scavenger hunt which started with preparatory work in Tahiti, where the travelers met several times at the headquarters of David's association and in Alain's office. The journey started as a tracking game before the spatial displacement itself, and the journey in China was its continuation.

It was Alain who did most of this detective work for both himself and the others. His genealogical work itself amounts to a set of problems to be solved, disparate pieces of information to be connected and voids to be filled by following clues. The preparatory work started with a set of linkage procedures destined to identify all of the travelers' villages of origin. "Using the archival source, I've been making some data reconciliations. It's like a puzzle," he explained. He had to combine and cross-check several different sources, the first being the matriculation files in which the Chinese immigrants had been registered and given a number upon arrival in the colony and which were completed later, although not always systematically, with the name and registration numbers of their spouse and children and dates of travel out of and back into the territory. The second was the French Polynesian Chinese population census carried out at the request of the newly appointed Consul of the Republic of China in 1945, which a member of the community had recently published on the internet, adding the romanized versions of family and place names, although not in *pinyin*, the official Chinese romanization, which added to the difficulty of the searches. This was how they found Elsa's grandfather's probable village of origin. Manoa and Heinui, however, found nothing more than their original family names.

The next step consisted of compiling a list of the places targeted for a visit and locating them. This involved identifying the villages on a map. The participation of several people who had studied Mandarin proved valuable in this operation. The old map of the area displayed in the entrance hall of the headquarters of the main and oldest Chinese association, the Si Ni Tong, where Alain pays a token rent for his office, was of little use as the text was only in Chinese characters. They converted the village names into pinyin and tried in vain to identify them on a digital map. There was a breakthrough when René produced a map of the Shenzhen area in both Chinese characters and pinyin that he had brought back from one of his journeys, which, as it was more than ten years old, showed the villages that were later urbanized, in 2004.

The entire first part of the journey in China was structured by visits to the different villages of origin. During the first three days, the travelers made these visits as a group, and then they split up into two or three subgroups according to their personal affinities and the proximity of the villages they wanted to visit. These were primarily the villages of the travelers' patrilineal kin, their fathers or grandfathers who had emigrated. Many are inhabited by members of one or two large lineages, and the ancestral temples dedicated to these lineages' founding ancestors were on the travelers' lists of sites that they wanted to find and visit. René, Michel, and David's fathers had all been born locally and had migrated to Tahiti; Michel and David's grandfathers had not migrated, but René's had, had then returned from Tahiti to China and thereafter left for Tahiti again.

Several of the travelers knew the names of their wives' villages, and some knew those of their mothers or grandmothers'. Alain and David visited their patrilineal village first and then turned to these other villages.

The travelers thus had varying degrees of knowledge about "their village." The men in the group and Maurice's wife knew more than the three women for whom this journey was not only their first visit to the region from which their grandfathers had originated but also their first visit to China. Their goal was not only to try to locate their villages of origin on the basis of just one or two clues but also to discover China.

The contrast between those in the group for whom the journey was a return to a place they had already visited and those for whom it was a whole new discovery was not as great as it may appear. Some had been only once for a flying visit: Alain had been to his village for just an afternoon in 1994. Even those who had visited their villages two or three times were wondering how it would look, whether the buildings raised with their families' donations from abroad were still standing, and other such questions. Neither did this contrast amount to a clear-cut opposition between those for whom the journey was more like a recreational tourist trip and those for whom the goal was more existential and centered on their relationship to their village of origin (Cohen 1979). The way the travelers decided their activities on an impromptu daily basis revealed that they considered both aspects of the journey complementary and equally desirable. All but Alain went to visit Splendid China and the China Folk Culture Village, amusement parks in downtown Shenzhen, and other tourist-oriented sites, and whereas the first two weeks of the journey were devoted to searching for the villages, the third was explicitly more leisure-oriented. Michel and his children, Jean, Maurice, Loïc, and Heinui left by plane for Xi'an and Beijing to visit Chinese scenic spots and museums and reconnect with their former teacher at the Confucius Institute. The others—David, René, André, Elsa, and Manoa—followed Alain's plan to dig deeper into their origins by visiting the Hakkas' area of provenance in the north of Guangdong Province; and while Alain went alone to search for the graves of Pine Mansion's founding ancestor's grandparents in rural villages around Meizhou City, the others visited the city's temples and its Hakka museum and enjoyed "Meizhou by night," as they called it.

Everyone in the group had a taste for research and reflection on genealogies, Hakka history, and Chinese culture and enjoyed discussing these topics at night around the dinner table. David and André are fervent Catholics and Michel is a Freemason, and intercommunity relations and religious syncretism came up in many conversations and led to discussions about the place of the Chinese in French Polynesian society. The local cuisine was another major topic; we sampled every Hakka restaurant in Pine Mansion and returned to those that served fish, comparing it to the raw and cooked fish dishes that are a central part of French Polynesian fare. Clearly, their intentions for this journey had been not just to discover the villages of origin but also to gather food for thought and action back home.

Everybody experienced the journey in a state of openness and readiness for adventure that was at once intellectual, spiritual, and somatic. They were in waiting mode, with an expectation of revelations. Manoa told me that when Elsa had gone to see her and talked about the project, "I asked if I could come. I did this on a sudden impulse. Surely, I must have been ready." A few days later, André used the same expression when he explained why, four years earlier, he had decided, for a variety of reasons, to end his stay in Shenzhen with his cousin René much earlier than he had planned. "At the time, I wasn't ready," he concluded. The travelers' state of readiness for discovery drove their hazardous quest for clues, traces, and tracks.

Wayfinding by Familiar Strangers

In Alain's correspondence with me during the weeks preceding their trip to China, I noticed that the program he had sent me was rather loosely defined. The villages to be visited were not listed or clearly scheduled, and the itineraries and modes of transport did not seem to have been thought through. This was a source of concern, as I saw myself having to take on the role of travel guide. I had been hoping to participate, certainly, but also to observe the ways in which the travelers proceeded on their quest and interacted with the local people in Pine Mansion and the other villages and how the latter received and treated the travelers and perceived them and their requests. I managed to occupy this position of an observer by hiding behind my camera as much as possible when I followed them, filming many of their interactions with their local hosts. I made it clear from the first evening that I was hoping to include a chapter about their peregrinations in the book I was writing. My position as researcher was all the more understandable for them because of the mimesis that pervaded our relations. The travelers, as well as the audiences at the talks I had been invited to give in Tahiti, which had included several members of the group, interpreted my research in the light of their own, as a quest for origins.

As it turned out, the fact that everything was improvised on the spot gave me a better overview of how they performed their search. Moreover, I came to understand that this improvisation was itself significant. Michael Jackson (2005, xii) writes that "most human action is less a product of intellectual deliberation and conscious choice than a matter of continual, intuitive, and opportunistic changes of course." Here, the group's intuitive and hazardous way of traveling, described below, appeared to be the paradoxical result of a deliberate and unconscious wish to leave things to chance. My fears proved groundless as the travelers seemed to want to rely on chance, and particularly chance encounters with local people, rather than on me. In Erving Goffman's (1967, 152) terms, they practiced "hazardous engagement": "for chanciness to be present, the individual must ensure he is in a position (or be forced into one) to let go of his hold and control on the situation."

Even if the villages could be located on a map, reaching them was a different game. Finding the way and the transport to reach them was difficult. The "villages" are no longer discrete spots in a rural landscape but highly densified urban quarters fused with newly built neighborhoods and industrial areas. Even where some of the old village houses are still standing, they are hidden from view by the surrounding buildings. Although this largely accounted for why the travelers had to find their way one clue at a time, there was something more to their method of proceeding. Locating some of the villages on a paper or a digital map was only the first step, the second being the journey to reach their aim, which was not just a specific place identified by a toponym but the tangible materialization of the traces of their forebears in the shape of a house once inhabited by their father or grandfather, an ancestral temple, a house or a school built by donations from overseas kin, a genealogical book. The travelers proceeded as if finding this precise item required them to grope their way forward rather than use a map, seeking fortuitous encounters.

David had visited his father's native village in 1974 and 2007. On the second occasion, his wife had accompanied him, and they had stayed in the region for several weeks, mainly to attend the Miss Overseas Chinese beauty contest in which their daughter was representing French Polynesia. He had been given the phone number of a remote cousin living in Hong Kong by one of his closer cousins in Tahiti. The Hong Kong cousin had driven them to the village, where he had met the cousin's sister and their mother, an elderly woman who had known his father. To my surprise, as we sat in the back of the car belonging to one of the Pine Mansion cadres who had offered to drive us around, David, usually very calm, started showing signs of nervousness at the idea that we might not be able to find the place. He asked me whether I could give him his Hong Kong cousin's phone number, which he had given to me a year earlier in case I would like to contact him, so that he could call him for guidance.

The fact that David had not brought this important contact detail along with him is just one instance among others that I noticed during the trip, when several of the travelers apparently deliberately forgot or neglected information tools that could have helped them in their search. These may have been instances of parapraxis. After noticing them with some surprise, I came to understand them as the product of their attitude of leaving things to chance. While were waiting to turn left and leave the wide two-lane boulevard we had followed almost since leaving Pine Mansion, I read the village's name on a signpost and pointed it out to David. His reaction was that "he would never have been able to recognize it," and he regretted "not having a GPS to record the exact coordinates." I offered to record them, but once we had parked in the village, David forgot about it. We went into the headquarters of the Old People's Association, where David and the Pine Mansion cadre talked in Hakka with one of the association's leaders, who took us across the village to a place where women and elderly people were playing mahjong. I recognized David's female cousin from the photographs and film he had shown me. She first took us to her brother, who still lived in the village (the other lives in Hong Kong, and she herself resides in downtown Shenzhen), leading us on foot to the "old streets" (*laojie*). As we approached the compound, David looked increasingly relieved and happy. What we were looking for turned out to be a very small house of barely eight square meters, which was completely hidden from view by a large building that encroached on David's family's terrain. His father had spent his childhood in this house, and the village officials considered that it now belonged to his heirs. David asked Elsa to take a picture of him posing as if he were about to open the walled-up door (figure 7.1).

FIGURE 7.1.   David posing in front of his father's house. Photo by author, October 2014.

The phenomenological idea that being takes the form of building and dwelling (Heidegger 1975, 145–61) has inspired anthropological approaches that foreground habitus and place making. "[The] objective world not only becomes endowed with, and animated by, our subjectivity; we come to feel that we incorporate and depend on the existence of the people and places with which we *habitually* interact" (Jackson 2005, 17, emphasis added). Ingold (2011, 12) conceptualizes "wayfinding" as inhabiting the world through movement by trail blazing or path following, differentiating wayfinding from navigating: "For the stranger, making his way in unfamiliar country, 'being here' or 'going there' generally entails the ability to identify one's current or intended future position with a certain geographic location, defined by the intersection of particular coordinates on the map" (Ingold 2011, 219). The "countryman," by contrast, does not need to consult an artefactual map to find his way. Ingold makes the case for a phenomenological approach (as opposed to cognitive theories) by building an opposition between the native and the stranger.[7] "It is the *knowledge of the region* . . . that distinguishes the countryman from the stranger" (Ingold 2011, 219, emphasis original). In short, Jackson and Ingold emphasize the intersubjective bond between ourselves and the world as the outcome of the habitual patterns of our practiced life *in a familiar place*.

The problem that this emphasis on habituation and familiarity raises may help in identifying the distinct singularity of diasporic return journeys. The French Polynesian travelers were strangers in China, either because it was their first visit or because the changes in the landscape provoked estrangement. Contrary to Ingold's contrast between the stranger who navigates by means of maps and the native person's wayfaring based on his or her "knowledge of the region," the travelers, though strangers, did not use maps. They did try to locate the villages on the map before leaving Tahiti, but once in China, they did not use maps to find the villages, nor did they feel the need to know their whereabouts on the map once they had found them. Whereas any person, including the average tourist, surely alternates what Kirsten Hastrup (1994, 169) calls "maps" and "tours," one succeeded the other in the course of this project.

The group's way of traveling overrode the dichotomy between strangers and natives. They could be called familiar strangers, not acquainted with the places they were looking for yet still able "to situate [their] current position within the historical context of journeys previously made" (Ingold 2011, 219). They were strangers in that they looked for places that some of them had never been to before, and so they could not rely on their own past experience, or only to a very small extent, as David's case has shown. However, they practiced wayfinding in the sense that they intersubjectively relied on the familiar experience of others—local people and the anthropologist—to find the villages. They tried to find places that their parents or grandparents had mentioned and their forebears had inhabited, places with histories rather than locations (Ingold 2011, 219) that are narrated rather than situated on a map. These histories were their own, but the places that encapsulated them were not yet part of their personal lived experience. What is at stake here is a mode of knowledge seeking that not so much reproduces prior familiarity as it produces refamiliarization.

Producing Refamiliarization

The travelers thus proceeded by exploratory movements, groping their way across the urban environment, often getting lost, looking for tangible traces of the past in the form of material artefacts, mainly in the form of buildings, and living people. They were hoping for chance encounters with inhabitants of the places they visited, potential witnesses of their forebears' existence in these places which might situate them in this past.

One night, Michel explained to me why he wanted to return to his village of origin the next day. The group had paid a collective visit to the village that afternoon. Michel did not have a precise address or name to contact in the village and started perambulating haphazardly. He spotted the name Wong, his patronym, on the facade of a "quite luxurious building." He loitered there for a moment. An elderly woman came out of the house, walked up to him and asked who he was. Michel gave his name and his father's, explaining that his grandfather had had five wives and his father had been the son of the fifth wife. "Different lines," as he put it, referring to the offspring from different mothers, had migrated to Tahiti. The woman answered that she could see which line it was and that his father had been born in the village. She took Michel's hand and invited him in. At this point, Michel stopped talking, overwhelmed by emotion, which resurfaced as he told the story. He paused, flushing and gasping for breath. Alain, who was sitting nearby and had overheard the narration, asked if he had entered the house. Michel said he hadn't because at that moment, other members of the group had joined him telling him that René was missing and they had to look for him. This was why he wanted to return the next day. He did return and later recounted how he had talked with the woman, who was eighty-five years old and had been married to one of his father's half brothers. "This is how she made the connection with me [*Elle a fait le lien avec moi*]." "*Faire le lien*" has two meanings in French: establishing contact or communication with someone and making a connection in the sense of a logical link between two things or events. Michel thereby revealed that he had been, in the Other's gaze, recognized for who he was, bringing him very close to his being-for-itself, his facticity. Whereas for Sartre (1969, 263), the objectifying effect of the Other's look is negative, "producing . . . the solidification and alienation of my own possibilities," for Michel, this momentary reduction to being-in-itself was precisely what he had been hoping for: to be situated within the genealogical line by someone who had known his father.

The travelers were not only looking for descendants of their ancestors, living people descended from collateral branches who might have known their forebears or who were at least part of the same lineage; they were also searching for a spiritual reconnection with their ancestors, a reunion that they felt most powerfully in particular places such as ancestral temples, and several reported having achieved this goal. In Manoa's case, both occurred, and the words she, and the others who witnessed it, used to describe her emotions and feelings were very strong: utmost happiness, ecstasy, almost a state of trance. Manoa had started with only one clue, her grandfather's patronym, Mu. She was helped by a van driver whom I had met the year before through other French Polynesian travelers and had introduced to the group.[8] He had been driving roots tourists for years and knew the region very well and immediately identified Manoa's village of origin thanks to her name, Mu, which is relatively rare. She thus found her grandfather's village, burned incense at the ancestral temple, and met a lineage cousin who had copied the Mu genealogy onto a USB stick for her.

Manoa was emotionally exhausted and went to bed early that evening. Michel enthusiastically showed me a photograph of her in the ancestral temple and another of her eating lunch with chopsticks, which she had not been able to manage before that, embarrassing them all when they ate in restaurants by asking for a fork. Elsa commented on this, drawing a parallel with her own situation. The Hakka language was "coming back," she explained, although she had never spoken it. Elsa had mainly been brought up by her half-Tahitian, half-Chinese mother from a wealthy Tahitian family of rather high status who had been intent on acquiring French cultural capital, a necessary instrument for social promotion in French Polynesia. She had learned to speak neither Hakka nor Tahitian.[9] She speculated, "I probably stored words deep in my memory that are coming out now that I'm in China." Elsa also suggested that Manoa suddenly knew how to use chopsticks now that she knew who she was, knew her grandfather's village and her place in her genealogy. Elsa too had found her village of origin, and having visited it, she said, was an immense step forward, but it "was not 100 percent satisfactory" because she had not found her genealogy, the temple, or anyone who might have known who she was. For the third Tahitian woman, Heinui, the journey was an immense disappointment, and she resented Alain for making what she held to be false promises. She did, however, "feel something," "a strong sensation" while they were visiting Jean's village and thought that this also might have been her grandfather's village.

In this, the travelers tended to self-essentialize—that is, to look for a coincidence between being-in-itself and being-for-itself, by recovering what they saw as an intrinsic part of themselves of which they had had no prior knowledge nor experience. The search to fill this gap is not an intellectual decision, an "individual will-to-be" (Jackson 2005, xii) but rather a sensorial exploration via encounters with places and people. This is why the search was also largely based on the principle of seeking intersubjective encounters with people who would recognize the travelers for what they were: the coincidence of the for-oneself and for-the-other (Sartre 1969). This was Michel and Manoa's experience.

The practice of reconnecting is as experiential as it is epistemic. The travelers' quest largely relied on the principle of serendipity: "making discoveries, by accident and sagacity, of things which they were not in quest of" (Ginzburg 1992, 110). While the last part of the definition does not entirely apply to these travelers, whose aims were quite precise, it does describe how they sought to fulfil them. Serendipity lies at the core of the evidentiary paradigm that Ginzburg (1989) highlights. It is specifically based on infinitesimal traces that permit the comprehension of a deeper, otherwise unattainable reality: on signs and signals ("*spie*" in Ginzburg's original title), and on tracks. This type of evidentiary practice anchored in concrete, empirical experience differs from the Galilean natural science paradigm, which distrusts the experience of the senses and seeks to reconstitute the laws of the universe independently of material data through the abstract language of mathematics.

The difference between navigating and wayfinding corresponds to that between the Galilean and the evidentiary paradigms. Navigating involves a totalizing, objectifying relationship to space. It involves a series of successive decisions, each preceded by a mental calculation that necessitates a map. Wayfinding, however, is anchored in concrete experience; "like the perception of the environment in general, [it] proceeds along paths of observation" (Ingold 2011, 229). Prior knowledge is not a prerequisite: it is the notion of finding that is central. The wayfinder explores by constantly "monitoring . . . the 'feel' of the environment" (Ingold 2011, 239), while the navigator, like the Galilean physicist, is "professionally deaf to sounds and insensitive to tastes and odors" (Ginzburg 1992, 98). Wayfinding is also an evidentiary practice in the sense that it foregrounds narration.[10] "[To] follow a path is also to retrace one's steps, or the steps of one's predecessors" (Ingold 2011, 237): it is less a course from one spatial location to another than "a movement in time, more akin to playing music or storytelling then to reading a map" (Ingold 2011, 238). The travelers found their way to and in the villages by seeking to connect with their ancestors.

Mana: Establishing Connections

Alain related his own experience of returning to the source after his first visit to the ancestral temple in Pine Mansion in the following terms: "The important thing is the *mana*. I use Western words to help you understand [laughing]. In Hakka, it's *shengong*, mind and work, as in qigong. According to my grandmother's explanations, the *mana* is like the *qi* of Shaolin monks. That's what I came to understand from my grandmother. It is spiritual." Alain repeatedly referred to his ancestors' *mana* during the group's stay in China. According to Roger Keesing (1984, 148), the concept of *mana* was—and still is, one might add—involved in two types of circumstance among Polynesian peoples: the unpredictability of the results of human action in fishing, horticulture, war, and the curing of illness, and the inequality between human beings in their enterprises, rank, and access to divinities and spirits.

Alain's use of the term *mana* to describe his experience of meeting his Chinese ancestors is intriguing. One possible analysis, following Claude Lévi-Strauss (1950, xlix), is that he was making use of it as an empty signifier such as the colloquial French word for "thing" (*truc*, thingy, *mea* in Tahitian) whose function is to "oppose the absence of meaning." However, as Pascal Boyer (1990) points out, this analogy does not hold: *mana* is not used like the joker in a card game. Moreover, the word does not refer to an indefinable mystical concept. Boyer argues, against structuralist theory, that the use of terms such as *mana* are not derived from abstractions but on the contrary must be considered in situations of real communication and interaction. Such terms are characterized by the fact that they reveal a very specific learning process in which their broad definitional traits are replaced by memories of singular situations.

In the particular context of this journey to China, Alain had put himself in a position in which he could live the unique experience of meeting his ancestors. The distant memories of what his grandmother had told him were actualized (in the double sense of brought up to date and realized in experience) through this concrete, bodily experience of coming into contact with his ancestors' places of origin. The term that Alain used refers to mystical forces: *mana* in the sense of a force possessed by the ancestors in the common Polynesian sense and in the sense of the Chinese *qi*—life breath, vital energy. Alain said that in China, he could "breathe the *mana*" of his ancestors. There is nothing meaningless about this experience, in fact quite the opposite. Although the use of the terms *mana* and *qi* does evoke a rather vague representative content or relative indeterminacy of what is potentially experienced through contact with ancestors—breath, spirit, energy—at the same time, it delivers a strong expression, perhaps made deliberately salient by the intervention of a Polynesian term in the Chinese context, of

Alain's barely communicable subjective experience at the moment of establishing contact.

This does not exhaust Alain's explanation of his use of the Tahitian word *mana*, however. He speaks fluent French and good Hakka and understands some Tahitian. His description of *mana* as Western may come as a surprise, as we know that Alain, who married a Tahitian woman after his first marriage to a metropolitan Frenchwoman, is perfectly aware of the Polynesian origin of the term. In interlocution with me, as someone who knows Polynesia, it may be a form of syllogistic short circuit (French Polynesia being French, this Polynesian term is well known by the French and more broadly by Westerners who know Polynesia, and therefore by me). It would be presumptive to think that I play the role of the shaman that Eduardo Viveiros de Castro (2012, 3) assigns to the anthropologist as the only type of person who can mediate between different ontologies. Alain did this very well by himself. Still, it is noteworthy that de Castro leaves the possibility of intercultural communication based on similitude rather than incommensurability between ontologies open.

Alain repeatedly used the expression "breathing the *mana*." In some Polynesian settings, *mana* is a force rather than a substance (Keesing 1984) but the latter in Hawai'i, where *mana* is close to breath (Valeri 1985). *Qi* in Chinese means both energy and (life) breath. By using *breathing* and *mana* together, Alain was clearly making a syncretic correspondence (Bastide 1978, 395) between the Chinese *qi* and the Polynesian *mana*. The situation of communication is broader than the situation of interlocution with the anthropologist—it is also a situation of Alain's interlocution with himself to which I bore witness. Alain started becoming interested in genealogical matters after researching the family of his Tahitian wife to resolve a dispute about some land. I often heard from the Tahiti Chinese that they were imitating the Tahitians in carrying out this type of research (Trémon 2010, 256, 367). For those who are of both Chinese and Tahitian descent, the Tahitian line is often already known or traced, while the Chinese line is surrounded by mystery related to its interrupted transmission or ignorance of ancestry beyond the grandfather who first settled in Tahiti. For Alain, who is descended from Chinese lines on both his father's and his mother's side, there is no such asymmetry of knowledge, but there was a gap in the line of transmission, manifest in the fact that it was his maternal grandmother who had told him about the ancestors' *qi*. His father and paternal grandfather had died when Alain was still a child, and his grandfather had broken the link with his village of origin by departing with his wife against his parents' will and had never returned to China (see chapter 8). Alain's father had died in 1975 when Alain was thirty years old and living in Paris, where his three daughters from his first marriage were born. He returned to French Polynesia in the early 1980s and married his current Tahitian wife, with whom he has two more daughters.

While proceeding to a syncretic equivalence of these notions, Alain also builds an opposition that differentiates Polynesia and the West, as merged into a Franco-Polynesian entity, from a Chinese otherness. Alain's wording can then be understood as having the effect of Franco-Tahitianizing his Chinese ancestors. He is both Chinese, in that his ancestors are in China, and Franco-Polynesian, in that he lives far from China and has a Tahitian wife and French-speaking daughters living in Paris and Tahiti. The seemingly deliberate repetition of the word *mana* in China, which I did not recall hearing from Alain in Tahiti, closely resembles what Carlo Severi (2007, 266) calls a paradoxical statement—that is, the way in which, in a situation of cultural contact, a traditional shaman opposes Christianity by calling himself Christ. A paradoxical situation emerges here in which "to be similar to someone is to be very different from him, and vice versa" (Severi 2007, 267). It is a statement of diasporic identity that is less hybrid than it is contradictory.

In this respect, pragmatic use is made of *mana* to which the word lends itself particularly well, since the term is not only a noun but also a verb and expresses both a state of being and a state of action (Mauss 1972, 108). It designated the experience that Alain was finding difficult to put into words and that he was seeking through contact with his remote ancestors during his Chinese journey; his father and his grandfather, his closest ancestors, are buried in the Chinese cemetery in Tahiti. Alain was making a syncretic amalgamation of the Chinese term *ling*, which means "spirit" but essentially means ancestral magical power or efficacy, and the Tahitian equivalent, *mana*. Alain's use of the notion of *mana* pragmatically established, by speech act, a connection between his Chinese ancestors and his dwelling place in Tahiti.

For roots tourists, travel is both a continuation and a means of research and knowledge practices: looking up genealogies but also learning Mandarin at the Confucius Institute and reading about the history of the Hakkas. The search for knowledge about the village of origin and China is intended to bridge a gap. At the heart of the human condition lies the problem of "not being what one is," as Sartre puts it. In the context of diasporicity, being-in-diaspora, this fundamental tension takes on a specific dimension of being torn between the sentiment of belonging to a faraway place and the past and at the same time being estranged from them. Not all descendants of Chinese migrants who identify themselves as Chinese experience this tension in this way, and some do not experience it at all; for this reason, it is important to maintain a distinction between identification as an ethnic Chinese and identification as part of the Chinese diaspora. Still, diasporic or roots tourism is often undertaken as a means of bridging the gap resulting from lack of knowledge about the village of origin and the culture of one's forebears that is variously the consequence of an absence of familial transmission, the premature death of parents, assimilation policies, the dispersal of kin as a result of migration, and troubled historical circumstances.

The members of the group all shared the same wish to reconnect with something they felt they had been deprived of, and therefore the journey itself was apprehended and even deliberately constructed as a set of enigmas to be deciphered. The considerable extent of improvisation during the journey was the result of this paradoxical will to surrender to chance. The serendipitous search for tracks based on the evidentiary collection of clues shaped a way of traveling that left open as many possibilities as possible. The search was as sensorial as it was intellectual, anchored in the bodily experience of groping forward, and included tasting local food as well as unexpected meetings with old buildings and living people. Through this experience, the travelers sought to refamiliarize themselves with something unknown, to recover something they considered they had once had or should have had. During the journey, what was little known or unknown became at least partly familiar *again*, and this is why the journey in search of one's roots is experienced as a return: it allows for an experiential recovery of knowledge, a refamiliarization. It is in the course of travel that what one has been estranged from becomes familiar *again*.

8

GLOBAL BROTHERHOOD WITHOUT CLOSE KIN

In the two decades following the reopening of China in 1979, overseas Chinese visitors were generally made welcome by the Qiaoban and Qiaolian liaison authorities, government and semi-government offices, respectively, that actively courted them. Madeleine Hsu (2000, 185) concludes her historical study of emigration from Taishan to the United States with the observation that ties between the emigrant communities and the overseas relatives had loosened. The large sign welcoming overseas visitors installed in front of Taishan City's main bus station in 1978 was removed in 1994 (Hsu 2000, 16), reflecting a change that I noticed myself during my stay in French Polynesia in 2013 when Tahiti Chinese showed me photographs of their trips to Shenzhen. Among those taken in the 1980s and 1990s, many show groups of travelers posing with village officials under a red-and-yellow banner welcoming overseas compatriots. This type of welcome is far less common in Shenzhen today.

In 2012, the Miaoyun Qiaolian office produced and published the book *One Hundred Years of Overseas Affairs* (*Bainian qiaoshi*). Like another official publication, *Encountering Miaoyun* (*Xiangfeng Miaoyun*), issued in 2005 by another subdistrict office, it depicts Miaoyun as a homeland of overseas Chinese, recounts the history of emigration, and portrays successful emigrants. It includes a group photograph taken during the visit of the president of the People's Republic of China (PRC), Jiang Zemin, to Tahiti in 2001 in which I recognize many of the Polynesian heads of Tahiti's overseas Chinese associations (Trémon 2010, 287). This stopover on Jiang Zemin's journey to Chile was the culmination of a series of visits to French Polynesia by high-profile Chinese officials as part of the PRC's

187

effort to reestablish ties with its overseas Chinese communities, and added to the Tahitian Chinese's collective reputation, already cemented by their generous support for village projects in China. A Pine Mansion Chen, Fuchang, sits beside President Jiang in the photograph. The prestige drawn by their overseas relatives from their proximity to the highest Chinese authorities spills over to Pine Mansion, as the inclusion of this photograph in the locally published book testifies.

However, besides these connections at the highest level, the village owes its reputation to the fact that compared to the surrounding former emigration villages, it has the largest number of emigrants and descendants of emigrants. The local community derives prestige from its many relatives overseas and their economic success. Lineage members hope that their ancestor will provide them with not only economic prosperity but also numerous descendants; large demographics are themselves a source of prestige. This was noticeable in the number of times proud Pine Mansioners and admiring inhabitants of neighboring villages told me how many of them come back to Pine Mansion for ancestral worship. When I first met the former village head Chen Shengyu in 2011, he declared, "The descendants of the ancestor Zhenneng of Pine Mansion, I think they are all over the world. . . . Of course, I wouldn't dare to say this myself: in fact, it is the *huaqiao* who, when they come back, say the Zhenneng lineage of Pine Mansion is global [*ba quanqiu*, literally 'dominates the whole world']."

This final chapter examines the ambivalence in the diasporic relationship, which lies in prejudice and misunderstandings about moral expectations (chapter 5) and about religious traditionalism (chapter 6), but also and perhaps more fundamentally in the tension between the global scale on which kinship with distant overseas relatives is located and the difficulty of maintaining ties when there is no longer a close kin relationship. One the one hand, this global scale is the scale at which the state liaises with the descendants of emigrants who are no longer Chinese nationals and is based on a rhetoric of blood ties, while on the other hand, it is the global scale of lineage kinship itself, which confers prestige on the local inhabitants of the former lineage villages. Both are based on a similar rhetoric of global brotherhood and eternal loyalty, and both are at odds with "practical kinship" between close kin (Bourdieu 1977). This tension between the global scalar ideal and practical close kinship is intrinsic to the lineage itself and is also homologous with that at the level of the Chinese state between the discourse on global kinship in the ethnic sense and its limitation by citizenship regimes' jurisdiction.

I examine the first dimension with a focus on the ambivalence that characterizes the Qiaolian, whose action and position is not only ambiguous but also changing due to its nature as a civic organization subordinated to the Chinese state and therefore obliged to speak in accordance with the Chinese government's position on the diaspora. A long interview with the chairman of the Qiaolian in October 2013 and a second visit the following year with the Tahitian travelers gave me the opportunity not only to assess the difficulties facing the Qiaolian, which he did not seek to hide, but also to observe the reception of visitors from overseas in practice.[1] This encounter confirmed what the Qiaolian had stated about the contradictions he faces, while also showing how he and his coworkers actively seek kinship ties, albeit with difficulty, to overcome these contradictions.

Building on Maurice Freedman's insights into lineage kinship, I attempt to open up new directions in the light of Marshall Sahlins's (2013) reflections on the "kinship I." Using observational material on the emigrants' descendants' visits to the village, I show how despite lineage leaders' rhetoric of global brotherhood interactions between locals and visitors from overseas are limited by the latter's absence of close kin. I conclude by returning to Sahlins's notion of "mutuality of being" and "mutuality of existence" and suggest that the two terms should be differentiated. It is the built-in tension within lineage kinship, the dialectics between public and private kin, that form the basis of the ambivalence experienced by diasporic visitors, who feel a sense of both global belonging and estrangement.

Impossible Bureaucratic Indifference

At the Miaoyun Qiaolian, I met President Chen Yunxiang and his employee, Ms. Weng. He asked me if I was an overseas Chinese and then if my book on the Tahiti overseas community had been published in Chinese. He pointed to a reproduction of a photograph of Chin Foo, the most famous of the Tahitian Chinese, in the book entitled *One Hundred Years of Overseas Affairs* (2012), which had just been released by the Qiaolian.[2] Chen Yunxiang and Ms. Weng are both from Yanghe, a village not far north of Pine Mansion. The Yanghe Chens form a separate lineage founded by a cousin of the Pine Mansion Chens' founding ancestor, Zhenneng. Chen Yunxiang showed me the genealogy (*zupu*) of the Yanghe Chens, which roughly follows the same format as that of Pine Mansion and is very similar to it, although much less substantial, suggesting that the Yanghe Chens' demographics are lower than those of the Pine Mansion Chens'. He also showed me pictures of their ancestral temple and the graves of their ancestors in Wuhua in the northeast of the province, where the founding ancestors of the Pine Mansion and the Yanghe Chens were born. He mentioned that about forty overseas Chinese return to Yanghe each year from Malaysia, Canada, and England for their founding ancestor's birthday.

He started to paint a picture of the organization: the whole interview oscillating between the subjective tone he used when speaking of his village and his involvement with overseas matters and a more impersonal and bureaucratic tone when explaining the laws and principles regarding these matters. He clarified that a distinction must be made between the Office of Overseas Affairs (the Qiaoban), a government entity, and the overseas liaison association, the Qiaolian, a civic organization (*minjian*). "However," he added, "they have common goals." Chen Yunxiang heads both organizations at the subdistrict level, his two functions printed on either side of his business card.[3] He had succeeded Chen Deqi, the vice president of the Zhenneng Foundation. The presidency rotates among the eight members of the board, which includes two Chen representatives of Pine Mansion: Deqi and the Hong Konger Xingchang, who were the vice president and president of the lineage foundation at that time. According to Chen Yunxiang, Pine Mansion and Yanghe predominate with two seats each because they stand out among the fifteen urbanized villages in Miaoyun with their large number of overseas Chinese: "The numbers of overseas Chinese [*Huaqiao*], dependents of relatives overseas [*qiaoshu*] and compatriots from Hong Kong and Macao [*gang'ao tongbao*] are relatively high compared with the rest of Miaoyun. Therefore, these are called central communities [*zhongdian shequ*]."

One Hundred Years of Overseas Affairs briefly presents the Qiaolian's history. The very first liaison association was founded in Bao'an County in 1950, abolished in 1954, and reintroduced in 1979, reflecting the chronology of the national bodies responsible for relations between China and the overseas Chinese. After coming to power in 1949, the Chinese Communist Party (CCP) maintained the Overseas Chinese Affairs Commission (OCAC) created by the previous nationalist Kuomintang government. However, the CCP had little experience in matters relating to overseas Chinese. It had called on them for financial assistance in the war effort against the Japanese occupation (1937–45), paying little attention to their specific problems (Fitzgerald 1972, 10).[4] After 1949, the nationalist government of the Republic of China in Taiwan put overseas Chinese at the forefront of its foreign policy while the CCP in mainland China focused on domestic problems. The administrative bodies for overseas Chinese in the PRC focused almost entirely on the national territory and returning overseas Chinese, and the OCAC had little direct contact with Chinese people living abroad (Fitzgerald 1972, 26; Wang 1991, 220). Having enjoyed privileged status from 1954 to 1957, organizations representing overseas Chinese in the PRC were then overlooked or even suspected of anti-communism due to their members' "capitalist" backgrounds. With the Cultural Revolution of 1966, this suspicion led to the harass-ment and persecution of the organizations' leaders and, more generally, of returned overseas Chinese and families with relatives overseas. The OCAC, re-named the State Council's Overseas Chinese Affairs Office (OCAO), or Qiao-ban, in 1954 was then abolished.

On September 29, 1977, at the very start of China's reforms, Deng Xiaoping announced that overseas Chinese affairs should be incorporated into the govern-ment's work plan. Two months later, the OCAO leader prior to the Cultural Revo-lution reentered the political arena and announced the abolition of the policies implemented after 1966 that persecuted Chinese overseas and their relatives in the PRC (Thunø 2001, 911). The Qiaolian was reestablished at central government level in 1978, followed by the restoration of some two thousand bodies in twenty-nine provinces, municipalities, and autonomous districts, and eight thousand af-filiated organizations at the county and village levels which were classified as qiaoxiang (see chapter 1). The Miaoyun Qiaolian was reestablished in 1982. Yunxiang's grandfather had migrated to Malaysia, and his father was a returnee. The fact that the sons of emigrants and returnees such as Chen Deqi and Chen Yunxiang were now presiding over the Miaoyun Qiaolian is a further sign of the return to grace in the 1980s of those who had suffered discrimination or even persecution due to their overseas connections (see chapter 3).

In the authorities' view, attracting remittances and investment from overseas depended on securing the status of those likely to receive and channel them. Re-mittances were therefore once again allowed as legal income, even when they were used to finance expensive funerals and ancestral worship rituals. However, in the late 1980s, the initial surge of foreign direct investment from Chinese people outside China declined sharply following the Tiananmen Square massa-cre in 1989. This led to a significant shift away from dependents and returnees (Thunø 2001, 921). A new policy was announced in May 1989 at the National Meeting on Chinese Overseas Affairs. It consisted of a transition from passive anticipation of resources that could be drained from Chinese citizens with rela-tives overseas to active cultivation of links with emigrants and the descendants of emigrants.

This new line broke away from the caution hitherto exercised and the care taken, mainly due to China's diplomatic ties with Southeast Asian countries, to distinguish between Chinese citizens and the descendants of Chinese nationals who did not have Chinese citizenship. The 1989 conference document shows that ethnic Chinese (huaren) are seen as closely linked to China by race and culture. Although the policy of liaison with the overseas Chinese was once again re-oriented in the mid-1990s (see chapter 1), the ethnicizing rhetoric has remained.

The long tirade that Chair Chen Yunxiang addressed to me revealed how he experiences the state's double categorization of overseas Chinese as legal foreigners and distant kin as a dilemma:

> The migrants who have left this area to [settle all over the] world still have their roots here: their place of origin [*ji*] has not changed. But now they and their descendants have become ethnic Chinese [*huaren*]. They are not Chinese citizens but foreigners. Now in the policy that is being implemented there is this differentiation [between citizens and foreigners]. How then can I say that overseas Chinese are "relatives" [*qinqi*]? There is this guiding principle. There is this separation. . . . They are not Chinese citizens; they are foreigners. However, [they are] all Chinese by blood [*xuetong*]. When they come back, we welcome them. They are relatives. They love the homeland; China is the country of their ancestors. Their countries of residence are the US, Canada, England, France, Germany, Malaysia. Their identity card has changed; they are no longer Chinese citizens, but by blood they are. If you come back, we welcome you [*huanyin*]. But there are differences in the services we provide for you. . . . Politics comes into play. But relatives can, if they have time, come back to see the old home [*laojia*], travel around, visit relatives. You can come and take a look at China's changes, feel affected. . . . However, [this] should not be confused with affairs of government, which must make distinctions. So we do not deal with the ethnic Chinese. They are [within the purview of] Yanghe, Pine Mansion villages. The two [policy] areas are not the same.

Chen Yunxiang's use of opposing statements ("they are foreigners," "however, all are Chinese by blood") highlights the tension in the government's separation of citizens and noncitizens among people that he thinks should all be considered blood relatives. The Republic of China's 1929 Nationality Law based on the principle of jus sanguinis introduced in 1909 initially remained in force in the PRC after 1949. However, this was inconsistent with China's quest for diplomatic recognition and threatened to exacerbate tension with Southeast Asian states. The PRC's policy therefore gradually shifted away from the principle of jus sanguinis, and from 1958 onward, its "three goods" (nationality, noninterference, and restoration) policy clarified its position: the government stated its wish to see overseas Chinese take the nationality of their countries of residence. This culminated in the Nationality Law of September 10, 1980, which renounced jus sanguinis (article 5) and excluded the possibility of dual nationality for any Chinese national (article 3), revoking Chinese nationality automatically in the event of voluntary or involuntary acquisition of the nationality of another country (article 9). It should be noted, however, that special provisions apply to citizens of Hong Kong and Macao, who do not automatically lose their Chinese nationality when they acquire another nationality, although they are expected to renounce it. If they do not do this, however, they remain Chinese nationals.[5]

According to Michael Herzfeld (1992, 10–11), the rationale behind bureaucratic identity management can be understood as a reflection of a sacred national order: bureaucratic actions are the rites of nationalism as religion. In spite of the rationalism of the state bureaucracy, national symbols and notions of blood are at play in the "social production of indifference" of street-level bureaucrats to non-ethnic non-nationals. Conversely here, the ethnicized nationalist discourse that categorizes the Chinese in China and overseas as *huaren*, which maintains a savvy ambiguity, legitimizes the impossibility for a state bureaucrat of welcoming them with complete indifference. The Chinese authorities are not always so clear in practice and deploy an active policy of liaising with Chinese communities overseas, including the overwhelming majority who have changed their nationality, as in the case of Tahiti (Trémon 2009, 2010). The state official Chen Yunxiang articulated the impossibility of producing such indifference: rational bureaucratic treatment would require them to treat overseas Chinese who do not have Chinese nationality as foreigners, which is very difficult when visiting overseas Chinese are both foreigners by law and relatives by blood, albeit distant ones.

The status of Miaoyun's Qiaolian as a local paragovernmental organization is even more ambivalent. It must follow the state line of preferential treatment of overseas Chinese nationals and "bureaucratic indifference" (Herzfeld 1992) toward those who have taken the nationality of their host countries. However, this is not easy in practice, as shown by the use of the first-person plural and the affirmative phrase "We welcome them" in Yunxiang's speech. This difficulty is not only due to the fact that the people of the Qiaolian are representatives of the emigrant villages; there is also a moral obligation to welcome overseas Chinese that, despite the governmental imperative, is difficult to resist when meeting kinsfolk.

"Let's Be Relatives!"

Although the Qiaolian is supposed to deal only with matters related to overseas Chinese nationals and not those who have taken the nationality of their country of residence, Chen Yunxiang indicates at the end of the quote that "the ethnic Chinese" are within the purview of former villages such as Yanghe and Pine Mansion. This suggests a division of tasks between the civic sphere (*minjian*)—the urban community (the former villages)—and the Qiaolian as part of the state apparatus operating at the subdistrict level.⁶ The positioning of the Qiaolian is delicate, as it is both a civic and a paragovernmental organization due to its administrative counterpart, the Qiaoban. The walls of the Qiaolian office are lined with photographs of delegations from overseas and of the annual meetings organized by the Qiaolian that bring returnees (*guiqiao*) together for New Year's Day and the Mid-Autumn Festival. Until the early 2000s, the village Qiaolian carried out these ceremonial functions. The Miaoyun Qiaolian still organizes receptions for emigrants, particularly those from Canada, with money to invest, but such official ceremonies are no longer coordinated at the former village level. This reflects the reorientation of liaison policy toward strategic business partnerships rather than simply reconnection with overseas relatives, as in the first two decades of the reform and opening era (chapter 1). Visits from overseas Chinese who are merely interested in spending an afternoon in their village of origin, especially now that travel to and within China has become so much easier than before, do not involve official channels. Although the Qiaolian's raison d'être is welcoming overseas Chinese and its field of action concerns relations between villages and villagers and people living overseas, these relations are mainly based on family ties maintained at the lower, civic level in the former villages and therefore escape its purview.

Added to this is the ambiguity around what the Qiaolian can actually do to assist overseas Chinese. Chen Yunxiang described the gist of its work as helping overseas Chinese with their quests, "for example, when they're looking for their ancestors' houses or searching for their roots." Yet, on real estate issues in particular, it can only inform overseas visitors of the existing legal provisions and has no means of making decisions on such matters. As an organization associated with its state counterpart, the Qiaoban, the Qiaolian is supposed to use government terminology and inform the public about the law when, for instance, people ask for assistance with the procedure necessary to get their house back. "So we look at how the house was passed on, if they haven't taken care of it for a long time, if it's used by relatives or other people, and we help them understand, we explain it to them." Chen Yunxiang refers here to the obstacles that overseas Chinese meet when claiming ownership and their difficulty in accepting that in most cases, they cannot claim back what is no longer considered theirs. In David's case, the native villagers considered him the legitimate heir of his father's house, and although his brothers, sisters, and cousins in Tahiti could all have claimed part of the property, he did not feel bad about claiming it for himself, as the house was tiny and he did so in order to be able to transfer its ownership to his remote Chinese cousins. Such ownership can be secured, but only if an overseas visitor can find people to act as witnesses in their favor. There are many stories of conflict between overseas Chinese and mainlanders over real estate.

In Tahiti, I met the Hong Kong–based second-degree niece of a set of six sisters aged seventy to eighty-five who originated from a village in Longgang. Two had been sent to live in their father's house during the 1940s and 1950s before they fled back to Tahiti. In China, they had lived with their father's first wife and an aunt who had come back from Tahiti with them with her two daughters and an adopted half-Tahitian son. After their half-Tahitian cousin's death, their Hong Kong niece, a lawyer, filed a claim to ownership of the house, but that cousin's son claimed to "have never had any connection with them" and even to have "no overseas connections whatsoever." Without his testimony, they were unable to prove that their father, who had emigrated to Tahiti in the late 1910s and had remained there all his life, had built the house.

The Qiaolian is expected to act as a gatekeeper, explaining Chinese law to overseas claimants but is unable to act on their behalf. It can only lend support when all the legal certificates required to prove ownership of a property have been secured, as happened in Fuchang's case. Ms. Weng, a Qiaolian employee, mentioned that she had dealt with him on a real estate matter: before his death, he had taken all the necessary steps to secure the transmission of his property to his son and grandchildren who live in Tahiti, who showed me the certificate of transfer of ownership.

Chen Yunxiang, Ms. Weng, and the book *One Hundred Years of Overseas Affairs* all describe the Qiaolian as an organization that connects and welcomes overseas Chinese. In reality, it does not devote a large proportion of its time to these activities. Andy, a student at Shenzhen University who originates from Tahiti, is Ms. Weng's sister's son, and his father is one of the rare third-generation French Polynesian Chinese who has married a Chinese wife. He told me that his aunt's job mainly consists of collecting money from the Qiaolian's tenants and depositing it in the bank. Andy spoke from a French viewpoint when he commented that he found this surprising, as such associations are normally nonprofit. His remark made me smile because the Chinese associations in Tahiti operate in exactly the same way: Tahiti Chinese and Shenzhen associations derive income from the buildings they own. The Qiaolian headquarters were built in 1982, the year it was reestablished in Miaoyun, and its income is derived from renting out the building's other floors.

Chen Yunxiang, Ms. Weng, and the other two Qiaolian employees all originate from the Miaoyun area and therefore have fairly extensive knowledge of the different local villages and their emigrants. Ms. Weng, who is married to a Yanghe Chen and comes from a nearby village, prides herself on "being acquainted with the thirty natural villages" (*zirancun*, subdivisions of the old villages) that make up Miaoyun. This knowledge of the surnames and the languages—Hakka and Cantonese—spoken in the villages allows them to help overseas Chinese in search of lost relatives or their forebears' villages: "All they have to do is give us the characters of the name of the place and we know right away" (see chapter 7).

The Pine Mansion workstation employee Chen Guanqiu led the Tahitian visitors to the Qiaolian in Miaoyun at their request. Throughout their stay in Pine Mansion, Guanqiu was Alain's main contact, and Alain visited him almost daily for advice and assistance. Guanqiu's attitude was noteworthy: on the one hand, he seemed willing to act as the main contact for travelers in the village, receiving them in his office without reservation, responding to their requests concerning, for example, transport to David's village (chapter 7); on the other hand, he behaved more like an escort or even one of the travelers than as a guide. He did not suggest possible places to visit. During the visit to David's village, he attended the discussion with the village officials and witnessed David's meeting with his cousins and his discovery of his grandfather's house. Throughout the visit, he photographed not only David's fellow travelers and cousins but also the village itself, its workstation, and its old houses with their tiled roofs and towers (*diaolou*). In this respect, he seemed to be taking advantage of the opportunity to become a visitor himself rather than to play an active role as a mediator; as it turned out (see below), he did this for publicity.

On the one hand, this attitude was the result of Guanqiu's functions as a social affairs officer (*shehui shiwu*), which cover a wide range of different areas including all matters related to what is "foreign" and potentially dangerous: he keeps records of returned overseas Chinese and, in the same set of binders, records of Taiwanese companies operating in Pine Mansion's urban community and a register of the populations of Pine Mansion's Chinese minority groups such as the Uighur Muslims (there were two Uighur families running noodle restaurants at the time of my fieldwork). Guanqiu is himself a Chen with overseas connections, as his brother-in-law has emigrated to the United Kingdom. With the workstation not a government body but an outpost for the local administration of municipal policy, Guanqiu's conduct reflects the double ambivalence mentioned by the president of the Qiaolian regarding the level at which overseas relatives should be hosted, within the civic sphere of former villages or the state sphere of the subdistrict, and their treatment as foreigners or kin. I noted some hesitance in Guanqiu's attitude as to whether it was appropriate to welcome visiting overseas Chinese. Unlike in the 1980s, when the village Qiaolian team, headed by Chen Tailai, organized official receptions for groups of overseas Chinese, nothing special was organized for the travelers I was accompanying, although their presence was acknowledged at the ancestor's birthday celebration (chapter 6). On the other hand, Guanqiu's photographs of the travelers were made public after they left: I saw them posted on the billboards next to the village workstation in 2017. This is part of the more general trend toward patrimonialization discussed earlier regarding the mausoleum, which has been designated a heritage spot, and the categorization of overseas Chinese as belonging to the past (chapters 4 and 6).

Guanqiu did not contact the Miaoyun Qiaolian on his own initiative, although he readily did so as soon as Alain expressed this wish.[7] He drove Alain and two other members of the group, René and André, to the meeting. President Yunxiang, who had just retired, was absent and we were met by Ms. Weng and two male members of staff. Ms. Weng was unaware that the visitors were from Tahiti and looked pleasantly surprised when she learned where they came from, as her sister is married to a Tahiti Chinese and lives in French Polynesia. The conversation, which I present here almost in full, reflects how the Qiaolian employees attempted to overcome the dilemma in which they were caught by welcoming the visitors as potential kin, devoting a large part of the conversation to searching for mutual relations in spite of the considerable language difficulties. Ms. Weng speaks both Hakka and Mandarin and the two male employees speak only Mandarin, which only René among the travelers understands well and speaks fairly proficiently. Only Alain and René of all the travelers in the group speak Hakka, although not fluently as they do not speak it on a daily basis.

> Ms. WENG (IN MANDARIN): Are you from Malaysia?
>
> ALAIN (IN HAKKA): No, from Tahiti. I'm a Pine Mansion Chen.
>
> Ms. WENG (IN HAKKA AND MANDARIN): Oh! Tahiti! Tahiti! Sit down, sit down, sit down!
>
> EMPLOYEE 1 (IN MANDARIN TO Ms. WENG): Isn't your grandmother a Chen?
>
> Ms. WENG (IN HAKKA): Yes, my grandmother! [*Ah po*]
>
> [. . . Guanqiu mentions the ancestor's birthday]
>
> ALAIN (IN HAKKA): People in Tahiti are not aware that there is a Qiaolian in Miaoyun. My grandfather went to Tahiti in 1911—
>
> GUANQIU (INTERRUPTING IN MANDARIN): The people in Tahiti number three thousand to four thousand; that's a lot. (He laughs and remains with his mouth wide open, looking stunned.) In Pine Mansion, the Chen are about 1,500, less than in Tahiti!
>
> Ms. WENG (IN HAKKA): My sister is in Tahiti.
>
> ALAIN (IN HAKKA): Who is your sister married to?
>
> Ms. WENG (IN HAKKA): Her husband is from Fonggong. His name is Huang [pronounced Wong in Hakka].
>
> ALAIN: Oh! Oh!
>
> Ms. WENG (IN HAKKA): They call him Ah Bing over there. He opened a business called *ngia ngia fong*.

ALAIN (IN HAKKA): Do you have a picture? Maybe if I see his face . . . (They get up and go to Ms. Weng's desk.)

Ms. WENG (IN MANDARIN TO ME AND ALAIN): They run a store. Tahiti is small, maybe you know it. The one in the middle is my brother-in-law.

ALAIN (IN HAKKA): Do you have a picture of the store? The name of the store?

Ms. WENG (IN MANDARIN): I don't know the French name. I know that in Chinese it's [in Hakka] *ngia ngia fong.*

ALAIN: *Ngia ngia fong.*

Ms. WENG (IN HAKKA): The shop sign isn't written in Chinese, but I know it's *ngia ngia fong.*

ALAIN (IN HAKKA): I'll only be able to read it in French.

Ms. WENG (IN MANDARIN): His son Andy has just left Shenzhen: he graduated. We Skype a lot. I'll call him.

ALAIN (IN HAKKA): All right.

[Alain and I discuss which French family name could be derived from the name Huang. Ms. Weng tells Alain that I met her nephew Andy last year.]

Ms. WENG (IN MANDARIN): What time is it there?

ME (IN FRENCH): Alain, what time is it in Tahiti?

ALAIN (IN FRENCH AND HAKKA): Five o'clock in the afternoon.

Ms. WENG (IN MANDARIN): Maybe they're still at the store.

[Ms. Weng makes the call on Skype, but no one answers.]

ALAIN (IN HAKKA): I want to share a concern with you: it is that the Tahiti overseas Chinese (*huaqiao*) don't know that there is a Qiao-lian in Miaoyun. . . . Maybe it would be possible to do something to make the Qiaolian known to the Tahitian *huaqiao*?

EMPLOYEE 2 (IN MANDARIN): Our Qiaolian is like a bridge, its role is to build bridges, so [in English] OK! OK!

ALAIN (IN HAKKA): Wouldn't that be a good thing?

GUANQIU (IN MANDARIN): I will give you the contacts.

Ms. WENG (IN MANDARIN): We can Skype; we can exchange emails.

EMPLOYEE 1 (IN MANDARIN): People here can't speak Hakka well any-more. They can't speak English either.

[They talk about how to maintain the relationship.]

Ms. WENG (IN MANDARIN): We've already had contact, with Fuchang. . . . You are welcome next time. . . . We have to reconnect. [In Hakka] We only have Fuchang's contact details.

ALAIN (IN HAKKA): Fuchang died at around the age of ninety.

RENÉ (IN MANDARIN): The Chen gatherings in Tahiti take place every year, the name Chen has an association, at these festivals people talk. If [they know that] there is a Qiaolian, they can connect with it . . . , we could do something to keep in touch.

[One of the two employees says he cannot read the email address Alain has given him and asks him to rewrite it in capital letters.]

ALAIN (IN FRENCH AND THEN IN HAKKA, INDICATING ANDRÉ): His mother is from Yanghe.

EMPLOYEE 1 (IN MANDARIN, POINTING TO THE OTHER EMPLOYEE): He is from Yanghe! You have the same ancestors [tong zuzong]. Give them a genealogy. We have to look for . . .

[Everyone is talking at the same time.]

ALAIN (IN HAKKA): Do you have any sisters to marry? [Laughs]

RENÉ (IN MANDARIN): Everywhere he asks, "Do you have a younger sister?" [Laughs]

Ms. WENG (IN MANDARIN): Come on! Let's be relatives [zuo qinqi le ba]! [Laughs]

Further conversation followed about the fact that the new generation no longer speaks Hakka and about the travelers' schedule. At noon, Ms. Weng suggested going for lunch—she asked Alain if they dared to eat dog—and then to visit Baopuchi's old village center in the afternoon. I did not attend the lunch and learned that they eventually visited a chinaware factory in another village.

This scene reveals the extent to which communication between representatives of the older Chinese diaspora, third-generation descendants of migrants, and contemporary inhabitants of the villages of origin is hindered by language: Hakka is used increasingly rarely in both China and French Polynesia. The name of Ms. Weng's brother-in-law's store in Tahiti, which she gave in Hakka and should be easily recognizable, all Tahiti's shopkeepers being known in the rather small Chinese community, could not be identified despite all their efforts. Even when Tahiti's Chinese stores have a Chinese name, they are primarily known by a French name or sometimes one mixing French and English such as Tropique Shop.

In spite of the language barrier, the conversation flowed easily. The participants did not seem to make a particular effort to either maintain the verbal interchange or avoid awkward silences. From a Goffmanian perspective, this was made possible by the fact that they all agreed on the "definition of the situation" (Goffman 1972): that the conversation was contributing to the aim of establishing of a connection between the Qiaolian and the Tahitian Chinese community. Yet, although there was clearly something of a ritual procedure in the way they were making contact, the interactional order did not so much entail face work—that is, maintaining one another's face—as the day-to-day interactions analyzed by Goffman. It was a collective effort of total strangers meeting for the first time to talk as if they were related based on the postulation that this must somehow be the case. This meeting illustrates the tension involved in the categorization of overseas Chinese as both foreigners and kin, which the Qiaolian employees pragmatically overcame by welcoming them hospitably and seeking kinship relationships. They even created them performatively, with the joke, which is also a speech act, "Let's be relatives!" The hortative construction "let us" is translated from the Chinese particle *ba*, but Ms. Weng's sentence already underscores the performativity of creating kinship via a speech act, as she literally says, "Let's do relatives" (*zuo qinqi le ba*). In addition, this first encounter involved looking for common acquaintances (Fuchang, Ms. Weng's brother-in-law) as well as hinting at potential family ties between Alain and Ms. Weng, whose grandmother was a Chen, and between André and the employee from Yanghe.[8] I explore these elements of the interactional procedure later, as they occurred in several encounters between the travelers and the locals.

Public and Private Kinship

Maurice Freedman's work has had a lasting influence on sinology and the anthropology of China. Until Freedman, sinological scholarship had a functionalist approach according to which the lineage community is the result of rules. Freedman introduced "the notion that the lineage was essentially a corporation, that is to say, a body that had a clear idea of membership and was able to hold property" (Faure 2007, 1). The lineage came to be defined as a corporation for which common descent was an essential feature of membership. However, in Freedman's view, descent does not constitute an autonomous logic; he argues that political and economic power account for the formation of lineage corporations (Freedman 1966, 39). Freedman (1958, 37) is thus careful to distinguish between lineages as corporate groups and the Chinese kinship system as a set of ideas. He emphasizes the difference between agnatic descent as an ideology legitimizing the formation of corporate descent groups and descent as the genealogical process by which such groups are formed (Freedman 1966, 30–31, 41–42).

Freedman (1970, 163–88) consistently criticizes the common misconception that the lineage is essentially an extension of the family. His analysis of the two different modes of ancestor worship, one oriented toward the common ancestors of the lineage as a whole or of a lineage branch and the other toward one's close ancestors, which he terms communal and domestic worship, respectively, are particularly valuable for understanding relations between the diaspora and the village of origin. In chapter 4, I introduced a distinction between public and private kinship. With this terminology, I am not suggesting that they are mutually exclusive, separate, and opposable domains. The Chinese anthropologist Fei Xiaotong argues that Chinese social relationships form a network of concentric circles around ego and are highly elastic. The number of people likely to be included in the kin category is indefinite, varying according to life circumstances and an individual's social properties. In such a mode of differential association (*chaxu geju*), the difference between private and public is always relative rather than absolute (Fei 1992, 69–70; see also King 1995). Lineage, or public kinship, relates all those who claim descent from a common ancestor. In China, this can be extended to all bearers of a common surname, but in the context of the lineage village, it includes all those who consider themselves descendants of the local founding ancestor.

The descent group is composed of agnates: men and women related by blood ties—a term often used is *xuemai*, blood vessels—through the male side. Although it includes women whose fathers are Chens, the emphasis is on fraternal kinship between the men, encapsulated in the Hakka expression *shuba kongdi* (*shubo xiongdi* in Mandarin), which means "younger uncle, elder uncle, elder brother, younger brother." This expression is a way of naming the relationship between uncles and nephews, brothers and cousins without specifying the exact nature of the relationship and bringing them back to a bond of brotherhood. For instance, when a man said upon meeting me that he knew Fuchang of Tahiti, I asked him to specify the relationship and he answered evasively, "We are *shubo xiongdi*." Two other expressions are more usually employed in the context of kin relations between members of the same branch: *tangxiongdi*, branch brothers, and *tangjiemei*, branch sisters, referring to second- and third-degree cousins.

Kinship terms make a distinction between lineage kinship, which is framed in the language of brotherhood and sisterhood, and close kinship, for which terms such as family members (*jiaren*; see chapter 5) and relatives (*qinqi*) are used. There is also a clear differentiation between common and more immediate ancestors, the latter being referred to by the widespread expression "own ancestors," *ziji de zuxian*. In circumstances where there could be confusion, people explicitly make the distinction, for instance by saying a "lineage relative, not a close relative" (*tangde, bu shi qinde*; see chapter 1).

Lineage kinship refers to ties beyond the realm of one's own immediate kin and branch. Richard Madsen (1984, 56), in his study of a single-lineage village in the same area as Pine Mansion in the Mao period, remarked that in the case of an external threat to the village, "a Confucian mode of moral reasoning . . . could lead people to conclude that they ought to sacrifice the narrow 'private' interests of their immediate families and closest neighbors for the good of a larger public group."

Freedman identifies this tension between common and individual kinship ties in his analysis of what he modelizes as the two opposing poles of the ancestral cult: geomantic burial practices—the self-interested desire to profit from the geomantic positioning of one's close ancestor's burial site—and communal ancestor worship. The accent in the first is on selfish interest, individualism, and competition and in the second, on the supremacy of the common good, harmony, unity, and collective behavior (Freedman 1966, 141, 143). Yet, the British structuralist preoccupation with descent groups has led him to overlook the implications of the tension between these two in the historical unfolding of lineage village political life. He sees the tension as structural, deriving from the lineage's tendency to segment into branches based on the fundamental principle of equal inheritance between brothers.

Such an approach, however, tends to overlook the historical dimension of the lineage as a unit that is the result of collective action and a political resource, although Freedman (1966) does stress the fundamental political dimension of lineage genealogies as a "blueprint for political action." As Steven Sangren (1984) cogently argues, Freedman's close association of estate formation with patrilineal inheritance resulted in the conflation of process or function (the transmission of property) and form (lineage corporations). Freedman sees other kinds of ancestral estate formation such as fusion (Cohen 1969) and aggregation (Pasternak 2002) merely as departures from the standard segmentary form through inheritance (Sangren 1984, 393).

This conflation of form and process hinders examination of the historical connections between them (Sangren 1984, 395). As chapter 4 has shown, several elements suggest that although there has been a tendency of the lineage to segment or divide into smaller segments for which later ancestors serve as reference points and nodes of identification, as emphasized by Freedman, there has also been a countertendency to foreground the founding ancestor in order to maintain unity in a strong context of strong emigration and more recently to protect the lineage's foundational sites from the threat posed by urbanization. Firth's (1956, 16) notion of a "group of potential mobilization" is useful to describe the efforts made to unify the lineage village to counteract the tendency toward segmentation and dispersion of its members. The notion of "groups of potential mobilization," although Firth coined it to refer to noncorporate groups, which are precisely the opposite of patrilineages according to their classic definition, usefully emphasizes the fact that public kinship ties are a resource that requires continuous political work and moral reassertion if they are to be maintained over time. Firth emphasizes the difference between the obligatory nature of extended kin ties in Tikopia and the optionality of their English equivalent, and yet what he writes of these ties—namely, that they allow the exchange of services and information and the expression of moral judgment—is largely applicable to the patrilineage, particularly where strong emigration further calls into question the automaticity of lineage ties and the solidarity derived from them. What has happened in Pine Mansion over the past century shows that lineage leaders have, possibly continually but at least at several key moments in its history, emphasized the unity of the lineage as a way of maintaining the loyalty of dispersed diasporic kin, just as much as overseas kin have contributed to maintaining the lineage's unity as a means of displaying their loyalty to the village of origin.

Zhenneng is at once the founding ancestor of the Chens and a wider symbol of village solidarity, including the minority native villagers who bear other surnames. His figure symbolically extends to stand for a community wider than the Chen descent group, but here, I focus on his status within the lineage *stricto sensu*. Because of his founding act—his migration and selection of Pine Mansion as the place to settle—and his perceived magical power as a generative source of development, his status can be likened to that of the rulers of what Sahlins (1985, 45) calls "heroic societies" in which historical practice becomes synonymous with the action of the sacred king or the chief endowed with magical powers. The "general life-conditions of the people" are "historically realized . . . by an hierarchical encompassment in the projects of kingship" (Sahlins 1985, 36).

In his essay *What Kinship Is—and Is Not*, Sahlins (2013) builds on the "heroic I," the use of the first person to refer to the collective, which he renames the "kinship I," largely drawing on Johansen's (2015 [1954]) account of the "collective I" among the Maori and his triple identification of kinship, fellowship, and mana. Johansen conceives mana "as the political-religious technique of fellowship, the active participation of one being with another" (Sahlins 2013, 36). Sahlins (2013, 28) extends this insight to kinship in general, characterizing it as "mutuality of being" or "mutuality of existence." His definition of kin thus takes the shape of an aphorism: kin are "people who participate intrinsically in each other's existence" (Sahlins 2013, 28). The sociocentric notion of intersubjective being is distinct from both individualistic epistemologies and person-centered approaches. It captures the ontological quality of kinship whereby one entity may be in discrete subjects "and conversely, one subject in discrete entities: the ancestor in his or her descendants" (Sahlins 2013, 34).

This notion of intersubjective participation is particularly interesting regarding how the figure of the founding ancestor turns the lineage into a framework for identification and action. Sahlins (1985, 44) contrasts the heroic formation of kingdoms and chiefships with the developmental process of the segmentary lineage. Yet, here we have a situation where the heroic mode serves as a counterpoise to segmentary tendencies. The common ancestor is an operator of unity and a directive principle of public good because he hierarchically encompasses all (chapter 4). He constitutes a "technique of fellowship" in that he is an operator of unity, working against tendencies to branch off and to prioritize the selfish concerns of one's "own" kin.

It is the structural relations between its component units, as embodied by the founding ancestor, that allow the lineage to remain global and a framework for identification for all faraway kin. They also make it possible for people such as Alain to travel to the village and connect with the local Chens. Walking around the village and engaging in conversation with local people without the benefit of fluent Hakka, he systematically started conversations by stating that he was a descendant of Zhenneng and of the eldest branch. As he put it, he used Zhenneng as a password to initiate conversations with Pine Mansioners. Alain also repeatedly invoked the Tahitian word *mana* when referring to the ancestors he had traveled to visit in China (chapter 7), another pragmatic use of language to make connections and overcome his unfamiliarity with his grandfather's village. Yet, despite the diasporic rhetoric of global brotherhood, the interactions between villagers and their overseas relatives are framed by bonding processes, one of these being the absence of close kin. I now turn to the second way in which the global scalar ideal is limited by practice—namely, through the practice of kinship between close kin.

The Limits of Having No Close Kin

Although travel back to one's roots is intended to create a global relationship, as Alain put it, interactions with locals reveal where the diasporic relationship is stretched to its limit and its breaking point. In the encounter between Alain and the vice president of the lineage foundation, Chen Deqi (chapter 6), the emphasis was on the vertical link connecting Deqi and Alain in their common descent from Zhenneng. They are from separate lineage branches: Alain from the first and Deqi from the third, and thus Zhenneng is their only ancestor in common. Deqi shows his full recognition of Alain as a member of the lineage and a lineage brother when he addresses him by his Chinese name, and especially with the address "elder brother" (*ah-ko*), referring to his seniority in years rather than in generation: Alain is of the ninth generation and Deqi, the eighth. If they had been closer kin, as members of the same branch, Deqi would have called Alain "nephew." The use of "elder brother" thus underlines a distant lineage brotherhood. The reference to the founding ancestor as an operator of unity and the ordering effect of the lineage genealogy are further emphasized by Deqi's statement that the founding ancestor is the grandfather of the grandfather of Alain's grandfather. He could simply have said, "You are a descendant of Zhenneng," but he was stressing the vertical patrilineal tie.[9] Had they been closer kin, he would probably have highlighted a more horizontal connection.

When Deqi asked Alain if he had close relatives (*qinren*) in the village, he received a negative answer. He then recommended that Alain turn to the branch closest to his ancestor Guoxuan's branch, that of Guobao, Guoxuan's older brother. With his question, Deqi underlined the importance of a close kin relationship and seemed to presuppose that finding close kin was Alain's main purpose in Pine Mansion. However, the likelihood that Alain would find someone of his branch in the village was very small. His grandfather was the fourth of five brothers, all of whom emigrated to Tahiti, and his great-grandfather was the only son of the fifth-generation ancestor Guoxuan, meaning that the entire branch left for Tahiti.

There was another reason why Alain was not really hoping to find any close kin, as his grandfather had died in 1961 without ever returning to China. Third-generation Tahiti Chinese are more likely to have kin in China if the grandfathers, the migrant pioneers, returned to China in the 1930s and 1940s, often with some of their sons and sometimes daughters. Or they might have sent their sons, and sometimes daughters, back to China, where they remained and had children of their own, in which case, those living in Tahiti have cousins in China. Another possibility is that the grandfathers, having returned to China, remigrated to Tahiti leaving one or two sons behind, and with a second spouse had more children in Tahiti, who have half brothers or half sisters in China. These scenarios account for most Tahitian Chinese with close kin in China. According to Alain, by not returning to China his grandfather fulfilled the curse voiced by his mother, who was very angry with him for taking his wife with him when he emigrated, as wives were supposed to remain in the village obediently caring for and serving their mothers-in-law. This was also a guarantee of their sons' return and the perpetuation of the family line in the village. Alain said that his grandfather was so much in love with his wife that he rebelled and disobeyed his parents. His mother let her hair down, a prerequisite to pronouncing a curse that I had heard of in several Tahiti Chinese stories, and told her son, "You will never return." Alain's grandfather's wife died in Malaysia when a tin mine collapsed, and her husband then left for Tahiti, leaving their two daughters there. In Tahiti, he married a Chinese woman from Southeast Asia, and they had four sons and five daughters, including Alain's father.

In spite of his pessimism about finding relatives on the trip due to this family curse, Alain looked up the descendants of an elder brother of his grandfather who had returned to China. "This branch is very scattered internationally," he said. "There's a pianist in New York and some representatives in Tahiti, and I've had a hard time trying to get them to talk." This great-uncle had two sons, one of whom lives in Hong Kong and the other in Shenzhen, but Alain showed no signs of attempting to trace them, seemed to rely instead on chance encounters with people in Pine Mansion itself. This way of proceeding resulted in interactions that, from my standpoint as an observer, were infelicitous, not so much because they made Alain appear unhappy or disappointed, although he did express boredom on one occasion, as because the necessary conditions for pursuing the conversational interaction or establishing contact were missing (Goffman 1972). Several encounters that I observed resulted in admissions of failure, in the sense that neither party was able to prolong the conversation by exchanging news about any kin they might have had in common. One example of this occurred near the workstation early in the morning of the ancestor's birthday with a man whose cap and shoulder bag suggested that he had traveled from Hong Kong. Chen Guanqiu introduced them, telling the man that Alain's name was in the genealogy (*zupu*) and that he was acquainted with Fuchang in Tahiti. It turned out that the man was from the Guobao branch.

> ALAIN: I am from Guoxuangong.
> CHEN: Maybe I know your father.
> ALAIN: No, no, no, he's not here. I'll show you the picture of my grandfather [he shows the man the photograph on his mobile phone].
> CHEN: I won't know your grandfather. Is he still alive?
> ALAIN: My grandfather emigrated in the 1900s.
> GUANQIU: His grandfather migrated; they're all over there.
> CHEN: Has he ever come here?

Alain said that he had not and clarified that his grandfather had died in 1961. The man looked a little puzzled, as if he was wondering what Alain wanted and what he could do for him. He pointed to Ganhua standing a little farther away and said, "Ganhua is my uncle." Ganhua then came over and started talking about the school celebration.

This conversation established contact but nothing more. The few bits of information were exchanged did not result in any real discussion but rather in the observation of a distance between them. The man probed to find whether they might have close relatives in common, asking if Alain's grandfather had possibly returned and whether he might know any of Alain's close relatives. Alain was by no means excluded or rejected as a foreigner: he was genealogically categorized as a descendant of Guoxuan. The language interaction was limited to acknowledging the different place each of them occupied in the lineage's genealogical order. The absence of close relatives in common prevented the extension of the interaction with what ideally constitutes the aim for such an encounter: the mutual exchange of news about shared relatives.

I also observed that although connections are quite close in the overseas community between people bearing the same surname and originating from the same village in China but from different branches, what separates them becomes more visible in the context of a return to China and the absence of close kin. In Tahiti, the Chens form the largest surname association and are a highly solidary group that monopolizes several key positions within the community's associational structure. Alain was very close to Fuchang, the dean of the Chens in Tahiti and head of the Chen surname association, and he often consulted him on genealogical matters and to learn more about Pine Mansion. Within the surname association, which includes some Chens who originated not from Pine Mansion but from other villages in the Pearl River delta, no references are made to ancestors in China. This surname association was the main means of channeling funding in response to calls for contributions from Pine Mansion; Alain made an ironic comment about Tahiti Chens originating from other villages who had donated to the mausoleum.

The dean of the Chens in Tahiti, Fuchang, was of the Guobao branch to which Deqi had referred Alain. He had died in 2005, but his son has very close ties with his cousin Weixin, the son of Fuchang's elder brother. Before leaving for China, Alain had asked Fuchang's son for Weixin's contact details, whereupon Fuchang's son muttered something about Alain needing to get in touch with his own family—his close relatives. Toward the end of the trip, Alain and I were discussing what had happened over the past couple of weeks, and I mentioned something about the Guobao branch, to which Fuchang and Weixin belong, being very united and forming a separate segment within the lineage. Alain related Fuchang's son's response to his request and added, "Now I understand it better." Although their relationship is ordinarily cordial and close, as they have the same surname in the overseas community and the same origin in China, a fairly unimportant difference, especially for Alain the genealogist, became salient when it came to visiting the village of origin.

Alain has undertaken a large-scale genealogical project to trace all the agnatic and uterine descendants of Pine Mansion Chens in Tahiti. By tracing the descent through both men and women, he has identified more than three thousand such descendants. He brought a copy of this bilateral genealogy to Pine Mansion and talked about his work to Guanqiu and Deqi, who were tremendously impressed by this number. During his speech at the ancestral ritual, Deqi cried out, "Here in Pine Mansion there are a thousand of us, but in Tahiti there are four thousand people!" Guanqiu also cited this figure during the meeting with the Qiaolian described earlier in this chapter. Bilateral kinship ties seem to generally increase in importance among overseas Chinese communities. Chinese Americans participating in the Guangdong Roots Program also work to establish American genealogies including both agnatic and uterine ties (Louie 2004, 32).[10]

The boundaries that emerge in the course of these interactions between overseas visitors and locals indicate a more general difference between social relations in the village of origin and those overseas. In the Tahitian Chinese community, everybody knows everybody else, kinship is both agnatic and uterine, and more generally the social bonds of relatedness are based on the common experience of living overseas, whereas in south China's lineage villages, agnatic and territorial neighborhood relations prevail. This view is very sketchy, and chapter 2 has shown how affinal ties also matter; however, in south China social relations are clearly shaped by the village frame of reference, while in Tahiti this is relatively unimportant as members of the overseas Chinese community relate to a diversity of villages of origin. Admittedly, most groups of travelers like the one I followed in October 2014 are based on rather loose ties of kinship, friendship, and interest rather than their origination from the same village. Issues come to light during such journeys that have little relevance to everyday life in Tahiti.

The course of the meeting with the Tahitian visitors at the Qiaolian reveals the shared desire to establish connections (*guanxi*) by actively seeking kinship relationships with the travelers, and to build them if none are discovered. The verbal interchange can be interpreted as a way of pragmatically overriding the dilemma faced by the Qiaolian, aggravated by his uncertain position between the state-imposed obligation to treat overseas visitors who are legally foreign with bureaucratic indifference on the one hand and the civic duty and moral obligation to help distant kin on the other hand. The ethnicized discourse on the solidarity between all Chinese descendants worldwide sits uneasily with their non-Chinese nationality but also, as the story of their meeting has shown, with their estrangement and difficulty of communicating resulting from the loss of Hakka as a common language, even though the PRC's efforts to promote China's official national language and culture had led to some of the visitors learning Mandarin at the Confucius Institute in Tahiti.

Alain's infelicitous interactions with people who were quick to remind him that he might have closer kin to contact beyond his remote connection to the common ancestors disclose the fundamental tension built into the lineage as a mode of organizing relationships between kin. At the level of the lineage, this tension refracts the tension between global Chineseness and legal foreignness; here, it is a tension between global brotherhood and close relatedness. Building on the approach of Freedman, who points to the structural contradiction between common and own, public and private kin ties that characterizes this kinship mode of social organization, I also emphasize the political dimension of the lineage as an organization for which kin mobilize support and which drives their mobilization in an attempt to maintain a commonality of being. There is a dynamic tension between actions and relationships that tend to emphasize commonality, and actions and relationships that tend to emphasize separateness.

These contradictory tendencies may reveal a weakness in Sahlins's (2013) recent conflation of kinship under the heading of mutuality of being. He remains evasive on issues of differentiation between kin, noting that the power of a Maori may be considered a "certain unbalance of mutual being" because it has "more fellowship, more mana, and more occasion for the 'kinship I' than others" (Sahlins 2013, 36–37) and that "mutuality of being among kinfolk declines in proportion to spatially and/or genealogically reckoned distance" (Sahlins 2013, 53). Here, his alternative use of "being" and "existence" may require clarification. On the basis of what I have shown in this chapter, I propose that brotherhood without close kin is commonality of being—the being shared by all the descendants of the founding ancestor—without the mutuality of existence in close kin's day-to-day sharing of one another's lives. This distinction accounts for the possibility of global belonging to a community of diasporic kin as well as the limits to this belonging posed by the absence of close relatives, for the lineage village inhabitants' pride in their large number of kin around the world, for the diasporic travelers' urge to visit their villages of origin, and for the experience of embarrassment and estrangement at actual meetings in these villages.

Conclusion

CHINESE GLOBALIZATION AND THE CHANGING VALUE OF SCALES

The book commemorating the centennial of the Zhenneng School (*School History* 2014) includes a photograph of me and a description of my research. This portrait is included in a chapter on overseas Chinese in a section about Chen Deqi, the vice president of the foundation. Chen Deqi is portrayed in that chapter because his grandfather and father emigrated, although he himself takes pride in having remained in China (see chapter 5). The irony is that he was the person who discovered that I was not an overseas Chen (see introduction). By returning, participating in collective celebrations, and encountering diverse actors, I came to be regarded as a researcher but a researcher associated with the overseas Chens and one who in part acted like them, especially those practicing roots tourism, as the following passage describes:

> It so happened that in 2009 [in fact, it was 2011] a Western researcher arrived in Pine Mansion and came to see Chen Deqi, introducing herself as engaged in research about ancestor Zhenneng. She said she was hoping to reach a deep understanding of the field by collecting first-hand material about Zhenneng (*guanyu zhenneng de diyi shou ziliao*). Chen Deqi found it strange that a Western researcher would be interested in Lord Zhenneng—how could this be? This researcher had previously been an assistant professor in Paris and had a doctorate from the Higher School in Social Research; her name is Taimeng Anlin (Anne-Christine Trémon). While studying the ethnology of France, Dr. Anlin had discovered a very interesting phenomenon on the island

of Tahiti in French Polynesia: the Chinese there have been highly successful, and among them the Zhenneng lineage is very affluent. They control a major part of the economy, and this is why the researcher has developed a profound interest in "Zhenneng" [quotation marks in the original]. She has traced the source (*zhuigen suyuan*) and from France, she came to Pine Mansion in China. By chance (*couqiao*), the twentieth day of the ninth lunar month in 2013 was the day of ancestral worship and also the celebration of ninety-nine years of Zhenneng School. She hurried back to Pine Mansion over thousands of kilometers and took part in the celebration.

The description likens me to a *huaqiao* and uses typical laudatory expressions for *huaqiao* visits such as "hurry back [to the village of origin]," but my research is seen as being "in depth." Most importantly, my research topic is presented as Zhenneng as a whole, although I would not have been able to describe it in this way the first time I met Chen Deqi.

This metonymization of the ancestor, his name representing the entire lineage and village, shows the extent to which lineage kinship is played out on a global scale with the aim of connecting people and sites that are both spatially and temporally distant. Lineage ties constitute a form of public kinship and shape a global fraternity that links remote relatives to the village. The founding ancestor's embodiment of the public good even allows the extension of the lineage, as a broader corporate community, beyond its genealogical limits to include all the native inhabitants of the village. Invocation of the ancestor's name, which represents the public good, channels donations toward projects for the perpetuation of the lineage and village entity.

The rituals performed twice a year produce a momentary spatiotemporal fusion, as if to negate the fragmentation that threatens the lineage as a global fraternity. However, they also reveal cracks in a community that aspires to be united. When I finished my research in Tahiti, I concluded that the very changes brought about by the investment of overseas Chinese in their home villages had altered their social, economic, and moral links to their localities of origin. Although the overseas Chinese contributed to these changes, today many regret them. I repeatedly heard the same nostalgic testimonies in the interviews I conducted in French Polynesia between 2000 and 2004: "Schools have been rebuilt. . . . We have been reforesting, contributing. But there's nothing left; it's been absorbed by the city," the Sino-Polynesian writer Jimmy Ly told me. He humorously depicted his disappointment at not finding his grandfather's village as he had imagined it in *Adieu l'étang aux chevrettes* (Farewell to Ha Gong Tam) (Ly 2003). The village's altered landscape plays a part in the emotional distancing of the majority of overseas Chinese from their villages of origin (Trémon 2007, 2010). When the anthropologist asks, "Did you visit your ancestors' village?"—thus recalling the moral imperative to "remember the source" instilled by parents and grandparents—it may even serve to justify their lack of interest in such a prospect: "There's nothing left anyway."

The emotional attachment to the village of origin felt by those who left it fades with subsequent generations, even though grandparents and parents try to impart it to their descendants. The younger generations tend to visit large cities and tourist attractions when they travel to China. Even if the majority in the diaspora do not accomplish it, the imperative to visit the village of origin at least once in their lifetime remains in the minds of the older generations. These journeys are completely separate from the business travel of overseas Chinese such as Lucien Ching, the greater part of which does not include the villages (see introduction). The travelers whose journey I followed have frenchified surnames and mixed-race children, like most Chinese in Polynesia. Lack of knowledge about their Chinese place of origin and culture, caused by an interruption to its transmission by their elders, drives their quest, as it does that of other overseas Chinese (chapter 7). Identity as practice as they travel amounts to a quest to close this gap in the form of a sensorial search for clues and through chance encounters with places and people. Their quest is impeded by the language barrier, and their difficulty locating their villages of origin is exacerbated by the transformation of the area around them.

The central concern of this book has been the diasporic relationship more than the diaspora as an entity. The use of the Tahitian notion of *mana* in China by Alain, one of the travelers, highlights the paradoxes of this relationship. I have argued that the echo between Chinese *ling*—the ancestor's magical potentiality—and *mana* is the result of a pragmatic establishment of "equivalences" (Bastide 1978) rather than a confusion of cultural categories. It is a speech act of the same kind as that whose ritual invocation manifests the ancestor's *ling*, as the rich Hong Kong entrepreneur Xingchang emphasized (chapter 6). Alain's use of the notion of *mana* pragmatically established, with this speech act, a double connection between disjointed elements: a genealogical connection between himself and his ancestors, and a spatial connection between French Polynesia, where he lives, and China, where his ancestors are. The paradoxical enunciation of a quest for the *mana* of the ancestors in China through travel thus underlies the tension at the heart of diasporic identification.

Although returning to one's roots is intended to create a global relationship, as Alain put it, the travelers' interactions with the locals that I observed in China in situations that connected my two main field sites indicated where the diasporic relationship is stretched to breaking point (chapter 8). If the vertical patrilineal line connects the descendants of emigrants to their village of origin, the absence of the horizontal lines of close kin marks their separation. Their desire to establish a link is thwarted by the absence of close relatives, and the desire for reciprocal exchange meets its limits in the asymmetry of the diasporic relationship to the village. The contradictory uses of culturally specific notions like that of Polynesian *mana* in China reveal the frictions that characterize the diasporic relationship.

From Multisited Ethnography to Scalar Action

Although the scale of diasporas far exceeds the here and now of ethnographic fieldwork, examining how social actors activate this global scale on the ground avoids the risk of substantialization that often accompanies overarching approaches to diasporas. Attention to scalar action offers a more viable solution to the problem of relations between local and global processes than the notion of abstract global forces impacting on the local, or than the flat ontology multisited ethnography tends to promote. The flexibility and low degree of prescription have enabled the wide adoption of the multisited method in the study of migration. However, it has attracted criticism for resulting in shallow ethnographic knowledge and thin description (Ferguson 2011), lack of attention to history, the diachronic production of the local situations under observation (Horst 2009; Leonard 2009), and its reintroduction of the notion of "the site" as a natural given awaiting discovery (Gille and O'Riain 2002). These weaknesses are qualifiable and easily remediable. Multisited ethnography can increase our intimacy with the subjects we follow, lending additional depth to our accounts. In migration studies, increased reflexivity regarding the choice of sites can be achieved by studying the different meanings that people ascribe to the places they have left, where they have settled, and between which they move or do not move (Gallo 2009; Coleman and Von Hellerman 2011).

Multisited ethnography has also been criticized for replicating the functionalistic holism from which it intended to escape, by displacing it from the local social system to the encompassing world system (Candea 2009, 2010). Rather than multiplying the number of research sites to constitute a totality that coincides with the object of study, can it not be just as productive to choose just one site and unveil its internal diversity and incoherence? The risk of overstating cohesion and homogeneity by focusing on the links and similarities that connect people across several sites is particularly acute when it comes to studying diasporas. However, the notion of "an arbitrary location" (Candea 2010) is only a reminder that the site is often the subject of an initial and most arbitrary choice, and as Van Velsen (1967) and others recognized early on, the object of study is never to be confounded with the single or multiple unit of observation. "Expectations of organic completeness" (Candea 2010, 31) may be equally disappointed. Neither the single site nor the multiple site are particularly exposed to the dangers of radical empiricism or functionalist holism. Even though Marcus aimed to empiricize the theoretical concept of the world system, we do not need to espouse a radical empiricism. The danger lies mainly in the lack of attention to the tensions and dynamics of change inherent in all social life.

Multisited ethnography is one way of breaking away from the functionalist monographic perspective of studying social life in a closed unit taken as the equivalent of a geographical unit, although Van Velsen (1967, 146) had pointed out that "isolation for analytical purposes should not be confused with *de facto* isolation," and the extended case method and situational analysis was designed by Manchester School anthropologists precisely for this purpose (Gluckman 2006, 10). However, although in Marxist-inspired ethnographies, the local field sites were situated within and articulated with the world system, in multisited ethnography the field sites should be locations allowing study "in/of," both in and of the world system (Marcus 1995). The world system was no longer to be understood as a "theoretically constituted holistic frame" within which the object of study is located: "it becomes in a piecemeal way, integral to and embedded in discontinuous, multisited objects of study" (Marcus 1995, 97). Globalization theorists went further, with wholesale rejection of the concept of a world system and its constitutive concepts, core, and periphery. There was nothing systematic at all, Appadurai (1996, 32) believed, in the "complex, overlapping, disjunctive order that cannot any longer be understood in terms of existing center-periphery models."

In this conclusion, I argue for an ethnographic analysis that maintains the analytical value of the local and the global and of core and periphery frameworks but grapples with them as relational rather than absolute terms. We can practice ethnography both within and of the world system by ethnographically reconstructing the roles of center-periphery and local-global polarities in people's lives, and how people participate in defining the dimensions of the worlds they inhabit and the value they accord them. This requires attention to pragmatic uses of scale. Increased anthropological attention to scale and to scalar action indicates its usefulness for understanding not just migration and diasporas but also many other aspects of the contemporary world (Strathern 1999; Tsing 2000, 2005; Corsin-Jimenez 2005; Xiang 2013; Smith 2014; Carr and Lempert 2016; Nonini and Susser 2019).

Fredrik Barth (1978), one of the first anthropologists to reflect on scale, argued that it must not arise as an artifact of analysis but must rather be dealt with as an empirical property of the things we study. He implied a distinction between scale as size and scale as scope—that is, between the *size* of the unit of observation (usually any micro-unit in ethnographically grounded studies) and the *scope* of the context of social interaction. However, he overlooked social actors' intentional manipulation of scales.[1] As discussed in the introduction, a substantial body of geographic scholarship has emphasized the social construction of scale, provoking a shift in focus from given sizes and preexisting levels to scaling and rescaling actions. This further implies introducing a more intentional dimension of scale than that Barth had in mind: scale as it is valued by social actors— that is, the scale(s) they consider important and appropriate (the local community, the city, the country, the world) and how they act according to this vision—that is, how they lead "scalar projects" (Tsing 2005, 57).

In battles over scale, social actors seek to determine the scale at which power is exerted (Nonini and Susser 2019, 3). The Chinese state and Shenzhen City reordered spatial hierarchies by creating the Special Economic Zone (SEZ) and eradicating the villages within it. Since existing spatial hierarchies are the residue of past scalar projects, such battles have a temporal dimension. Scalar projects invoke past and future arrangements. Different timescales are also at play in the struggles between the competing temporalities of capitalist production and daily reproduction (Gardiner and Lem 2018). Scalar action moreover involves temporal strategies of acceleration or delay (Nonini and Susser 2019, 2).

At the start of China's economic reforms, the country's central authorities used the regional and local scales of the main emigrant areas in the coastal provinces as a springboard for attracting overseas capital, encouraging their inhabitants to invite their overseas relatives to visit to stimulate the potential for diasporic reconnection. The SEZ and the city of Shenzhen, although often presented as an ex nihilo creation, have largely relied on global capital at two levels. The zone as a whole has depended on investment from Hong Kong and multinational companies without necessarily involving kinship ties. At the village level, overseas relatives have largely funded the building of transport, water, and electricity infrastructure to attract investment.

Locally, the maintenance of collectives in the form of shareholding companies—distant heirs of the lineage corporations—was designed to ensure the transition to a market economy. They participated in the industrialization of Shenzhen by building infrastructure on agricultural land that provided the means for manufacturing companies to settle in the area at low cost. The collective economy has thus been made to serve capital accumulation by generating conditions that allowed the rental of factories to foreign multinationals and housing to workers from other Chinese provinces, and the establishment of a manufacturing zone that has enabled China to join the global capitalist system.

As such, the collective economy participates in capitalism but is internally organized according to noncapitalist principles. Hybrid in nature, the shareholding companies embody the community's moral economy (chapter 3).

These dynamics have restored the power of the lineage, an institution that provides for the community's public good locally and mediates the diaspora's transnational networks globally. In spite of its increased religious tolerance in the reform era, the Chinese state does not officially endorse lineage institutions; however, since the country's reopening, the authorities have de facto encouraged their revival. The ambivalent relations between the state and lineage institutions dates back to the latter's origin in sixteenth- and seventeenth-century China as a way for the state to control society and levy taxes (Faure 1989, 2007; Faure and Siu 1995).[2] It was an organization subordinate to the state and was supposed to act as a proxy for state power, but it tended to autonomize itself and act on its own behalf. The imperial state's creation of the lineage institution was considered "morally good and politically useful," but these very attributes meant that it could become a threat if it got too powerful (Freedman 1966, 29).

The labeling of lineage and village projects as aimed at the public good (*gongyi*), a phrase borrowed from the state authorities, reflects this scalar battle for power. It indicates the former peasants' detention of a "claim [to promote the public good] that *originated* in the revolutionary state" (Brandstädter 2013, 14, emphasis in original) but also a longer tradition of lineage investment in schools and philanthropic works. Lineage activities are legitimized by their contribution to the public good as both a goal and a principle. The villagers' invocation of the public good is far from purely instrumental here, but it is nonetheless highly strategic in its relationship with the state: the state cannot oppose an action carried out according to the very principle it defends or is supposed to defend (chapters 2 and 4).

Although the contemporary account of the pioneering foundation of Shenzhen echoes the local narrative of the foundation of the Pine Mansion Chen lineage as an "enterprise" (chapter 3), Shenzhen is paradoxically defined in opposition to the very villages that enabled its creation. It was built in a twofold relationship with the local villages that the city engulfed, relying on them while transforming them and then seeking to abolish them, first by reclassifying their administration and now through urban renovation policies. And yet, while urbanization and its associated rationalization policies aimed to shape the "backward" peasants into modern "civilized" citizens, that very urbanization, far from being entirely imposed from above, is inscribed in a logic of development that echoes what the people of Pine Mansion ask for in their rituals. Paradoxically, the very act of preserving heterotopic and heterochronic sites, whose ritual uses are at odds with the ideology of modernization-cum-urbanization, brings homotopia and homochronia into play. The mobilizations for protecting the grave site and the school (chapter 4) did not involve open opposition to the urban authorities so much as the exploitation of gray areas left open to interpretation. They required a temporal scalar strategy, acting at "Shenzhen speed." The game amounted to overtaking the authorities, acting even faster than they did to present them with a *fait accompli* by erecting monumental buildings that correspond to the expectations and standards of Shenzhen modernity.

The Moral Economy of Scale

Although China's emergence as a core in the world system makes it a central node in global flows of money and power, it also increases the importance of the local and national Chinese scales. There is a distinction to be made between scale as scope and scale as valence. *Scale as scope* is the temporarily stabilized "product," the spatial and temporal reach of social systems or chains of interdependence resulting from actions and interactions that lend them a certain extension in space and time. It is relational in that far-reaching spatial or temporal extension is measured relative to lesser extension. *Scale as valence* is the attractiveness and desirability of a scale in relation to other scales.[3] In distinguishing between scope and valence, I build on Marilyn Strathern's (1999) distinction between two types of scalar action, scaling and matching. Scaling applies to scale as magnitude. The measuring tool (e.g., the mile, the Richter scale) is fixed; the scale is that against which the scope of the action can be measured (the scope of an earthquake, the scope of social networks). In matching, "what is held constant is not the values on the scale but a relation between values"—for example, a ratio such as purchasing power (Strathern 1999, 205). Valence is a relationship between values; applied to scale, it refers to the value that can be generated by a certain level, to a locality's attractiveness and potentiality.

An analytical distinction between value and valence is in order here. Value is generated by the actions of a human community to provide for its own material and existential continuity. In David Graeber's (2001; 2006, 73) definition, it is "the way in which actors represent their actions as part of a larger whole." Whereas value can be understood as the significant totality that is the product of social actions, valence is the expected horizon against which these actions take place and are evaluated. Valence is about potentiality—the capacity to generate value—and desirability—the moral dimension of values. What is at stake here is the relative capacity of scales to be sources of value creation, and the desirability of different scales in moral terms.

First, the valence of the local scale in China refers to the locality's attraction and value-generating potential. The land's profitability has greatly increased, with two-thirds of the current villagers no longer planting grain but drawing their income from real estate as rentiers (chapter 3). And although the people of Pine Mansion often chose their emigration destinations according to how they judged their development potential, they consider that this potential has now "returned" to the center. The change in geomantic action or return of the magical power (*ling*) of the ancestor and the mountain in which he is buried also indicate a relocation or at least a rebalancing of value generation. The burial site's geomantic power is closely associated with both fertility—the power to give life— and economic success, hence the involvement in ritual of mobile entrepreneurs such as Xingchang (chapters 1 and 6). Under Mao, the conditions for performing the rite were not met. Unable to feed the ancestors, the living were deprived of the rite's value-generating potential.

Its relocation overseas, where the economic and political conditions needed to accomplish it were in place, ensured the cult's continuity. As the rites can now be performed locally once again, it is not surprising that the feng shui is said to be "turning" to benefit those who have the means to exploit its value-generating potential. Furthermore, the influx of so-called floating migrants, whose presence is officially temporary but whom the people of Pine Mansion know will probably remain (chapter 3) is, in the eyes of the village natives, in line with the attractiveness of the place.

Second, the valence of the local scale also refers to its desirability: to value as "a conception, explicit or implicit, distinctive of an individual or characteristic of a group, of the desirable which influences the selection from available modes, means, and ends of action" (Kluckhohn 1962, 395). The former village's prosperity is interpreted as a return to order, and a more just order, after the disorder of the Mao period. This was explicit in the community members' comments on the equalization of the ancestral tomb's geomancy. The increase in the number of female donors (chapter 2), the reduced importance of agnatic ties in overseas communities (chapter 8), and several villagers' allusions to the inversion of the male and female ancestors' graves (chapter 5) all provide clues as to why geomancy, said in the past to favor women and migrants, is now perceived to have at least equalized, if not reversed, over the past decades. At play here is a Confucian hierarchy of values wherein male power once again prevails over female power, and order over disorder or anomie (*luan*).

Nowhere is the intricate relationship between value and values more manifest than in the way native villagers who remained in the village and worked the land paid a lower entry price for a share in the companies that draw income from the collective land (chapter 3). The very creation of the category of "native villagers" signals the moral revaluation of local residence. What I have called sociodicies of (im)mobility—narratives of the trajectories of those who stayed compared to those who emigrated—are sustained by a meritory logic of past virtue rewarded in the present (chapter 5).

The notion of valence helps us to understand the difference between the case of Pine Mansion and that of Gawa, studied by Nancy Munn (2007). In Gawa, scope (space-time expansion) is the parameter of value. In the case of Pine Mansion, the relationship between spatiotemporal extension (scalar scope) and the desirability of this extension (scalar valence) is not linear; valence does not necessarily increase with scope. In Gawa, generative actions give shape to spatiotemporally extended exchange circuits. Value is "characterized in terms of an act's relative capacity to extend or expand," or what Munn calls "intersubjective spacetime." "Value is as it were 'measured'" in terms of a parameter or "level of potency" which is the "relative expansive capacities of the spacetime formed" (Munn 2007, 8–9). Spatiotemporal extension is the spatial reach of personal and collective fame, and the length of time for which an object travels the inter-island *kula* circuit. Positive value, such as fame, is an outcome of positively transformative actions of hospitality and remembering, and a product of the evaluation of the actor by significant others. Similarly, in Pine Mansion, flows of people and of money are constituted of the value-generating actions of migrating and donating money: the flow of people generates social value or worth for the lineage, while the flow of money that results from emigration in turn generates value for the migrant community. The extension of the lineage on the global scale—its scope—is itself a source of value and prestige: the lineage's demographics alone are prestigious, and the lineage's global spread adds further status.

Ideally, however, migrants should return and social reproduction should take place in the village of origin. The diaspora's circuit differs from the *kula* circuit in that it is not based on the principle of reciprocal donation but on its Sino- and village-centered circuit in which migrants constitute a population flow to the periphery and the money they return establishes a financial flow to the center. The capitalist practices of contemporary mobile entrepreneurs are embedded in the lineage's moral economy, which requires the demonstration of virtue and merit via donations. Donations helped to build schools in the village to which the children of migrants were sent back from abroad, and with China's reopening, the range of public goods that the migrants could finance expanded. The mausoleum, the school, and the temple are sites from which value is generated. They are public goods in that they enable the community to care for their dead, educate their children, and gather with visiting relatives.

As shown in chapter 2, most importantly these public goods have ensured the social reproduction of the local community over time. Under Mao, this social reproductive function was delocalized to Hong Kong and overseas where migrants had settled. Hong Kong in particular took over from the village as the central node of the diasporic networks. The lineage's resurgence in the 1980s and 1990s was therefore, at least in the case of Pine Mansion and probably also of other emigration villages in Shenzhen, a relocation. There was certainly a local recovery after an interruption, yet this recovery amounted to a return to the center. The repatriation of the private foundation bearing the name of the ancestor testifies to this process of relocalization (chapter 2).

Maurice Freedman (1958, 127) described the pre-1949 "corporate" functioning of the lineage as feeding a centripetal force: "The surplus economy of the region, mediated by the institution of collective ownership, created a fund of property that tended to keep lineage members at home." Remarkably, Freedman, who began his career as an anthropologist with a study of kinship among the Chinese in Malaysia and Singapore, barely touched on the subject of emigration in his later work on the Pearl Delta lineage villages, although they had seen one of the largest migration flows in human history. This phenomenon of massive emigration is contrary to the centripetal ideologic of lineage communities. Those who have stayed in the village or have returned to live there point out that China's new prosperity now makes it possible to live a good life at home without having to leave. This can be seen as an achievement of the ideal according to which the local community can ensure the livelihoods of its members without having to try their luck elsewhere, made possible by the reappearance of what Freedman (1958, 127) refers to as a surplus economy and of what I call surplus ethics (chapter 3). From this standpoint, the restored local order is seen as both ideal and more just.

Chapter 5 has argued that although the conditions of life locally and abroad used to be incomparable, their regained commensurability allows implicit moral statements about the undesirability of emigrating. The adjectives *local* and *global* not only qualify measurable items—how far networks extend or flows reach—but they also refer to incommensurable polar opposites (Strathern 1995). For a long time, the inhabitants of rural villages wanted to escape from the local and aspired to the global, which might have seemed unattainable. Although they were long seen as incommensurable, they have become commensurable. The valence of local and global scales is now seen by the inhabitants of Shenzhen as equal, if not reversed: there is a growing *equivalence* between scales.

Competing Scalar Projects

Even though analytically differentiating scale as scope and scale as valence is fruitful, it is equally important to examine the interplay between the two. Valence implies an evaluation, and actioning one particular scale rather than another is related to its potentiality and moral desirability. The strategies of the actors involved for defending or promoting a particular scale of action depend on the scope of the resources available to them, while spatial and temporal extensions offer resources for value-generating action. The temporal and spatial extension of the lineage as a social entity provided local members with both economic and symbolic assets that played a substantial part in the transformations described in this book: the making of Shenzhen and the opening up of China, and also the cunning resistance to the state's attempt to dissolve the former lineage villages, opposing their preferred scale to that of the Chinese state's project. This preferred scale is to some extent global—the local members value their lineage's global scope in space and time and draw legitimacy and prestige from it. It is, however, increasingly superseded by a local scale aligned with the Chinese central and Shenzhen municipal governments' scale projects.

At first sight, the global does not seem to be devalued. The global extension of flows in space and time, and the interactions and transactions across the locales linked by these flows, seem to bear unequivocally positive valence: spatial and temporal extensions provide resources for value-generating action. Pine Mansioners have made strategic use of the global scalar properties of their lineage, whose extension in space enhanced the potential for raising funds from the most successful overseas relatives. The value of the diasporic donations is acknowledged on the donation plaques and in the genealogy, which records how overseas relatives have participated in the public good.

In terms of temporal scale, the long history of the lineage village has conferred prestige upon it and helped to perpetuate it as an entity. Spatially extended kinship networks have not only provided financial resources, but their temporal extension has also provided a political resource in terms of the local community's relationship with the state. Pine Mansioners justified their opposition to the primary school's closure with the fact that it had been built with overseas donations (chapter 4), and its centennial history now raises the value of the newly built apartments nearby, creating further value (figure 9.1). Similarly, the villagers used diasporic relatives, who supposedly cling to old beliefs officially condemned as superstition, as a convenient pretext for safeguarding the founding ancestor's tomb in contravention of the funeral reform, again with a processual effect as the tomb's history allowed for its heritage protection and hence the legitimization of the mausoleum.

However, even if the Pine Mansion lineage's extension in space and time brings value, the local members of this emigrant community tend to devalue this global scale. This *ambivalence* in the diasporic relationship—the local community's mixed feelings and contradictory ideas about their overseas relatives—results from the tension between the global scale on which kinship with distant

FIGURE 9.1. View of Pine Mansion's new high-rise buildings from the school's flag podium. Photo by author, 2018.

overseas relatives is located via the lineage's rhetoric of global brotherhood and the state's rhetoric of blood ties linking all ethnic Chinese (*huaren*) to the homeland on the one hand and the difficulty of maintaining ties when there is no longer a close kin relationship on the other hand. This was particularly visible in the dilemma expressed by the Qiaolian, the head of the overseas liaison association, in his tirade (chapter 8).

Although there is a cultural intimacy between the locals and their relatives from the diaspora which makes them complicit in their projects to resist the Chinese state's encroachments, another type of cultural intimacy connects people in the village to their state citizenship, distinguishing them from their overseas relatives. The revival of the ancestral rites and return of the lineage institution from Hong Kong was based on an alliance between two sections of society that hold the memory of the ritual: the local elders, persecuted under Maoism for having relations who had emigrated, and the emigrants in Hong Kong, who had continued to perform the rites during the Maoist prohibition. This alliance is publicly expressed in ancestor worship, which is jointly conducted by two leading figures with contrasting pasts: the foundation's president, Xingchang, who left China for Hong Kong and then Canada, and the vice president, Deqi, who remained in the village (chapter 6). The representation in the community's leadership of these two social classes—those who owe their social prestige to their education and their career with the Chinese state administration and those who owe it to their entrepreneurial audacity and economic success abroad—generates tensions about how the rites are conducted, resulting in a compromise between tradition and modernization. The same differentiation exists between graduates who have been able to pursue a career outside the village and those who have remained farmers. Villagers' relationships with their overseas relatives also vary according to social class (chapter 5).

Although the notion of cultural intimacy is useful when dealing with issues such as the modernization of ritual, something more is at play here. The participation of overseas relatives in ancestral ritual legitimizes practices that are heterodox with regard to the modernity advocated by the state and even makes it possible to fulfill local aspirations such as seeking prestige for the lineage, which are difficult to confess in a context where lineage organizations are still officially illicit. In other words, it is a way for the local lineage to assert power. I find Hans Steinmüller's (2013) reformulation of intimacy as complicity useful here; it underlines a form of strategic alliance whereby the local community allies with the diaspora against the Chinese state, and also, and increasingly, tends to side with the Chinese state against the diaspora to emphasize the national over the global, transnational scale. However, ultimately the community itself, in spite of the class differentiation among its members, cultivates a moral economy at the local scale that seeks autonomy from both the diaspora and the state. The rejection of indefinite accumulation in favor of a good life at home, as revealed by the moral prestige granted to overseas Chinese who have returned to live in the village, contrasts with the state's encouragement of the pursuit of wealth and constitutes oblique criticism of the class of Hong Kong–based mobile entrepreneurs, whose obsession with money and belief in geomancy is viewed with a certain ironic distance.

The fundamental ambivalence at the heart of the financial relationship with overseas relatives is also located in the discrepancy between the valorization of overseas donations and the villagers' widespread suspicion of remittances. The restored prosperity of the former village, now part of Shenzhen, and the desire for financial self-reliance and an end to dependence on overseas donations have brought a stop to the flow of people and money from abroad. The diasporic network is being "cut" (Strathern 1996)—it is the end of emigration and the end of donations. The latest fundraising campaign for the renovation of the ancestor's temple in 2014 was not even circulated globally, being presented in the form of an open letter to only those who were present at the annual ancestral festival in the former village.

The negative valence accorded to the global scale is further visible in the categorization of overseas relatives as living in the past, which members of the local community conspicuously pit against their own and China's modernity (chapter 6). The people of Pine Mansion tend to view overseas emigration as a phenomenon of the past and *huaqiao* as a historical category dating from the early twentieth century rather than existing in the present, partly because the incentive to migrate is now much less urgent than it was a century ago thanks to the local opportunities for a comfortable retirement, employment and education, social advancement, and simply, a good life. It is also due to the passing of time and the succession of generations, with the former local and overseas connectors now almost all dead.

In spite of the lineage elders' efforts to preserve the memory of past linkages and global donations there are also signs of deliberate forgetting. In Gawa, forgetting a debt entails a breakdown in the spatiotemporal process connecting exchange partners across islands (Munn 2007, 67). Negative value (spacetime contraction) occurs as a result of selfish consumption and forgetting. In Shenzhen, the Confucian imperative to "remember the source" is oriented toward the ancestors in the village center rather than relatives in the diaspora. Misremembrance is partly due to the emigrant community's members concern to save face and their desire to not be seen as beggars, but it is also encouraged by the state's nationalist discourse, which encourages letting the period preceding the creation of Shenzhen fade into oblivion and insisting on the Chinese authorities' role in creating the SEZ ex nihilo. It is then not so much a negation of value generation as a counteremphasis on the local and national scales as alternative sources of value creation. The state's increased intervention in the financing of public goods formerly funded by relatives in the diaspora constitutes an alternative project of scalar valence. The building of a new home for the elderly housing an association sponsored by the state included the destruction of the plaque listing the names of those who had funded the original building (chapter 6). New infrastructure and additional buildings for the now provincially funded primary school have also involved the loss of the original plaque, and the redevelopment of the village is also destroying many other traces of its past.

The fact that Lucien's grandfather's house had recently been demolished, with someone else pocketing the compensation money (see introduction) is indicative of the change that has occurred since the 1990s, with a distancing of the diasporic relationship following the transformation and now the wholesale destruction of the villages of origin to make way for urban redevelopment. The generation after Tailai, who was in his late seventies when I met him, is largely unaware of the extent to which Shenzhen's creation has relied on foreign investment and diasporic donations. The provincial and municipal governments are implementing a scalar project that amounts to placing the city, regional, and national scales center stage. Taken together, all these recent changes since China reopened and Shenzhen was created have led to the diaspora's past contributions fading into oblivion and denial of the major role of overseas Chinese in the generation of value. Although overseas visits were frequent and attracted much governmental and scholarly attention in the 1980s and 1990s, this wave of collective effervescence had already receded by the time I started my research. The number of visitors has declined and their visits have become more routine, although they are still emotionally charged. Today, overseas Chinese visiting their villages of origin find it easier to see how their contributions have been used to create localized sources of income such as rented-out factory buildings than to view the direct results of their family's donations. The houses their donations helped to build in the past have all been torn down, the only exceptions a few sites that have been safeguarded using overseas money, which stand out as remnants of the past diasporic relationship in a radically altered landscape.

Processual Anthropology in and of the World System

If we are attentive to the pragmatics of scale, core-periphery relations remain useful analytical tools. They can be used processually and on the ground to account for social actors' spatial mobility strategies and exploitation of varying opportunities within the world system according to the valence that they attribute to different scales. Attention to the activation of scales as scope and valence also helps us go beyond the alternatives offered by theories that see globalization as an autonomous force and those that emphasize people's worldviews of the global (Nash 1981): the focus is on both the spatial and the temporal scope of action, led by individual actors and collectives, institutions, states, and on the attractiveness and desirability of the scale at which things should be happening and reality interpreted in relation to other scales. This fosters an analysis combining an epistemology of "distanciation" with one of "intimacy" (Keane 2003). Whether multisited or "strategically single-sited" (Marcus 1995, 111), multiscalar ethnography can thus reveal how the world system is lived and produced by people, complicating teleological periodizations and decollapsing global and local scales. This allows the reconciliation of global transformations such as those that have occurred in China with the actual practices of people within situated localities.

The connections between the village and its diaspora are articulated by center-periphery relations in the classic sense of relations between the homeland and the places of destination, the village being the center or heart of a global network of social and kinship ties that radiate from it. These connections are also framed by the core-periphery relations that constitute the world system, with China emerging as a new core. For more than a century, the people of Pine Mansion and many other surrounding villages have been migrating from the periphery to the cores and semiperipheries of the world system. Many donations have been recorded as sent from colonial ports, which typically have semiperipheric functions. The village has been the recipient of financial flows from migrants that have been instrumental in tempering the damage resulting from the anti-Japanese and civil wars, and to a lesser extent from China's closure under Mao from the late 1950s to the late 1970s, and ensured its prosperity before and after that period. Changes in the donation landscape reveal the peripheralization of former destinations that disappear from the donation records along with the death of first-generation immigrants and the distancing of their offspring from the "homeland," but they also reveal strategies for remigration to the cores of the world system and, more generally, the upward social and spatial mobility of migrants and descendants who have remained connected to the village and therefore the strategic use made of semiperipheral positions in the world system (chapter 2).

I have taken a processual view of the effects generated by the diasporic reconnections that followed China's reopening and their contemporary consequences. Capitalizing on their moral duty to visit and support their village of origin, Pine Mansioners launched several rounds of fundraising in the 1980s and 1990s for a variety of public projects to which the diaspora contributed the largest amount. These donations and investments made the village financially autonomous and secured the infrastructure necessary for the success of the SEZ and China's economic emergence. Today, relations between the homeland and the diaspora are becoming equalized, if not reversed, in the context of China's emergence as a core in the world system, whose dynamics are based on cycles of capital accumulation and hegemonic expansion followed by capital decentralization and hegemonic transitions during which systems are reshaped around new hegemonic centers (Friedman 1994; Ekholm Friedman and Friedman 2008). From this perspective, globalization is the empirical manifestation of the transformation of the world system. China's globalization (Pieke 2009) is the driving force behind contemporary global transformations. Shenzhen is one of the main instruments via which the country has become a major actor in an increasingly Sinocentric world that has "re-reoriented" (Frank 1998) the global system.

This nuances the depictions of globalization theorists who view the 1980s as the start of a new epoch. Such an approach obscures and simplifies the past, neglecting how far-reaching mobilities have been part of human history all along (Mintz 1998; Friedman 2002; Waldinger and Fitzgerald 2004); "furthermore, because such past mobilities lead into the present, it obscures how the shift from past to present involves [the] reworking of older patterned flows into new sets of flows" (Heyman and Campbell 2009, 136). Challenging the teleological periodization of macroanthropological accounts that view the global flows at the end of the twentieth century as radically new and a cause of deterritorialization, the Chen lineage has been globalized by a century of emigration that has enhanced the village's status as a territorial reference point (chapter 4).

Even if Harvey (1989) emphasizes the long-standing nature of spatiotemporal compression, the flow of capital, people, and information is certainly accelerated. While recognizing its consequences in terms of facilitating the formation of diaspora and transnational communities, it is important to avoid technological determinism and overstatement of the effect of this acceleration. Easier international travel, due both to the sharp reduction of China's restrictions on leaving the country and the acceleration of transport and communication opportunities, have changed perceptions of emigration and replaced it with new strategies for global mobility. Although often involving extended stays abroad, these new opportunities are no longer classed as emigration (chapter 1), and even though they facilitate new forms of mobility, they are not a necessary or sufficient condition for maintaining ties with the diaspora over time.

Inhabitants of Shenzhen categorize their relatives in the diaspora as pertaining to a remote past and consider emigration *passé*, favoring practices of transnational mobility such as living abroad for part of the year and in China for the rest. There may be more continuity between past and present practices than they acknowledge. The novelty of the transnational as a concept (Glick Schiller, Basch, and Blanc-Szanton 1992) should not make us oblivious to its duration as a phenomenon (Waldinger and Fitzgerald 2004). Historians of Chinese migration have accounted for the long-standing links between emigrant and immigrant communities in the nineteenth and twentieth centuries (Chan 1990; Dirlik and Wilson 1995; Ong and Nonini 1997; Hu-Dehart 1999; Hsu 2000; Benton 2003; Azuma 2005). Even if migrants stayed away for many years in the past, they often returned and thus became members of transnational households: the difference is only one of degree. Still, the rise of China has made a difference, as this book has explored. Today, relations between the homeland and the diaspora are equalizing or inverting in the context of this rise to become a major player in the world system. The village is no longer dependent on overseas financial support and the desirability of migration has declined. The people of Pine Mansion increasingly identify development and modernization with Shenzhen and China at large, rather than with overseas.

In the migration through which the Pearl Delta region became a pioneering front in the sixteenth to eighteenth centuries, local communities and newcomers registered their land in the names of their ancestors and thereby formed lineages. In the pioneering opening (*kaihuang*) of the Shenzhen SEZ, the native villagers (*yuancunmin*) reinvented their lineages with the intervention and financial support of their overseas relatives and now seek to ensure their perpetuation in the context of the arrival of a new wave of newcomers (chapters 2 and 3). This is not history repeating itself: between the two periods, the lineage has gradually developed as an institution and become globalized, and today it is being revived in a context where its legitimacy, questioned since the beginning of the twentieth century, is fragile. The construction of the lineage over time is concomitant with the globalization of its networks. The inauguration of the mausoleum in 2000 was the climax of the reactivation of lineage activities and diasporic connections that began in the early 1980s. The building of the mausoleum was a turning point, as it was not entirely in line with previous lineage renewal activities but was rather a consequence of the village's urbanization.

The global extension of the lineage networks over the long duration of the twentieth century was accompanied by the accentuation of the figure of the founding ancestor in a long-term process of lineage desegmentation. This process was accelerated by the funeral reform of the late 1990s during China's transition to market socialism and urbanization, but it can be traced back to the building of the primary school in the immediate aftermath of the Chinese Republican Revolution of 1911, when the separate lineage branches' private schools were merged into one. It was further evident in the 1961 establishment of the foundation to unite all the villagers who had found refuge in Hong Kong in the ancestor's name. Lineage desegmentation was both a response to emigration, as a means of channeling funding for a unitary cause by invoking the founding ancestor's name, and a result of emigration, as migrants tended to bring funding as well as new ideas back from overseas (chapter 4).

A diachronic dialectic of globalization and localization is therefore at play: the creation of Shenzhen, one of the main instruments and most striking manifestations of Chinese globalization, led to the relocation and refocusing of the diaspora's deterritorialized networks in the villages of origin. Contemporary Chinese globalization has not come out of nowhere: in the Shenzhen SEZ, it is partly the outcome of processes by which lineage villages such as Pine Mansion have been globalized for more than a century, from the 1880s to the 1980s, through the massive emigration of their members. The relationship with the diaspora thus follows the pulse of the world system and its successive waves of globalization. The globalization of kinship networks originating from the village began with the wave of globalization in the late nineteenth century, characterized by European hegemony in the world system, and a century later these networks have provided funding that has processually led to the end of dependency and the emergence of China as a core of the world system—that is, to contemporary Chinese globalization.

Notes

INTRODUCTION

1. Lo Wu (in Cantonese, used in Hong Kong) or Luohu (in Mandarin, used in Shenzhen) is an urban district that straddles the Hong Kong–Shenzhen border and is also the name of its MTR stop.

2. Lucien's and Alain's grandfathers were brothers who migrated from Pine Mansion to Tahiti in the 1890s and early 1910s, respectively.

3. In the Ming and Qing dynasties, the area of today's Hong Kong and Shenzhen was called Xin'an County. After the first Opium War, Hong Kong Island was ceded to the British in 1842, followed by the Kowloon Peninsula (1860) and the New Territories (1898). North of the border, in 1913 Xin'an was renamed Bao'an County by the Nationalist government, and in August 1980, an area of 327.5 km^2 was carved out of it to create the Shenzhen SEZ.

4. The Four Modernizations (of agriculture, industry, national defense, and science and technology) were announced at the third plenum of the eleventh Central Committee of the Chinese Communist Party on December 12–18.

5. See Trolliet 1994; Lever-Tracy, Ip, and Tracy 1996; Ong and Nonini 1997; Wang and Wang 1998; Pan 1990, 1999; Ma and Cartier 2003; Reid 2008.

6. They caution that it might lead to overstating cultural homogeneity across communities that have changed culturally as a result of being overseas and their adjustment to their host countries (Wang 1991, 1999; Ang 1994; McKeown 1999; Chun 2001; Skeldon 2003; Nonini 2015).

7. Most focus on the transnational or diasporic actors involved. See Lever-Tracy et al. 1996; Weidenbaum and Hughes 1996; Hsing 1997; Smart and Smart 1998; Douw, Huang, and Godley 1999; Kuah 1999; Huang and Zhang 2003; Tan 2007.

8. They use meso (urban and regional) units of analysis. See Woon 1990, 1996; Johnson 1993, 1994, 2007; Hoe 2013.

9. The few recent anthropological studies of emigrant communities in China are mostly ethnographies of peripheral rural areas from which people still migrate, although increasingly to domestic destinations such as Shenzhen rather than abroad.

10. The relationship between China's imperial government and the empire's subjects residing in foreign places has seen ebbs and flows for several centuries (Chen 1939; Lombard and Aubin 1995; Reid 2001; Skinner 2001; Brook 2010; Hoe 2013).

11. Wang Gungwu (1993) argues for the term *Chinese overseas* rather than *overseas Chinese* or *Chinese diaspora* to include both Chinese nationals and ethnic Chinese holding another nationality. People in the emigrant villages use the term *huaqiao* indiscriminately for all their overseas relatives. Since the focus here is on the inhabitants of the regions of origin, who use the term *huaqiao* in ways that echo official discourse, throughout this book I use either the Chinese term or its translation as "overseas Chinese."

12. Although such urbanized villages can be found all over China, because of the recent specific history of Shenzhen's creation, they constitute a central feature of its urban space (O'Donnell, Wong, and Bach 2017, 7). The characterization of such places as "villages in the city" results not only from the chaotic urban landscape that stems from their "spontaneous urbanization" (Shen, Wong, and Feng 2002) but also from the social entity formed by the villages' native inhabitants, who are powerful economic actors.

13. *Guxiang* and the similar term *jiaxiang*, both of which are used to refer to one's village of origin, include an emotional connotation.

14. The genealogy, privately published in 2000, has a title but no official authors. It was edited by a "compilation committee" whose members are presented on the first pages. The first part contains texts by two named lineage elders, but they are not the authors of the genealogy as a whole.

15. Freedman (1958) attempts to apply the Africanist anthropologists Evans-Pritchard and Fortes's (1940) descent theories to the Chinese case. He stresses that their applicability is limited due to China's strong lineage organization within a centralized political system and underlines the importance of overcoming the dichotomy between segmentary and state societies.

16. See R. Watson 1985; Ebrey 1986; Ebrey and Watson 1986; Faure 1989, 2007; Faure and Siu 1995; Zheng 2001; Szonyi 2002.

17. See Judd 2005; Yan 1996; Brandstädter 2000; Stafford 2000a; Brandtstädter and Santos 2009.

18. Particularly in the south: see Potter and Potter 1990; Woon 1990, 1996; Johnson and Woon 1997; Kuah 1999; Kuah-Pearce 2011; Ku 2003; Shu 2004; Pan 2006; Tan 2007; Tsai 2007; Chan et al. 2009; Santos 2009; Chen 2013; He and Xue 2014; Guo and Herrmann-Pillath 2019.

19. Polarity refers to center and periphery; I subsume it under "valence", defined next.

20. See Brubaker (2005:7) on the importance of temporal continuity in making diasporas "sociologically"—and anthropologically—interesting.

21. They have shown that scales are not natural but rather an outcome of processes of capitalist production (Smith 1984, 2008; Brenner 1999), social and political struggle (Delaney and Leitner 1997; Herod 1997; Jones and MacLeod 2004), and social reproduction (Marston 2000).

22. Not all Tahiti Chens originate from Pine Mansion: some are from other Hakka villages nearby, and a minority came from Cantonese villages on the Pearl River's west bank. However, the Pine Mansion Chens are dominant in number among both the Chens in Tahiti and the Tahitian Chinese population.

23. Due to my limited understanding of Hakka, I conducted interviews in Mandarin, which even the older leaders speak well, or in Hakka with the help of assistants. During my first stays, Luo Jiting, Zhang Rou, and Liu Tingting, graduates from Sun Yat-sen University in Guangzhou and the Chinese University of Hong Kong, helped me to translate and transcribe Hakka into Mandarin.

1. A GLOBALIZED LINEAGE

1. The genealogy was first set down on paper in 1822 and was revised in 1842, 1925, 1987, and 1996. In 2000, it was published as a printed book for the first time.

2. The term *coolie* was used by Europeans, usually pejoratively, to refer to the mainly Indian and Chinese contract (or indentured) laborers recruited to work on plantations in European colonial areas in response to the labor shortage brought on by the abolition of slavery. "*Mai zhuzai*," to sell oneself as a pig, is the more colloquial and widespread expression used in Pine Mansion and the surrounding emigrant villages.

3. Rather than continuing to see Europeans as barbarians living on the periphery of the Qing empire as their nineteenth-century predecessors had, the Jinan intellectuals were acutely aware that China was on the periphery of Europe, and they "contemplated a Chinese settler colonialism" (Chan 2018, 50).

4. The Guo ancestors of the fifth generation are listed in descending generational order in an index referring to the relevant pages.

5. Figures for individual countries are not given.

6. Cadres (*ganbu*) are civil servants or elected heads of shareholding companies and residents' committees. Until 2018, the latter were not necessarily members of the Communist Party; membership is now mandatory.

7. Some guesswork is needed to locate these: this is easy to do in the case of a mother and her son or daughter because in many cases, the mother has a name other than Chen. For the rest, I used their professional occupation as an indicator; when the respondent had no profession but stated that the declared person was a worker, it is very likely that the latter was residing in Hong Kong.

8. The number of returns to China is estimated to have been about twenty thousand per year in the second half of the 1980s (Skeldon 1994, 30).

9. I came to this conclusion after searching the per-country lists for the names of people whom I knew for certain had left for a particular destination. For example, Tailai's father, who returned from Indonesia, is not on the Southeast Asia list. This is confirmed by the fact that major donors at successive fundraising events are absent from the lists— they often returned (see chapter 2).

10. They are written in Chinese characters in the genealogy.

11. Since 1942, the Tahiti Chinese had been represented by a consul of the Republic of China, and this continued after the Kuomintang government retreated to Taiwan in 1949.

12. Migration from Pine Mansion probably began as early as the 1860s, but the genealogy mentions the 1870s as the starting period and records show a clear uptick from the 1880s onward.

13. I arrived at these estimates by manually searching through the per-country lists in the genealogical material, a tedious task that made it possible to identify their generational ranking.

14. It stopped altogether with the Japanese occupation of Hong Kong in 1941 (Hsu 2000, 179).

15. Chapter 7 returns to the difference in legitimacy (and not just legality) between migration to Hong Kong and migration abroad over time, and the associated moral assessments.

16. This explains why a larger number of UK Chens are included in the official 2010 census than on the list of UK residents in the 2000 genealogy (see table 1.2).

17. Business immigration programs were put in place in Canada, the United States, Australia, and New Zealand. They favor the admission of entrepreneurs and investors and have contributed to the shaping of a transnational capitalist class (Sklair 2001). The other preferred destinations for remigration from Hong Kong were Australia, Singapore, and New Zealand, but the people of Pine Mansion rarely chose these.

18. Overseas Chinese family dependents (*huaqiao juanshu* or *qiaojuan*) and returned residents (*guiqiao*), hereafter "returnees," were together categorized as people with overseas connections and were all subject to the same policies.

19. Even in the 1970s, women's very significant work on private plots of land clearly distinguished Hakka villages from Cantonese villages (Parish and Whyte 1978, 207).

20. From the data in the genealogy, I estimate that more than one-third of the marriages between the 1950s and the 1980s occurred between Chens, usually between kin relatives related beyond the fifth degree. The new Marriage Law of 1950 lifted the prohibition on marriages between bearers of the same surname (Croll 1981, 80). More generally, the increase in the number of such intermarriages can be attributed to strong local retrenchment during the collectivist period (Potter and Potter 1990, 156) and to the encouragement of cadres to set an example by renouncing old customs. Moreover, they enabled the consolidation of networks of political influence (Parish and Whyte 1978, 176). At the time of

my fieldwork, the majority of Pine Mansion leaders, both in office and retired, were Chens married to Chens.

21. In spite of this, the extended family seems to have remained widespread in the collectivist era (Huang 1992).

22. Bao'an District, in which Pine Mansion was located, and Longgang District remained separated from the SEZ by a barbed-wire border and checkpoints until 2010, when the SEZ expanded to include the whole of Shenzhen.

23. Since 2005, all Chinese citizens have been entitled to a passport and can be granted an exit visa if they have sufficient income.

24. These privileges were first granted in 1955 but, seen as a contradiction in the construction of a socialist country, were reduced in 1958–59 and withdrawn altogether in 1966–67 (Fitzgerald 1972, 55–65, 167; Peterson 1988).

25. The 1990 Protection Act protected the rights and interests of returned overseas Chinese (*guiqiao*) and the dependents of relatives overseas (*qiaojuan*), adopted by the National People's Congress on September 7, 1990.

26. Overseas emigration continues in other regions with a long tradition of emigration such as Fujian Province and Wenzhou in Zhejiang Province (Pieke and Mallee 1999; Pieke et al. 2004; Chu 2010). Other Chinese regions in the interior and the north have become new areas of emigration.

27. Qiaoban is the State Council's OCAO. For the full names, see Note on Anonymization, Romanization, and Translation. Each administrative level—provincial, municipal, district, and subdistrict—has both a Qiaolian and a Qiaoban; at the village level—that is, outside the formal administrative apparatus—there used to be only the Qiaolian, but now that the villages have been urbanized, the Qiaolian have been removed (see chapter 2).

28. From 1979 to 1991, total foreign direct investment in China amounted to US$26.8 billion, of which an estimated US$13.9 billion came from Hong Kong and Macao, US$2.5 billion from Taiwan, and only US$1.5 billion from people of Chinese origin living elsewhere (Lin 1999).

29. *School Centenary 2014.* This book was published in 2014 for the Pine Mansion school's centenary and includes the portraits of many Pine Mansioners. To protect the anonymity of my informants and the former village, I have not translated the full title.

30. Its mission is the same as in the early days of the PRC: to close ranks around the Communist Party and gain support from representatives of parties other than the Chinese Communist Party or nonaffiliated persons, as also from intellectuals, national minorities, religious figures, returnees, and "compatriots" in Hong Kong and Macao. It is closely controlled by the Communist Party and plays a purely consultative role (Chen 2018).

31. The others are the Chinese Zhigong Party, the National People's Congress OCAO, and the All-China Federation of Returned Overseas Chinese. It was recently announced that OCAO will become a subdepartment of the Chinese Communist Party's Unified Front Working Department (*Zhonggong zhongyang tongyi zhanxian gongzuobu*), whose guidelines are implemented by the Political Consultative Conference. The Central Committee of the Communist Party of China published the "Plan for Strengthening Institutions and Political Parties," Xinhuanet, March 21, 2018, http://www.xinhuanet.com/2018-03/21/c_1122570517.htm.

2. THE SHIFTING LANDSCAPE OF DONATIONS

1. However, most emigrants' children attended schools run by Chinese sociopolitical associations in their host countries (Trémon 2010, 65–70).

2. These were remittances of not only money but also of goods. Foodstuffs were sent during the famine years following the Great Leap Forward (Woon 1990, 142; Guldin

1995, 90; Tan 2007, 81) and after the hardest years of the Cultural Revolution. Cooking oil in particular was cruelly lacking, according to some of my Chinese respondents in Tahiti. Chapter 7 returns to the distinction between remittances and donations and the prestige derived from being a donor.

3. Hsu (2000, 35–38) describes how remittances were transferred up until the 1940s.

4. Processing these data requires patience, as the lists present only the name of each individual donor followed by the amount they donated, with the amounts not in numerals but in capital form (*daxie shuzi*), such as that used on bank checks and official documents.

5. The 1929 records list the donations in *yuan*, the currency in circulation in Guangdong Province since the late ninteenth century. In 1946, 1987, and 1998, the donations are listed in the national currency of the country of origin. Taking into consideration the depreciation of the Chinese currency in 1946 and the use of US dollars in several donor locations, I have converted all the amounts on the 1946 list to US dollars and the 1987 and 1998 amounts to Hong Kong dollars, using the average exchange rates for each year (http://fxtop.com/fr/historique-taux-change.php).

6. Republican Cuba also imported several thousand Chinese laborers during and after World War I.

7. Seven hundred Chinese contract laborers were brought to work on the railway in the 1850s, a catastrophic recruitment with many dying of illness or committing suicide. The French brought around three thousand workers from Guangdong Province in the late 1880s to build the canal, but many also immigrated without a contract. The Americans completed the canal without recruiting laborers (Siu 2005).

8. A fifth-rank official (*wupin*) gave the largest amount (500 yuan); among the thirty-three who gave 100 yuan were four *jiansheng* (students of the Imperial Academy) and another fifth-rank official. *Jiansheng* was an honorary title whose purchase was common in the late-Qing dynasty (only those who passed the imperial examinations at the highest level were guaranteed an official position). Its holders enjoyed exemptions from taxes and chores and constituted a social stratum of scholar-farmers who acted as intermediaries in local government (Siu 1989, 46).

9. The value of the yuan dropped considerably in 1946, two years before the issuance of the new yuan in 1948 (Ebeling 2010).

10. The emergence of single-lineage villages is often the result of the progressive domination of one lineage that gains control of the territory and seeks to oust others (Freedman 1966, 12). When the founding ancestor Zhenneng picked Pine Mansion to settle in, the territory was already inhabited by Cantonese-speaking families bearing the surnames Huang, Ye, Wei, and Qiu. The genealogy states that there were only one or two households per surname. It seems that those named Ye arrived together with Chen Zhenneng; one Ye Manzhu is said to have been his servant. The Chens formed matrimonial alliances with all of these families except the Huang, who are still present in Pine Mansion today and form a minority stronghold. The party secretary was a Huang in 2010, and he still held the same position the last time I was in the field in 2018.

11. On the Hakkas in La Réunion see Live (2003).

12. See Trémon (2010, 75) on Tahiti, Tjon Sie Fat (2009, 50, 183) on Suriname and Leo (2015, 54, 75–76, 87) on Jamaica and Malaysia. The Hakkas are not the majority in Malaysia overall; they constitute about 23 percent of the Chinese population (Hoe 2013, 46).

13. Aruba was placed under British and then American protection during the Nazi occupation of the Netherlands. Suriname became a US airbase and was the world's largest supplier of bauxite, which is used in military aircraft (http://www.archievenwo2.nl /thema-overzicht/Surinamee/oorlogsindustrie-bauxiet).

14. Wallerstein's framework tends to replicate the "methodological territorialism" of state-centric approaches on a global scale (Brenner 1999, 68). The historical dynamics of the world economy are described in terms of the differential positions occupied by states within the core-periphery structure: semiperiphery countries are industrializing, mostly capitalist countries geographically located between periphery and core countries.

15. This was also the case for the home for the elderly in 1994.

16. At 9 percent, non-Chen participation is slightly higher than the proportion of native non-Chen inhabitants of Pine Mansion (less than 8 percent).

17. I was able to confidently identify 190 of the 213 donations as local, including fifty-one non-Chens at least half of whom were women from the village with minority surnames or women from other villages who had married Chens.

18. I present the notions of public good(s) in the singular and plural in chapter 3.

19. China's average yearly wage amounted to 1,459 yuan in 1987, 6,470 yuan in 1998, and 84,744 yuan in 2017 (https://tradingeconomics.com/china/wages).

3. COLLECTIVE FUNDS AND THE MORAL ECONOMY OF SURPLUS

1. While urban workers' annual net wages grew about thirty-fourfold from 1980 to 2001, the annual per-capita income of the rural population increased sixty-fivefold over the same period (Ng 2003, 430).

2. A fourth-generation descendant of Zhenneng had resettled there in the mid-nineteenth century and his ancestral temple still stands, although the temples of third- and fourth-generation apical ancestors in Pine Mansion have all been destroyed. The segment has remained ritually connected to the Pine Mansion Chen lineage.

3. The foundation participates in financing scholarships for Pine Mansioners. See this chapter's last section.

4. Eight *fen* (0.8 *mu*) of land were allocated per person, 3.2 *mu* for a family of four (a *mu* is equal to one-sixth of an acre or 0.0667 of a hectare). *Tian* land was for rice and *di* for vegetables, sweet potatoes, and sugar cane.

5. Former village head, interviewed August 2011.

6. A 1983 Central Committee circular separated government administration from economic management (O'Brien 1994, 37; see also Shue 1984, 259).

7. This principle was reasserted in the revised constitution of 1982 (Zhao 2009, 97).

8. On the transition from a rural to an urban public goods regime and the increased involvement of the state, see Trémon, forthcoming 2023.

9. The *shequ* is a hybrid of administrative (*minzheng*) and civil society (*minjian*) (Derleth and Koldyk 2004; Ngeow 2010). In 2016, the workstation was renamed the Party Service Center (*dangqun fuwu zhongxin*).

10. In many villages in Guangdong Province, where the land reform took longer than in other provinces (Vogel 1969, 49), political control of the "bad classes" only really occurred during the Cultural Revolution and was relaxed soon after. Residents of rural villages were generally very uncomfortable with the idea of attacking property acquired by emigrants' hard work. (Siu 1989, 127), and in some single-lineage villages, the landowners have never been criticized (Parish and Whyte 1978, 100; Woon 1984, 104).

11. When I asked for data about overseas Chinese who had returned to live in Pine Mansion, Chen Guanqiu took out a very thin folder in which two elderly people who had returned from Malaysia were registered—the only ones who had been able to reclaim their local *hukou*, or rather obtain it, because they had probably left China before the *hukou* system was set up in its current form. Guanqiu admitted that there are many more returnees in Pine Mansion, mostly from Hong Kong, but he explained the problem away by saying that this register is only kept on a voluntary basis (*ziyuande*).

12. The residence registration system in the 1960s and 1970s prevented migration to cities as it was not possible to change *hukou* (Chan and Zhang 1999). In 1985, for the first time, rural migrants were allowed to register as temporary residents in urban areas. Although the system has been liberalized, it remains difficult to change one's *hukou*, especially in large cities (Chan and Buckingham 2008). The *hukou* system still discriminates against migrants, who are unable to access many social services in the locality where they live and work (Yu 2002; Pun 2005; Wang 2005; Solinger 2006; Fan 2008; Chan 2012; Huang 2014).

13. Of the 122 individuals in the "unemployed or retired" category, 115 declared that they had no occupation, 2 declared themselves retired, and 3 stated that they were homemakers (*jiating zhuren*).

14. Deng's trip to Shanghai and Shenzhen was intended to revive support for his economic program. He thereby renewed a long-standing tradition of imperial tours (Oksenberg 2001).

15. Liu Shaoqi instituted this sending-down policy of urban cadres in the early 1960s to redistribute excess urban population following the Great Leap Forward's famine to do manual labor and assist agriculture (Cell 1979). Mao Zedong later reinstituted this policy under the Cultural Revolution.

16. See Chan (2013) for a literature review and study of how female property and inheritance are allowed in Hong Kong's New Territories lineage villages despite the traditional notion that only males should inherit.

17. They were called figurehead households (*jiakonghu*). However, in contrast to the case discussed by Guo and Herrmann-Pillath (2019), shares were not distributed to households but to individuals.

18. On this and on plans to reform joint-stock companies, see Trémon 2015 and 2018.

4. SAVING THE ANCESTRAL SITES, MOBILIZING FOR THE PUBLIC GOOD

1. These understandings are very close to economists' definitions of public goods (Ostrom and Ostrom 1977; Gazier and Touffut 2006; Tsai 2007).

2. The first character, *ye*, means business, occupation, estate, property. *Chuang* means to begin, to initiate, to create. *Chuangye* signifies to venture and, as a noun, refers to entrepreneurship.

3. The practice of making ancestors can be traced as early as Shang China (Keightley 2004).

4. Bill no. 63, dated March 3, 1997, available at http://www.szgm.gov.cn/publish/main /1/9/12/15/20121101110740875740296/index.html.

5. In ancient China, the cremation or pulverization of an enemy's remains was believed to be the best way of permanently annihilating them (Lewis 2006, 59–60).

6. Confucianism has been reactivated in the last two decades both by intellectuals close to the circles of power and by ordinary citizens (Billioud 2007).

7. In this Hakka village, double burial was customary, the bones being dug up seven to ten years after burial and placed in large jars called *jinta*, which were then reburied (see J. Watson 1982, 1988b). The bones of particularly important and wealthy deceased persons were placed in small buildings called *yinzhai* or *yincheng*. The act of digging up the deceased for cremation is similar to that required for reburial and could explain the relative acceptance of, or at least lack of resistance to, cremation (Jackson 2008, 128).

8. Its etymology derives from the religious functions of nobles and dignitaries. *Gong* thus refers to public in the sense of communality and collectivity rather than the political sense of the public sphere (Li 2014, 101).

9. See Faure (2007, 346) for a similar example of lineage desegmentation elsewhere in the Pearl River delta.

10. I rely here on the history of the building of the school, "The Developmental Process of the Zhenneng Schools over a Hundred Years: A Discussion of the Zhenneng Lineage People's 100 Years of Emotional Involvement in Running Schools" by three senior, high-status retired Chens who live in Shenzhen, where I met them twice, in August 2011 and October 2013.

11. This prefigured Pine Mansion later becoming a "supervillage." Zhe Xiaoye and Chen Yingying (1997) mention among the typical traits of supervillages such as industrialization and "natural urbanization" the fact that they have developed public goods and services to the point at which they have become local "cultural and social service centers."

12. See endnote 10.

13. Chinese schools are ranked as local, municipal, or provincial according to their size and the quality of their infrastructure. Their ranking determines their funding, which varies according to the level of government that funds them. Provincial schools are the best resourced and most prestigious.

14. As noted in chapter 3, at the time of the urbanization, the Shenzhen government refrained from taking over the collective land due to its lack of budget for compensation and the financial responsibilities that would have ensued in terms of public goods. Over the past two decades, one widespread solution in Shenzhen and elsewhere in China has been to persuade village collectives to sign contracts for urban renovation with real estate developers, who assume the compensation costs. Many collectives thus work out tripartite deals with the municipal government and developers (Hsing 2006). The government benefits by taking over the use rights (*shiyongquan*) from individuals and companies and will receive 200 RMB per square meter in rental, plus taxes from the real estate company. See Trémon (2020 and forthcoming 2023) on the conditionality of public goods provisioning on such renovation projects.

5. REVERSED FENG SHUI AND SOCIODICIES OF (IM)MOBILITY

1. I take up several of the challenges issued by the "regimes of mobility" approach advocated by Glick Schiller and Salazar (2012). One of these is to take into account the territorial and power constraints mainly exercised by nation-states, without remaining theoretically bound by methodological nationalism (Glick Schiller and Salazar 2012, 9); another is to theorize the dynamics of mobility and immobility "in ways that normalize neither mobility nor *stasis* [immobility]" (Glick Schiller and Salazar 2012, 2).

2. As also recently noted by Steinmüller (2013, 61) and Stafford (2000a, 34).

3. Confucianism accentuates agnation, separating dualities and establishing a hierarchical order between them. Among the Hakkas of northern Guangdong and southern Fujian, from where Chen Zhenneng is said to have originated, Confucianism was grafted onto a strongly established local tradition of Taoism (Chan 1995). Some traces of Taoism can still be found in the ancestral status granted to Zhenneng's wife. Yet, an indirect effect of the funeral reform has been to reestablish a Confucian order by erasing most remnants of unorthodox Taoist practice in ancestor worship. Lineage leaders today invoke only Confucianism to legitimize their lineage-related practices.

4. The inscriptions form a symmetrical set of corresponding characters, followed at the bottom of the tablet by the phrase *er wei shen zhu*, "seat of the two spirits." It is thus a dual tablet containing the spirits of both the male and the female ancestor. On the altar, there is only this one tablet, consistent with what has often been observed among the Hakkas in Guangdong Province and southern Taiwan (Aijmer 1967, 57; Cohen 1969, 170; Johnson 1988). The Cantonese have a tablet for each ancestor.

5. At Chunfen, two jars, holding the remains of Zhenneng's wife and his third son's wife, and seven urns containing those of his servant who came with him from Wuhua, his eldest son, his wife, his second son and his two wives, and his third son are taken from their shelves and placed before Zhenneng's tomb. All members of the first two generations are worshipped "in what is, for the lineage, a declaration of its corporate and genealogical solidarity" (Cohen 1990, 514).

6. On the history of Hakka migration and settlement see Leong (1997); on the role of migration and boundaries between established and newcomers in the creation of the Hakka ethnic group, see Cohen (1996).

7. A test is always "a test of strength," the determination of a certain degree of strength or status of the respective parties; a "legitimate test" rests on a *judgment* not only of their strength (or status) but also of "the just character of the order disclosed by the test" (Boltanski and Chiapello 2005: 31).

8. That is, people justify their decision on the basis of what has occurred since then, and it is extremely difficult to retrospectively identify their reasoning during the lead-up to their decision to migrate or to stay.

9. See Trémon (2018) for a more developed version of this argument.

10. Oxfeld (2010) does not mention the idea of not wanting to be perceived as a beggar, perhaps because the rural village in which she worked is much less prosperous than Pine Mansion.

11. The official and sociological term for remittance is *qiaohui*.

12. *Xin* is often translated as "heart," but in Chinese, it connotes both "heart" and "mind" and is where moral virtue is located (Oxfeld 2010, 52). On the relation between the gift and prestige, see Yan (1996) and between reputation and morality, see Chen Meixuan (2018).

6. RITUAL RENEWAL AND SPATIOTEMPORAL FUSION

1. Besides these occasions, Zhenneng's father and mother are worshipped about two weeks before Chunfen and the ancestor's birthday. Young male delegates of the lineage perform the collective pilgrimage to Wuhua, not far from Meizhou (I did not take part in it).

2. The verbs *jisi* and *jibai* more specifically designate the sacrificial actions that take place at the tomb and the temple.

3. This is still the case today: in Pine Mansion, few villagers have domestic altars, and none have domestic tablets. Instead, they have photographs of deceased parents and grandparents.

4. For instance, the Guan Lineage Association of Kaiping, on the other side of the Pearl Delta, had its headquarters in Hong Kong and worship activities restarted in Kaiping in 1983 in collaboration with the locally restored lineage association (Woon 1990, 161; 1996, 510; see also Nelson 1974).

5. Freedman (1958, 67) emphasizes the distinction between "theoretical primogeniture," evident in the custom that gives the elders the status of continuer of sacrificial rites, and "practical equality between sons" defined by law and generally applied (Freedman 1966, 7). Such sacrifices to ancestors of the older branch are halfway between the "associative" and "fixed" genealogical modes distinguished by Cohen (1990) and qualify the contrast between them.

6. Two suckling pigs are offered on his birthday. These are sacrificial offerings, different from the pig meat bought in large quantities for the communal meal.

7. Definition of *song* in the Great Preface to Mao's Poetry in the *Shijing* cited by Kern (2000:50). The *song* is an ancient genre that appears in the *Shijing* Book of Odes, a compilation of 305 poems dated from the eleventh to seventh centuries BC. These poems were

sung during political-religious ceremonies of sacrifice to the ancestors of the Zhou (eleventh to third centuries BC). Even when intended to commemorate historical events, they were not simply recited but ritually performed in the form of a dance (Kern 2000).

8. Far from being devoid of semantics (Bloch 1974), the propositional locutory aspect is embedded in the illocutionary act in this ritual language.

9. The genealogy displays a handwritten and a printed version of the eighty-four verses of text written by the head of the Zhenneng Foundation in Hong Kong in the fall of 1972.

10. Zhenneng was born in 1694; traditional lunar age calculation in *sui* includes all the lunar years experienced since birth.

11. Although the *qilin* dance is found elsewhere in China, in Guangdong Province it is peculiar to the Hakkas. Each village used to have its own band of musicians and dancers who were also martial arts practitioners. The groups challenged each other, and this tradition is now being resumed in the context of patrimonialization.

12. However, Chen Ta (1939, 243) describes an ancestral worship ritual in 1934 that included nineteen *koutou*.

7. RETURNING TO ONE'S ROOTS THROUGH JOURNEYS AND QUESTS

1. I have given the travelers pseudonyms that reflect their original names' religious (Christian) and cultural (French or Tahitian) backgrounds. The majority of French Polynesian Chinese converted to Catholicism in the 1950s and 1960s.

2. Several criticisms of Clifford's writings have been voiced (Hutynk 1998; Friedman 2002; Russell 2007).

3. "*Recherche des racines*" or "*retour aux racines*" are the French translations of the Mandarin *xungen* or *guigen*. The Hakka terms are very similar.

4. Being-for-itself is the internal negation or nihilation of being-in-itself on which it depends. We are always beings in situation, and any situation is a mixture of transcendence and facticity.

5. Until then, the Chinese community in Tahiti had been under the legal jurisdiction of the Republic of China in Taiwan.

6. In Tahiti, three associations use variations of Kuomintang (romanized following the Wade-Giles system that prevails in Taiwan). David is the head of the Kuo Min Tang Association. Following the 1911 revolution in China, the Tahiti Chinese were divided between those who wanted to support Sun Yat-sen's revolutionary action and those who were in favor of the imperial reformists. The former created the Tahiti Kuomintang Association in 1918 following the creation of the political party in China, and the latter set up the Philanthropic Association (Chungfa Fuikon or Zonghua Huiguan). The Tahiti Kuomintang later split into three rival associations.

7. Ingold criticizes cognitive theories that assume the difference between the countryman and the stranger resides in the former relying on a mental map and the latter holding a paper map.

8. Considering the small size and extensive interconnectedness of the Chinese community in French Polynesia, it is surprising that they had not gathered this type of logistical information before leaving. Although this could have been to save face by not appearing to depend on others, it might also have been another instance of deliberate forgetting.

9. Elsa had learned Tahitian only as an adult after starting work at the Bureau of Land Affairs, where she often interacts with Tahitian speakers.

10. The idea of narration may have originated from relating the experience of deciphering tracks (Ginzburg 1989, 93). Ginzburg outlines how this type of evidentiary method began to assert itself as a paradigm in the human sciences in the 1870s, although

its roots can be traced much further back to hunter-gatherers' cynegetic and divinatory practices.

8. GLOBAL BROTHERHOOD WITHOUT CLOSE KIN

1. "Qiaolian" refers to both the liaison organization and the person who chairs it.

2. I do not give this book's full reference to keep the subdistrict Miaoyun anonymous.

3. Chen Yunxiang works for the Qiaoban as a civil servant and probably receives a share of the association's rental income as part of his involvement with the Qiaolian.

4. The Japanese occupation is most commonly known in China as the War of Resistance against Japan (*kangri zhanzheng*).

5. If they complete a declaration of nationality change, they lose their Chinese nationality but keep their status as permanent resident of Hong Kong or Macao unless they live abroad for more than thirty-six months, in which case, their status changes to that of nonpermanent resident.

6. Recall that the subdistrict is the lowest level of the state's administrative hierarchy. At this level, there is a separation between the Qiaolian (the civil society association) and the Qiaoban (the administrative body in charge of overseas affairs), while before urbanization, there was only the Qiaolian at the village level.

7. Alain inquired about the existence of a Qiaolian in Miaoyun because earlier in their stay, they had already met the Longgang Qiaolian, whose former chair had been a cousin of his mother.

8. There was no traceable link to René, who presented himself as a native of Longgang.

9. Granet (1998, 114) highlights the importance of alternate generations—links between grandfather and grandson—in Chinese kinship. Here, the enumeration has the effect of rhetorically reinforcing the proximity of the relationship between Alain and the common ancestor.

10. See Wolf (1972) on the uterine family and Johnson (1988, 142) and Oxfeld (1993, 168) on the importance of women as property owners among the Hakkas in the New Territories and in Calcutta; Inglis (1991) and Trémon (2010) discuss women's property and involvement in trade as well as uterine families among overseas Chinese.

CONCLUSION

1. See Trémon (2021) for a fuller discussion of Barth's approach.

2. The dual nature of the lineage has been noted repeatedly (Hu 1948, 98; Liu 1959, 33; Hsiao 1960, 353; Freedman 1966, 29; Potter 1970, 136; Woon 1984, 1; Siu 1989, 37).

3. See definition of valence in the introduction.

References

Ahern, Emily. 1973. *The Cult of the Dead in a Chinese Village*. Stanford, CA: Stanford University Press.

Aijmer, Goran. 1967. "Expansion and Extension in Hakka Society." *Journal of the Hong Kong Branch of the Royal Asiatic Society* 7:42–49.

Anagnost, Ann. 1994. "The Politics of Ritual Displacement." In *Asian Visions of Authority: Religion and the Modern States of East and Southeast Asia*, edited by Charles F. Keyes, Laurel Kendall, and Helen Hardacre, 221–54. Honolulu: University of Hawai'i Press.

Ang, Ien. 1994. "On Not Speaking Chinese: Postmodern Ethnicity and the Politics of Diaspora." *New Formations* 24:1–18.

Appadurai, Arjun. 1996. *Modernity at Large: Cultural Dimensions of Globalization*. Minneapolis: University of Minnesota Press.

Arrighi, Giovanni. 2007. *Adam Smith in Beijing: Lineages of the Twenty-First Century*. London: Verso.

Azuma, Eiichiro. 2005. *Between Two Empires: Race, History, and Transnationalism in Japanese America*. Oxford: Oxford University Press.

Bach, J. 2010. "'They Come in Peasants and Leave Citizens': Urban Villages and the Making of Shenzhen, China." *Cultural Anthropology* 25 (3): 421–58.

Baptandier, Brigitte, ed. 2001. *De la malemort dans quelques pays d'Asie*. Paris: Karthala.

Barnett, Clive, Nick Clarke, Paul Cloke, and Alice Malpass. 2008. "The Elusive Subjects of Neo-liberalism: Beyond the Analytics of Governmentality." *Cultural Studies* 22:624–53.

Barth, Fredrik. 1966. *Models of Social Organization*. Oslo: Universitetforlaget.

Barth, Fredrik. 1967. "On the Study of Social Change." *American Anthropologist* 69 (6): 661–69.

Barth, Fredrik, ed. 1978. *Scale and Social Organization*, Oslo: Universitetforlaget.

Bastide, Roger. 1978. *Les religions africaines au brésil: Vers une sociologie des interpénétrations de civilisations*. Paris: PUF.

Benton, Gregory. 2003. "Chinese Transnationalism in Britain: A Longer History." *Identities: Global Studies in Culture and Power* 10:347–75.

Besnier, Niko. 1996. "Heteroglossic Discourses on Nukulaelae Spirits." In *Spirits in Culture, History and Mind*, edited by J. Mageo and A. Howard, 75–97. New York: Routledge.

Billioud, Sébastien. 2007. "Confucianism, 'Cultural Tradition,' and Official Discourse in China at the Start of the New Century." *China Perspectives* 3:50–64.

Bloch, Maurice. 1974. "Symbols, Song, Dance and Features of Articulation: Is Religion an Extreme Form of Traditional Authority?" *Archives européennes de sociologie* 15 (1): 55–81.

Bolt, Paul J. 1996. "Looking to the Diaspora: The Overseas Chinese and China's Economic Development, 1978–1994." *Diaspora* 5 (3): 467–96.

Boltanski, Luc, and Eve Chiapello. 2005. *The New Spirit of Capitalism*. London: Verso.

Boltanski, Luc, and Laurent Thévenot. 2006. *On Justification: Economies of Worth*. Princeton, NJ: Princeton University Press.

Bonacich, Edna. 1973. "A Theory of Middleman Minorities." *American Sociological Review* 38:583–94.

Booth, William. 1994. "On the Idea of the Moral Economy." *American Political Science Review* 88 (3): 653–67.

Bourdieu, Pierre. 1977. *Outline of a Theory of Practice.* Cambridge: Cambridge University Press.

Bourdieu, Pierre. 1994. "Stratégies de reproduction." *Actes de la recherche en sciences sociales* 105:3–12.

Boyer, Pascal. 1990. *Tradition as Truth as Communication: A Cognitive Description of Traditional Discourse.* Cambridge: Cambridge University Press.

Brandstädter, Susanne. 2000. "Hierarchy or Alliance: The Moral Economy of Gender Relations in Rural Taiwan and China." PhD diss., Freie Universität Berlin.

Brandstädter, Susanne. 2013. "Counterpolitics of Liberation in Contemporary China: Corruption, Law, and Popular Religion." *Ethnos* 78 (3): 328–51.

Brandtstädter, Susanne, and Gonçalo D. Santos, eds. 2009. *Chinese Kinship: Contemporary Anthropological Perspectives.* Abingdon, UK: Routledge.

Brenner, Neil. 1999. "Beyond State-centrism? Space, Territoriality, and Geographical Scale in Globalization Studies." *Theory and Society* 28:39–78.

Brenner, Neil. 2001. "The Limits to Scale? Methodological Reflections on Scalar Structuration." *Progress in Human Geography* 25 (4): 591–614.

Brook, Timothy. 2010. *History of Imperial China.* Vol. 6, *The Troubled Empire.* Cambridge, MA: Harvard University Press.

Brubaker, Rogers. 2005. "The 'Diaspora' Diaspora." *Ethnic and Racial Studies* 28 (1): 1–19.

Bruner, Edward M. 1996. "Tourism in Ghana: The Representation of Slavery and the Return of the Black Diaspora." *American Anthropologist* 98 (2): 290–304.

Bruun, Ole. 2003. *Fengshui in China: Geomantic Divination between State Orthodoxy and Popular Religion.* Honolulu: University of Hawaiʻi Press.

Bruun, Ole. 2013. "Social Movements, Competing Rationalities and Trigger Events: The Complexity of Chinese Popular Mobilizations." *Anthropological Theory* 13 (3): 240–66.

Burawoy, Michael. 1998. "The Extended Case Method." *Sociological Theory* 16 (1): 4–33.

Candea, Mattei. 2009. "Arbitrary Locations." In *Multi-sited Ethnography: Theory, Praxis and Locality in Contemporary Research*, edited by Mark-Anthony Falzon, 25–46. Aldershot, UK: Ashgate.

Candea, Mattei. 2010. *Corsican Fragments: Difference, Knowledge, and Fieldwork.* Bloomington: Indiana University Press.

Carr, E. Summerson, and Michael Lempert. 2016. *Scale: Discourse and Dimensions of Social Life.* Oakland: University of California Press.

Cartier, Carolyn. 2001. *Globalizing South China.* Oxford: Blackwell.

Cell, Charles P. 1979. "Deurbanization in China: The Urban-Rural Contradiction." *Bulletin of Concerned Asian Scholars* 11 (1): 62–72.

Chan, Anita, Richard Madsen, and Jonathan Unger. 2009. *Chen Village: Revolution to Globalization.* Berkeley: University of California Press.

Chan, Kam Wing, 2012. "Crossing the 50 Percent Population Rubicon: Can China Urbanize to Prosperity?" *Eurasian Geography and Economics* 53 (1): 63–86.

Chan, Kam Wing, and Will Buckingham. 2008. "Is China Abolishing the Hukou System?" *China Quarterly* 195:582–606.

Chan, Kam Wing, and Li Zhang. 1999. "The Hukou System and Rural-Urban Migration in China: Processes and Changes." *China Quarterly* 160:818–55.

Chan, Kwok-shing. 2012. *A Localized Culture of Welfare: Entitlements, Stratification, and Identity in a Chinese Lineage Village.* Lanham, MD: Lexington Books.

Chan, Kwok-shing. 2013. "Women's Property Rights in a Chinese Lineage Village." *Modern China* 39 (1): 101–28.

Chan, Shelly. 2018. *Diaspora's Homeland: Modern China in the Age of Global Migration.* Durham, NC: Duke University Press.

Chan, Sucheng. 1990. "European and Asian Immigration into the United States in Comparative Perspective, 1820s–1920s." In *Immigration Reconsidered: History, Sociology and Politics,* edited by Virginia Yans-McLaughlin, 37–79. Oxford: Oxford University Press.

Chan, Wing-Hoi. 1995. "Ordination Names in Hakka Genealogies: A Religious Practice and Its Decline." In *Down to Earth: The Territorial Bond in South China,* edited by David Faure and Helen F. Siu, 65–82. Stanford, CA: Stanford University Press.

Charney, Michael W., Brenda S. A. Yeoh, and Chee Kiong Tong, eds. 2003. *Chinese Migrants Abroad: Cultural, Educational and Social Dimensions of the Chinese Diaspora.* Singapore: Singapore University Press.

Chase-Dunn, Christopher K., and Thomas D. Hall. 1997. *Rise and Demise: Comparing World Systems.* Boulder, CO: Westview.

Chau, Adam Yuet. 2006. *Miraculous Response: Doing Popular Religion in Contemporary China.* Stanford, CA: Stanford University Press.

Chau, Adam Yuet. 2011. "Introduction: Revitalizing and Innovating Religious Traditions in Contemporary China." In *Religion in Contemporary China: Revitalization and Innovation,* edited by Adam Yuet Chau, 1–31. London: Routledge.

Chen, Jie, and Bruce J. Dickson. 2010. *Allies of the State. China's Private Entrepreneurs and Democratic Change.* Cambridge, MA: Harvard University Press.

Chen, Bing'an. 2011. *Dataogang* [The flight to Hong Kong]. Hong Kong: Zhonghe Publishing.

Chen, Meixuan. 2013. "'Eating *Huaqiao*' and the Left Behind: The Moral and Social-Economic Consequences of the Return of Overseas Chinese to a South China Village." PhD diss., University College London.

Chen, Meixuan. 2018. "Reputation, Morality and Power in an Emigrant Community: *Qiaoxiang* in Guangdong Province." In *Cooperation in China,* edited by C. Stafford, E. Judd, and E. Bell, 137–52. London: Bloomsbury.

Chen, Minglu. 2018. "Inside the 'Flower Vase': The Chinese People's Political Consultative Conference." In *Local Elites in Post-Mao China,* edited by Guo Yingie, 39–52. London: Routledge.

Chen, Ta. 1939. *Emigrant Communities in South China: A Study of Overseas Migrations and Its Emigrants.* Shanghai: Kelly and Walsh.

Chu, Julie Y. 2010. *Cosmologies of Credit: Transnational Mobility and the Politics of Destination in China.* Durham, NC: Duke University Press.

Chun, Allen J. 1989. "Pariah capitalism and the overseas Chinese of Southeast Asia: Problems in the definition of the problem." *Ethnic and Racial Studies* 12(2): 233–256

Chun, Allen. 1996. "The Lineage-Village Complex in Southeastern China." *Current Anthropology* 37 (3): 429–50.

Chun, Allen. 2001. "Diasporas of Mind, or Why There Ain't No Black Atlantic in Cultural China." *Communal/Plural* 9 (1): 95–109.

Chun, Allen. 2002. *Unstructuring Chinese Society: The Fictions of Colonial Practice and the Changing Realities of "Land" in the New Territories of Hong Kong.* New York: Routledge.

Chung, Him. 2010. "Building an Image of Villages-in-the-City: A Clarification of China's Distinct Urban Spaces." *International Journal of Urban and Regional Research* 34 (2): 421–37.

244   **REFERENCES**

Clifford, James. 1988. *The Predicament of Culture: Twentieth-Century Ethnography, Literature, and Art.* Cambridge, MA: Harvard University Press.
Clifford, James. 1997. *Routes: Travel and Translation in the Late Twentieth Century.* Cambridge, MA: Harvard University Press.
Cohen, Erik. 1979. "A Phenomenology of Tourist Experiences." *Sociology* 13:179–201.
Cohen, Myron L. 1969. "Agnatic Kinship in South Taiwan." *Ethnology* 8:167–82.
Cohen, Myron L. 1976. *House United, House Divided.* New York: Columbia University Press.
Cohen, Myron L. 1990. "Lineage Organization in North China." *Journal of Asian Studies* 49 (3): 509–34.
Cohen, Myron L. 1996. "The Hakka or 'Guest People': Dialect as a Sociocultural Variable in Southeastern China." In *Guest People: Hakka Identity in China and Abroad*, edited by Nicole Constable, 36–79. Seattle: University of Washington Press.
Coleman, Simon, and Pauline von Hellermann, eds. 2011. *Multi-sited Ethnography: Problems and Possibilities in the Translocation of Research Methods.* New York: Routledge.
Collins, Jane L. 2017. *The Politics of Value: Three Movements to Change How We Think about the Economy.* Chicago: University of Chicago Press.
Comaroff, J and Comaroff, J. L. 1999 "Occult Economies and the Violence of Abstraction: Notes from the South African Postcolony." *American Ethnologist* 26, 2: 279–303.
Corsin-Jimenez, Alberto. 2005. "Changing Scales and the Scales of Change: Ethnography and Political Economy in Antofagasta, Chile." *Critique of Anthropology* 25 (2): 157–76.
Croll, Elisabeth. 1981. *The Politics of Marriage in Contemporary China.* Cambridge: Cambridge University Press.
Dean, Kenneth. 1993. *Taoist Rituals and Popular Cults in Southeast China.* Princeton, NJ: Princeton University Press.
Dean, Kenneth. 2003. "Local Communal Religion in Contemporary South-East China." *China Quarterly* 174:338–58.
Delahaye, Hubert. 2002. "The Duilian, Parallel and Converging Sentences: A Few Sociological Aspects." *Études chinoises* 21 (1–2): 41–66.
Delaney, David, and Helga Leitner. 1997. "The Political Construction of Scale." *Political Geography* 16 (2): 93–97.
Derleth, James, and Daniel R. Koldyk. 2004. "The *Shequ* Experiment." *Journal of Contemporary China* 13 (41): 747–77.
Ding, Yuling. 2004. "*Kuaguo wangluo zhong de qiaoxiang: haiwai huaren yu fujian shudoucun de shehui bianqian*" [Transnational networks and social change in a Fujian emigrant]. PhD diss., Chinese University of Hong Kong.
Dirlik, Arif. 2004. "It Is Not Where You Are From, It Is Where You Are At: Place-Based Alternatives to Diaspora Discourses." In *Worlds on the Move: Globalization, Migration and Cultural Security*, edited by J. Friedman and S. Randeria, 141–66. London: I. B. Tauris.
Dirlik, Arif, and Richard Wilson, eds. 1995. *Asia/Pacific as Space of Cultural Production.* Durham, NC: Duke University Press.
Douw, Leo, Cen Huang, and Michael R. Godley. 1999. *Qiaoxiang Ties: Interdisciplinary Approaches to "Cultural Capitalism" in South China.* Leiden: International Institute for Asian Studies.
Du, Juan. 2008. "Don't Underestimate the Rice Fields." In *Urban Transformation*, edited by I. Andreas and R. Andreas, 218–25. Berlin: Ruby Press.
Duara, Prasenjit. 1997. "Nationalists among Transnationals: Overseas Chinese and the Idea of China, 1900–1911." In *Ungrounded Empires: The Cultural Politics of Mod-

ern Chinese Transnationalism, edited by A. Ong and D. Nonini, 39–60. New York: Routledge.

Dufoix, Stéphane. 2011. *La dispersion: Une histoire des usages du mot diaspora*. Paris: Éditions Amsterdam.

Dzenovska, Dace. 2012. "The Great Departure: Rethinking National(ist) Common Sense." *Journal of Ethnic and Migration Studies* 39 (2): 201–18.

Ebeling, Richard M. 2010. "The Great Chinese Inflation." Foundation for Economic Education. Accessed November 25, 2016. https://fee.org/articles/the-great-chinese-inflation/.

Ebrey, Patricia. 1986. "The Early Stages in the Development of Descent Group Organization." In *Kinship Organization in Late Imperial China, 1000–1940*, edited by Patricia Ebrey and James L. Watson, 16–61. Berkeley: University of California Press.

Ebrey, Patricia. 1991. *Confucianism and Family Rituals in Imperial China: A Social History of Writing about Rites*. Princeton, NJ: Princeton University Press.

Ebrey, Patricia. 2003. *Women and the Family in Chinese History*. New York: Routledge.

Ebrey, Patricia, and James L. Watson. 1986. *Kinship Organization in Late Imperial China, 1000–1940*. Berkeley: University of California Press.

Ebron, Paulla L. 1999. "Tourists as Pilgrims: Commercial Fashioning of Transatlantic Politics." *American Ethnologist* 26:910–32.

Edin, Mark. 2003. "State Capacity and Local Agent Control in China: CCP Cadre Management from a Township Perspective." *China Quarterly* 173:33–52.

Ekholm Friedman, K., and Jonathan Friedman. 2008. *Historical Transformations: The Anthropology of Global Systems*. Walnut Creek, CA: Altamira.

Evans-Pritchard, Edward E., and Meyer Fortes. 1940. *African Political Systems*. London: Oxford University Press.

Falk Moore, Sally. 1999. "Reflections on the Comaroff Lecture." *American Ethnologist* 26 (2): 304–6.

Fan, Shun Ching. 1974. *The Population of Hong Kong*. Hong Kong: Committee for International Coordination of National Research in Demography.

Fan, C. Cindy. 2008. *China on the Move: Migration, the State, and the Household*. Routledge Studies in Human Geography 21. London, New York: Routledge.

Fassin, Didier. 2009. "Les économies morales revisitées." *Annales. Histoire, Sciences Sociales* 64 (6): 1237–66.

Faure, David. 1989. "The Lineage as a Cultural Invention." *Modern China* 15 (1): 4–36.

Faure, David. 2006. *China and Capitalism: A History of Business Enterprise in Modern China*. Hong Kong: Hong Kong University Press.

Faure, David. 2007. *Emperor and Ancestor: State and Lineage in South China*. Stanford, CA: Stanford University Press.

Faure, David., and Helen F. Siu, eds. 1995. *Down to Earth: The Territorial Bond in South China*. Stanford, CA: Stanford University Press.

Fei, Xiaotong. 1992. *From the Soil: The Foundations of Chinese Society*. Berkeley: University of California Press.

Fenwick, Ann. 1984. "Evaluating China's Special Economic Zones." *International Tax and Business Law* 2 (2): 376–97.

Ferguson, James. 2011. "Novelty and Method: Reflections on Global Fieldwork." In *Multisited Ethnography: Problems and Possibilities in the Translocation of Research Methods*, edited by Simon Coleman and Pauline von Hellermann, 194–208. New York: Routledge.

Feuchtwang, Stephan D. 1974. *An Anthropological Analysis of Chinese Geomancy*. Vientiane: Vithagna.

Feuchtwang, Stephan D. 1998. "What Is a Village?" In *China's Rural Development: Between State and Private Interests*, edited by E. Vermeer, F. Pieke, and W. L. Chong, 46–74. New York: M. E. Sharpe.

Feuchtwang, Stephan D. 2000. "Religion as Resistance." In *Chinese Society: Change, Conflict and Resistance*, edited by E. J. Perry and M. Selden, 161–77. New York: Routledge.

Feuchtwang, Stephan D. 2002. "Tales of Territoriality: The Urbanization of Meifa Village, China." *Études rurales* 163–164 (3): 249–66.

Firth, Raymond. 1956. *Two Studies of Kinship in London*. London: Athlone.

Fitzgerald, Stephen. 1972. *China and the Overseas Chinese: A Study of Peking's Changing Policy, 1949–1970*. Cambridge: Cambridge University Press.

Flower, John M. 2004. "A Road Is Made: Roads, Temples, and Historical Memory in Ya'an County, Sichuan." *Journal of Asian Studies* 63 (3): 649–85.

Foucault, Michel. 1998. "Different Spaces." In *Aesthetics, Method, and Epistemology: Essential Works of Foucault*, Vol. 2, edited by J. D. Faubion, 175–185. New York: New Press.

Frank, Andre Gunder. 1998. *Re-orient: Global Economy in the Asian Age*. Berkeley: University of California Press.

Freedman, Maurice. 1958. *Lineage Organization in Southeastern China*. London: Athlone.

Freedman, Maurice. 1966. *Chinese Lineage and Society: Fukien and Kwangtung*. London: Athlone.

Freedman, Maurice, ed. 1970. *Family and Kinship in Chinese Society*. Stanford, CA: Stanford University Press.

Friedman, Jonathan. 1994. *Cultural Identity and Global Process*. London: Sage.

Friedman, Jonathan. 2002. "From Roots to Routes: Tropes for Trekkers." *Anthropological Theory* 2 (1): 21–36.

Fu, Chen. 2003. *Nongcun shequxing gufenhezuozhiyanjiu* [Research of the rural community-based shareholding cooperatives]. Beijing: Zhongguo jingjichubanshe.

Gallo, Esther. 2009. "In the Right Place at the Right Time? Reflections on Multi-sited Ethnography in the Age of Migration." In *Multi-sited Ethnography: Theory, Praxis and Locality in Contemporary Research*, edited by Mark-Anthony Falzon, 87–102. Oxford: Ashgate.

Gardiner Barber, Pauline, and Winnie Lem, eds. 2018. *Migration, Temporality, and Capitalism: Entangled Mobilities across Global Spaces*. Cham: Palgrave Macmillan.

Gates, Hill. 1987. "Money for the Gods." *Modern China* 13 (3): 259–77.

Gazier, Bernard, and Jean-Pierre Touffut. 2006. "Public Goods, Social Enactions." In *Advancing Public Goods*, edited by Jean-Pierre Touffut, 1–12. Cheltenham, UK: Edward Elgar.

Gernet, Jacques. 1995. *Buddhism in Chinese Society: An Economic History from the Fifth to the Tenth Centuries*. New York: Columbia University Press.

Gille, Zsuzsa, and Seán O'Riain. 2002. "Global Ethnography." *Annual Review of Sociology* 28:271–95.

Ginzburg, Carlo. 1989. "Clues: Roots of an Evidential Paradigm." *Clues, Myths, and the Historical Method*, 96–125. Baltimore: Johns Hopkins University Press.

Glick Schiller, Nina, Linda Basch, and Christina Blanc-Szanton. 1992. *Towards a Transnational Perspective on Migration: Race, Ethnicity, and Nationalism Reconsidered*. New York: New York Academy of Sciences.

Glick Schiller, Nina, and Noel Salazar. 2012. "Regimes of Mobility across the Globe." *Journal of Ethnic and Migration Studies* 39 (2): 1–18.

Gluckman, Max. 2006. "Ethnographic Data in British Social Anthropology." In *The Manchester School: Practice and Ethnographic Praxis in Anthropology*, edited by Terry M. S. Evens and Don Handelman, 13–23. New York: Berghahn.

Goffman, Erving. 1967. *Interaction Ritual: Essays on Face-to-Face Behavior.* Garden City, NY: Doubleday.

Goffman, Erving. 1972. *Relations in Public: Microstudies of the Public Order.* New York: Basic Books.

Goossaert, Vincent, and Ling Fang. 2008. "Les réformes funéraires et la politique religieuse de l'état chinois, 1900–2008." *Archives de sciences sociales des religions* 144:51–73.

Gordon, Edmund T., and Mark Anderson. 1999. "The African Diaspora: Toward an Ethnography of Diasporic Identification." *Journal of American Folklore* 112 (445): 282–96.

Graeber, David. 2001. "Turning Modes of Production Inside Out: Or, Why Capitalism Is a Transformation of Slavery." *Critique of Anthropology* 26 (1): 61–85.

Graeber, David. 2006. *Toward an Anthropological Theory of Value: The False Coin of Our Own Dreams.* New York: Palgrave-Macmillan.

Granet, Marcel. 1998. *La religion des Chinois.* Paris: Albin Michel.

Gu, Minkang. 1999. "The Joint Stock Cooperative Enterprise: A New Independent Legal Entity in China." *Hastings International and Comparative Law Review* 23 (1): 125–48.

Gu, Minkang. 2010. *Understanding Chinese Company Law.* Hong Kong: Hong Kong University Press.

Guerassimoff, Éric. 2006. "Des coolies aux Chinois d'outre-mer: La question des migrations dans les relations sino-américaines. années 1850–1890." *Annales. Histoire, sciences sociales* 1:63–98.

Guldin, Gregory E. 1995. "Toward a Greater Guangdong: Hong Kong's Sociocultural Impact on the Pearl River Delta and Beyond." In *The Hong Kong–Guangdong Link*, edited by Reginald Yin-Wang Kwok, Alvin Y. So, and Ming K. Chan, 89–118. Armonk: M. E. Sharpe.

Guo, Xiaolin. 2001. "Land Expropriation and Rural Conflicts in China." *China Quarterly* 166:422–39.

Guo, Man, and Carsten Herrmann-Pillath. 2019. "Exploring Extended Kinship in Twenty-First-Century China: A Conceptual Case Study." *Journal of Current Chinese Affairs* 48 (1): 50–75.

Gupta, Akhil, and James Ferguson, eds. 1997. *Culture, Power, Place: Explorations in Critical Anthropology.* Durham, NC: Duke University Press.

Handelman, Don. 2005. "The Extended Case: Interactional Foundations and Prospective Dimensions." *Social Analysis* 49 (3): 61–84.

Hann, Chris. 2011. "Embedded Socialism? Land, Labour and Market in Eastern Xinjiang." In *Market and Society: The Great Transformation Today*, edited by Chris Hann and Keith Hart, 256–81. Cambridge: Cambridge University Press.

Harrell, Steve. 1974. "When a Ghost Becomes a God." In *Religion and Ritual in Chinese Society*, edited by A. P. Wolf, 193–206. Stanford, CA: Stanford University Press.

Harvey, David. 1989. *The Condition of Postmodernity: An Enquiry into the Origins of Cultural Change.* Cambridge, MA: Blackwell.

Harvey, David. 2000. "Cosmopolitanism and the Banality of Geographical Evils." *Public Culture* 12 (2): 529–64.

Hastrup, Kirsten. 1994. "Anthropological Knowledge Incorporated: Discussion." In *Social Experience and Anthropological Knowledge*, edited by Kirsten Hastrup and Peter Hervik, 1–12. London: Routledge.

He, Shenjing, and Desheng Xue. 2014. "Identity Building and Communal Resistance against Landgrabs in Wukan Village, China." *Current Anthropology* 55 (S9): S126–37.

Heidegger, Martin. 1975. *Poetry, Language, Thought.* New York: Harper.

Herod, Andrew. 1997. "Labour's Spatial Praxis and the Geography of Contract Bargaining in the US East Coast Longshore Industry, 1953–89." *Political Geography* 16 (2): 145–69.

Hertz, Ellen. 1998. *The Trading Crowd: An Ethnography of the Shanghai Stock Market*. Cambridge: Cambridge University Press.

Herzfeld, Michael. 1992. *The Social Production of Indifference: Exploring the Symbolic Roots of Western Bureaucracy*. Oxford: Berg.

Herzfeld, Michael. 2016. *Cultural Intimacy: Social Poetics in the Nation State*. New York: Routledge.

Heyman, Josiah, and Howard Campbell. 2009. "The Anthropology of Global Flows: A Critical Reading of Appadurai's 'Disjuncture and Difference in the Global Cultural Economy.'" *Anthropological Theory* 9 (2): 131–48.

Ho, Elaine, and Julia Kuehn, eds. 2009. *China Abroad: Travels, Subjects, Spaces*. Hong Kong: Hong Kong University Press.

Hoe, Yow Cheun. 2013. *Guangdong and Chinese Diaspora: The Changing Landscape of Qiaoxiang*. New York: Routledge.

Horst, Cindy. 2009. "Expanding Sites: The Question of 'Depth' Explored." In *Multi-sited Ethnography*, edited by Mark-Anthony Falzon, 119–34. London: Routledge.

Hsiao, Kung-chuan. 1960. *Rural China: Imperial Control in the Nineteenth Century*. Seattle: University of Washington Press.

Hsing, You-Tien. 1997. "Building Guanxi across the Straits: Taiwanese Capital and Local Chinese Bureaucrats." In *Ungrounded Empires*, edited by Aihwa Ong and Donald Nonini, 143–64. New York: Routledge.

Hsing, You-Tien. 2006. "Land and Territorial Politics in Urban China." *China Quarterly* 187:575–91.

Hsu, Francis L. K. 1963. *Clan, Caste and Club*. Princeton, NJ: Van Nostrand.

Hsu, Madeline Y. 2000. *Dreaming of Gold, Dreaming of Home: Migration and Transnationalism in Taishan County, Guangdong, 1882–1943*. Stanford, CA: Stanford University Press.

Huang, Yeqing. 2014. "The Continuity and Changes of the Hukou System Since the 1990s: A Critical Review." In *Urban China in the New Era*, edited by Zhiming Cheng, Mark Wang, and Junhua Chen, 25–43. Berlin, Heidelberg: Springer Berlin Heidelberg.

Hu, Hsien Chin. 1948. *The Common Descent Group in China and Its Functions*. New York: Random House.

Hu-Dehart, Evelyn. 1999. *Across the Pacific: Asian Americans and Globalization*. Philadelphia: Temple University Press.

Huang, Kunzhang, and Yinglong Zhang, eds. 2003. *Huaqiao huaren yu zhongguo qiaoxiang de xiandaihua* [Overeas Chinese and the modernization of *qiaoxiang* in China]. Beijing: Overseas Chinese Publisher.

Huang, Shu-Min. 1992. "Re-examining the Extended Family in Chinese Peasant Society: Findings from a Fujian." *Australian Journal of Chinese Affairs* 27:5–38.

Hui, Yew-Foong. 2011. *Strangers at Home: History and Subjectivity among the Chinese Communities of West Kalimantan, Indonesia*. Leiden: Brill.

Hutynk, John. 1998. "Clifford's Ethnographica." *Critique of Anthropology* 18 (4): 339–78.

Inda, Jonathan X. 2005. "Analytics of the Modern: An Introduction." In *Anthropologies of Modernity: Foucault, Government, and Life Politics*, edited by Jonathan Xavier Inda, 1–22. Malden, MA: Blackwell.

Inglis, Christina. 1991. "Women and Trade: A Chinese Example from Papua New Guinea." In *An Old State in New Settings. Studies in the Social Anthropology of*

China: In Memory of Maurice Freedman, edited by H. Baker and S. Feuchtwang, 44–69. Oxford: Jaso.

Ingold, Tim. 2011. *The Perception of the Environment: Essays on Livelihood, Dwelling and Skill*. London: Routledge.

Jacka, Tamara, and Sally Sargeson. 2001. *Women, Gender and Rural Development in China*. Cheltenham, UK: Edward Elgar.

Jackson, Jonathan C. 2008. "Reforming the Dead: The Intersection of Socialist Merit and Agnatic Descent in a Chinese Funeral Home." PhD diss., University of California Los Angeles.

Jackson, Michael. 2005. *Existential Anthropology, Events, Exigencies and Affects*. New York: Berghahn.

Jing, Jun. 1996. *The Temple of Memories: History, Power, and Morality in a Chinese Village*. Stanford, CA: Stanford University Press.

Johansen, J. Prytz, introduction by Marshall Sahlins. 2015 (1954). *The Maori and his religion in its non-ritualistic aspects*. Hau books. https://haubooks.org/the-maori-and-his-religion/.

Johnson, Ellen L. 1975. "Women and Childbearing in Kwan Mun Hau Village." In *Women in Chinese Society*, edited by Margery Wolf and Roxane Witke, 215–42. Stanford, CA: Stanford University Press.

Johnson, Ellen L. 1988. "Grieving for the Dead, Grieving for the Living: Funeral Laments of Hakka Women." In *Death Ritual in Late Imperial and Modern China*, edited by James L. Watson and Evelyn S. Rawski, 135–63. Berkeley: University of California Press.

Johnson, Graham E. 1993. "The Political Economy of Chinese Urbanization: Guangdong and the Pearl River Delta Region." In *Urban Anthropology in China*, edited by Gregory Guldin and Aidan Southall, 185–220. Westport, CT: Greenwood.

Johnson, Graham E. 1994. "Open for Business, Open to the World: Consequences of Global Incorporation in Guangdong and the Pearl River Delta." In *The Economic Transformation of South China: Reform and Development in the Post-Mao Era*, edited by Thomas P. Lyons and Victor Nee, 55–87. Ithaca, NY: Cornell University Press.

Johnson, Graham E. 2007. "Comings and Goings: Pearl River Delta Identities in an Era of Change and Transformation." In *Chinese Transnational Networks*, edited by C. B. Tan, 23–48. New York: Routledge.

Johnson, Graham E., and Fong-Yuen Woon. 1997. "The Response to Rural Reform in an Overseas Chinese Area: Examples from Two Localities in the Western Pearl River Delta Region." *Modern Asian Studies* 31 (1): 31–59.

Jones, Martin, and Martin MacLeod. 2004. "Regional Spaces, Spaces of Regionalism: Territory, Insurgent Politics and the English Question." *Transactions of the Institute of British Geographers New Series* 29 (4): 433–52

Judd, Ellen R. 2005. *Gender and Power in Rural North China*. Stanford: Stanford University Press, 1994.

Kalb, Don, and Herman Tak, eds. 2005. *Critical Junctions: Anthropology and History beyond the Cultural Turn*. New York: Berghahn.

Kapferer, Bruce. 2000. "Star Wars: About Anthropology, Culture and Globalisation." *Australian Journal of Anthropology* 11:174–98.

Keane, Webb. 2003. "Self-Interpretation, Agency and the Objects of Anthropology." *Contemporary Studies in Society and History* 45 (2): 222–48.

Keesing, Roger. 1984. "Rethinking Mana." *Journal of Anthropological Research* 40:137–56.

Keightley, David. 2004. "The Making of the Ancestors: Late Shang Religion and Its Legacy." In *Chinese Religion and Society: The Transformation of a Field*, Vol. 1, edited by John Lagerwey, 3–63. Hong Kong: Chinese University of Hong Kong Press.

Kern, Martin. 2000. "*Shi jing* Songs as Performance Texts: A Case Study of 'Chu Ci' (Thorny Caltrop)." *Early China* 25:49–111.

King, Ambrose Y. C. 1995. "Zhongguoren de 'gong,' 'si' guannian. Jianlun zhongguo ren dui gong si de lijie" [Chinese people's concepts of public and private]. In *Gong yi si, renquan yu gongmin shehui de fazhan* [Public and private. The development of human rights and civil society in China], edited by Sihui Wen and Canhui Zhang, 151–66. Hong Kong: Humanities Publishing.

Kipnis, Andrew. 2006. "School Consolidation in Rural China." *Development Bulletin.*

Kipnis, Andrew. 2016. *From Village to City: Social Transformation in a Chinese County Seat.* Oakland: University of California Press.

Kluckhohn, Clyde. 1962. "Values and Value-Orientations in the Theory of Action: An Exploration in Definition and Classification." In *Toward a General Theory of Action*, edited by Talcott Parsons and Edward Shils, 388–433. Cambridge, MA: Harvard University Press.

Ku, H.-B. 2003. *Moral Politics in a South Chinese Village: Responsibility, Reciprocity, and Resistance.* Lanham, MD: Rowman & Littlefield.

Kuah, Khun Eng. 1999. "The Singapore-Anxi Connection." In *Qiaoxiang Ties: Interdisciplinary Approaches to "Cultural Capitalism" in South China*, edited by Leo Douw, Cen Huang, and Michael R. Godley, 143–57. Leiden: International Institute for Asian Studies.

Kuah-Pearce, Khun Eng. 2011. *Rebuilding the Ancestral Village: Singaporeans in China.* Hong Kong: Hong Kong University Press.

Kuah-Pearce, Khun Eng, and Siu-Lun Wong. 2001. "Dialect and Territorial-Based Associations: Cultural and Identity Brokers in Hong Kong." In *Hong Kong Reintegrating with China: Political, Cultural and Social Dimensions*, edited by Pui-Tak Lee, 203–18. Hong Kong: Hong Kong University Press.

Kulp, Daniel H. 1925. *Country Life in South China: The Sociology of Familism.* Vol. I. *Phenix Village, Kwantung.* New York: Columbia University Press.

Lagerwey, John. 1996. Preface to *Meizhou diqu de miaohui yu zongzu* [Temple festivals and lineages in Meizhou], by Fang Xuejia, 1–14. Hong Kong: International Association of Hakka Studies and École française d'Extrême-Orient.

Lai, Walton Look. 2007. "The Chinese of Trinidad and Tobago: Mobility, Modernity and Assimilation during and after Colonialism." In *Chinese Transnational Networks*, edited by Chee-Beng Tan, 191–210. London: Routledge.

Lan, Yuyun. 2004. *Dushi lide cunzhuang* [Villages in the city]. Beijing: Sanlian shudian.

Leite, Naomi. 2005. "Travels to an Ancestral Past: On Diasporic Tourism, Embodied Memory, and Identity." *Antropologicas* 9:273–302.

Leo, Jessieca. 2015. *Global Hakka: Hakka Identity in the Remaking.* Leiden: Brill.

Leonard, Karen. 2009. "Changing Places: The Advantages of Multi-sited Ethnography." In *Multi-sited Ethnography*, edited by Mark-Anthony Falzon, 165–79. London: Routledge.

Leong, Sow-Theng. 1997. *Migration and Ethnicity in Chinese History: Hakkas, Pengmin, and Their Neighbors.* Edited by T. Wright. Stanford, CA: Stanford University Press.

Lever-Tracy, Constance, David F. K. Ip, and Noel Tracy, eds. 1996. *The Chinese Diaspora and Mainland China: An Emerging Economic Synergy.* London: Macmillan.

Lévi-Strauss, C. 1950. *Introduction à l'œuvre de Marcel Mauss.* Paris: Presses universitaires de France.

Levitt, Peggy, and Nina Glick Schiller. 2004. "Conceptualizing Simultaneity: A Transnational Social Field Perspective on Society." *International Migration Review* 38 (3): 1002–39.

Lewis, Mark E. 2006. *The Construction of Space in Early China*. Albany: State University of New York Press.

Li, Minghuan, ed. 2005. *Fujian qiaoxiang diaocha: qiaoxiang rentong, qiaoxiang wangluo yu qiaoxiang wenhua* [Emigrant villages in Fujian: Identity, networks and culture]. Xiamen: Xiamen University Press.

Li, Peilin, 2004. *Cunluo de zhongjie* [The end of villages]. Beijing: Shengwu Yinshuguan.

Li, Ruojian. 2006. *"Diwei huode de jiyu yu zhangai: Jiyu wailai renkou juji qude zhiye jiegou fenxi"* [Advantages, opportunities and obstacles of locality: An analysis of the structural occupation of areas with high concentrations of migrant population]. *Zhongguo renkou kexue* 5:69–78.

Li, Xiangping. 2014. *"Zongjiao shehuixing ji qi biaoda—zhongguo zongjiao shehuixue de qiben mingti"* [The social dimension of religion and its representation: A fundamental thesis of Chinese sociology of religion]. In *Marxism and Religion*, edited by D. Lü and X. Gong, 95–133. Leiden: Brill.

Liao, Chiyang. 2015. *Kuayue shijie: Liu xuesheng yu xin huaqiao* [A transnational world: Overseas students and new migrants], Vol. 2. Shanghai: Chinese Academy of Social Sciences Press.

Lin, George C. S. 2006. "Peri-urbanism in Globalizing China: A Study of New Urbanism in Dongguan." *Eurasian Geography and Economics* 47 (1): 28–53.

Lin, Jiajing. 1999. *"Jindai Guangdong qiaohui yanjiu"* [Research on remittances in modern Guangdong]. *Dongnanya Xuekan* [Southeast Asian studies] 4:46–59.

Liu, Guofu. 2007. *The Right to Leave and Return and Chinese Migration Law*. Leiden: Martinus Nijhoff.

Liu, Hong, and Els Van Dongen. 2016. "China's Diaspora Policies as a New Mode of Transnational Governance." *Journal of Contemporary China* 25 (102): 805–21.

Liu, Hui-chen Wang. 1959. *The Traditional Chinese Clan Rules*. New York: J. J. Augustin.

Liu, Yaling. 2009. *"Zhongguo dushihua guochengzhong xinxing de nongmin shouzujieji: Wenzhou yu wuxi chengzhongcun de zhuanxing lujing, jiti kangzheng yu fuli zhengce"* [The new "peasant rentier" class in urbanizing China: Resistance of the collectives and welfare politics in Wenzhou and Wuxi]. *Taiwanese Sociology* 18:5–41.

Liu, Yuting, Shenjing He, Fulong Wu, and Chris Webster. 2010. "Urban Villages under China's Rapid Urbanization: Unregulated Assets and Transitional Neighborhoods." *Habitat International* 34:135–44.

Live, Yu-Sion. 2003. "Illusion identitaire et métissage culturel chez les 'Sinoi' de la Réunion." *Perspectives chinoises* 78. http://journals.openedition.org/perspectiveschinoises/160.

Lombard, Denys, and Jean Aubin, eds. 1995. *Marchands et hommes d'affaires asiatiques dans l'océan Indien et la mer de Chine: XIIIᵉ–XXᵉ siècles*. Paris: Éditions de l'EHESS.

Lora-Wainwright, Anna. 2013. *Fighting for Breath: Living Morally and Dying of Cancer in a Chinese Village*. Honolulu: University of Hawai'i Press.

Louie, Andrea. 2000. "Re-territorializing Transnationalism: Chinese Americans and the Chinese Motherland." *American Ethnologist* 27 (3): 645–69.

Louie, Andrea. 2001. "Crafting Places through Mobility: Chinese American 'Roots-Searching' in China." *Identities* 8:343–79.

Louie, Andrea. 2004. *Chineseness across Borders. Renegotiating Chinese Identities in China and the United States*. Durham, NC: Duke University Press.

Lowenthal, David. 1972. *West Indian Societies*. New York: Oxford University Press.

Ly, Jillt. 2003. *Adieu l'étang aux chevrettes*. Tahiti: Éditions Te Ite.

Ma, Laurence J. C., and Carolyn Cartier, eds. 2003. *The Chinese Diaspora: Space, Place, Mobility and Identity*. Lanham, MD: Rowman & Littlefield.

Ma, Laurence J. C., and Fulong Wu, eds. 2005. *Restructuring the Chinese City: Changing Society, Economy and Space.* New York: Routledge.

Madsen, Richard. 1984. *Morality and Power in a Chinese Village.* Berkeley: University of California Press.

Makovicky, Nicolette, Anne-Christine Trémon, and Sheyla S. Zandonai. 2018. *Slogans: Subjection, Subversion, and the Politics of Neoliberalism.* London: Routledge.

Marcus, George. 1995. "Ethnography in/of the World System: The Emergence of Multi-sited Ethnography." *Annual Review of Anthropology* 24:95–117.

Marston, Sallie A. 2000. "The Social Construction of Scale." *Progress in Human Geography* 24 (2): 219–42.

Mauss, Marcel. 1972. *A General Theory of Magic.* Translated by Robert Brain. London: Routledge and Kegan Paul.

McKeown, Adam. 1999. "Conceptualizing Chinese Diasporas, 1842 to 1949." *Journal of Asian Studies* 58 (2): 306–37.

McKeown, Adam. 2000. "From Opium Farmer to Astronaut: A Global History of Diasporic Chinese Business." *Diaspora* 9 (3): 317–61.

McKeown, Adam. 2010. "Chinese Emigration in Global Context, 1850–1840." *Journal of Global History* 5:95–24.

Mintz, Sidney W. 1998. "The Localization of Anthropological Practice: From Area Studies to Transnationalism." *Critique of Anthropology* 18 (2): 117–33.

Mitchell, James Clyde. 1983. "Case and Situation Analysis." *Sociological Review* 31 (2): 187–211.

Mueggler, Erik. 2001. *The Age of Wild Ghosts. Memory, Violence, and Place in Southwest China.* Berkeley: University of California Press.

Munn, Nancy D. 2007. *The Fame of Gawa: A Symbolic Study of Value Transformation in a Massim (Papua New Guinea) Society.* Durham, NC: Duke University Press.

Naquin, Susan, and Evelyn Rawski. 1987. *Chinese Society in the Eighteenth Century.* New Haven, CT: Yale University Press.

Nash, June. 1981. "Ethnographic Aspects of the World Capitalist System." *Annual Review of Anthropology* 10:393–423.

Nelson, H. G. H. 1974. "Ancestor Worship and Burial Practices." In *Religion and Ritual in Chinese Society,* edited by Arthur P. Wolf, 251–77. Stanford, CA: Stanford University Press.

Neveling, Patrick. 2015. "Export Processing Zones, Special Economic Zones and the Long March of Capitalist Development Policies during the Cold War." In *Negotiating Independence: New Directions in the Histories of the Cold War and Decolonization,* edited by Leslie James and Elisabeth Leake, 63–84. London: Bloomsbury.

Ng, Mee Kam. 2003. "Shenzhen." *Cities* 20 (6): 429–41.

Ngeow, Chow Bing. 2010. "Democratic Development in China's Urban Communities." PhD diss., Northeastern University.

Nonini, Donald. 2008. "Is China Becoming Neoliberal?" *Critique of Anthropology* 28 (2): 145–76.

Nonini, Donald. 2015. *"Getting By": Class and State Formation among Chinese in Malaysia.* Ithaca, NY: Cornell University Press.

Nonini, Donald, and Ida Susser. 2019. *The Tumultuous Politics of Scale: Unsettled States, Migrants, Movements in Flux.* London: Routledge.

Nyíri, Pál. 2002. "From Class Enemies to Patriots." In *Globalizing Chinese Migration,* edited by Pál Nyíri and Igor R. Saveliev, 208–41. Aldershot, UK: Ashgate.

Nyíri, Pál. 2010. *Mobility and Cultural Authority in Contemporary China.* Seattle: University of Washington Press.

O'Brien, Kevin. 1994. "Implementing Political Reform in China's Villages." *Australian Journal of Chinese Affairs* 32:33–59.

OCAO (Overseas Chinese Affairs Office), ed. 2000. *Deng Xiaoping's Speeches on* Qiaowu. Beijing: Zhongyang Wenxian chubanshe.

O'Donnell, Mary Ann. 2001. "Becoming Hong Kong, Razing Bao'an, Preserving Xin'an: An Ethnographic Account of Urbanization in the Shenzhen Special Economic Zone." *Cultural Studies* 15 (3–4): 419–43.

O'Donnell, Mary Ann, Winnie Wong, and Jonathan Bach, eds. 2017. *Learning from Shenzhen: China's Post-Mao Experiment from Special Zone to Model City*. Chicago: University of Chicago Press.

OECD (Organisation for Economic Co-operation and Development). 2017. "OECD Initiative for Policy Dialogue on Global Value Chains, Production Transformation and Development." Accessed November 11, 2018. https://www.oecd.org/dev/PTPR-PM_Shenzhen.pdf.

Oi, Jean C. 1989. *State and Peasant in Contemporary China: The Political Economy of Village Government*. Berkeley: University of California Press.

Oksenberg, Michael. 2001. "China's Political System: Challenges of the Twenty-First Century." *China Journal* 45:21–35.

Ong, Aihwa. 1999. *Flexible Citizenship: The Cultural Logics of Transnationality*. Durham, NC: Duke University Press.

Ong, Aihwa. 2006. *Neoliberalism as Exception: Mutations in Citizenship and Sovereignty*. Durham, NC: Duke University Press.

Ong, Aihwa, and Donald Nonini, eds. 1997. *Ungrounded Empires: The Cultural Politics of Modern Chinese Transnationalism*. New York: Routledge.

Ostrom, Vincent, and Elinor Ostrom. 1977. "Public Goods and Public Choices." In *Alternatives for Delivering Public Services: Toward Improved Performance*, edited by Emanuel S. Savas, 7–49. Boulder, CO: Westview.

Oxfeld, Ellen. 1993. *Blood, Sweat and Mahjong: Family and Enterprise in an Overseas Chinese Community*. Ithaca, NY: Cornell University Press.

Oxfeld, Ellen. 2010. *Drink Water, but Remember the Source: Moral Discourse in a Chinese Village*. Berkeley: University of California Press.

Palomera, Jaime, and Theodora Vetta. 2016. "Moral Economy: Rethinking a Radical Concept." *Anthropological Theory* 16 (4): 413–32.

Pan, Hongli. 2006. "The Old Folks' Associations and Lineage Revival in Contemporary Villages of Southern Fujian Province." In *Southern Fujian: Reproduction of Traditions in Post-Mao China*, edited by Chee-Beng Tan, 69–96. Hong Kong: Chinese University Press.

Pan, Lynn. 1990. *Sons of the Yellow Emperor: A History of the Chinese Diaspora*. Boston: Little, Brown.

Pan, Lynn. 2000. *Encyclopédie de la diaspora chinoise*. Paris : Les Éditions du Pacifique.

Parish, William L., and Martin K. Whyte. 1978. *Village and Family in Contemporary China*. Chicago: University of Chicago Press.

Parry, Jonathan, and Maurice Bloch, eds. 1989. *Money and the Morality of Exchange*. Cambridge: Cambridge University Press.

Pasternak, Burton. 1972. *Kinship and Community in Two Chinese Villages*. Stanford, CA: Stanford University Press.

Pasternak, Burton. 1973. "Chinese Tale-Telling Tombs." *Ethnology* 12 (3): 259–73.

Pasternak, Burton. 2002. "The Disquieting Chinese Lineage and Its Anthropological Relevance." In *The Chinese Family and Its Ritual Behavior*, edited by Jih-chang Hsieh and Ying-Chang Chuang, 165–91. Taipei: Academia Sinica.

Paton, Michael J. 2007. "Fengshui: A Continuation of 'Art of Swindlers'?" *Journal of Chinese Philosophy* 34 (3): 427–45.

Pei, Xiaolin. 2002. "The Contribution of Collective Land Ownership to China's Economic Transition and Rural Industrialization: A Resource Allocation Model." *Modern China* 28 (1): 279–314.

Perry, Elisabeth J., and Mark Selden, eds. 2000. *Chinese Society: Change, Conflict and Resistance*. New York: Routledge.

Peterson, Glen. 1988. "Socialist China and the *Huaqiao*: The Transition to Socialism in the Overseas Chinese Areas of Rural Guangdong 1949–1956." *Modern China* 14 (3): 309–35.

Peterson, Glen. 2012. *Overseas Chinese in the People's Republic of China*. Abingdon, UK: Routledge.

Pieke, Frank N. 2003. "The Genealogical Mentality in Modern China." *Journal of Asian Studies* 62 (1): 101–28.

Pieke, Frank N. 2009. "Introduction: A Chinese Century in Anthropology?" *Social Anthropology* 17 (1): 1–8.

Pieke, Frank N., and Hein Mallee. 1999. *Internal and International Migration: Chinese Perspectives*. New York: Routledge.

Pieke, Frank N., Pál Nyíri, Mette Thunø, and Antonella Ceccagno. 2004. *Transnational Chinese: Fujianese Migrants in Europe*. Stanford, CA: Stanford University Press.

Po, Lanchih. 2008. "Redefining Rural Collectives in China: Land Conversion and the Emergence of Rural Shareholding Cooperatives." *Urban Studies* 4:1603–23.

Potter, Jack M. 1970. "Land and Lineage in Traditional China." In *Family and Kinship in Chinese Society*, edited by Maurice Freedman, 121–38. Stanford, CA: Stanford University Press.

Potter, Jack M. 1974. "Cantonese Shamanism." In *Religion and Ritual in Chinese Society*, edited by Arthur P. Wolf, 207–31. Stanford, CA: Stanford University Press.

Potter, Jack M., and Sulamith Heins Potter. 1990. *China's Peasants: The Anthropology of a Revolution*. Cambridge: Cambridge University Press.

Pratt, Jean. 1960. "Emigration and Unilineal Descent Groups: A Study of Marriage in a Hakka Village in the New Territories, Hong Kong." *Eastern Anthropologist* 13:147–58.

Puett, Michael. 2013. "Critical Approaches to Religion in China." *Critical Research on Religion* 1 (1): 95–101.

Pun, Ngai. 2005. *Made in China*. Durham, NC: Duke University Press.

Reid, Anthony. 2001. "Flows and Seepages in the Long-Term Chinese Interaction with Southeast Asia." In *Sojourners and Settlers: Histories of Southeast Asia and the Chinese*, edited by Anthony Reid, 15–50. St. Leonards, Australia: Allen & Unwin.

Reid, Anthony, ed. 2008. *The Chinese Diaspora in the Pacific*. Aldershot, UK: Ashgate.

Rose, Nicholas. 1999. *Powers of Freedom: Reframing Political Thought*. Cambridge: Cambridge University Press.

Rouse, Roger. 1991. "Mexican Migration and the Social Space of Postmodernism." *Diaspora* 1 (1): 8–23.

Ruf, Gregory. 1998. *Cadres and Kin: Making a Socialist Village in West China, 1921–1991*. Stanford, CA: Stanford University Press.

Russell, Andrew. 2007. "Writing Traveling Cultures: Travel and Ethnography amongst the Yakkha of East Nepal." *Ethnos* 72 (3): 361–62.

Sahlins, Marshall. 1985. *Islands of History*. Chicago: University of Chicago Press.

Sahlins, Marshall. 2013. *What Kinship Is—and Is Not*. Chicago: University of Chicago Press.

Salmon, Claudine. 1996. "Ancestral Halls, Funeral Associations, and Attempts at Re-sinicization in Nineteenth Century Netherlands India." In *Sojourners and Settlers: Histories of Southeast Asia and the Chinese*, edited by Anthony Reid, 197–98. St. Leonards, Australia: Allen & Unwin.

Sangren, P. Steven. 1984. "Traditional Chinese Corporations: Beyond Kinship." *Journal of Asian Studies* 43 (3): 391–415.

Sangren, P. Steven. 1987. *History and Magical Power in a Chinese Community*. Stanford, CA: Stanford University Press.

Santos, Gonçalo. 2009. "The 'Stove-Family' and the Process of Kinship." In *Chinese Kinship: Contemporary Anthropological Perspectives*, edited by Susanne Brandt-städter and Gonçalo D. Santos, 112–36. Abingdon, UK: Routledge.

Sartre, Jean-Paul. 2003 (1943) *L'être et le néant, Essai d'ontologie phénoménologique*. Paris: Gallimard. [1969. *Being and Nothingness: An Essay on Phenomenological Ontology*. London: Routledge.]

Sayad, Abdelmalek. 1977. "Les trois 'âges' de l'émigration algérienne en France." *Actes de la recherche en sciences sociales* 15:59–79.

Scott, James C. 1977. *The Moral Economy of the Peasant: Rebellion and Subsistence in Southeast Asia*. New Haven, CT: Yale University Press.

Shen, Jianfa, Kwan-yiu Wong, and Zhiqiang Feng. 2002. "State Sponsored and Spontaneous Urbanization in the Pearl River Delta of South China, 1980–1998." *Urban Geography* 23:674–94.

Shenzhen Statistics Bureau. 2020. *Shenzhen Tongji Nianjian 2020*. [Shenzhen Statistical Yearbook 2020.] http://tjj.sz.gov.cn/attachment/0/811/811560/8386382.pdf.

Shu, Ping. 2004. "Lineage Making in Southern China since the 1980s." In *Asia Examined: Proceedings of the 15th Biennial Conference of the Asian Studies Association of Australia*, edited by Robert Cribb. Canberra: Asian Studies Association of Australia.

Shue, Vivienne. 1980. *Peasant China in Transition: The Dynamics of Development towards Socialism, 1949–1956*. Berkeley: University of California Press.

Shue, Vivienne. 1984. "The Fate of the Commune." *Modern China* 10 (3): 259–83.

Sinn, Elisabeth. 1997. "*Xin xi guxiang*: A Study of Regional Associations as a Bonding Mechanism in the Chinese Diaspora." *Modern Asian Studies* 31 (2): 375–97.

Siu, Helen F. 1989. *Agents and Victims in South China: Accomplices in Rural Revolution*. New Haven, CT: Yale University Press.

Siu, Helen F. 1990. "Recycling Tradition: Culture, History, and Political Economy in the Chrysanthemum Festival of South China." *Comparative Studies in Society and History* 32 (4): 765–94.

Siu, Helen. 1994. "Cultural Identity and the Politics of Difference in South China." In *China in Transformation*, edited by Tu Wei-ming, 19–44. Cambridge, MA: Harvard University Press.

Siu, Helen F. 2007. "Grounding Displacement: Uncivil Urban Spaces in Post-reform South China." *American Ethnologist* 34:329–50.

Siu, Lok C. D. 2005. *Memories of a Future Home: Diasporic Citizenship of Chinese in Panama*. Stanford, CA: Stanford University Press.

Skeldon, Ronald. 1994. "Hong Kong in an International Migration System." In *Reluctant Exiles? Migration from Hong Kong and the New Overseas Chinese*, edited by Ronald Skeldon, 163–86. New York: M. E. Sharpe.

Skeldon, Ronald. 2003. "The Chinese Diaspora or the Migration of Chinese Peoples?" In *The Chinese Diaspora: Space, Place, Mobility and Identity*, edited by Laurence Ma and Carolyn Cartier, 51–68. Lanham, MD: Rowman & Littlefield.

Skinner, William G. 2001. "Creolized Chinese Societies in South East Asia." In *Sojourners and Settlers*, edited by A. Reid, 51–93. St. Leonards, Australia: Allen & Unwin.

Sklair, Leslie. 1991. "Problems of Socialist Development: The Significance of Shenzhen Special Economic Zone for China Open Door Development Strategy." *International Journal of Urban and Regional Research* 15 (2): 197–215.

Sklair, Leslie. 2001. *The Transnational Capitalist Class*. Malden, MA: Wiley-Blackwell.

Smart, Alan, and George C. S. Lin. 2007. "Local Capitalisms, Local Citizenship and Translocality: Rescaling from Below in the Pearl River Delta Region, China." *International Journal of Urban and Regional Research* 31 (2): 280–302.

Smart, Alan, and Josephine Smart. 1998. "Transnational Social Networks and Negotiated Identities in Interactions between Hong Kong and China." In *Transnationalism from Below*, edited by Michael P. Smith and Luis E. Guarnizo, 103–61. New Brunswick, NJ: Transaction.

Smart, Alan, and Josephine Smart. 2001. "Local Citizenship: Welfare Reform, Urban/Rural Status and Exclusion in China." *Environment and Planning A* 33 (10): 1853–69.

Smith, Gavin. 2014. *Intellectuals and (Counter-)Politics: Essays in Historical Realism*. New York: Berghahn.

Smith, Neil. 1984. *Uneven Development: Nature, Capital and the Production of Space*. New York: Basil Blackwell.

Smith, Neil. 2008. "Scale Bending and the Fate of the National." In *Scale and Geographic Inquiry: Nature, Society, and Method*, edited by E. Sheppard and R. B. McMaster, 192–212. Malden, MA: Blackwell.

Smith, Robert C. 2006. *Mexican New York: Transnational Lives of New Immigrants*. Berkeley: University of California Press.

Solinger, Dorothy. 1999. *Contesting Citizenship in Urban China: Peasant Migrants, the State, and the Logic of the Market*. Berkeley: University of California Press.

Solinger, Dorothy. 2006. "The Creation of a New Underclass in China and Its Implications." *Environment and Urbanization* 18 (1): 177–93.

Song, Yan, Yves Zenou, and Chengri Ding. 2008. "Let's Not Throw the Baby Out with the Bath Water: The Role of Urban Villages in Housing Rural Migrants in China." *Urban Studies* 45:313–30.

Stafford, Charles. 1999. "Separation, Reunion and the Chinese Attachment to Place." In *Internal and International Migration: Chinese Perspectives*, edited by Frank N. Pieke and Hein Mallee, 315–30. Richmond, UK: Curzon.

Stafford, Charles. 2000a. "Chinese Patriliny and the Cycles of *Yang* and *Laiwang*." In *Cultures of Relatedness: New Approaches to the Study of Kinship*, edited by Janet Carsten, 37–54. Cambridge: Cambridge University Press.

Stafford, Charles. 2000b. *Separation and Reunion in Modern China*. Cambridge: Cambridge University Press.

Steinmüller, Hans. 2013. *Communities of Complicity. Everyday Ethics in Rural China*. New York: Berghahn.

Strathern, Marilyn. 1995. *Shifting Contexts. Transformations in Anthropological Knowledge*. New York: Routledge.

Strathern, Marilyn. 1996. "Cutting the Network." *Journal of the Royal Anthropological Institute* 2:517–35.

Strathern, Marilyn. 1999."Puzzles of Scale." In *Property, Substance and Effect: Anthropological Essays on Persons and Things*, 204–61. London: Athlone.

Suryadinata, Leo. 2004. *Chinese and Nation-Building in Southeast Asia*. Singapore: Marshall Cavendish Academic.

Szonyi, Michael. 2002. *Practicing Kinship: Lineage and Descent in Late Imperial China*. Stanford, CA: Stanford University Press.

Tambiah, Stanley J. 1985a. "The Magical Power of Words." In *Culture, Thought and Social Action: An Anthropological Perspective*, edited by Stanley Tambiah, 17–59. Cambridge, MA: Harvard University Press.

Tambiah, Stanley J. 1985b. "A Performative Approach to Ritual." In *Culture, Thought and Social Action: An Anthropological Perspective*, edited by Stanley Tambiah, 123–66. Cambridge, MA: Harvard University Press.

Tan, Gang. 2005. *"Chengzhongcun jingjizhuti jingji huodong ji zhuyao tezheng"* [Characteristics of economic actors and economic activities of villages-in-the-city]. *Kaifang daobao* 3:51–55.

Tan, Chee-Beng. 2007. "The Shishan Ye People in Malaysia and the Ancestral Homeland in China." In *Chinese Transnational Networks*, edited by Chee-Beng Tan, 73–91. London: Routledge.

Tang, Wing-Shing, and Him Chung. 2002. "Rural-Urban Transition in China: Illegal Land Use and Construction." *Asia Pacific Viewpoint* 43 (1): 43–62.

Thireau, Isabelle, and Linshan Hua. 2001. "Du présent au passé: Accords et désaccords concernant les affaires communes villageoises." In *Disputes au village chinois: Formes du juste et recompositions locales des espaces normatifs*, edited by Isabelle Thireau and Hansheng Wang, 79–124. Paris: Éditions de la Maison des sciences de l'homme.

Thireau, Isabelle, and Linshan Hua. 2010. *Les ruses de la démocratie: Protester en Chine.* Paris: Seuil.

Thireau, Isabelle, and Kong Mak. 1996. "Village Leadership in an Emigrant Community." In *South China: State, Culture and Social Change during the 20th Century*, edited by Leo M. Douw and Peter Post, 205–20. Amsterdam: KNAW Verhandelingen.

Thompson, Edward P. 1971. "The Moral Economy of the English Crowd in the Eighteenth Century." *Past and Present* 50 (1): 76–136.

Thompson, Stuart E. 1988. "Death, Food and Fertility." In *Death Ritual in Late Imperial and Modern China*, edited by James L. Watson and Evelyn S. Rawski, 71–108. Berkeley: University of California Press.

Thornton, Patricia M. 2002. "Framing Dissent in Contemporary China: Irony, Ambiguity and Metonymy." *China Quarterly* 171:661–81.

Thunø, Mette. 2001. "Reaching Out and Incorporating Chinese Overseas: The Transterritorial Scope of the PRC by the End of the 20th Century." *China Quarterly* 168:910–29.

Tian, Li. 2008. "The Chengzhongcun Land Market in China: Boon or Bane? A Perspective on Property Rights: The Chengzhongcun Land Market in China." *International Journal of Urban and Regional Research* 32 (2): 282–304.

Tjon Sie Fat, P. 2009. *Chinese New Migrants in Suriname: The Inevitability of Ethnic Performing.* Amsterdam: Amsterdam University Press.

Tölölyan, Khachig. 1996. "Rethinking Diaspora(s): Stateless Power in the Transnational Moment." *Diaspora* 5 (1): 3–36.

Trémon, Anne-Christine. 2007. "Les liens transnationaux en diaspora: Le cas des Chinois de Polynésie française." *Diasporas, histoire et sociétés* 10:217–27.

Trémon, Anne-Christine. 2009. "Cosmopolitanization and Localization: Ethnicity, Class and Citizenship among the Chinese in French Polynesia." *Anthropological Theory* 9 (1): 103–26.

Trémon, Anne-Christine. 2010. *Chinois en Polynésie française: Migration, métissage, diaspora.* Nanterre, France: Société d'ethnologie.

Trémon, Anne-Christine. 2015. "Local Capitalism and Neoliberalization in a Shenzhen Former Lineage Village." *Focaal* 2015 (71): 71–85.

Trémon, Anne-Christine. 2017. "Flexible Kinship: Shaping Transnational Families among the Chinese in Tahiti." *Journal of the Royal Anthropological Institute* 23 (1): 42–60.

Trémon, Anne-Christine. 2018. "'Start Here': Foundational Slogans in Shenzhen, China." In *Slogans: Subjection, Subversion, and the Politics of Neoliberalism*, edited by Nicolette Makovicky, Anne-Christine Trémon, and Sheyla S. Zandonai, 50–76. London: Routledge.

Trémon, Anne-Christine. 2020. "Variegated Valuation: Governance and Circuits of Value in Shenzhen." *Focaalblog.* http://www.focaalblog.com/2020/07/20/anne-christine-tremon-variegated-valuation-governance-and-circuits-of-value-in-shenzhen/.

Trémon, Anne-Christine. 2021. "Diagnostic Contradictions and Scales of Change." In *Snapshots of Change: Assessing Social Transformations in Qualitative Research*, edited by Anoushka Derks, Yasmine Berriane, and Aymon Kreil, 22–59 London: Palgrave Macmillan.

Trémon, Anne-Christine, ed. Forthcoming, 2023. *From Village Commons to Public Goods. Graduated Provision in Urbanizing China.* New York: Berghahn.

Trolliet, Pierre. 1994. *La Diaspora chinoise*, Paris : Presses Universitaires de France.

Tsai, Lily L. 2007. *Accountability without Democracy: Solidary Groups and Public Goods Provision in Rural China.* Cambridge: Cambridge University Press.

Tsing, Anna Lowenhaupt. 2000. "The Global Situation." *Cultural Anthropology* 15 (3): 327–60.

Tsing, Anna Lowenhaupt. 2005. *Friction: An Ethnography of Global Connection.* Princeton, NJ: Princeton University Press.

Unger, Jonathan. 2002. *The Transformation of Rural China.* Armonk, NY: M. E. Sharpe.

Valeri, Valerio. 1985. *Kingship and Sacrifice: Ritual and Society in Ancient Hawaii.* Translated by Paula Wissing. Chicago: University of Chicago Press.

Van Velsen, Jaap. 1967. "The Extended-Case Method and Situational Analysis." In *The Craft of Social Anthropology*, edited by A. L. Epstein, 29–53. London: Tavistock.

Viveiros de Castro, Eduardo. 2012. *Radical Dualism.* Berlin: Hatje Cantz.

Vogel, Ezra. 1969. "Land Reform in Kwangtung, 1951–1953: Central Control and Localism." *China Quarterly* 38:27–62.

Vogel, Ezra. 1989. *One Step Ahead in China: Guangdong under Reform.* Cambridge, MA: Harvard University Press.

Vogel, Ezra. 2011. *Deng Xiaoping and the Transformation of China.* Cambridge, MA: Belknap.

Waldinger, Roger D., and David S. Fitzgerald. 2004. "Transnationalism in Question." *American Journal of Sociology* 109 (5): 1177–95.

Wallerstein, Immanuel. 1974. *The Modern World System I: Capitalist Agriculture and the Origins of the European World-Economy in the Sixteenth Century.* New York: Academic Press.

Wallerstein, Immanuel. 1976. "Semi-peripheral Countries and the Contemporary World Crisis." *Theory and Society* 3 (4): 461–83.

Wang, Fei-Ling. 2005. *Organizing through Division and Exclusion: China's Hukou System.* Stanford: Stanford University Press.

Wang, Gungwu. 1981. "A Note on the Origins of Hua-ch'iao." In *Community and Nation: Essays on Southeast Asia and the Chinese*, selected by Anthony Reid, 118–27. Singapore: Heinemann.

Wang, Gungwu. 1991. *China and the Chinese Overseas.* Singapore: Times Academic Press.

Wang, Gungwu. 1993. "Greater China and the Chinese Overseas." *The China Quarterly* 136: 926–48.

Wang, Gungwu. 1999. "A Single Chinese Diaspora? Some Historical Reflections." In *Imagining the Chinese Diaspora: Two Australian Perspectives*, edited by Wang Gungwu and Annette Shun Wah, 1–17. Canberra: Centre for the Study of the Chinese Southern Diaspora.

Wang, Gungwu. 2000, *The Chinese Overseas : From Earthbound China to the Quest for Autonomy*, Cambridge, Harvard University Press.

Wang, Lan-Chih, and Gungwu Wang, eds. 1998. *The Chinese Diaspora: Selected Essays.* Singapore: Times Academic.

Wang, Ya Ping, Yanglin Wang, and Jiansheng Wu. 2009. "Urbanization and Informal Development in China: Urban Villages in Shenzhen." *International Journal of Urban and Regional Research* 22 (4): 957–73.

Watson, James L. 1975. *Emigration and the Chinese Lineage: The Mans in Hong Kong and London.* Berkeley: University of California Press.

Watson, James L. 1982. "Of Flesh and Bones: The Management of Death Pollution in Cantonese Society." In *Death and the Regeneration of Life*, edited by Maurice Bloch and Jonathan Parry, 155–86. Cambridge: Cambridge University Press.

Watson, James L. 1988a. "The Structure of Chinese Funerary Rites: Elementary Forms, Ritual Sequence, and the Primacy of Performance." In *Death Ritual in Late Imperial and Modern China*, edited by James L. Watson and Evelyn S. Rawski, 3–19. Berkeley: University of California Press.

Watson, James L. 1988b. "Funeral Specialists in Cantonese Society: Pollution, Performance and Social Hierarchy." In *Death Ritual in Late Imperial and Modern China*, edited by James L. Watson and Evelyn S. Rawski, 109–34. Berkeley: University of California Press.

Watson, James L. 2004. "Presidential Address: Virtual Kinship, Real Estate, and Diaspora Formation—The Man Lineage Revisited." *Journal of Asian Studies* 63 (4): 893–910.

Watson, Rubie S. 1985. *Inequality among Brothers: Class and Kinship in South China.* Cambridge: Cambridge University Press.

Watson, Rubie S. 1988. "Remembering the Dead: Graves and Politics in Southeastern China." In *Death Ritual in Late Imperial and Modern China*, edited by James L. Watson and Evelyn S. Rawski, 203–27. Berkeley: University of California Press.

Watson, Rubie S. 1994. "Making Secret Histories: Memory and Mourning in Post-Mao China." In *Memory, History and Opposition under State Socialism*, edited by Rubie Watson, 65–86. Santa Fe, NM: School of American Research Press.

Weber, Max. 1970. "Religious Rejections of the World and Their Directions." In *From Max Weber: Essays in Sociology*, edited by C. Wright Mills and Hans H. Gerth, 323–59. London: Routledge.

Weidenbaum, Murray L., and Samuel Hughes. 1996. *The Bamboo Networks: How Expatriate Chinese Entrepreneurs Are Creating a New Economic Superpower in Asia.* New York: Martin Kessler.

Whyte, Martin K. 1988. "Death in the People's Republic of China." In *Death Ritual in Late Imperial and Modern China*, edited by James L. Watson and Evelyn S. Rawski, 289–316. Berkeley: University of California Press.

Wolf, Arthur P. 1974. "Gods, Ghosts and Ancestors." In *Religion and Ritual in Chinese Society*, edited by Arthur P. Wolf, 131–82. Stanford, CA: Stanford University Press.

Wolf, Margery. 1972. *Women and the Family in Rural Taiwan.* Stanford, CA: Stanford University Press.

Woon, Yuen-Fong. 1984. *Social Organization in South China 1911–49: The Case of the Kuan Lineage of K'ai-ping County.* Ann Arbor: University of Michigan Press.

Woon, Yuen-Fong. 1990. "International Links and the Socio-economic Development of Rural China." *Modern China* 16:139–66.

Woon, Yuen-Fong. 1996. "The Guan of Kaiping County in the 1990's: Still a Cohesive Group?" In *China: State, Culture and Social Change during the 20th Century*, edited by Leo M. Douw and Peter Post, 221–30. Amsterdam: KNAW Verhandelingen.

World Shipping Council. 2019. "Top 50 World Container Ports." Accessed March 30, 2019. http://www.worldshipping.org/about-the-industry/global-trade/top-50 -world-container-ports.

Wu, Yiching. 2014. *The Cultural Revolution at the Margins: Chinese Socialism in Crisis.* Cambridge, MA: Harvard University Press.

Xiang, Biao. 2003. "Emigration from China: A Sending Country Perspective." *International Migration* 41 (3): 21–48.

Xiang, Biao. 2013. "Multi-scalar Ethnography: An Approach for Critical Engagement with Migration and Social Change." *Ethnography* 14 (3): 282–99.

Xie, Zhikui. 2005. *"Cunluo ruhe zhongjie: zhongguo nongcun chengshihua de zhidu yanjiu"* [How to end villages-in-the-city: A study of the urbanization institutions of peasant villages in China]. *Chengshi fazhanyanjiu* 1 (5): 22–29.

Xue, Desheng, and Fulong Wu. 2015. "Failing Entrepreneurial Governance: From Economic Crisis to Fiscal Crisis in the City of Dongguan, China." *Cities* 43:10–17.

Yan, Yunxiang. 1992. "The Impact of Reform on Economic and Social Stratification in a Chinese Village." *Australian Journal of Chinese Affairs* 27:1–23.

Yan, Yunxiang. 1996. *The Flow of Gifts. Reciprocity and Social Networks in a Chinese Village*. Stanford, CA: Stanford University Press.

Yang, Ch'ing-k'un. 1957. "The Functional Relationship between Confucian Thought and Chinese Religion." In *Chinese Thought and Institutions*, edited by J. K. Fairbank, 269–90. Chicago: University of Chicago Press.

Yang, Ch'ing-k'un. 1961. *Religion in Chinese Society: A Study of Contemporary Social Functions of Religion and Some of Their Historical Factors*. Berkeley: University of California Press.

Yang, Mayfair Mei-Hui. 1994. *Gifts, Favors and Banquets: The Art of Social Relationships in China*. Ithaca, NY: Cornell University Press.

Yang, Mayfair Mei-Hui. 2000. "Putting Global Capitalism in Its Place: Economic Hybridity, Bataille, and Ritual Expenditure." *Current Anthropology* 41 (4): 477–509.

Yang, Mayfair Mei-Hui. 2004. "Spatial Struggles: Postcolonial Complex, State Disenchantment, and Popular Reappropriation of Space in Rural South East China." *Journal of Asian Studies* 63 (3): 719–55.

Yeh, Anthony G. O. 2005. "Dual Land Market and Internal Spatial Structure of Chinese Cities." In *Restructuring the Chinese City*, edited by Laurence J. C. Ma and Fulong Wu, 59–79. New York: Routledge.

Yeoh, Brenda, and Kathy Willis, eds. 2004. *State/Nation/Transnation: Perspectives on Transnationalism in the Asia-Pacific*. New York: Routledge.

Yu, Depeng. 2002. *Shehui: Cong geli zouxiang kaifang* [Urban and rural societies: From isolation to openness]. Jinan: Shandong renmin chubanshe.

Zha Zhenxiang. 2008. *"Shenzhen shi chengzhongcun jitigufen hezuo gongsi biange yanjiu"* [A study of the transformation of collective cooperative companies of villages-in-the-city in Shenzhen]. *Tequjingji* 5:15–18.

Zhang, Li. 2001. *Strangers in the City: Reconfigurations of Space, Power, and Social Networks within China's Floating Population*. Stanford, CA: Stanford University Press.

Zhang, Li. 2010. *In Search of Paradise: Middle-Class Living in a Chinese Metropolis*. Ithaca, NY: Cornell University Press.

Zhang, Li, Simon X. B. Zhao, and J. P. Tian. 2003. "Self-Help in Housing and Chengzhongcun in China's Urbanization." *International Journal of Urban and Regional Research* 27 (4): 912–37.

Zhao, Bo. 2009. "Land Expropriation, Protest, and Impunity in Rural China." *Focaal* 9 (54): 97–105.

Zhe, Xiaoye. 1997. *Cunzhuang de caizao: Yi ge "chaojicunzhuang" de shehui bianqian* [Reconstructing a village: Changes in a "super village"]. Beijing: Zhongguo shehui kexue chubanshe.

Zhe, Xiaoye, and Chen Yingying. 1997. *"Chaoji cunzhuang de jiben tezheng ji 'zhongjian' xingtai. Shehuixue yanjiu"* [Basic characteristics and "middle" form of supervillages]. *Sociological Research* 6:37–45.

Zheng, Zhenman. 2001. *Family Lineage Organization and Social Change in Ming and Qing Fujian.* Honolulu: University of Hawai'i Press.

Zhu, Jieming. 2004. "From Land Use Right to Land Development Right: Institutional Change in China's Urban Development." *Urban Studies* 41 (7): 1249–67.

Zhuang, Guotu, and Jingying Zhang. 2012. *"Zhongguo xinyimin de leixing he fenbu"* [Categories and distribution of new migrants]. *Shehui kexue* 12:4–11.

Zou, Hua. 2014. *Zongzu bian gongsi: Guangzhou zhangban cun cunmin zuzhi jiegou de bai nian yanbian* [From lineage to corporation: A century of changing rural organizational structures in Zhangban Village, Guangzhou]. Beijing: Contemporary China Publishing House.

Index

Page numbers in *italics* indicate illustrations. Chen family members are listed by first name, with the exception of published authors.

abolition of slavery, 230n2

Alain: author mistaken for daughter of, 2; close kin in China, lack of, 204–9; Deqi and, 161–62, 204–5, 207, 239n9; emigration of grandfather to Tahiti, 205–6, 229n2; fieldwork by author and, 1, 2, 18; on financial donations from emigrants, 139; at founding ancestor's birthday celebrations, 2014, 156, 161–63; journeys and quests to Chinese origins, 166, 169, 170, 172–76, 180, 181, 183–85; Lucien introduced to author by, 1; on *mana*, 183–85, 204, 212; on mausoleum, 8; Qiaolian and, 196–200, 239n7

All-China Federation of Returned Overseas Chinese Association. *See* Qiaolian

ambivalence about emigration/overseas Chinese, 24, 124–43; ancestor worship/ancestral cult and, 222–23; "being Chinese"/Chineseness, 130, 131–32, , 165; feng shui discourse and, 122, 123–27; financial support from overseas Chinese and, 121, 123, 134–42, *139, 140,* 211–12, 223; global brotherhood versus practical close kinship, tension between, 188, 209; *huaqiao* viewed as separate class, 133–36, 141–42, 143; moral valorization of remaining, 121–22, 127–31; at Qiaolian, 187–89; regimes of mobility approach and, 263n1; return and nonreturn, 131–33; Shenzhen versus Pine Mansion Chens, 141; sociodicies of (im)mobility and, 23, 122, 125, 133, 142, 218–19

ancestor worship/ancestral cult, 23–24, 144–65; ambivalence about emigration/overseas Chinese and, 222–23; birthday celebrations of 2014, 155–60, *157, 160;* bowing and prostration at, 156–57, 158, 238n12; Chunfen, 20, 108, 110, 125, 146, 147, 150–51, *152,* 154, 159, 164, 237n5; communal meal, 101, 150–52, *152,* 237n6; Communist regime and, 12, 148–49,

157–58; defined and described, 144–46, *145;* delocalized to Hong Kong, 146, 148–50, 155; domestic versus collective or lineage worship, 145, 146, 200–201, 237n3; feng shui and, 123–24; founding ancestor's birthday, 11, 26, 31, 109–10, 113, 115–16, 118, 137, 146–51, 153–64, 190, 196, 197, 206, 237n6; funeral reform and, 104; invention of tradition, 147–48; lineage ties and, 10, 12–13; mausoleum and, 150; moral economy and, 75, 94; not regarded as official religion, 12; overseas Chinese and, 146–47, 155, *157,* 158–65, *160;* paper, burning, 144, *145;* Qingming, 20, 108, *145,* 145–46, 151; *renao* at, 159; revival/return/relocalization/re-creation of, 146–47, 150–55, *152;* "tomb sweeping," 145, 147; "worshipping the mountain," 145

ancestor Zhenneng/founding ancestor: Chunfen ritual and, 237n5; diaspora/emigrant community and, 2, 10; emigration from Pine Mansion and, 26, 28, 188; financial support from overseas Chinese and, 53, 233n10; kinship ties, as mediator of, 203–5; moral economy and, 73, 74, 89, 234n2; saving ancestral sites and, 100, 102, 110–11, 118. *See also* ancestor worship/ancestral cult; ancestral tomb

ancestral sites, saving, 23, 97–120; funeral reform in China and, 97–98, 103–5, 107–8, 112; as geomantic power spots, 102, 104; as heterotopias and heterochronias, 98, 99–103, 216–17; mausoleum, construction of, 103–8, *105, 106;* mobilization of Pine Mansion for, 97–98; primary school, campaign to save, 97–98, 111–16, *115;* as public goods, 98; redevelopment of Pine Mansion and, 116–19, *117;* temple, renovation of, 98, 118–19; territorial boundaries, importance of keeping ancestral remains in, 108–11

shui of, 110; financial support from overseas Chinese for, 8–9, 51, 107; layout of, *105*, 105–7, *106*; lineage activities, reactivation of, 228; lineage slogan on, 106; naming of, 107–8; ritual meals at, 109–10; territorial boundaries, importance of keeping ancestral remains in, 108–11; Zhenneng foundation and, 66

memory/remembering, 34, 101, 104, 133, 138–39, 154, 163, 164, 181, 212, 219, 222, 224. *See also* misremembrance and forgetting

Miaoyun (subdistrict), 1–2, 47, 66, 77, 89, 94, 187, 190

Miaoyun People's Association, Hong Kong, 68–69

Miaoyun Qiaolian. *See* Qiaolian

Michel, 156, 161, 172–75, 180–82

migrant workers. *See* internal migration, migrants, and migrant workers

migration out of Pine Mansion. *See* emigration

minority (non-Chen) surnames in Pine Mansion, 33, 55–56, 60, 62, 66, 75, 105, 107, 114, 115, 124, 233, 234n16

misremembrance and forgetting, 163–64, 224–25

mobility/hypermobile entrepreneurs, 3, 10, 43–48, 231n17

mobilization, 9, 13, 22, 23, 28, 39, 54, 64, 76, 91, 97–99, 107–8, 111–12, 118–19, 125, 202, 209, 216; *tuanjie* (to unite or rally), 110–11. *See also* ancestral sites, saving; protest

modernity/modernization: ancestor worship/ ancestral cult and, 146, 149, 157–58, 164–65; diaspora relationship and emigration, 15, 17, 24, 46; financial assistance of overseas Chinese and, 60; Four Modernizations, 229n4; globalization and, 216–17, 223, 227; moral economy and, 79, 87, 95, 96; saving ancestral sites and, 98, 101, 104, 111, 113, 118, 119

moral economy, 22–23, 72–96; categorization of population in, 82–86, *85*; current economic prosperity of Pine Mansion, 72–73, 87–90, *89*, 234n1; decollectivization and cooperatives, 78–80; defined, 93–94; economic development companies, 78–79; land reform and collectivization, 75–78, *76*, 95; lineage persisting as corporate group in, 73–75, 81, 91, 93, 94; real estate/rental income, 87–90, 94; scales and, 215–16;

217–20; shareholding companies, 78–82, *82*, 90–96, 156, 215–16, 218; social benefits, access to, 92–93, 94–95; subsistence ethics, 12, 74, 93–94; surplus ethics, 12, 74, 93, 94, 220

multisited positionality and fieldwork, 2, 3, 14, 17–22, 213–15

Munn, Nancy, 16, 138, 219, 224; space-time/ spacetime and study of kula circuit by, 219, 224.

mutuality of being/existence, 24, 189, 209

Nationality Law in China, 192–93

neighborhoods/*wei*, 73, 75, 80; natural villages and, 75, 78, 195; Xianwei neighborhood, 40, 112, 131–32; Zhongxin neighborhood, 73, 75, 94, 95; *See also* village

Netherlands, 36, 44, 57, 58, 59

non-Chens. *See* minority (non-Chen) surnames in Pine Mansion

Oceania. *See* Tahiti/Tahiti Chens

one-child/single-child policy, 37, 50

Ong, Aihwa, 7, 44–45

overseas associations. *See* associations overseas

overseas Chinese. *See* diaspora/emigrant community and relationships; *huaqiao; specific countries*

Overseas Chinese Affairs Office/Commission (OCAO/OCAC), 48, 190–91, 232n27, 232n31. *See also* Qiaoban; Qiaolian

Oxfeld, Ellen, 135, 237n10

Panama/Panama Canal, 52, 55, 56, 57, 58, 62, 129, 233n7

the past, association of overseas Chinese with, 15, 23, 121, 160–65, 197, 223–24

phenomenology, 176, 179

Philanthropic Association, Tahiti, 19

Pine Mansion. *See* village

pioneers and pioneering *(kaihuang)*, 8, 27, 28, 33, 34, 39, 40, 42, 56, 100, 103, 113, 205, 216, 227

plantation colonies, emigration to, 32, 33, 50, 52, 55, 56, 129, 230n2. *See also* indentured/ contract laborers

Polynesian/Tahitian kinship, 203, 209

primary school. *See* schools, Pine Mansion

processual approach, 13–17, 225–28

Protection Act (1990), 46, 232n25

protest, 99, 103, 111–16. *See also* ancestral sites, saving; mobilization

CPSIA information can be obtained
at www.ICGtesting.com
Printed in the USA
LVHW040730031122
732268LV00002B/298

9 781501 767951